"This warts-and-all biography recounts the
America's most colorful, accomplished, and _____ _____ _____,
Benjamin Morris ("Alphabet") Browne. At once a rabbi, a doctor, and a lawyer,
Browne befriended Ulysses S. Grant, bested the atheist preacher Robert Ingersoll,
corresponded with Theodor Herzl, and sprang innocent men from jail. Acquainted
with many of the leading figures of his day, he championed causes both great and
small, and occupied pulpits from Boston to Peoria. Few recall Browne today, but as
this prodigiously researched volume demonstrates, they should. His life illuminates
significant chapters in the history of American Judaism."

   – Jonathan D. Sarna

   Joseph H. & Belle R. Braun Professor of American Jewish History, Brandeis
   University, and author of American Judaism: A History

"Readers will quickly discover that by examining Browne they will supplement their
knowledge of numerous vitally important topics relating to the history of American
Jewry, including American Reform Judaism, American Zionism, the American
Jewish press, American Jewry and politics, and much more. Janice Rothschild
Blumberg deserves much credit for assiduously reconstructing her great grandfather's
complicated, intriguing, and truly illuminating biography. The story of Rabbi
"Alphabet" Browne is as instructive as it is enthralling."

   – Gary Phillip Zola

   Executive Director of the Jacob Rader Marcus Center of the American Jewish
   Archives and Professor of the American Jewish Experience at Hebrew Union College
   Jewish Institute of Religion, Cincinnati, Ohio

"The narrative is meticulously documented, but lovingly related by Janice Rothschild
Blumberg who remembers her great grandfather from her childhood. Browne is
honestly depicted as a prophetic figure who held strong and controversial opinions
in a generation of rabbis who were committed to compromise. The book is an
important contribution to an understanding of American Jewry during the post Civil
War era, and particularly the relationship between reform and traditional Jewish
beliefs in this era. I would characterize the narrative as a "delightful" read, a term
which I would ordinarily restrict to a work of historical fiction."

   – Rabbi Harold S. White

   Senior Advisor and Founder, The Program for Jewish Civilizatiom,
   The School of Foreign Service, Georgetown University, Washington D.C.

Prophet in a Time of Priests

Rabbi "Alphabet" Browne
1845-1929

a biography

Janice Rothschild Blumberg

Apprentice House
Baltimore, Maryland

Printed in the United States of America

Cover and internal design by: Alyssa Link

ISBN: 978-1-934074-73-2
First Edition

Published by Apprentice House
The Future of Publishing…Today!

Apprentice House
Communication Department
Loyola University Maryland
4501 N. Charles Street
Baltimore, MD 21210

410.617.5265
410.617.2198 (fax)
www.ApprenticeHouse.com

TABLE OF CONTENTS

FOREWORD

Since the 1890s numerous rabbis have occupied pulpits in particular congregations for decades. Especially in Reform temples, but also in some Conservative and modern Orthodox synagogues, their responsibilities have included service as ambassadors to the gentiles." This broad role includes interaction with the general community, ecumenical endeavors, participation in civic and social service projects and organizations, and acting as major spokespeople and faces of the Jewish community. Although conflicts frequently occurred, rabbis have tended to enjoy power and prestige within their congregations and within the broader Jewish and secular societies.

These patterns have not always been the rule. As Janice Rothschild Blumberg makes clear in this path breaking study of Rabbi E.B.M. ("Alphabet") Browne, virtually all of those who followed Rabbi Abraham Rice, the first ordained rabbi to hold an American pulpit, in 1840, did not do so. During the next decade the vast majority were either fired or resigned under pressure. Laymen (women did not vote, hold office, or even membership in congregations) accustomed to making congregational decisions, refused to relinquish power to rabbis. Rabbis and congregations also came into conflict over reforms—which ones, how many, and how quickly were they to be implemented. From the 1870s into the 1890s rabbis were hired and fired on a regular basis as either the more Reform or traditional faction within their congregation held sway.

The Pittsburgh Platform's stress on social service over religious observance, the availability of rabbis trained at the Hebrew Union College, the trend toward three separate movements within American Judaism—

Reform, Orthodox, and Conservative—and the firm move of congregations into those camps, among other factors intertwined and contributed to the rise of prestige of the rabbinate and the shift of power within congregations toward the rabbis. Consequently, this extended rabbinic tenures.

For the nineteenth and into the early twentieth centuries with few exceptions, the important" rabbis—institution builders and thinkers like Isaac Leeser, Isaac M. Wise, David Einhorn, Kaufmann Kohler, and Emil Hirsch— have drawn the greatest historical attention. Yet itinerant rabbis like Alphabet Browne who struggled from one pulpit to another are perhaps far more representative of the typical rabbinical experience of their era.

As readers of this biography will see, Hungarian-born Browne earned degrees in law and medicine besides rabbinical training and ordination. Well read, fluent in several languages, an international traveler and speaker, Browne was a Renaissance man with an ego to match. I.M. Wise's protégé and newspaper competitor, he made friends (including President Grant and other public figures) and enemies at every stop.

One of the things that made writing about him so difficult and reading about him so interesting is that he proves impossible to pigeonhole. He is a Reform rabbi with strong tendencies toward Conservative practices and beliefs. Whereas most Reform rabbis rejected political Zionism and remained aloof from the East European Jewish immigrants who flooded into America especially between 1881 and 1924, Browne ardently supported Zionism and became a champion of the poor Jewish immigrant. He ascribed to the authority and prestige of the modern, professional rabbinate but seemingly went out of his way to foment controversy and antagonize powerful opponents. During a period in which rabbis tended to eschew politics, Browne ardently campaigned for candidates, emphasized Jewish bloc voting, and lobbied for patronage positions. A direct descendent, his biographer depicts him in all of his strength as well as his numerous weaknesses.

I first became familiar with Janice Rothschild Blumberg's work when I began studying southern Jewish history during the late 1970s. She had written a history of Atlanta's Hebrew Benevolent Congregation (The Temple), which she revised twenty years later. She followed this with two insightful articles on the early history of Atlanta Jewry for the *Publications of the American Jewish Historical Society* (now *American Jewish History*). Janice also wrote a memoir treating her first husband, Rabbi Jacob Rothschild, and their experiences with the civil rights movement. We share devotion to the Southern Jewish Historical Society (SJHS), an organization over which she presided, and where we meet regularly at annual conferences.

I have had the pleasure of editing three of Janice's articles. She provided a fascinating memoir of Rabbi Rothschild and her experiences for an anthology, *Quiet Voices: Southern Rabbis and Black Civil Rights*, I co-edited with Berkley Kalin. Her preliminary articles on Rabbi Browne's Atlanta years and on his wife, Sophie Weil Browne, as a rabbi's wife and clubwoman appeared in the SJHS journal I edit. In all of these works as in her biography of Browne, Janice Rothschild Blumberg melds the literary verve of the journalist with the critical, analytic skills of the historian.

Those who know Janice view her as the model of the southern lady in the highest sense of the concept. Far from being perched on the proverbial pedestal, she is rather a brilliant conversationalist and thinker, who in her eighth decade, has completed a scholarly project that has taken years of research, writing, and repeated revision. In these pages she offers readers great insights into immigration and identity, the roles of rabbis and their wives, interaction between rabbis and between rabbis and congregations, religious ideas and debates, divisions within Judaism, the nature of nineteenth century politics and political figures, regionalism and movement across sections, foreign affairs, and the life and travels of an unusual but also often typical individual of his class, vocation, and age. Enjoy!

Mark K. Bauman

Editor, *Southern Jewish History*

INTRODUCTION

Little has been written about the numerous rabbis who came to America in the mid-nineteenth century except for those few who sustained long tenures in important pulpits. The vast majority served small communities throughout the country, often moving from place to place or to other professions with rapidity that suggests incompetence and lack of achievement. Such was not the case, however, with the peripatetic Edward B. M.. Browne, LLD, AM, BM, DD, MD (called "Alphabet" because he signed his name with all the letters.) Browne's simultaneous careers as rabbi, public orator, journalist, pro bono attorney, and lobbyist provide rare insights to the Jewish experience during the formative period of American Judaism within our country's dynamic, tumultuous era from Reconstruction through the First World War. His story is one of American history, Jewish history, and the history of church-state relations. His passion was America's fulfillment of its promise of equal rights for all, a doctrine deeply imbedded in the hearts of most immigrants.

Browne held thirteen pulpits in eight states during a rabbinate that spanned half a century. He invited controversy at every turn, endearing himself to Christians and Eastern European Jewish immigrants while alienating the leading power brokers of American Jewry. He was admitted to the bar in two states; lectured in chemistry as well Talmud and the life of Jesus, taught at a medical college, wrote for and edited newspapers, and embraced political Zionism at a time when it was anathema to most members of his congregation. His lectures drew enthusiastic applause across America. He traveled frequently to Europe and at least twice to the Middle East on missions of mercy for his fellow Jews, played a significant role in the presidential campaign of Benjamin Harrison, served as an honorary pall bearer in the state funeral of Ulysses S. Grant, sympathized with the labor movement, embraced the theories of Henry George, was referred to in New York newspapers as "The Poor Man's Friend" and in the mid-West as "The Man Who Challenged Ingersoll." Yet his name is hardly a footnote in American Jewish history.

One is tempted to ask why. Why is it that few Jewish scholars recognize his name, that fewer yet mention him in their published work, and even then in negative context? Why did biographers ignore him? Why have his achievements been overlooked and only his foibles remembered? Was he an unsung hero, a charismatic braggart, or merely an annoying gadfly? Was his failure due entirely to his own eccentricities, or because he was ahead of his time and dared to buck the mainstream? Those are questions for the reader to decide. This study seeks to illuminate the issues, not to resolve them.

Edward B. M. Browne was my great-grandfather. He and his only grandchild, my mother, formed a close bond which led to his spending much time with us in Atlanta during the last five years of his life and the first five of mine. I retain a brief but vivid memory of him as a warm, witty old man with a full head of curly white hair and a walrus mustache, who sometimes teased me and always seemed to enjoy my company. Family tradition, far from endowing him with a halo, cast suspicion on almost everything that he was purported to have done, perhaps due to the jaundiced memory retained by my grandmother who endured childhood as "the preacher's kid." Her attitude is not hard to understand. Moving from place to place and hearing public criticism of one's parent does not make for a happy childhood. Furthermore, her father by words and actions upheld Jewish distinctiveness at a time when she and her Jewish Victorian friends most wanted to blend into the mainstream. Her only glowing reminiscence of those days was that of viewing Grant's funeral procession from an area outside New York's posh Fifth Avenue Hotel reserved for celebrities and families of the participants, an awesome experience for a romantic nine-year-old. She never tired of showing me the identifying black armband that her father wore that day, a souvenir that unfortunately disappeared during ensuing decades.

My interest in writing about Browne began when I discovered the partial galley of a book intended as a tribute to him from an organization of "downtown" New Yorkers whom he inspired. It detailed how he saved the life of a seventy-year-old Hungarian Jewish immigrant who was falsely accused, convicted and sentenced to death for the murder of his wife. What a perfect plot for a play or a novel! I thought, and determined to write it someday.

That day came fifty years later. By then I realized that the story deserved serious attention as a poignant portrayal of handicaps confronting immigrants in the 1880s. Here was a rabbi born and educated for success in the elitist world of German Jewry, who ignored the accepted rules of "uptown" society and befriended the deeply observant refugees from persecution and poverty in Eastern Europe. He approached them not as a benefactor but as a fellow Jew and fellow immigrant who understood their language and their angst. It read like fiction but it was not fiction. It was an account of suffering due to discrimination against immigrants, something that many of our forebears experienced when they came to America. He confronted it as a prophet acting on his own, not as a conventional rabbi who in those days was expected to be a priest representing acknowledged authority. Fearless and independent, he pursued the realization of America's promise as his conscience demanded, undeterred by opposition and its consequence. He spoke not primarily to please his listeners, but to lead them.

One can easily get hooked on writing history. At times my quest resembled a game, similar to a scavenger hunt in which each clue leads to another. For example, an inquiry at the New York Public Library yielded nothing on the requested issue but, thanks to a diligent staffer, opened a treasure trove of information on even more significant points in Browne's life. A chance acquaintance with Tweed Roosevelt, great-grandson of Theodore Roosevelt, led me to the microfilm collection of presidential correspondence at the Library of Congress that yielded a jackpot of Browne's correspondence not only with T.R. but also with Presidents Benjamin Harrison, William Howard Taft and Woodrow Wilson. Most surprising of all, in a scrapbook of newspaper clippings about Browne that my mother assembled after he died, I noticed the report of a 1912 lecture memorializing Theodor Herzl in which the rabbi was identified as "a close personal friend" of the Zionist leader. This astonished me because, prior to the Holocaust, I had never heard anyone in my family mention Zionism or Herzl. Browne's descendants were staunch anti-Zionists in those days. Did my mother realize the significance of this news when she pasted it in the scrapbook? It was too late to ask her but not too late to inquire at Central Zionist Archives in Jerusalem if Herzl's papers contained anything about E. B. M. Browne. The answer came in two file folders of correspondence (1897-1898) wherein Browne gave Herzl his unvarnished view of American Jewish life, its leaders, their negative attitude toward Zionism, and his readiness to resign his pulpit in order to work full time promoting Herzl's vision.

These are the sorts of nuggets that delight unsuspecting historians who stumble upon them while following well defined paths of research. For this writer, the journey promised additional joy by illuminating the life of a revered forefather, previously ignored but deserving of remembrance. As the fourth generation of his progeny, I derive deep satisfaction and take great pleasure in dedicating his story to the generations that follow, to my beloved children Marcia and Bill Rothschild and my incomparably beloved grandson, Jacob M. Rothschild. May they enjoy the heritage as my mother and I have enjoyed it before them.

Janice Rothschild Blumberg

May, 2011

I - WUNDERKIND AND THE PROMISE
OF AMERICA

On Saturday afternoon, May 27, 1884, a stocky, five-foot five Hungarian
immigrant ascended the platform of the United States Senate to invoke
God's blessing upon the decisions to be made that day. A year later the
same man represented the Jewish citizens of America as one of the fourteen
honorary pall bearers for President Ulysses S. Grant, walking rather than
riding with the others because the elaborate state funeral took place on the
Jewish Sabbath.

The man was Rabbi Edward Benjamin Morris Browne, called
"Alphabet" by his colleagues because he signed his name "E. B. M.
Browne, LLD, AM, BM, DD, MD." He had earned all of the academic
degrees—three before the age of twenty—yet his contemporaries more
often pronounced "Alphabet" in derision than in admiration. Controversial
as much as charismatic, Browne inspired either love or hate, but rarely
indifference. A prominent Christian clergyman declared him "the stoned
prophet of our day" and a notable Orthodox rabbi eulogized him as "a
great-hearted Jew," yet he attracted powerful enemies among the leaders of
Reform Judaism in America.

Deeply patriotic as most immigrants were, and profoundly moved by
the promise of America, Browne devoted his formidable talents to testing
that promise wherever he perceived it to be threatened. Unlike most of his
contemporaries, he believed that here one could be both fully Jewish and fully
American without compromising Jewish values or jeopardizing credentials
of citizenship. Likewise, he accepted the scientific advances of his age as
completely compatible with religious belief, embracing Darwinism and biblical
criticism as enhancements rather than denials of religion—this despite the fact

that most other ministers and rabbis, including his teacher, Isaac Mayer Wise, initially opposed them. An outspoken loner and independent, oblivious to personal considerations, his frequently unorthodox means of pursuing human rights drew public attention frowned upon by Jewish community leaders, who preferred their own brand of quiet diplomacy. The wide diversity of his activism and the range of people whose lives he touched present a rarely seen image of Jewish life in America during a period of formative growth in American Judaism as well as in the nation itself.

During the last quarter of the nineteenth century and the beginning of the twentieth, American Jews strove to identify themselves both as Americans and as Jews. The vast majority were immigrants, and few, even among the highly successful, were thoroughly free of the fears that informed their lives in Europe. Most of them came from areas where, although legally included as citizens and partially acculturated, in reality they were largely excluded and treated as pariahs. In America where their skills were needed and generally welcomed, city councils, Masonic lodges and literary societies opened to them. Their Christian neighbors, many of whom also came from Germany and shared their nostalgia for its culture, found them congenial and respected them as descendants of the "Old Testament" Prophets. Together they enjoyed German music, German literature, and German dance.

On the other hand, it was difficult to practice Judaism in America. While many Jewish communities provided makeshift Sunday schools for the children, until the mass immigrations of the 1880s there was little opportunity for more than the most basic Jewish education. Nor was it easy to obtain kosher food, and it was all but impossible for most Jews to keep the Sabbath because they could not afford to remain idle on Saturday—payday and the busiest workday of the week. In such an environment, the problem for these western European Jews who had begun to enjoy emancipation was no longer how to be accepted by their Christian neighbors, but how to remain Jewish.

In the pre-modern Europe from which these immigrants came, Jewish communities were ruled by a chief rabbi appointed by and answerable to the civic government. Unless a Jew dared to break tradition, every aspect of his or her life was regulated by the local rabbi's interpretation of Talmudic law. With the beginning of emancipation in western and central Europe in the late eighteenth century, attempted reforms—including modern interpretations of the law—began to loosen the rabbinic stranglehold for many Jews. Most of them were only too happy to interpret those rules for themselves upon arrival in the "Jewish wilderness" of America. This absence of control along with fluctuations of the economy resulted in significant instability, affecting both the congregations and the rabbis who served them. Also there were hardly any Jewish educational institutions in America, none as yet for the training of rabbis. The situation invited charlatans and fly-by-nights as well as true exponents of Jewish learning.

Jacob Rader Marcus, the godfather of American Jewish history, dismissed the majority of nineteenth century American rabbis as being "of little learning and less character." Almost entirely foreign born, most were loners who emigrated as individuals seeking job opportunities and freedom from government control. They tried to establish their own choice of reforms in order to sustain Judaism in America with its relatively open society, but with few amenities to facilitate maintaining Jewish tradition. Lay leaders, often with the same goals in mind, but also at times with an additional personal agenda, frequently disagreed with the paths favored by their rabbis. Tempers were volatile, synagogue membership fluid and financial support inadequate. As a result, historian Jonathan Sarna reminds us, "Most rabbis were quick to find jobs and equally quick to lose them."[1]

Such a rabbi was "Alphabet" Browne. He did not fit the characterization described by Marcus, however, for he was unquestionably learned and of strong character. He was a maverick in a time and place of many mavericks. They came mostly from central Europe, where governments and their own religious hierarchies were grappling with the effect of the Enlightenment, tightening their grip on independent thought in order to preserve the status quo. America beckoned to individualists, especially the intellectuals among them.

In 1845, the year of Browne's birth, the Austro-Hungarian Empire had for decades dealt with political turmoil, regional insurrections, and the movement of Jews from one province to another due to economic conditions and post-rebellion reprisals against those who had fought with the insurgents. At that time relatively few Jews had settled in Browne's home town of Eperies, in Slovakia, barely enough to have recently built a synagogue within the town. They came largely from the west and north, from German states or the neighboring Austro-Hungarian provinces of Croatia and Bohemia, seeking better opportunity in less developed regions of the empire. Slovakia attracted them primarily because Jews there, having remained neutral during provincial revolts, escaped the backlash of reprisals against communities where Jews largely joined the insurgents.[2]

Later, during Browne's youth, the Jewish population of Eperies increased due to heavy migrations of Hasidic Jews from Transylvania crossing the mountains westward into Slovakia to escape persecution and poverty in Rumania. As a child, however, Browne had encountered Jewish neighbors who were much like his own family, German speaking settlers imbued with the spirit of emancipation and Enlightenment, open to secular education and in some cases to religious reform.

Western European Jews, having been freed from the ghetto and given citizenship beginning with Napoleonic edicts at the close of the previous century, tended to embrace the intellectual questioning prevalent among their fellow citizens. Some even dared to interpret the Bible in the light of new scientific studies, which drew strong opposition from the Orthodox rabbinic establishment who viewed it as heresy and feared that it would lead to the breakdown of Jewish community structure and eventual assimilation. Believing the Talmud to be perfect, its laws immutable, they feared secular education as an invitation for scholars to challenge that precept. One rabbi notably declared that anyone who studied at a university was unfit for the rabbinate.[3]

Proponents of mild change often remained under the umbrella of Orthodoxy. Describing themselves as "modern Orthodox," they sought to make peace with modernity, as historian Michael Meyer writes, while "attempting to establish the fully observant Jewish life within it." They were willing to alter practices that were merely traditions, not rooted in Talmudic law. More radical reformers sought to change not only the liturgy and outward manifestations of their belief, but the very structure of the Jewish community itself. They became known as "Neologs."[4]

By the 1840s, the call for decorum in the synagogue and a more intellectual approach to worship could be heard in many places. While notable controversy took place in the Germanic states, reforms occurred more quietly in the Austro-Hungarian empire, especially in the north and west. In Eperies where Browne lived, for example, the congregation held confirmation services for boys and girls together as early as 1846. This nod to gender equality was one of the earliest innovations of Reform.[5]

Only in the capital city did tensions rise to a boiling point. There a group of young people had established a service with mild modernization, similar to one being used in Vienna. For a while they were allowed to practice as they wished. In 1847 a brilliant young rabbinic candidate, Ignaz Einhorn, became their leader and took them speedily into the more radical reforms being carried out in a few synagogues in Germany, mainly in Hamburg and Berlin. Einhorn and his followers formed the Central Association of Hungarian Israelites, hoping to create a league of like minded congregations. This failed, but they continued locally, renaming their group the Pesth Israelite Reform Association. Emboldened by the revolution of 1848, they went even further, holding worship services on Sunday, abandoning the wearing of hats, instituting the use of an organ and choir in their synagogue, and preaching in the vernacular, even reciting some of the prayers in Hungarian. When this also failed, Ignaz Einhorn fled to Germany.[6]

Whereas the revolution inspired Magyarization (Hungarianization) among Jews, its failure brought a fierce backlash against them. This caused the Orthodox leaders to become ever more nervous about Jewish radicalism and increasingly harsh in suppressing it. In 1852, they persuaded the government to close the synagogue of the Pesth Reform Association. This sent an unmistakable message to Hungarian Jews that changes would not be tolerated. The winds of change continued to blow, however, and more strongly in some outlying communities than in the capital city. Initial movements of reform were felt in Eperies in 1845, the very year that Moshe ben (son of) M'hader Yaakov—subsequently Rabbi "Alphabet" Browne—was born.[7]

Moritz and Katje Sonnenschein Braun (pronounced "brown") enjoyed high standing in their community. Moritz was a judge and president of the synagogue, a man of means and influence. Katje came from a family able to provide her with lasting indications of affluence, one of which was a set of huge, intricately carved ivory cufflinks bearing the monogram of her father, probably later worn by her husband and their son. Their home displayed such elegant accouterments as tall monogrammed silver candlesticks, fine linen damask towels, and oil on canvas portraits of themselves as bride and groom.[8]

As customary in the German speaking social stratum to which the Brauns belonged, Moshe and his two sisters, Teresa and Ilona, were initially educated at home by private tutors. They were taught French as well as high German, in addition to which Moshe studied Hebrew as every Jewish boy was required to do. He later learned Yiddish and Magyar (Hungarian), the languages spoken on the streets of Eperies.

The boy could read Talmud—the books of exegesis and commentary on the Torah—at a very early age. This was an astonishing feat because, while custom demanded that all Jewish boys learn Hebrew initially by memorizing the Torah, then by memorizing the entire Hebrew Bible, they were rarely permitted even to begin the complicated study of Talmud with its arguments and legalisms until after becoming bar mitzvah, at age thirteen. As a very young child, Moshe Braun was frequently called upon to recite randomly designated Talmudic passages in public, which he did verbatim, for charitable events in the synagogue. Being so encouraged to show off, this adored only son of prominent parents received ongoing adulation from the entire community. The exploitation may have affected his character for his adult ego appeared to be over-developed, but apparently it did not detract from his popularity as a child. One elderly woman remembered him as bold and outspoken "but always beloved by all," and another as "a hard student" and very kindhearted.[9]

During Moshe's bar mitzvah year, a new rabbi, Mayer Austerlitz, came to Eperies. A disciple of Rabbi Azriel Hildesheimer, renowned teacher of modern Orthodoxy before Reform became an established movement, Austerlitz may well have sparked the boy's interest in becoming a rabbi dedicated to reforms.[10]

Both science and religion fascinated young Moshe. This was not surprising because German culture placed special importance on the study of science. It was likewise not unusual for German speaking Jews to combine this discipline with the study of Judaism. For millennia great rabbis were known to combine medicine with religion. Now the prescient among enlightened nineteenth century Jews foresaw the risk of assimilation, the logical antidote to which was an increased emphasis on Jewish education.[11]

At seventeen Moshe Braun entered a government technical college to study science. He gave some lectures on the subject while there, and graduated two years later. Then, perhaps influenced by the Modern Orthodox background of his home town rabbi, he enrolled in an early outpost of modern Judaism, the Fünfkirchen Theological Seminary. Its director, Rabbi I. H. Hirschfeld, gave him a theological degree after only one year. Then Braun came to America.[12]

There is no sure answer as to why he came. His daughter, having heard that he charmed the ladies during his bachelor years in America, imagined that he had perhaps done so to excess in Europe, departing in order to escape the consequences of a careless romance. This, however, went contrary to the view of the elderly woman from his home town who had known him since his childhood. She recalled that he was a straight-laced young man whose friends often chided him for not joining in their student revelries. A contemporary who came to America with him remarked on his "uprightly and independent behavior," noting that he "never cared for money . . . never buys on credit, never owes a cent . . . never asks for a favor . . . never drank and is not a society man" a characterization backed by accounts of his future life. Many years later, Browne described his lifestyle in approximately the same words to Theodor Herzl, the visionary of modern political Zionism. "I find it important to tell you," he wrote in support of his offer to work for Zionism, "that I do not drink, I don't smoke, I don't gamble, I am not a gourmet, make no visits and receive no guests and work 18 hrs a day."[13]

Although such testimonials do not disprove the possibility that he fled Europe to avoid a shotgun wedding, it seems far more likely that he left in order to pursue a career in a progressive form of Judaism. Many others from Central Europe, among them the renowned liberal rabbis Samuel Adler, Max Lilienthal, Isaac M. Wise, and David Einhorn, did likewise during the middle and late nineteenth century.

Einhorn, no relation to the fiery Ignaz Einhorn of the Pesth congregation, had in fact followed his namesake as rabbi in Pesth in1852, but had to leave after two months because the government closed his synagogue. Having so inflamed the powers governing European Judaism, David Einhorn came to America as rabbi of Temple Har Sinai in Baltimore, where he became known as this country's uncompromising leader of radical Reform. A generation older than Braun, he shared much of the younger man's temperament, possibly because both were influenced by their native environment in Hungary.[14]

When Moshe ben M'hader Yaakov Braun came to America in late August, 1865, he became Edward Benjamin Morris Browne—Ed to his intimates. At least one of his friends was among the many young men who traveled with him that year, just a few months after the American Civil War ended. Adding to the attraction of new opportunities for work and individual enterprise was the novelty of crossing the Atlantic by steamship which had just begun when the war ended. Although this radically improved mode of travel was launched in the early 1860s, it was used exclusively for government priorities and not available to the public until after the war. Thus did the voyage hold exceptional promise for young men like Browne who were embarking not only on a new form of transportation, but on a new life as well.[15]

Such an experience remains a milepost in memory, easily becoming romanticized and embellished. Years later Browne recalled standing on the docks in Hamburg, "with a longing look [toward] this land of freedom . . . watching in wonder the many different kinds of ships "ungearing, loosening their tackles, heaving anchor, developing steam, setting sails and saluting with a cannon ball a farewell to old Europe."[16]

Musing on the destinations of so many ships, the young rabbi asked an old mariner on a small schooner where he was going. "New York," the man answered.

Next, Browne noticed a bark and asked its skipper, "Where to, good friend?"

He, too, replied "New York."

Then Browne spied another ship, the "Red, White and Blue." It was manned by two sailors and a dog, also going to New York. Browne considered this an indication of American foolhardiness.

Then, according to his memoir, the young emigre watched hundreds of vessels start for New York, "with proud or humble masts, with swelled or baffled sails, with steam, with screws, and with side wheels. . . ." Following them in the distance as they scattered in different directions, he saw them "float on for awhile, and finally rise and sink and recede in the mist. . . ."

Weaving this image into a sermon years later, Browne noted that his ship had reached New York before the others. After three weeks ashore he returned to the docks and encountered the skipper of the "Red, White and Blue," which had just arrived. Greeting him, Browne mentioned that this crossing had taken much longer than his own, whereupon the seasoned seaman replied, "You traveled by steam. . . . I had to travel by sail. . . . The steamer can no more deride the sail than the sail the rudder, for they are the developments of each other. First the rudder, then the sail, then the steam, next electricity. Or the sunbeam, for all we know."[17]

Even assuming that Browne concocted the story to enhance a sermon, the words provide evidence that his early interest in science and technology continued throughout his life, as indeed it did. In 1912 he designed an airplane which, after the United States entered the first World War, he offered to the War Department. Even more revealing was his reference to sailing toward the same place by different routes and diverse sources of power, which became a metaphor for his entire life. As shall be seen, he sought the same basic goals as others did, but by different vehicles and different routes. More often than not, he plied the waves alone on uncharted seas, powered solely by his own resourcefulness.[18]

Browne stayed a short while in New York before departing for Cincinnati at the invitation of Rabbi Isaac Mayer Wise, a leader of Reform in America, then in its initial stages of development. Reform had no national organization, no standard of observance, and no American-trained rabbis. Wise, who became its chief organizer and institution builder, emigrated from Bohemia in 1846, and after a stormy eight-year tenure in Albany, New York, accepted a call to Congregation B'nai Jeshurun (now known at Wise Synagogue) in the well established German Jewish community of Cincinnati. Soon renowned throughout the country, it was he whom most congregations other than those in the large Jewish centers of New York, Philadelphia and Baltimore consulted when they needed a rabbi. In this capacity Wise was constantly on the lookout for promising young scholars with rabbinic potential.

Wise probably heard of Browne from mutual friends or colleagues in Europe. The renowned rabbi soon took the neophyte under wing and into his home, treating him like a member of the family. Theresa Bloch Wise, the rabbi's wife, became a surrogate mother to Browne, and he became the brotherly confidant of her children, especially the rebellious son Leo who was only a few years his junior. I. M. Wise nurtured and instructed Browne, supervised his secular education, and masterminded his moves for the foreseeable future.[19]

The Wises mingled freely in gentile society and introduced Browne to it as one of their own. They were the only Jews living on College Hill, so named because of several institutions of higher learning located there, including Farmer's College, the Medical College of Ohio, and the Ohio Female College. Browne, while studying privately with Wise for the Reform rabbinate, enrolled in Farmer's College to further his general education and entered the medical school to follow his interest in science. At the Ohio Female College, where the Wise daughters were the only Jewish students, he spent a sufficient amount of time to become friends with some of more literary minded ladies.[20]

Although he did not study English before coming to America and later claimed to have had little fluency in it during his initial stay in Cincinnati, Browne made himself understood well enough by members of the Hesperian literary society of the Ohio Female College for them to invite him to contribute to their publication, The Hesperian Gazette. He obliged by submitting a number of humorous, romantic verses. In 1869, Browne inscribed these poems along with others in a 276 page handwritten album entitled "Floral House Weeds," which he dedicated to Wise and presented to him and Theresa on their twenty-fifth wedding anniversary. Browne's first body of work in English, it also included four items in other languages that Wise understood—one in Hebrew, one each for Rabbi and Mrs. Wise in German, and a translation of Lord Byron's "Maid of Athens" in Hungarian. The verses were mostly romantic and about women, probably tongue-in-cheek. One that was both serious and touching he dedicated to his sister Ilona.[21]

Despite a disclaimer that his views, "religious or otherwise, should by no means be inferred from these writings," they often foreshadow issues that he would espouse in the future. In one that suggests the rising voice of organized labor, which he vigorously supported as the movement grew, he seemed to be scolding those who demanded higher wages without having earned them.

> *We are always complaining, we have less than our neighbor,*
> *Why man! do compare your reward with your labor!*
> *If he works more than you, more reward he may claim;*
> *And he receives that reward. 'Tis yourself you must blame.*

Certainly no Walt Whitman, the would-be bard tended to imitate Algernon Charles Swinburne and Edgar Allen Poe, often emulating their meter and rhyming schemes as well as their flowery romanticism. Yet for all his sophomoric versifying, the ardent youth revealed an astonishing breadth of knowledge and interests. His metaphors ranged from copious use of scripture to such references as mythology, ancient and modern history, astronomy, botany, and Dalton's law on the use of gasses. He also displayed, for one so recently arrived in America, a surprising knowledge of national politics. The impeachment of President Andrew Johnson inspired him to write the last poem in his collection, entitled "North and South."

> *To you in the North*
> *Whose arrows go forth*
> *To strike a fallen hero,*

Whose venomous mouth

Denounces the South:

"Remember the end of a Nero!"

And the South in despair

I remind: "be aware,

There are roses enough among thorns.

Wade and Butler the beasts

The devil's best priests

Have lost the power of their horns.

Though radical wrath

Presages but death

And sends you defying the challenge;

Up on high watches God

With righteousness' rod,

Adjusting the uneven balance!"

Browne's apparent sympathy for the South, particularly the allusion to Generals Benjamin Wade and Benjamin Butler as "the beasts," probably stemmed from Wise's influence. Although there is no evidence to suggest that either man ever condoned slavery—Browne, in fact, as shall be seen, displayed unpatronizing friendship for African Americans even while serving Southern congregations—it is likely that as Wise's disciple he absorbed his teacher's views that the South should have been allowed to secede unchallenged in order to avoid war. Browne probably dedicated the poem to Johnson out of personal sympathy rather than endorsement of the president's political decisions.[22]

After one year Wise sent Browne to Savannah, Georgia, for "seasoning" and to improve his English while teaching Hebrew at the Savannah Hebrew

Collegiate Institute. It is possible that he also wanted to divert his protégé's attentions from Cincinnati's social life. The wily mentor may even have tried to arrange a suitable marriage, a *shittoch*, for Browne, as he reputedly did for future rabbinic candidates at Hebrew Union College, cautioning them to take a wife before signing on with a congregation. He secured lodgings for Browne in Savannah at the home of the school's superintendent, Rabbi Raphael Lewin, whose wife, Adeline, had an unmarried sister. They were daughters of Abraham Einstein, one of the city's wealthiest Jews and a founder of the Hebrew Institute. According to rumor, the Einsteins encouraged Browne to become their son-in-law and never forgave him for declining the favor. Over a decade later, when false charges were brought against Browne in New York, his nephew believed that they had been instigated by the Einstein family in revenge.[23]

Besides teaching at the Hebrew Institute, Browne matriculated at the Savannah Medical College, and also gave several lectures there in chemistry. His experience in the laid-back city of colonial origins and wartime captivity enabled him to deepen his understanding of American history, to acquaint himself directly with a segment of the South under the burden of Reconstruction, and to intensify his sympathy for southerners of both races.[24]

Browne returned to Ohio the following year, resumed his medical studies at the institution that later became the Medical School of the University of Cincinnati, and earned his Doctor of Medicine degree by the end of the term. At the same time Wise gave him *s'micha*—rabbinic ordination—possibly the first and only one conferred in America before the first graduation at the Hebrew Union College in 1883.

Now Wise believed that his protégé was ready to test his skills as an American rabbi. Browne was well connected, well endowed intellectually, and no less well suited sartorially for the very visible position of Jewish leadership in the rising middle class communities of the United States. Photographs reveal him as a courtly youth with a full head of brown hair above a wide oval face, sporting a neatly trimmed mustache and goatee, garbed in black cutaway with a medal dangling from his watch chain, posed proudly in Napoleonic stance with right hand in vest and gray eyes determinedly forward. Although only five foot three and three quarters inches tall—slightly less than average height—he was slim, fashionable and debonair, suggesting affluence and sophistication, attributes much admired and eagerly sought by nineteenth century American Jewry.

Happily, Browne had none of the negative characteristics generally associated with the typical "greenhorn." What he lacked was not visible, its absence not quickly detected. It was, however, an ephemeral quality highly necessary for success as a congregational rabbi. As Wise later expressed the need, one must be "very circumspect, particularly in an age and in a country where rabbis are looked upon as ice cream only."[25]

Browne could not be compared to ice cream. His persona more closely resembled the culinary specialty of his native land. Hungarian goulash is highly seasoned, greatly nutritious, and for many people hard to digest.

II - UNCHARTED WATERS AND SOPHIE

Browne sailed forth into the uncharted, turbulent seas of the American rabbinate only partially prepared for the conditions that awaited him. Although Wise had ostensibly introduced his protégé to the real world of the American rabbinate by taking him along on some of his travels, the fledgling rabbi had yet to observe the far reaching ramifications of the power struggle that divided American congregations and their rabbis.

This was a period of transition, a time when many were undecided about the degree of reform that would best serve their needs both as new Americans and as Jews. Congregations fluctuated back and forth between the modern orthodoxy taking root in Europe, and the emerging neologism—radical reform—that they were now free to practice without restraint in America. Much depended on the views of congregational presidents and their boards of directors. No longer ruled by a government-appointed rabbi as in Europe, laymen rebelled against rabbinic domination and often relegated their spiritual leader to the position of mere functionary, an employee to be curbed or fired at the will or whim of an influential member. Personal egos ran high on both sides of the bima (pulpit).[1]

A few exceptionally well-qualified rabbis prevailed over this condition by gaining "star power," through authorship of periodicals and prayer books, as well as by crowd- pleasing oratory. Occasionally a congregation would import an already renowned rabbi from Europe, as did New York's B'nai Jeshurun in 1849 when it lured Morris Raphall from Birmingham, England, with the promise of high salary and life tenure. Such rabbis represented a range of Jewish thought from the uncompromising orthodoxy of Abraham Rice, who immigrated in 1840 and was the first ordained rabbi to serve an American congregation, to the extreme Reform of David Einhorn, who arrived in

1855, unable to hold a pulpit in Germanic states because of his radical views. Between these poles others maintained their own agendas for the salvation of American Jewry, some remaining adamant proponents of particular views; others compromising to further their various missions, and some genuinely moved by a change of philosophy.[2]

Isaac Leeser, although educated in America and unordained, was a traditionalist who nevertheless advocated Americanizing Judaism. Despite his German background, he had served as hazan (cantor and reader) of Mikveh Israel, Philadelphia's historic Portuguese Congregation. Widely known for his efforts to educate American Jews through his many publications including the first Jewish-oriented translation of the Bible into English, and the Occident, the first nationally disseminated American Jewish periodical, he traveled extensively performing weddings, dedicating synagogues, and persuading far flung communities such as that of Atlanta to form congregations. As early as 1841, he attempted to organize a congregational union. The only rabbi of his day to approach him in output or travel was his energetic younger colleague, I. M. Wise of Cincinnati.[3]

By the time of Leeser's death in 1868, Wise had become the recognized leader of "Western" Jewry—Jews living west of the Alleghenies. Congregations in need of a rabbi typically asked him for recommendations, which gave him increasing power and influence, putting younger rabbis in his debt as their benefactor. Knowing how fluid these positions were, such rabbis were reluctant to risk Wise's disapproval even after achieving their immediate goals.

Leading Wise's competition in the East were the cutting-edge liberals, David Einhorn, who by that time had moved from Baltimore to Philadelphia and then to Adath Israel (now Temple Beth El) of New York, and Samuel Adler of New York's prestigious Temple Emanu-El, the wealthiest congregation in America. Unlike Wise, who immigrated as an unknown, they had attracted attention in Europe arriving in America as recognized scholars and ardent reformers. They were older than Wise, and despite being more traditionally educated than he, were even more determined to break with tradition. In 1869, they published a weekly newspaper, the Jewish Times, to promote their views.[4]

Wise had already established his two weekly newspapers, the Israelite (English) and Die Devorah (German), as well as a publishing house for Jewish books. Having little formal education but a mind quick to absorb and retain, he was, in Browne's words, "a self-made man, [who] had much business enterprise. . . ." He organized the so-called Western Jews "on a business-like basis, and . . . continually [went] for his opponents so that they became mortal enemies."[5]

A major point of controversy was competition over the selection of prayer books. With few exceptions, congregations in post-colonial America used either the traditional Minhag Ashkenaz to which they were accustomed, or a liturgy composed by their rabbi in response to members' request for more modernization. The earliest of these was Leo Mersbacher's Order of Prayer, published in 1855, then quickly followed by Wise's Minhag America in 1856, which reflected his purpose of uniting American Jewry, thus being seen as "middle of the road." Einhorn, who had no desire to compromise or Americanize, competed the same year as Wise by publishing his Olat Tamid in German as an appeal for intellectualized radical Reform in the German tradition. Among others who published later according to their own precepts were Adolph Huebsch of New York, Raphael da Cordova Lewin of Brooklyn, David Levy of Charleston, Max Landsburg of Rochester, Aaron Hahn of Cleveland, Solomon Sonneschein of St. Louis, and Browne himself in New York. Not only did the purchase of these books produce income for their authors, it also indicated the degree to which congregations approved a particular rabbi's views on liturgy. They served as weapons in the rabbis' war for control of American Judaism, a conflict frequently marked by unbridled accusations in the Jewish press, notably in journals published by the rabbis themselves.[6]

Wise and Einhorn divided on more basic, inherent differences, however. The latter, an ideologue and uncompromising revolutionary, refused to bend his convictions even temporarily in order to gain wider support. He was an intellectual; Wise was not. Wise was a politician whose great appeal lay in his popular style and affable approach, his ability to relate to the public. His most compelling issue was uniting American Jewry in order to support a seminary for the training of rabbis who would then spread his interpretation of Reform across America. He often bent his tactics to further his progress, but never deviated from his goal of establishing a seminary.

In this spirit of compromise Wise spearheaded a conference in Cleveland in 1855. It was a third attempt to unite all American Jewish congregations. This infuriated Einhorn, who arrived in America just as the conference was about to begin and refused to attend. Although its adopted platform failed when traditional leaders recognized it as a tactic for establishing Reform, its most virulent opponents were Einhorn's supporters at the opposite pole. They abhorred compromise, however temporary or practical it may have been.

Einhorn responded by immediately producing yet another competing prayer book, Olat Tamid, and establishing Sinai, a monthly German language periodical. The journal lasted only six years, whereas Wise's weekly, The Israelite, in publication before Einhorn's began, is still being published today and enjoyed a wide circulation during Wise's lifetime, especially across the mid-west and the south. Ironically, although Wise's views prevailed at the time, Einhorn's, known as radical reform, ultimately emerged as the winner, becoming the foundation of Classical Reform through the leadership of his distinguished sons-in-law, Rabbi Emil G. Hirsch of Chicago and Rabbi Kaufmann Kohler who, after Wise died, became president of the Hebrew Union College.[7]

Browne was drawn into the Wise versus Einhorn (moderate versus radical Reform) controversy in September 1868, when Wise took him to New York for the dedication of Temple Emanu-El's outstanding new synagogue. The congregation's rabbi, Samuel Adler, pulled Browne aside to advise him that the occasion presented "a very favorable opportunity" for reconciling the conflict between Einhorn and Wise. Believing that their "entire enmity comes from their prayer books," Adler thought that they might be persuaded to collaborate on a new *minhag* as replacement for their existing ones. He offered to bring Einhorn to the table if Browne could bring Wise. Wise agreed. Einhorn refused.[8]

Competition among rabbis over philosophy and control, fueled by their overarching egos, exacerbated differences between Wise and his opponents. Freed from the restraints of censorship as in Europe, they publicly insulted each other in vitriolic terms that would be unacceptable today. Einhorn, for example, memorably referred to Wise's lowly position in Europe and questionable ordination as rabbi with the statement that he, "would not set with that Bohemian ex-schochet [ritual slaughterer] 'Rev. Dr.' under one roof." He called Wise "the Barnum of the Jewish pulpit" who "arrogates to himself the role of dictator," and declared Wise's Minhag America "an abortion." Wise responded in The Israelite, calling Einhorn and his friends a pack of "unprincipled nobodies."[9]

One of those friends was the revered scholar Marcus Jastrow, who after earning a rabbinical degree and doctorate of philosophy, had been jailed in Poland for speaking out on human rights. In 1866, Congregation Rodeph

Shalom of Philadelphia brought Jastrow to America with a generous life contract and salary of $4000 a year, thus assuring his status as a "celebrity" rabbi. In contrast to his east coast colleagues Einhorn and Adler, Jastrow was a more temperate reformer who immediately enabled his congregation "to feel the pulse of the times in Judaism in America," and was later instrumental in establishing Conservative Judaism. His opposition to Wise stemmed from theological differences and the fact that he viewed the Cincinnati rabbi as a radical reformer without principle or learning. He opposed Wise's idea of a Union of American Hebrew Congregations and the seminary that it would support.[10]

Jastrow apparently called Wise a liar in a published pamphlet, whereupon Browne recalled having gone to Philadelphia "with the sole purpose of cowhiding Dr. Jastrow." Fortunately the hot-headed acolyte reconsidered, but not without having called attention to himself as a quick-triggered spokesperson for Wise.[11]

Montgomery, 1868

With this already dubious reputation, Browne entered his career as a rabbi. Steering him clear of the volatile east coast communities, Wise sent him to a pulpit safely within the protective confines of his own "western" influence. In 1869, when the turbulence of Reconstruction gave Southern Jews more pressing issues to contend with than disputes over differing views of Judaism, Wise sent his protégé to the "Cradle of the Confederacy," Montgomery, Alabama.

Congregation Kahl Montgomery (now Temple Beth Or) although incorporated in 1852, had actually been in existence for twenty years and its membership—mostly German, Alsatian, and Polish in origin—had increased far beyond its original thirty founders. In 1862, the congregation acquired a synagogue building, largely through a bequest from New Orleans philanthropist Judah Touro.[12]

The congregation had been served by numerous readers, whose duty it was to lead the services and sometimes to teach the children. They had to know Hebrew, but were neither ordained rabbis nor necessarily scholars. Only one actual rabbi, James K. Gutheim, served in Montgomery before Browne. A staunch Confederate, distinguished scholar and advocate of moderate Reform, Gutheim left New Orleans rather than sign a pledge of allegiance to the United States when the city fell to Federal forces. He survived the war by settling his family with his wife's parents in Mobile and earned a minuscule income by serving the congregations both of Montgomery, Alabama, and Columbus, Georgia, to which he commuted on a part-time basis. At war's end he returned to New Orleans, having led the formerly traditionalist Kahl Montgomery well into Reform.[13]

Browne might have anticipated encountering special problems in this Deep South community still anguished by defeat in what local residents referred to as the "War of the Northern Aggression." When he arrived, the Alabama capital, original capital of the Confederacy, was still under military rule and far from having healed its war wounds. Montgomery's Jews, although largely residents of long standing ostensibly comfortable in their gentile environment, under the stress of war had become ever more sensitive to their neighbors' view of them. Although economic disaster engendered by the war affected Jews and Christians alike, it aroused some envy of those Jews who noticeably prospered, one example of which was a Jewish shoe manufacturer appointed to supervise production of shoes for the Confederate army. This stirred previously dormant antisemitism, and among Jews dredged memories of enduring persecution in Europe which intensified their resolve to be acknowledged as fervent defenders of the Lost Cause. It was not unusual to see framed Confederate money and army discharge papers mounted on the walls of their homes.[14]

The post-bellum situation called for utmost discretion in public discourse, especially in regard to patriotism and social justice. Browne refrained from overt reference to these subjects in his first lecture in Montgomery, which he gave on Sunday morning, August 1, 1869. Because in those days lectures were a major source of entertainment and it was understood that some Christians would attend, he chose "Ethics of the Talmud," an apparently nonpolitical subject to which he had given much thought over a long period of time and for which he held passionate convictions. As a devotee of the Talmud since childhood, he strongly disagreed with Einhorn and the radical reformers who decried it. Considering his congregants' sensitivity to Christian scrutiny however, some of his ideas may nevertheless have caused them discomfort.

In his preamble Browne stated that Talmudic ethics could be understood only "in close alliance with modern sciences," which clearly indicated that he viewed sacred texts from a scientific perspective. The latter, a relatively new and disputed form of study known as Biblical criticism, was being developed primarily by Christian scholars in Europe, some of whom were reputedly anti-Semitic. Browne contended that few people of either faith understood Talmudic ethics because "only a few gentlemen of the old European Hebrew school" were sufficiently trained to comprehend the text, and they had been taught to regard it as "a study claiming the implicit faith of the student, a work which should not pass the speculative processes of the mind . . .beyond the test of mental synthesis or analysis." Christian scholars, in turn, while devoting "much of their time to the investigation . . . according to the means at their command" had even less possibility of understanding it because they were "confined to mere translations, frequently very defective, generally very unsystematically arranged, and nothing more than trifling fragments."[15]

Browne followed with a brief definition of the Talmud, including the fact that it was written over a period of six centuries, "and perhaps much longer . . . ." Furthermore, he noted, current knowledge depended upon men who collected and compiled the traditions long after their authors had died.

In the body of his lecture Browne examined four divisions of Talmudic ethics: reverence toward father and mother, charity and benevolence, preservation and restoration of peace, and study and instruction above all. He illustrated its ethical superiority by contrasting such examples as Sophocles' reprimand of his son for disrespecting his mother Xantippe, and the story of Cleobis and Biton according to Herodotus and Plutarch, with the Talmudic account of Rabbi Tarphon having placed his hands under his mother's feet to protect her from stepping on barren ground.

Browne then cited Talmudic sections on charity and peace, referring to Bar Kaprah's "glimpse into heaven" to demonstrate that angels harbored no hatred despite their differences. Underscoring ecumenism, he quoted the Talmudic passage, "All that are toiling for the restoration and preservation of peace, without religious distinction, shall inherit of the Lord peace and happiness here and hereafter," adding the similar passage from Jesus' Sermon on the Mount, "Blessed are the peacemakers, for they will be called the children of God."[16]

Regarding the Talmudic injunction to study and teach, he reminded listeners that the Jewish tradition of public education dated from the time of Ezra, and described the zeal with which ancient rabbis pursued their own studies. To illustrate the excess of that zeal (and demonstrate his attitude toward the traditionalists) he noted that the rabbis of the Talmud, "like the ultra-orthodox of our days, carried everything to the extreme." Scholars were so revered, he said, that they were exempted from such ordinary concerns as providing for their own sustenance. He cited as an example the story of Rabbi Simon Bar Yochai secluding himself in a cave for thirteen years, sustained by fruit from a tree that miraculously grew in the depths of the cave for that purpose. To emphasize such heavenly provision for poets and scholars, he translated and quoted Friedrich Schiller's poem "Die Theilung der Erde" (The Division of Earth), its lesson being "that real devotion to knowledge cannot be coupled with the enjoyments of earthly pleasures."

In closing, Browne apologized for inability to do full justice to the subject in the given time, and again referred with slight disparagement to the ultra-orthodox who continued to accept Scripture and Talmud literally. He noted that it was his intention "simply to remove part of the prejudice entertained against the Talmud" not only by outsiders, but also by "Israel's own sons [who] add now to its misrepresentations." In America, some of the blame for those misrepresentations could be attributed to its scarcity of trained rabbis.

Turning from the fundamentalists to their opposites, Browne then criticized radical reformers who rejected the Talmud:

> the American Jewish pulpit, like all professions, has its parasites, being blessed (?) with a great number of so-called Rev. Drs. . . . [whose] titles consist in a dozen or two of white cravats and a waist-coat buttoned up to the chin. . . . Yet they wish to be reformers, and to be that, they believe it a contingency to decry the Talmud, which they cannot even read. But that is a great mistake. The Talmud is a treasure of learning, and Israel's leading reformers quote it freely in their daily works and writings.

Although Browne's Montgomery audience may have been impressed with his knowledge, overall approval of these remarks was questionable.

Few Jews, regardless of their degree of reform, were ready to accept biblical criticism, even fewer to shed their long ingrained belief in divine revelation. Also, some listeners may have taken umbrage at his condemnation of "so-called" rabbis or of those radical reformers who thought that the Talmud was irrelevant. Still others, sensitive to the reaction of Christians in the audience, may have been disturbed by his candor in criticizing conditions within the "American Jewish pulpit."

While this does not appear to have been a prudent discourse for Browne's debut in Montgomery, it obviously pleased his mentor in Cincinnati, whose own beliefs he so devotedly reiterated. Wise published the lecture in its entirety, spreading it over his next three issues of the Israelite.

A few weeks later, Browne preached a sermon for Rosh Hashana, the Jewish New Year, much milder and only a fraction as long as his lecture on the Talmud. The title, "Comparative Mythology - The Book of Life," described it well, his premise being that we should not dismiss as myths the religious literature of other ancient peoples while continuing to accept as literal truth equally anthropomorphic imagery in our own. Citing the traditional Jewish New Year's blessing "May you be inscribed in the book of life for a good year," as a timely example, he contradicted the general assumption that it referred to an actual notation, presumably by the hand of God. He said that it was a metaphor which meant that we should inscribe ourselves for life metaphorically by the manner in which we live. Even this innocuous nod to the scientific approach, however, was apparently more radical than some of his Montgomery congregants could accept. Temple Beth Or dismissed Browne forthwith because of that sermon.[17]

Despite so short a tenure, the exposure of his scholarship, eloquence, and unorthodox views gained Browne recognition elsewhere. There were few rabbis in America then with a sufficient command of English for use on the pulpit, and an increasing number of congregations anxious to infuse more English into their services that were still conducted in Hebrew and German. Browne received an invitation from Philadelphia's Reform congregation Keneseth Israel, where the fiery Einhorn had once served, to be its English preacher alongside the German speaking Rabbi Samuel Hirsch. Wary of Einhorn's lingering influence and not yet ready to leave the orbit of his mentor, Browne declined, opting instead for Wise's recommendation that he become the first rabbi of a newly formed, second congregation in Milwaukee.[18]

Milwaukee, 1869

The move took him from a southern city decimated by the Civil War to a northern city enriched by it. Congregation Emanu-El had broken off from Milwaukee's long established Congregation B'nai Jeshurun only the year before, instigated by the community's burgeoning Jewish population which expanded from a maximum of seventy families in the 1850s to more than two thousand individuals by 1869. Pioneer Jews who only a few years earlier had been country peddlers, small grocers, and clothiers had suddenly become manufacturers, meat packers, purveyors of grain, and moguls of transportation on the Great Lakes. Upwardly mobile and flexing their muscle, leaders of the new congregation readily offered their rabbi a three- year contract at an annual salary of $2500.[19]

Again Browne promptly displeased his congregants, but apparently not due to a sermon. On the grounds that he lacked the necessary qualities demanded of the position, the board asked him to resign within three months, paying him only $700 for his efforts. Having been given no specific reason for dismissal, he complained in Wise's paper, now renamed the American Israelite. He demanded an explanation but did not receive one.

His later claim that he resigned because the congregation had no building seems somewhat specious because the congregation acquired a building the following year. In light of his future reluctance to deal with financial matters other than personal ones, it is reasonable to suppose that he refused to become involved in the congregation's building campaign and that perhaps this was the major quality in which the trustees found him lacking. It is also possible that he expressed his position in less than diplomatic terms. The former *wunderkind* was developing a knack for sarcasm and a short fuse for dealing with those whom he considered pompous incompetents.[20]

Before leaving Milwaukee, Browne had the joy of celebrating the fifth anniversary of his arrival in America—i.e., the date on which he became eligible to apply for citizenship. He lost no time in doing so. Accompanied by two Milwaukee friends, A. S. Singer and attorney Max N. Lando, who co-signed his application, Browne appeared before the municipal court of Milwaukee on January 25, 1871, to become a naturalized citizen of the United States.[21]

Madison, 1870

By that time he had moved to Madison and enrolled in two courses at the University of Wisconsin School of Law. In June of the same year that he became a citizen, he received his bachelor of law degree, the only foreigner and apparently the only Jew in a graduating class of twenty. With that event he completed the collection of academic letters that inspired his nickname, "Alphabet."[22]

As Browne later testified, his reason for studying American law was to deepen his understanding of Talmudic law, for he was currently engaged in writing a commentary on the Talmud. Unfortunately no copy exists by which to appraise it, but in an excerpt from its introduction he clarified the connection between the two systems of law. "The Talmud as a 'corpus juris'" he explained, "is to the Jew what the Congressional Globe [now Record] is to the American citizen." In other words, this was the record of Jews' beliefs and practices, whereas the Torah was their Constitution.[23]

Because the Talmud is written primarily in Aramaic, which few Christian scholars understood, Christians did not realize that the lex talionis ["eye for an eye" etc.] and other primitive rulings were never carried out by Jewish courts. Likewise, they did not realize that Judaism had been developing for more than fifteen centuries before the Talmud was written. As a result, Christian scholarship fostered the perception that Judaism was a religion based on violence rather than love, and that its God was a god of wrath. These ideas fueled anti-Semitism. Now the recently developed Biblical criticism, also largely promulgated by Christian scholars unfamiliar with the intricacies of Talmud and led by the notoriously anti-Semitic Julius Wellhausen, furthered these misconceptions. The flawed scholarship gave fresh support to prejudice in Europe, which was currently being spread across America by evangelists in their mission to convert Jews to Christianity. The growing movement of Protestant evangelism and its Social Gospel understandably alarmed America's small Jewish community, struggling to retain its Judaism.

In step with nineteenth century Reform's emphasis on ecumenism as an antidote for prejudice, and especially as a means of ending the misguided interpretation of Talmud that furthered it, Browne used his lecture platform to interpret Talmud for non-Jews. A more powerful tool was needed, however, and along with Wise, his teacher, he foresaw the benefit that could be derived from an authoritative translation of the Talmud accessible to all English readers.

Wise, who later edited an English-language Talmud commentary written by Michael L Rodkinson, introduced Browne to the idea of writing one much earlier when Browne was his student. While present during a discussion between Wise and his Cincinnati colleagues Rabbi Max Lilienthal and Unitarian Reverend Thomas Vickers, Browne responded happily to Wise's suggestion that he undertake writing such a volume. As Wise later noted in the American Israelite, "we advised Dr. Browne to go to that piece of work which would be appreciated very highly by English readers, especially preachers, writers and students of history...We receive numerous letters of persons who want the Talmud translated; they would be much pleased...with a good English compilation of its numerous gems, stories, parables, sayings and maxims."[24]

Browne accepted the challenge. When he completed it, in 1872, E. Claxton and Company of Philadelphia asked to publish it but required that it be submitted on stereotyped plates. These cost some $4000, which delayed publication for several years while Browne sold subscriptions to pay for it. Despite the fact that he received orders from nearly 250 people, including Horace Greeley, Henry Wadsworth Longfellow, and President James A. Garfield, for reasons that will be discussed in a subsequent chapter, Claxton canceled the work and it was never published. Although Browne's work did not survive as a book, he used much of it in lectures and later published portions of it in popular form, entitled The Encyclopedia of Talmudic Beauties. Unfortunately, no copies of this volume have been found.[25]

With Protestant revivalism and missionary zeal spurring interest in the Old Testament, a growing number of American Christians became sufficiently curious about the current descendants of its people to seek knowledge of Jews and Judaism. Rabbi Isidor Kalisch, forced to leave Germany in 1849 because of his liberal views, while serving congregations in several mid-western American cities including Milwaukee, had spoken to

Christian audiences on "Ancient and Modern Judaism." Like him, Browne became known as one of the relatively few Jewish scholars in America with sufficient fluency in English to appear before non-Jewish audiences, and sufficiently conversant with early Christianity to effectively present the Jewish point of view.[26]

It is likely that Browne's expertise became known through social as well as academic involvement during his year in Madison. Although known to avoid parties while a student in Europe and avowedly doing so in later life, the young rabbi apparently diverged from this practice in his years before settling down as a married man. In the Wisconsin capital he reportedly danced with the daughter of Chief Justice Salmon Chase and met other notables, probably including some of the state's politicians. They learned of his oratorical ability and invited him to address the Wisconsin State Senate as well as to serve as its chaplain. This launched him on a series of public lectures that soon developed into a successful second career.[27]

The neophyte was not discouraged from continuing in his profession when, soon after receiving his law degree, he was hit by one of the mud-slinging anonymous writers who habitually hounded American rabbis. Someone purporting to be "M.F., a true friend of Judaism," had written to officers of the Montgomery congregation claiming that Browne had been jailed in Hungary for stealing money and other valuables, and escaped to America leaving his destitute wife and two children in Europe. The same person also wrote to the congregation in Milwaukee before Browne arrived there, not only repeating the libel but also alleging that the rabbi had eloped with a senator's daughter after stealing $500 from Wise's safe with which to finance his honeymoon. Browne believed that the slanderer was a contender for his job in each of those cities. Hoping to identify his accuser, he responded in the American Israelite, "It is below the dignity of anybody to attempt an excuse emanating from such a 'friend of Judaism.'"[28]

Wise disagreed with Browne's theory as to the reason for the libel. He was convinced that the culprit was "no disappointed candidate, [but] a Hungarian peddler whom we have met somewhere . . . and who is as malicious and unscrupulous a friend as we have met one in human shape." He not only published that opinion in his newspaper, but reaffirmed his confidence in Browne by inviting him to preach from the master's own pulpit in Cincinnati's magnificent B'nai Jeshurun, Plum Street Temple.[29]

Preaching a regular weekly sermon was a Protestant innovation adopted into Judaism by Reform that became an increasingly popular addition to Jewish services in America. This was especially true when delivered in English rather than German, the language then used in most American synagogues. Not only did it attract the younger members who spoke English and wanted to improve their fluency, but it also drew non-Jews to the synagogue since lectures were a popular form of entertainment and synagogues did not charge admission fees. Thus did the sermon grow in importance and become significant both as a factor in the process of Americanization as well as in the all-important function of combating antisemitism. As a result the role of the rabbi, which in Europe had been that of scholar and teacher with rarely any synagogue-related responsibility, changed in late nineteenth century American congregations to that of pastor, teacher, leader of the worship service, and public advocate for the Jewish community. In the words of historian Jacob Rader Marcus, the modern rabbi was expected to be "a lodestar for the youth and an ambassador to the admiring Gentiles," an image which Wise and his immediate followers as president of the Hebrew Union College assiduously cultivated.[30]

Browne, well qualified in respect to pleasing non-Jews, had no trouble finding another pulpit after failing in his first two. He received a call from Charleston's historic Congregation Beth Elohim to be its English reader alongside the Dutch-born, German-speaking Rabbi Joseph H. M. Chumaceiro. While traveling to that Deep South post, however, he made what he thought would be a temporary stop to speak for the Evansville, Indiana, lodge of B'nai B'rith, the international Jewish service organization founded in 1843. There he encountered a combination of circumstances that changed his life.[31]

Evansville, 1871

Jewish communities up and down the Ohio River from Cincinnati knew Isaac Mayer Wise and frequently sent him news to be published in the American Israelite. In September, 1871, he received a report from Samuel Meyer, a furniture manufacturer in Evansville, who wrote:

> *It is with feelings of greatest pleasure that I write to inform you that we have selected the Rev. Dr. Browne as Rabbi of our congregation, and I congratulate myself on the fact that our society is indebted to me for that piece of good fortune. While on a visit to Cincinnati, I had the pleasure of making Dr. Browne's acquaintance, and I requested him to visit Evansville, feeling that he was just the man of whom we stood in need. . . . Dr. Browne declined my proposal . . . being about to start for Charleston, S.C., where he had been called to a position as rabbi, of which any minister might be proud. I thereupon entreated him to take the route to Charleston via Evansville & Nashville, the distance being about the same as via Louisville. Dr. Browne agreed . . . and on the evening of his arrival, the B'nai B'rith invited him to address them. . . . The Doctor spoke extempore for over an hour, and the congregation were quite charmed . . . Many present declared that no foreigner could*

acquire greater proficiency in the English tongue. . . . We offered Doctor
Browne every inducement in our power to accept the position . . . but
he replied that he felt himself called to Charleston. We found, however
that he was favorably impressed with our temple and congregation, and
we contrived to detain him among us a little longer. He subsequently
delivered his lecture on the Talmud before the largest and most intelligent
audience in Evansville, and our Gentile brethren were loud in his praises,
while the city press spoke in very high terms of his discourse. But just
when it seemed that we were about to lose Dr. Browne, news suddenly
reached him that the yellow fever had broken out in Charleston, and this
intelligence caused him to accept our invitation. . . .

It may have been more than the news of yellow fever that persuaded
Browne to remain in Evansville. In addition to mentioning that the
congregation had previously considered five other candidates, each old
enough to have been Browne's father, Meyer also wrote that Wise might be
called upon shortly to perform a marriage ceremony for the young man, it
being "not unlikely that some of the most beautiful young ladies in our city
are setting their caps for him."[33]

Wise had dedicated Evansville's first synagogue in 1865, and was well
acquainted with its Jewish community. The congregation of B'nai Israel,
then known as the Sixth Street Temple, was largely composed of 1840s
immigrants from Bavaria and Wüerttemberg. It leaned toward Reform from
the beginning, was among the first to join the Union of American Hebrew
Congregations in 1873, and proudly claimed to be the very first to pay
dues. Well situated for river traffic, its citizens prospered during the war and
subsequently enjoyed the fruits of their good fortune.

Soon after Browne accepted the position in Evansville, the local B'nai

B'rith lodge sponsored a ball to benefit its Hebrew Orphan's Home in Cleveland. Since its inception B'nai B'rith had established orphanages, hospitals and other public facilities, nurturing them until they could exist on their own or were no longer needed. Balls such as these—ubiquitous as a means of supporting communal institutions and supported by Christians as well as by Jews—were scheduled to celebrate almost any occasion, especially festive Jewish holidays such as Purim and Simchat Torah at the end of Succoth, which was the case with this one. When asked to speak at the event, the rabbi noted that, although the congregation did not utilize the lulav, ethrog and succah, traditional objects for the holiday celebration, the joyous tone and charitable purpose of the event brought it closer than any other to the spirit of the festival as specified in Scripture.

Evidence of the importance that Jews placed on the approval of Christians may be seen in the report of this ball that appeared in the American Israelite. It noted that "the first American families" (i.e., native born Christian) participated, and that the local newspapers, "especially the leading and most aristocratic Journal, accorded all praise to our ladies...due homage to the beautiful 'oriental type of our Jewesses. . . .'" This avowal of admiration, combined with the lingering perception that Jews were somewhat foreign and exotic, reflected a well meant though mixed message on the part of Christians.[34]

Another note in the Evansville Journal declared, "In ball dresses amiable Miss S. W. was pronounced the most exquisite in her modest buff. . . ." The initials identified Sophie Weil, the sixteen-year-old daughter of Moses and Clara Loewenthal Weil, well established leaders in the community.

Moses Weil had come to the region from Bavaria in 1839 as a boy of twelve, settling there even before Evansville became chartered as a city. He studied law independently while working as a grocery clerk. Although admitted to the bar in later years, he never practiced law, but chose instead to remain in business. His record is similar to that of other immigrants of the time. In 1872 he was listed as a pawn broker, living on Vine Street between 7th and 8th. He later opened the first Midwest branch of the New England Mutual Life Insurance Company. Active both in civic affairs and in the Jewish community, he was also instrumental in establishing Evansville's first synagogue.[35]

The men of Clara's family, the Loewenthals, were likewise active in the community and founders of B'nai Israel. Her parents had immigrated when she was a child, bringing her, her sister Sara and their two brothers from Wüerttemburg, Germany, not far from Moses Weil's birthplace. Sister Sara married Emil Brentano, son of another German Jewish family in Evansville and brother of the bachelor August Brentano, founder of the New York bookstore that bears his name. They became the parents of the three men credited with expanding the company onto the world stage. Clara wed Moses Weil in 1853 and produced a family of four boys and three girls. Sophie, born December 12, 1854, was their first child.[36]

A childhood memory that Sophie often repeated suggests that the Weils may have offered their home as a station on the Underground Railroad. She recalled her parents having instructed her and her siblings that whenever they saw a dark-skinned person hurrying across the Ohio River from Kentucky, Indiana's slave-holding southern neighbor, they should close their eyes, point to the basement of their house, and keep their eyes closed until the fugitive had time to get inside. The reason given to the children was that a white man would soon come and ask them if they had seen where the escapee went, and they must be able to say "no" truthfully—not having *seen* where he went.[37]

Pro-slavery sentiment in that corner of Indiana was so strong that those who tried to help runaways did so at the risk of their own lives and the safety of their families. For that reason abolitionists kept no records and such recollections cannot be verified. Considering the danger, it seems truly extraordinary that immigrant Jews, themselves vulnerable and easily suspected of disloyalty, would risk their own safety by defying the prevailing sentiment of their neighbors. Perhaps it was precisely the fact that they were Jewish, however, with the memory of exodus from Egypt reinforced annually at their Passover Seder, that these fervent patriots sympathized with the Union, the government of their newly adopted Promised Land, and dared to assist others escaping slavery. It must have required enormous courage.[38]

Whether the Weils actually were abolitionists or not, they unquestionably gave their children worthy values. Sophie, like other daughters of upwardly mobile families of her day, probably first attended public schools and later enrolled in a private seminary for girls. She mastered French and German, read the classics in those languages as well as in English, and excelled at the piano. Her mother Clara taught her the finer points of homemaking and introduced her to daily prayers with the help of a personalized Jewish prayer book for the home, written mostly in English and published in America.[39]

Clara taught Sophie strict German standards of cleanliness as well as culinary skills in the German Jewish tradition, nourishing recipes that avoided pork products but probably contained no other Jewish dietary restriction since Reform Jews rejected kashruth in principle. Biblical injunction against other food such as shellfish was selectively ignored by most, but ham, pork, bacon, and sausage remained taboo. Sophie retained vivid memories of the day her father took her and her siblings to a slaughter house to see its unsanitary conditions and unsavory atmosphere in order to impress upon them the reason then espoused by logic-loving Reform Jews for not eating pork.[40]

As a serious sixteen-year-old, Sophie wasted no time in cultivating friendship with the new rabbi. When immediately upon arrival he organized the Evansville Literary Society, a staple offering of most Jewish communities, she joined her father and some sixty others as a founding member. Her lawyer-educated father served as the club's "prosecutor," and she volunteered as corresponding secretary. In early November she reported to the American Israelite that the group had accepted a "tilt" (a challenge to debate) with the Young Men's Hebrew Association of Henderson, Kentucky, Evansville's neighbor across the river. This was another activity characteristic of German Jewish communities.[41]

Comely, intelligent, and well schooled in amenities valued by the increasingly acculturated Jews of her day, Sophie appeared to be an ideal match for an American Reform rabbi. Readily smitten, Browne courted her in proper Victorian fashion. Recognizing that her intellectual interests paralleled his own, he thought that she would like to have a copy of a particular reference book that he favored, but apparently believed that it was bad form to bring her a gift and therefore hesitated to do so. After their betrothal, announced October 9, 1871, he presented the chosen volume, accompanied by a card on which he wrote, "Miss Sophie Weil, My lady– Not being entitled to bring presents to young ladies, I only lend you the use of this dictionary. Use it freely. Your most obedient servant, Dr. EBMB."[42]

Formidable formality, even for Victorian times!

The book, hardly a romantic offering, was entitled A Biblical and Theological Dictionary: Explanatory of the History, Manners and Customs of the Jews and Neighboring Nation. Nearly twelve hundred pages long and three inches thick, it undoubtedly challenged the physical as well as the intellectual capacity of anyone attempting to use it. Originally compiled by Richard Watson in 1831 and published in a new edition by the Southern Methodist Publishing House in 1860, its cover page identified the contents as "History, Manners, and Customs of the Jews and Neighboring Nations, with an Account of the Most Remarkable Places and Persons Mentioned in Sacred Scripture, an Exposition of the Principal Doctrines of Christianity, and Notices of Jewish and Christian Sects and Heresies." It also included an Alphabetical Table of the Proper Names in the Old and New Testaments with "their proper pronunciation and the chief meaning or significance of each word in the original language," as well as tables of weights, measures and money mentioned in the Bible, statistics on the religious denominations in the United States according to the 1850 census, a Biblical atlas with numerous maps, and a "Scripture Gazetteer" with engravings of ritual objects and priestly vestments as they were then imagined to have been.[43]

The new American edition of this tome reflected the growth of Christians' interest in ecumenism, a positive development despite its purpose being that of conversion. Browne probably considered the encyclopedic volume interpreted by and for Christians as a useful tool for implementing his facility in relating to them. Sophie's intellectual curiosity and dedication to her future role as rabbi's wife likely suggested that she would derive both pleasure and benefit from it. Rabbis' wives were often asked by Christians to elucidate remote points of Scripture that have little relevance for Jews, and this biblical dictionary readily provided authentic answers.

On the lighter side, puns were popular, and Sophie was the target of one published in the Evansville Journal, submitted by J. S. Lowenstein, secretary of the congregation. It posed the question of why Miss Sophie Wile (sic) was like an oyster being fried. The answer was, "because she will become Browne after a Wile." The pun sheds light on popular culture as well indicating a degree of successful "fitting in."[44]

Sophie and Ed were married on March 12, 1872, in a ceremony typical of those then in vogue with increasingly affluent, middle class Jewish families.

Five bridesmaids and five groomsmen attended the couple. Wise and his wife Theresa journeyed from Cincinnati, he to officiate and she to stand under the chuppah, the bridal canopy, as surrogate mother for the groom. It was customary for Christian friends to be invited and for relatives from distant cities to attend, as many of them did. As reported in the local newspaper, "There was not room enough in the Sixth Street Temple last evening for the people who came to see the Rev. Dr. E.B.M. Browne married to Miss Sophie, daughter of Moses Weil, Esq." The same newspaper recalled the event fifty years later.[45]

The lavish wedding gifts that the Brownes received testified to the acculturation of immigrant Jewish families who benefitted from the post-war economy. A pair of three-pronged Tiffany crystal candelabra, a large insulated hand-painted porcelain pitcher framed in silver on a stand with two silver goblets and drip bowl, a six piece silver coffee service with oil lamp warmer for the urn, and countless other items of heavy silver supplied what those of the Weils' milieu considered standard necessities for the household of an American rabbi. Remarkably, Sophie preserved them intact through the many moves that characterized her life with Browne.[46]

For their honeymoon, the newlyweds boarded a river boat and plied the Mississippi, going ashore in several cities where Browne had been invited to speak. Leisurely days on the water provided time to reflect, perhaps inspiring the young rabbi to look back on his seven years in America, and assess his career to that moment.

His experiences had brought him knowledge of six post-Civil War Jewish communities, two of them Southern, and introduced him to a very negative aspect of Jewish public life as rabbis competed for control of American Judaism. After quickly failing in two congregations, he met great success in another, became initially recognized as a public orator and earned a law degree which gave him access to American courts. He had almost finished translating the Talmud so that Christians could better understand Judaism, and he had become an American citizen, married to an American-born daughter of a well-to-do Jewish family. If he had been truly circumspect, he should have perceived where his strengths and interests lay, where to watch for pitfalls, and how to deal with the exigencies of married life.

A few months after their marriage, Browne gave his bride a gold locket inscribed "To my Sophie, Ed, July 30, 1872." Although the date itself has no identifiable significance, the anchor embossed on its cover could have been intended to carry a message. Still choosing the sea as his metaphor, Browne may have been suggesting that he was ready to drop anchor permanently in Evansville.[47]

III - EVANSVILLE

Browne came to Evansville well prepared for the diverse duties of an
American rabbi. Already an acclaimed public speaker, he fulfilled the highest
hopes of his congregants as their representative to the gentile world. He led
them in intellectual activities by organizing the Evansville Literary Society
and encouraging study among young adults. He pursued scholarly projects on
his own, writing, translating, teaching and publishing. Most significant of all
insofar as pleasing his congregation was concerned, he married Sophie. She
was intelligent, personable, and one of their own. From all appearances the
two were securely set to live "happily ever after."

For his inaugural sermon at B'nai Israel, on the eve of the Jewish New
Year, 1871, Browne chose the text of Jeremiah 1:47, wherein the prophet
seeks God's help with the words, "Behold, I cannot speak, for I am a boy."
Humbly acknowledging his own youth and inexperience, the rabbi reminded
his listeners that the injunction to teach was meant not only for Jews but
"unto the nations" and that he would welcome their guidance in this
endeavor, clearly indicating outreach to the gentile community. He then spoke
of a rabbi's duties to his congregation and those of the congregation to its
rabbi. Citing the instructions given to Moses in Exodus 27:20 and Leviticus
24:2,3 for the Israelites to bring to Aaron, the high priest, pure oil of olives
for the eternal light, Browne drew the parallel to himself and his Evansville
congregants. It was his duty to tend the lamp of enlightenment, but theirs to
supply the oil.[1]

The subject was not unusual for rabbis of that era, but its message is
worth noting for its relation to the times and the man. Addressing women
especially, Browne invoked the Jewish view of motherhood. By asking them
to help him educate their children, he drew upon the biblical injunction

for mothers to introduce their children to the Torah. Also, with the intense patriotism typical of new Americans, he conjured the image popularized by novelist Harriet Beecher Stowe of mothers as primary purveyors of moral authority, charging them to "enlist as soldiers in the great army of the republic which shall free the mind from the sway of old despotic views."

To illustrate his role as principal teacher, he drew from his medical studies a tongue-twisting ophthalmological metaphor about people "afflicted with photophobia . . . myopia and presbiophia," (meaning that they either hated light or were farsighted or nearsighted) and concluded that they "contracted those morbid tendencies by bad habits, by looking either too much at the sun and becoming dazzled, or by closing their eyes altogether." Such patients, he said, "must have an artificial light overseen and regulated by a good oculist. The priest has to be the optician here. He must shape lenses . . . which will gather the eye beams in the right focus, and thus assist their vision to behold things in the true light." The imagery, reflecting his continued fascination with science, also suggested the presence of the eye disease that soon manifested itself and plagued him throughout most of his life.[2]

No sooner was Browne installed as Evansville's rabbi than he announced a series of public lectures. He opened with "The Genesis of Christianity," which the city newspapers asked him to repeat. Entering community affairs, he headed the Charitable Burial Association, served by his father-in-law, Moses Weil, as treasurer. He also began publishing an English periodical, the Jewish Independent, headquartered in Chicago. Within a few months the Evansville Medical College offered him faculty chairs in medical jurisprudence and diseases of the mind, and dispatched him as its delegate to the United States Medical Convention in Philadelphia.[3]

Rabbis were often called upon by Jewish communities other than their own to officiate at weddings, dedicate new synagogues, and deliver lectures for charitable purposes. In Petersburg, Indiana, Browne conducted its county's first Jewish wedding. Celebrated in the Presbyterian Church, church bells summoned all residents to the ceremony and the church choir provided music. At the luncheon that followed, guests asked the rabbi to lecture that evening at the courthouse, and he agreed on condition that they contribute the admission fee to victims of the recent Chicago fire. The townspeople printed posters for the lecture, entitled "Social Features, Ancient and Modern," and recruited boys to go through the streets as town criers clanging large bells to announce it. The event enabled Petersburg to send more than $100 to Chicago for victims of the devastating fire.[4]

In Vincennes, Indiana, Browne addressed the Moral and Social Union on "Science and the Bible," described in the local newspaper as "the principal features of the Hebrew laws and traditions." It was well received by most, but not all listeners. According to the report, some clergymen "did not like the idea of being lectured to by Jews and see them carry off the palm of public applause. . . ." One Catholic priest became so agitated that he provoked Browne into challenging him to debate the subject.[5]

While we cannot know if the priest objected to the message or the messenger, the lecture's title suggests that his reaction reflected that of many religious leaders, both Christian and Jewish, to the scientific view of religion. Biblical criticism and Darwinism posed a threat to those unable to come to terms with modernism. Clergymen of all faiths feared them and believed that those who advocated them were largely responsible for the disturbing decline in attendance then apparent at worship services in their churches and synagogues alike.

Reform rabbis had good reason for alarm. They recognized that most of their rapidly acculturating, German-born constituents, however rational their thinking on other issues, still clung to the traditional beliefs in creation by design, man's creation in God's image, and God's revelation of the complete Torah at Sinai. The rabbis posited that if such devotees of logic were influenced by academic biblical scholarship or Darwinism to the extent that they abandoned those underlying tenets of their religious background, they would be left with no intellectual basis to sustain their Judaism. Indeed, some had already found expression of their socio-religious views in Unitarianism and Ethical Culture. As historian Naomi W. Cohen explained, when inquiring minds began to question their inherited beliefs, " . . . those [denominations] that boasted of their rational nature or their adaptability and relevance to modern society were hard-pressed to reinterpret essential articles of their faith. . . ."[6]

Although Browne and the highly respected Rabbi Bernhard Felsenthal, of Chicago, maintained that rational inquiry did not threaten Judaism, the vast majority of their colleagues condemned it. Wise gave space in his newspapers to advocates of Darwinism and biblical criticism, but he accepted neither, charging that they were based on unverified hypotheses. For once in agreement with Einhorn, who called Darwinism the "brutalization of our species," Wise called it "Homo-Brutalism" and "the gorilla theory," and held that it robbed humans of their "preeminence" making all of nature a battleground.[7]

Browne, trained in both medicine and theology as was Darwin, viewed evolution from a vantage point similar to that of the evolutionist himself. Backed by his knowledge of biblical criticism and influenced perhaps by having read the works of the American philosopher-historian John Fiske and British philosopher-biologist Herbert Spencer, Browne emulated them in seeking a means of reconciling religion and science rather than undermining the science. Few philosophers, theologians or scientists in the Victorian era shared that view.

Philosophical disagreement did not diminish Wise's support for Browne's work, however. Wise continued to promote it, praising Browne's Jewish Independent for its "rich variety of original reading matter," and applauding the young rabbi's start on a new book, "The Encyclopedia of Talmudic Beauties."[8]

Browne also began translating The Book Jashar, one of the lost books of the Bible (literally, "The Correct Book"), mentioned in Joshua 10:13 and II Samuel I:18, which contained stories from creation to the time of the judges. Late twentieth century scholars believed that The Book Jashar was a collection of war songs already known at the time of the Bible's canonization, some of which, including Miriam's Song at the Sea (Exodus 15:1), were preserved in other sections of Scripture without attribution to earlier sources.

According to Browne, the book had been "in the hands of our people" since time immemorial, although not translated into English until the nineteenth century. Scholars disputed the authenticity of the version most recently discovered, which included dates, genealogies, and full explanations of many obscure passages, and which Emanuel Deutsch, foremost Jewish exponent of biblical criticism, endorsed. Despite the fact that Julius Wellhausen, most famous of the critics, called it a fraud, Browne chose that newest version for his translation.[9]

Browne completed the work in 1875, with advance orders including one from the Savannah Lodge of B'nai B'rith. Wise praised its "correct and fluent Hebrew." He also noted that "The Book Jashar" had been first published in Venice in 1625, and that the American politician and playwright Mordechai Noah had reportedly translated it into English earlier in the nineteenth century. Apparently lost, the knowledge of Noah's work may have inspired Browne to undertake his own translation.[10]

Much as he enjoyed these intellectual pursuits, as a congregational rabbi Browne did not have the luxury of hiding in an ivory tower. He soon became involved in one of the petty conflicts that Victorian codes of conduct frequently ignited within status-conscious, middle class society. Ostensibly it began shortly after the Brownes returned from their honeymoon. At that time David Heiman, an influential member of the Evansville congregation, complained that he and his wife had been insulted by the rabbi at the latter's wedding dinner: when the Heimans attempted to sit at the table reserved for the bridal party, someone—presumably Browne—referred them to seats at the head of a different table. A local newspaper learned of the perceived affront and asked Browne about it. The rabbi remained silent until a persistent but seemingly friendly reporter from a rival paper persuaded him that he should tell his side of the story in order to defend himself.[11]

Acknowledging that the incident had occurred, Browne noted that Heiman did not appear to be offended until months later after returning from a business trip to Metropolis, Indiana. There Heiman claimed to have heard that Browne invoked the name of Jesus Christ in a lecture. While this apparently constituted a crime in Heiman's view, several people who had attended the lecture testified that it was untrue, which put the rumor to rest. Then Heiman tried again, charging that Browne, after lecturing in Paducah, Kentucky, embezzled proceeds that were designated for charities, one of which was the B'nai B'rith Hebrew Orphan's Home in Cleveland.

Again exonerated and supported by numerous congregants, Browne offered to forgive Heiman in return for an apology and a large contribution to the Hebrew Orphan's Home. He received the apology and a small contribution for the home, but only after an unduly long wait. This incensed him to the point of returning the wedding gift that he and Sophie had received from the Heimans.[12]

The incident evidently struck a deep chord within Browne, for despite continued support from the congregation, in a subsequent interview he unleashed growing grievance over a related situation. The reporter first asked if he would sue for damages, to which Browne replied that he probably would not. If he did, he said, he would represent himself, assisted by Captain W. Frederick Smith, one of the "genial Southern gentlemen and scholars" who had recently come to practice law in Evansville. Then he noted that he thought it would help the clergy if the issue went to court because ministers— rabbis, especially—were being mistreated. They were "disfranchised in every way," he said, and required to work around the clock for an average salary less than that of a street laborer. Browne noted that it was less onerous with Christians because their ministers could appeal to a conference or synod, whereas rabbis, left to the mercy of their congregants, suffered "all sorts of abuse patiently" because complaints were of no use. In his case, he claimed, if his accuser had succeeded in getting thirty votes against him he would "now be left homeless and under the bans of proscription without relief."[13]

Browne did not stop there. In what he may have intended as an innocent plug for Wise's projected Hebrew Union College, he told the reporter, "You know, sir, that we have no seminaries in this country, and every Tom and Dick who can read a little Hebrew may be accepted at the pleasure of the congregation as a minister. Those parasites spoil the ministry. They have no independence because [they have] no substance."[14]

However true this may have been, it was not likely to have pleased members of Congregation B'nai Israel to see it in the city newspaper because it revealed an unseemly aspect of Jewish communal behavior. Nevertheless, no repercussions arose. Shortly after it appeared, a reconciliation took place between Browne and Heiman, who then hosted an elaborate "peace banquet" to celebrate. The Israelite's Evansville correspondent, reluctant to blame either contender for the unseemly brouhaha, reported, "By some inexplicable way, one of our most respected members allowed himself to be influenced by a malignant party to avenge an imaginary insult. . . ." Presumably the "malignant party" did not live in Evansville.[15]

Such was the temper of the times. It was not unusual, especially in small communities such as Evansville, for rabbis to be treated as mere employees. In many cases they were not allowed to sermonize without their president's permission, and one minister was fired because he preached against playing poker.[16]

Meanwhile, Browne tendered his resignation. The congregation refused to accept it, notifying the Israelite, "we could not afford to part with the man, whom, all artifices of two or three parties notwithstanding, we reelected almost unanimously." The report also mentioned that the New York-based, Jewish Times, edited by Moritz Ellinger about whom more will be seen subsequently, had published the story "in an aggravated form by a unanimous [sic.] correspondent," but that it would probably be the last such libel "for our rabbi is not to be trifled with, being a lawyer himself, it is easy for him to file a complaint. . . ."[17]

Nonetheless, the slander continued, although it is unclear whether the next attack–part of the continuing battle between rabbinic factions of the East and West—was intended as a personal thrust against Browne or a statement opposing Darwinism and biblical criticism. Wise's Evansville correspondent had previously reported seeing Wise cited in the Jewish Times as author of a pamphlet entitled "Attila" that argued against the traditional view of creation as revealed in Genesis. More recently the paper carried a half-page statement identifying the author of the pamphlet as "a western rabbi, not residing in Cincinnati." Then Browne read in the Jewish Times that "a Hungarian western rabbi whose initials are E.B.M.B." had written "a scurrilous pamphlet" of the same description.[18]

Wise debunked the accusation, saying that he had seen the pamphlet three years before, read a favorable review of it in the esteemed London Saturday Review, and found nothing wrong with it. He believed that the letter was an attempt to keep Browne from getting the recently vacated post of English preacher at New York's prestigious Temple Emanu-El. There was no indication that Browne was seeking any new position. He was still in Evansville and despite the incident with Heiman, ostensibly very happy there. Referencing the ongoing struggle between East and West, Wise observed, "There seems to be a secret purpose hidden in that attack on Dr. Browne. . . ." Citing the vacancy at Temple Emanu-El, he argued that, since the press had praised Browne as an extemporaneous and successful English preacher, "somebody might have the idea this young orator could be engaged in the Emanuel Temple . . . and must therefore be abused in advance so that the hierarchical fraternity of the metropolis be not disturbed by an independent link in the chain forged on the New York reform congregations."[19]

The strength of that chain would affect Browne in the not-so-distant future. At this time, however, Wise was actually addressing his own agenda, as he continued,

> We know to a certainty that the Jewish Times has abused us beyond measure, by order of the New York hierarchs, because it was rumored one day [that] we might be a candidate for some New York pulpit and, we are told, it is abusing us now, and we suppose also Browne, because it fears, by order of course, he or we might have such an idea now. We can assure those terrified gentlemen that we are no candidate for any office, ecclesiastical or political, and in regard to Dr. Browne we can add that he is well situated in Evansville. It is not necessary on this ground that the Times should continue in unprincipled meanness to attack,

especially as we never condescend to make a reply to a sheet enslaved by

its taskmasters and conducted by a man without honor or integrity.[20]

The man was Wise's rival, Rabbi David Einhorn, and it was not the last time that his newspaper libeled Browne. Within a few months Browne informed Wise of further abuse, but indicated that he would not sue because "the Times is not worth one cent, hence a suit would only incur to my loss."[2211]

Wise responded:

> *"while it is acceded that slander is contemptible, no matter who the parties concerned are, we believe the crime is greatly increased when it aims at the honor of a young man. We old ones can stand a great deal without being hurt, but as regards a young man some people will believe something, let it come from any source."*[22]

Still the attacks continued. Someone launched a rumor about Browne in Quincy, Illinois, apparently in an attempt to limit attendance at a lecture that he was scheduled to give there. Officers and trustees of the Evansville congregation rose to his defense, responding with a signed declaration in the Israelite:

> *"Having heard that slanderous reports and letters have been sent to Quincy, Illinois, aiming at the character of Rev. Dr. Browne, member of the B'nai Israel Congregation, we, the undersigned, therefore declare that as a minister and as a gentleman Dr. Browne has always met with the fullest approval of the congregation, and the outsiders thereof. Several parties, though, on account of petty personal affairs, started up trouble in said congregation, still no one can or dare question that as a*

preacher, as a teacher in his Sunday-school, which was a model of order and decorum, and in all his duties, Dr. Browne stands as pure as any minister in this or in any other country. The slanderer who attempts to blacken the fair reputation of an honest and upright public man like Dr. Browne, deserves his unqualified contempt of every one."[23]

Even after moving to another city Browne could not relinquish anger over his treatment by Heiman. Almost a year later he revived the unseemly controversy in his journal, the Jewish Independent. The article, entitled "Why I Left Evansville," drew vitriolic response from Evansvillians who reversed their previous opinion and sent resolutions to the Israelite calling him "Meanest liar in creation," "Most contemptible, self conceited fool," and "Most abominable hypocrite." Wise published them, but "with the utmost regret . . . not only because the words used . . . are unbecoming this journal and any religious community, but also we admire the talent and ability of Dr. Browne as an eminent pulpit orator, and know that he is no hypocrite, and there is no wickedness in him." That said, Wise conceded that he did "sincerely mourn over the follies of our young friend, who possesses all the gifts to make his mark in the pulpit, and yet mistakes notoriety for reputation, and transient sensation for fame."[24]

The incident, in addition to revealing Browne's impetuous nature and unbending pride, reflects both the naïveté and the mercurial temper of the average congregation. While Browne unquestionably invited reproof, considering his previous strong support by the congregation, the vindictive tone of the Evansville resolution suggests that it was written by members not formerly in control. Such behavior, traceable to changes in the congregation's lay leadership, was also often affected by financial problems. A sidelight worth noting is the fact that although the Evansville congregation engaged Browne at a generous $3000 a year, it offered only $1000 for his successor and was required to double that figure when no one acceptable applied. This suggests economic concerns as well as contention within the ranks of leadership.[25]

Although Wise defended Browne publicly, he was not blind to behavioral flaws in his young friend that might have added to his problems. In a personal letter written while Browne was still in Evansville, his mentor began with a sad report on Mrs. Wise's health and then admonished in these words:

> "Allow me to tell, if I had had four places in five years or so, and gone away quarreling from either, beyond a doubt, I would have come to the conclusion that the fault is in me. In this case I would have shelved myself for a year or two in a quiet retreat, to overcome my own follies, evidently in my way to success, and I would have given my attention exclusively to scientific pursuits and not let hear of me one word, until the old Adam be out of me. Can you not see the failure you have made? Starting out as you did, after five years, you have landed in Peoria. Are you blind to all that? Publish no cards, rather seek quietly to reconstruct your wrecked fortune, by good sermons without sensation or humbug, by diligent study especially of Jewish sources which you have forgotten, and by careful attention to conduct in society, where prudence, forbearance and moderation are as necessary as a good moral character. I am your friend who tell you what I have to say, others may persecute you. The world is cold. Now you may do as you please; I have done my duty as a friend. If you want to remain in the ministry you must build up a reputation not only as a scholar and orator but also as a quiet, earnest and peaceable man who manages well. This will take time, resolution and self-government."[26]

Browne did not take Wise's advice. His reason is unclear but it invites speculation. Although Wise's reference to Peoria implies that Browne's move there was a step downward in his career, some aspects of the city and the history of its congregation suggest otherwise. The feud with Heiman had taken its toll on Browne's popularity, and despite the strength of his remaining support, he was left with a residue of ill will that clouded his outlook for a future in Evansville. Sophie was very young—barely nineteen— and presumably loathe to leave her parents; however, she and the rabbi retained a close relationship with them and visited often. He had established his reputation throughout the mid-west as an eloquent orator and progressive thinker, an advocate of biblical criticism and Darwinian evolution, and the offer of a position in the larger city with its proximity to Chicago beckoned enticingly. All known facts considered, it seems that Browne simply decided that it was a good time to go.

IV - PRESIDENT GRANT AND THE MAN WHO CHALLENGED INGERSOLL

Browne ignored Wise's advice and accepted a call to the pulpit of Congregation Anshe Emeth of Peoria, Illinois, the oldest Jewish community in the state other than Chicago. Originally comprised of Western Europeans some of whom had arrived in the 1840s, Peoria Jewry had grown considerably in recent years due to the arrival of immigrants from Eastern Europe. Congregation Anshe Emeth, Peoria's first synagogue, had established a religious school and a burial association in the 1850s, and completed its building by 1863. The rabbi who preceded Browne had remained there for ten years, an unusual longevity in those times that spoke well not only for him but—significantly—for the character and stability of the congregation. It was a congenial community, where Jews mingled freely with their non-Jewish neighbors as they did in Evansville and elsewhere.[1]

The Brownes settled comfortably in lodgings at 406 Jefferson Street and embraced the cultural life of the city. In the "First Grand Entertainment" of the Standard Literary Association, the rabbi recited Edgar Allen Poe's "The Raven" and Sophie performed several pieces on the piano. Browne joined the local lodge of B'nai B'rith as he had probably also done in Evansville. Membership in the philanthropic fraternity was considered de rigeur for Jewish men of position. Browne was no stranger to the Peoria lodge, having spoken there while still serving as rabbi in Evansville. At that time he so pleased the local committee that it sent a series of resolutions to the Israelite declaring him "one of the foremost ministers in America," and "a preceptor under whose guidance we can safely trust our noble cause, and our motto and watchword Progress be actually correct in the effect." [2]

The same emphasis on image is seen in the report of a lecture that

Browne gave in Burlington, Iowa. It inspired Jews there to advise the Israelite that it "would be an honor for Judaism if our talented rabbis would occasionally make a tour, especially to places which are not so fortunate. . . . It creates a good influence. . . ."[3]

These kudos aptly identify a primary goal of Jews in mid-nineteenth century America: acceptance for themselves and their religion in their Protestant-dominated land. Browne served Peorians well in this role of ambassador to the gentiles. Then a new role for rabbis, it soon became a major requirement for those serving acculturated American Jews. Peorians emphasized this yearning as they expressed to Wise their pride in having "the most able Jewish rabbi in the West," thus permitting them to "feel with dignity our elevation among an enlightened community" and to declare, "This, Dear Editor, is what Judaism here and elsewhere long has sought—to have the right man to lead us in our synagogues, and represent us among our Christian friends. . . ."[4]

The same dispatch reported that "the Rev. Doctor has created quite a new life" in the city, that religious services were "splendidly attended," that a Young Men's Social Club had recently been established "for literary and dramatic purposes," and that the B'nai B'rith lodge was "in most excellent condition, numbering now fifty-one members, with a fund of $1200."[5]

Peorians especially appreciated Browne's public lectures outside of the synagogue. The city's mayor introduced him on one such occasion, a B'nai B'rith sponsored benefit to help yellow fever victims in two southern cities. Thanks to the rabbi's popularity the lecture raised the substantial amount of $500. Another time, he addressed the Illinois State Senate and was voted "one of the very best, wholly extempore, eloquent and interesting throughout."[6]

At the county court house, where he spoke on "The Jewish God" for the Free Thought Association, Browne said that if the Bible were fully understood and read in the light of the times in which it was written, there would be no need for further "infidel meetings." This inspired Wise to quip that such free thinking probably pleased the speaker's free-thinking listeners. Despite lingering reservations about biblical criticism, Wise also praised the speech for having "sustained the Bible and its connection with science clearly shown and in perfect accord."[7]

The reference to infidel meetings applied to the hugely popular lectures of another Peoria resident, the brilliant lawyer, teacher, preacher and war hero, Colonel Robert G. Ingersoll. Known as the Great Agnostic because of his strong opposition to religion, Ingersoll's popularity increasingly threatened religious leaders. With Darwinism looming as a thunder cloud over the church, Protestants felt especially vulnerable to agnosticism. Church leaders organized tent revivals in an effort to reinvigorate the faith, but Ingersoll's rhetoric was highly entertaining and soon exceeded Darwinism as a perceived threat to Christianity. The preacher cleverly manipulated facts to support his case against God, communicating directly and charmingly to his eager listeners. The power of his words and his personality exemplified the religious community's worst fears.[8]

In January 1874, the Peoria Democrat announced that "Rev. Dr. Browne, of the Hebrew Church" successfully challenged Ingersoll. When after his oration the Great Agnostic invited comments from the audience, Browne rose to his feet and refuted Ingersoll's "unjust attacks...upon the Bible and religion." According to one witness, the young rabbi "handled the theories of the speaker without gloves" for twenty minutes, using "a keen-edged dissecting knife with the skill of an old master." Thereafter newspapers referred to Browne as "The Man Who Could Challenge Ingersoll."[9]

Debates between Ingersoll and such personages as Jeremiah Black,

Reverend Henry Field and British Prime Minister William Gladstone made news for over two decades. During these years public controversy grew more heated, and likewise spurred the demand for Browne to refute the agnostic. In 1881, Bishop John P. Newman of New York recommended Browne as "the only man who can answer Ingersoll." Ten years later, a reporter in Lincoln, Nebraska, wrote, "After hearing Dr. Browne, it could be easily understood why the bold and eloquent Ingersoll is afraid to meet him. . . . Dr. Browne, like Colonel Ingersoll, has full sway over his audience, but the rabbi holds his people spellbound by the earnestness of his reasoning, addressing himself to the souls of his hearers, and binding them to his own deep religious convictions."[10]

Although Browne continued to denounce Ingersoll, it is uncertain if they ever confronted each other in person after their initial encounter in Peoria. Had Browne devoted himself to preaching the compatibility of science and religion with the same intensity as Ingersoll preached against it, he might have hastened the day when the world could accept both. He might even have averted the Scopes "Monkey" Trial or the current twenty-first century brush with Creationism.

Browne had other interests though, and as a congregational rabbi, other responsibilities. In 1873, he represented Peoria at the founding conference of the Union of American Hebrew Congregations, Wise's first landmark achievement in his mammoth effort to organize American Judaism. Besides serving on the committee for permanent organization, Browne proposed reforms that addressed such ongoing issues as the still competing prayer books and problems caused by self-proclaimed rabbis who had neither training for the position nor compensating intellectual achievements. He wanted the UAHC to exercise jurisdiction over its congregations and their rabbis, appoint a council to adjudicate problems arising between them, and form a committee (from which he excluded himself) to examine the credentials of men who claimed to be rabbis, licensing those who were qualified and exposing the fraud of those who were not.[11]

Both motions were ruled out of order. Lay leaders remained wary of any suggestion that implied imposition of authority, and Wise, having witnessed Isaac Leeser's failed attempts to form a union, was not disposed to entertain any proposal that threatened divisiveness. He understood the delicate balance needed to keep all parties at the table, and knew that in order to achieve his goal of a rabbinical seminary, he must gather under his banner all of the dissident factions. Eventually— when the timing was right—he embraced Browne's issues as his own.[12]

Although social anti-Semitism had not yet highlighted an obvious need for rabbis to be ambassadors to the gentiles, Peoria's Jews increasingly appreciated their rabbi's spectacular success in that role. They reelected him unanimously in 1874, and again sent him to the UAHC conference. Whereas business at the first conference had centered on organization, delegates at the second one concentrated on resolutions concerning ecumenism and patriotism, religious education, obtaining English Bibles, circuit preaching (apparently needed due to the scarcity of qualified rabbis fluent in English), the sharing of rabbis for communities too small to support one full time, properly honoring major donors, and organization of the rabbinical seminary. No rabbis were listed as members of reporting committees. Browne again pressed for regulations to improve the treatment of qualified rabbis and weed out the unqualified, still without success.[13]

Later that year, Browne became inadvertently involved in the personal life of his mentor. The Wise family had not heard from son Leo or known his whereabouts for four years, at which time he had absconded with funds entrusted to his father for the forthcoming Hebrew Union College. Long considered a "wild boy," Leo had run away from home at least once before, supposedly to join the Mexican army. Browne had been like an older brother to Leo while living in Cincinnati, sometimes interceding for him with his father. Fully realizing that the boy might resent him for doing so, Browne nonetheless occasionally tried to "put him straight" with brotherly counsel.[14]

On November 5, 1874, Leo sent Browne a note indicating that he was in Peoria and needed to see him. Browne welcomed him and listened to his confession. Leo admitted having spent all of the stolen money, then signing onto an English ship bound for Africa, and frequently landing in the brig. Despairing that his life was hopeless, he told Browne, "If they give me an unkind word at home, I shall leave at once and forever."[15]

Browne tried to console Leo, assured him of a home if he ever needed one, and then hurried him off to Cincinnati where his mother lay dying. At her funeral a month later, Leo told Browne that he felt he had killed her.[16]

Theresa Wise had been like a mother to Browne, and her death was as much a blow to him as to her own children. Wise understood his grief and acknowledged it by including him in the family circle for the mourning rituals. As they observed Theresa's casket being taken from her home to the hearse and on to Wise's Temple B'nai Jeshurun for the funeral, it was Browne who read from Psalms and led the recitation of kaddish, the traditional mourner's prayer. At the service itself Browne co-officiated with Wise's distinguished Cincinnati colleague and dearest friend, Rabbi Max Lilienthal.[17]

That sorrowful event marked the end of an era for Browne as well as for the Wises. The patriarch soon remarried, sired more children, and changed forever the ambience at Floral House on College Hill. Its new mistress, Selma Bondi Wise, busy with her own growing family, had neither time nor interest in cultivating her husband's former student.

Leo vowed to repent and promised Browne to become "a different man"in the future. Within a year he again appealed for help, this time in a frantic plea for medication with which to abort a friend's pregnancy. Browne balked at that one. Ethics, law and morality overrode his sense of brotherhood. Leo never forgave him for refusing. Soon thereafter Leo became his father's surrogate as editor of the American Israelite, an ongoing position that enabled him to exact revenge upon those who offended him. Browne was not alone in receiving that revenge as years went by.[18]

Soon after Theresa Wise's death, Browne received a terrifying prognosis from Dr. Joseph Aub, the famous Cincinnati ophthalmologist who had been treating him for a serious eye disease. Browne learned that his condition had greatly deteriorated and in Aub's opinion, he would lose his sight completely unless he left the rabbinate for work in a profession less demanding on his eyes. He had no choice but to resign his position and seek other employment.[19]

Because he knew his subjects and spoke extemporaneously without further study, lecturing to the public seemed a viable option not likely to worsen his condition. The lecture circuit, however, required him to be away from home for long periods of time touring the country. He was loathe to leave Sophie because they were trying to start a family and she had already suffered several miscarriages. He considered moving to Chicago, headquarters of his journal, the Jewish Independent, as well as that of his lecture bureau. Although he inquired about renting office space there, he ultimately opted to keep his residence in Peoria, intermittently sojourning with Sophie at her parents' home in Evansville.[20]

In addition to signing onto the lecture circuit, Browne applied for a position in the diplomatic corps, a move that led to his friendship with

President Ulysses S. Grant.

While still in Wisconsin, the summer of 1871, the rabbi had initially written to Grant applying for the chaplaincy at West Point. This seemed odd at the time, for Browne had just received his law degree and had been invited to serve a prestigious congregation. His action becomes somewhat plausible in hindsight, however, as we shall see. Possibly he wanted to make a point rather than obtain a job when he addressed the president:

Your Excellency:

I figure upon the full amount of your charity in allowing myself this importunity, emanating wholly from motives selfish in their nature. Having learnt of the vacancy created in the West Point Academy by the resignation of Prof. French, I ventured my application to the Secretary of War for the position of Chaplain to West Point. The press throughout the land dwells largely on the claims of the Episcopalians and Methodists to that office, so much so that President Grant is at a loss to make a choice between them...

Now I fail to see (I am convinced your Excellency will side with my views) what claims any particular denomination can have upon that office. It appears to me that we, the Jews, have equal rights with them, hence I applied and lay my prayer before your Excellency. In fact it seems to me that the Jews have perhaps more just claims as the Christian clergy, because no Jewish minister has yet been given a single office while the Christian clergy is very well represented in the offices of the U. S. I am the rabbi of Emanuel Temple in this city, duly graduated Rev. A.M., M.D.,LL.B, 26 years of age, and am willing to fill besides the chair of any branch in the academy falling in the line of my professions, ready to undergo the necessary examination. My references are the Revs. Isaac M. Wise and Max Lilienthal of Cincinnati, Ohio, James K. Gutheim of N.Y., Robert Collier of Chicago, J.N. Dudley and D. Graham of Milwaukee. In conclusion I would state that I was Chaplain to our State Senate during the last session.[21]

This was the first of many attempts that Browne would make to pique the government's conscience on its promise of equal opportunity for all. As will be discussed in subsequent chapters, throughout his life he advocated for immigrants—especially Jews—to receive justice and recognition in whatever area he perceived their need and his ability to help.

Although Browne did not get the appointment at West Point, his letter may have drawn Grant's attention and thus caused him to remember Browne's name. In 1875, the rabbi really did need a job and approached Grant for a diplomatic post, either domestic or foreign. He was endorsed by influential friends such as Illinois Senator Richard J. Oglesby, who wrote to the president that Browne was "a gentleman of high scientific and literary attainments now suffering from a disease of the eyes" which necessitated a change of employment, and that he was highly recommended also by Indiana Senator O. P. Morton as well as by "members of the Jewish church."[22]

Wise, having known Grant since before the Civil War, also advised him that Browne's "prominent talents and learning are appreciated by a large number of our people," and that the "particular favor . . . in his time of distressing sickness, if granted, would make a very favorable impression on very many of your zealous friends, and also many of your political opponents."[23]

No mean politician himself, Wise, an avowed Democrat who was considered by many to be the voice of American Jewry, diplomatically flattered the Republican President with a personal expression of "utmost respect for your many virtues as the chief magistrate of our blessed country." He did not mail the letter, but gave it to Browne to deliver personally. The enterprising job-hunter had used his status as a journalist to obtain an interview with Grant and soon made his appearance at the president's vacation home in Long Branch, New Jersey.[24]

Although already into his second term, Grant still suffered from the effects of his anti-Semitic General Order No. 11 that temporarily expelled all Jews from the Department of the Tennessee during the Civil War. He claimed to have signed the document under pressure and immediately regretted doing it, but even after becoming the nation's enormously popular national hero he never overcame his inner need to convince Jews that he was not an anti-Semite.[25]

Browne, who at the time of the American Civil War was a teenager in faraway Hungary, probably never heard of Order No. 11 until the 1868 presidential campaign when he was living with the Wises in Cincinnati. Wise, although he opposed Grant politically, remained his friend throughout and even refrained from harshly criticizing Grant editorially during the presidential campaigns of 1868 and 1872. As to Order No. 11, Wise declared that he had "long ago forgiven him that blunder." Wise was convinced that Grant had made sufficient atonement and "had been adequately punished right after having issued it."[26]

Experts have long debated the degree to which Grant was personally responsible for the order, arguing the point most heatedly in the years immediately after the war when Republicans looked to the general as a shoo-in for the White House. Grant himself courageously admitted his mistake and asked forgiveness, and recent historians have concluded that he could "in no wise be held responsible, personally and solely, for the anti-Jewish regulations which he dictated and signed." Historian Jacob Rader Marcus, while not disputing Grant's own acknowledgment of guilt, asserted that, although he was "an inept administrator and an egregious failure as a President . . .[he]. was no Jew baiter."[27]

In the White House, Grant tried to dispel that reputation by giving more appointments to Jews than had any of his predecessors. While it seems that as president, with influential Jewish supporters such as Washington lobbyist Simon Wolf and New York's powerful Seligman banking family whom he had known since he was a junior officer in the army and they were small town storekeepers upstate, Grant would have had little need for the good will of an unemployed young rabbi. Apparently that logical conclusion was offset by the fact that Grant understood the power of the press. Browne applied for the meeting in his capacity as journalist, not rabbi. The president probably welcomed his interview as an opportunity to improve his image with readers of Browne's Jewish Independent. The journal was based in Chicago, home to America's largest Jewish population outside of New York.[28]

The President received Browne cordially. Not surprisingly, he lauded Jews whom he had known, recalling that he had met many in the social settings of Cincinnati and in his father's home across the river in Covington, Kentucky. The discourse with which he continued was disappointing, but likewise no surprise. It seemed to imply, as philo-Semitic statements often do, deep and frequently unrecognized anti-Semitism. The President told Browne:

> *I think the Jew lives longer because he loves his life more. It is certain that the Jew takes no risk of life and limb, while even in the many railroad accidents Jews, though much more given to traveling, are rarely injured. And yet I have found Jewish soldiers among the bravest of*

the brave. The Jew risks his life only to show his patriotism and then he is fearless. The Jewish soldiers, as stated, I have found wonderfully courageous in our Army and in the Rebel lines as well. But there were army followers among us. It happened one day that a number of complaints reached me and in each case it was a Jew and I gave the order excusing the Jewish traders. You know that during war times these nice distinctions were disregarded. We had no time to handle things with kid gloves. But it was no ill-feeling or want of good-feeling towards the Jews. If such complaints would have been lodged against a dozen men each of whom wore a white cravat, a black broadcloth suit, beaver or gold spectacles, I should probably have issued a similar order against men so dressed. . . ."[29]

However disconcerting those words appear to Jews, Grant undoubtedly meant them to be friendly and conciliatory, affirming his admiration for Jewish people and their values. In closing, he encouraged Browne about the job possibility and advised him to send his application to Secretary of State Hamilton Fish.

Browne wrote to Fish, indicating that the president promised to nominate him for a currently open spot in the diplomatic corps and thoughtfully enclosing an item from the Chicago Times that mentioned his disability. He added that, although he had expressed a preference to be posted in Europe or South America, he now understood that there would be an opening in Turkey and preferred that above all others. Constantinople had been a center of Jewish activity since 1492 when the Ottoman Empire welcomed Jews expelled from Spain. Now the American government treated it as a "Jewish" post.

In stressing his qualifications, Browne modestly informed Fish that he did not "claim the favor as a mere gratuity," for he was known "in every Jewish family throughout the U.S., am not without some influence abroad and especially in my own state." He also noted that he was recognized as one of the best lecturers and campaign speakers in the country, that he had lived in the South for three years, was "posted in the history of our politics," and had promised to return the following year "to stump the United States both in the English and German languages for the Republican party. . . ."[30]

Grant wrote to Fish, suggesting a South American consulate for Browne if one was available. When Fish informed Browne that at present there were no favorable openings in South America, Browne replied that an unfavorable one would do, since he needed only a "small income" to support his family. This apparently yielded him a choice of posts, either in Argentina or in Mexico. Dr. Aub, his ophthalmologist, vetoed the latter because of its climate. Ultimately Browne rejected both because neither paid enough to support him, even if he left Sophie with her parents in Evansville and went alone.[31]

So ended Browne's brush with the diplomatic corps, but it was by no means the end of his relationship with Fish and Grant. These blossomed into friendship years later when all three lived in New York and Browne took a more active interest in politics. For the present, Browne still needed a job. Discouraged about finding one in government, he relied on lecturing.[32]

As usual, Wise tried to help him. He announced that the young rabbi, being threatened with blindness, proposed to tour the country speaking "upon all popular and Jewish subjects." In addition to the already acclaimed "Types of Manhood" and "The Talmud, Its Ethics and Literary Beauties," Browne suggested the following topics: "The Religion of Temperance, or How the Chosen People Keep Sober" a response to the Protestants' intensifying anti-alcohol campaign which he would soon present successfully in Atlanta; "The Genesis of Christianity;" which he later developed into a popular treatise on the Jewish role in the Crucifixion; "The Talmud on Diseases of the Mind;" "The Devil as Viewed by the Ancient Hebrews;" "The Modern Problem of the Southern People, Social not Political;" "The Young Men of the South and their Present Duties;" "The American Crown;" "Women's Religious and Social (not political) Emancipation;" "The Education of Mankind;" and "Moses Handling Electricity, or The Science of the Bible and Talmud."

There is no evidence that he ever spoke on other than the first four of these subjects, and little evidence of contemporary rabbis addressing public audiences on any of them. The one known exception was Wise, who spoke widely on early Christianity as well as on certain aspects of the Talmud. Browne evidently chose to avoid commenting on political issues.[33]

Lectures became an even more popular form of entertainment with the birth of Chautauqua in 1874. The flourishing institution that began as a summer study course for Christian religious school teachers at a camp site in New York State, quickly burgeoned into a program for cultural improvement emulated in other attractive pastoral settings throughout America. It brought to its stages the greatest speakers, actors, writers and musicians of the day, with the most charismatic orators vigorously promoting their various beliefs.

Chautauqua also added impetus to a mushrooming of evangelical tent assemblies and other religious revival programs among the many Protestant sects competing for predominance.

Because of its emphasis on the Christian religion, this original Chautauqua was not a venue for rabbis, although it is possible that Browne occasionally appeared on its programs because of his lectures geared to Christians. Protestants in America at that time took great interest in learning about Jews and Judaism because the Jewish Bible—the Old Testament for Christians—was at the core of their religious belief. They considered Jews to be current descendants of the classical prophets whom they greatly revered.

In 1893, Rabbi Henry Berkowitz and other Jewish scholars founded a similar organization, the Jewish Chautauqua Society, with the cooperation of the existing Christian institution and along the same lines as the original. In this and other fields of communal service in the nineteenth century, American Jewry developed its outstanding system of social welfare and service institutions from models originally provided by denominations of the Christian Church.

Protestants at that time greatly feared that America would be negatively influenced by the large Catholic immigration from Ireland and Mediterranean countries, working people who were not prohibited as were most Protestants from the use of alcohol. Exploitation of labor was rampant, which led many immigrant workers to dilute their frustrations in saloons and barrooms. This produced still more misery for their families, many of which were abandoned by husbands and fathers unable to cope.[34]

Church groups responded by organizing a forceful anti-alcohol crusade, establishing mission houses and stepping up efforts to convert those whom the zealous missionaries regarded as non-believers. In such an atmosphere, Browne easily attracted crowds with his most popular subjects, "The Jews and Temperance; or How the Chosen People Keep Sober and Straight," "The Talmud: Its Ethics and Literary Beauties;" and "The Crucifixion of Christ, or Have the Jews Actually Crucified Jesus of Nazareth?"[35]

After hearing Browne's presentation on the Talmud, a reviewer in Chicago noted that it was written for Christians, "and for them the Talmud had an unusual interest.. . . The Rabbi is a lecturer of no mean attainments, and the subject he has chosen . . . of unusual interest and beauty . . . treated with rare judgement and skill, and to this is added a good voice and excellent delivery." Another Chicago paper reported that Browne's lecture on the

Talmud was considered "one of the finest and more unique ever delivered in this city, the lecturer evincing a knowledge of the ancient literature of the Hebrews possessed by few persons."[36]

Later, as a result of similar publicity, Browne was urged to address the General Assembly of the Presbyterian Church. In 1885, he delivered the same message at the Methodist Episcopal Conference in New York. Invitations for the Talmud lecture increased, one of them producing a lengthy synopsis that revealed more historic and philosophic perspective than his original version presented in Montgomery eight years earlier. This time he added interesting historic background, noting that the Talmud had been condemned by Christian monarchs until the fifteenth century when the French king ordered that it be taught at the University of Paris; that the Holy Roman Emperor Maximilian had protected it because it embodied the records of Jesus's "closest relatives;" and that Martin Luther refrained from burning it along with Catholic documents at Wittenberg in 1520, coincidentally the same year that it was first published by a Jewish press in Venice.[37]

Browne also added an anecdote about Rabbi Gamaliel that emphasized the Jews' regard for education. He recalled that when Emperor Vespasian offered to grant the rabbi one wish before destroying Jerusalem, instead of asking him to spare the Temple, Gamaliel asked the emperor to spare the universities and yeshivas. This, said Browne, taught that "religion is useless unless based on knowledge." The statement bordered on heresy for many religious people of his day who believed that faith—belief in Jesus as the Messiah—was the sole requirement.[38]

Concluding his address with an example of "what a liberal creed implies," Browne used the metaphor of a doctor prescribing the same medication in three different forms for three patients with different preferences and needs but suffering from the same disease. When the doctor himself needed the prescription, he eschewed sweeteners and other means of making the medicine more palatable, swallowing the ingredients in their natural form. "So on with all the denominational recipes," Browne declared. "When we come to the great physicians of the soul, like Christ and the Rabbi Hillel, we find the creed of love taught in its simple purity, without any denominational trimmings. . . ."[39]

Thus did Browne seek to bring Judaism and Christianity together by stripping both of their diverse marketable embellishments. This tactic apparently resonated more with Christians than with Jews. A reviewer in Indianapolis wrote of Browne, "In point of brilliant scholarship and fine liberal tone, the most remarkable one heard in this city. . . he has no prejudices and expresses his views with the earnestness of an apostle and the liberality of a large minded scholar. . . . In manner the Doctor is vivacious, clear and highly entertaining."[40]

A Jewish listener questioned the ecumenical aspect of the speech, objecting to Browne's conclusion that both Jews and Christians would share equally in the hereafter if each lived up to his own religious beliefs. "Judaism and Christianity," declared the dissenter, "cannot reasonably be accepted as two corresponding pieces of the same excellent article: if one is true, the other is not true."

Wise identified the critic as one "who appears to have a distrust of all the present approved forms of religion, and who is classed among the very intelligent and shrewd freethinkers of the city." This highlighted a tension between the Jewish yearning for acceptance via ecumenism and the inability on the part of many Jews to accept the validity of any other faith than their own or to view their own with its embellishments stripped away. Browne had attacked their conventional approach to ecumenism. Then and in the future, as he continued to speak frankly, he gained approval and admiration from Christians while drawing the disapproval of Jews.[41]

In November, 1876, Wise notified readers that Browne would leave shortly for a tour through the Southwest (then meaning west of Atlanta and east of Houston.) Noting that Browne "has engagements for all the larger cities . . . but we have no doubt that arrangements for smaller places can be made," Wise urged people not to miss the opportunity "to procure a Jewish lecturer in places where there is no congregation . . . especially as the Doctor is able, eloquent and his lecture well worth hearing." [42]

That spring Browne traveled eastward across the Gulf states from Louisiana, where a reporter for the New Orleans Times praised his talk at the Rampart Street Synagogue as "the most entertaining and instructive . . . the people of New Orleans have ever heard or missed hearing for a long time." [43]

Crossing the Chattahoochee into Columbus, Georgia, Browne spoke on the historic Jewish view of the crucifixion, addressing an enthusiastic crowd of 125 that included "one colored Baptist Minister," in the city's historic Springer Opera House. A local reporter described the speaker as "able, systematic and forcible as we have ever had the pleasure of listening to. . . ." He extolled Browne's "power of illustration by analogizing" and his "vein of almost imperceptible humor, which was as subtle as is possible to conceive [as] fine, rich and highly enjoyable, though accompanied with due reverence." Then the reporter, apologizing that he could not give the two and a half hour lecture a "thorough synopsis" due to its length, reviewed it at a length proportionate to its delivery.[44]

In this presentation Browne made some startling assertions about Jesus's trial and betrayal, indicating that he knew about an obscure source, the Judas Gospel, that was mentioned in some medieval Christian texts, but not discovered in the original until the 1970s and undisclosed to the general public until 2006. Based partially on information contained in that document, Browne maintained that Jews were not responsible for the crucifixion because the timing and mode of Jesus's trial was contrary to Jewish laws, because it was carried out by "scalawags" and Romans, because the judges and officers were bribed, and because all but two of the judges were illiterate in Hebrew (presumably meaning Hebrew law, because the people spoke Aramaic, not Hebrew, and the rulers spoke Latin.) Browne exonerated Judas on the grounds that the alleged betrayer was really trying to save Jesus, who had asked to be delivered to the priests for protection. Furthermore, since Judas was the disciples' treasurer, he could have escaped with far more than thirty pieces of silver if profit had been his motive. Browne tagged Peter as the guilty one but did not say why.

Browne began his explanation of the crucifixion to his mostly Christian audience by giving a fictitious legal example set in 19th Century America. He then described a parallel case under Roman rule in Judea, where false messiahs constantly appeared promising to liberate the people. Their messianic claim was a political crime, for which the penalty was crucifixion.

"The captive nation cried in bitterness for the Messiah that would save it," Browne asserted, for the nation was torn in fragments, many of which Jesus had been able to reconcile. Then, "in an unguarded moment, by Jesus's dearest friend, he was declared to be the Messiah, the son of David, he who was to rescue the Jews from Roman bondage." The indiscreet announcement caused the Nazarene to be betrayed and indicted for high treason.

Browne noted that the trial could not have been a Jewish one because 1) it lasted only a few hours, whereas "by Jewish law then prevailing" it would have taken three days; 2) it took place on a Friday, which was also contrary to Jewish law; and 3) it was said to have taken place on the Passover, "again impossible according to Jewish law." A later reviewer quoted Browne as saying that, "in an unguarded moment" Peter declared Jesus to be the Messiah, come to rescue the Jews from Roman bondage--a crime greatly feared by the Roman authorities, and punishable by death.

By advancing the theory that an inadvertent remark rather than purposeful betrayal had led to Jesus's death, Browne sought to disabuse Christians of the notion that Jews were responsible for the crucifixion. It is doubtful that he succeeded with many. Imbedded within centuries of indoctrination, the theory prevailed unchallenged by the Church until almost a century later.[45]

The Columbus reviewer wrote that Browne "attributed to Jesus a much more dignified character than is credited to him by Christians," saying that he was "truly liberal throughout his discourse," and possessed noble sentiments "worthy of any man . . . a gentleman of high culture, of profound thought, backed by extended [sic] reading. . . . We wish that his entire lecture would be published that the people might read and study."[46]

While fate decreed otherwise about its publication, Browne's lecture that evening did bring him good fortune. In the audience were four leaders of Atlanta's Hebrew Benevolent Congregation. It is possible that they were there on a mission to choose a rabbi, for Browne had lectured in Atlanta the previous year on "The Talmud, Its Ethics and Literary Beauties" to good reviews. The Atlanta delegation was so impressed that the men returned home offering personally to pay for the completion of their synagogue building, halted due to lack of funds, if the congregation would engage Browne as its rabbi. Fortunately, Browne had just undergone an operation by an eminent eye surgeon in Texas which improved his condition sufficiently for him to accept the offer.[47]

The timing was fortuitous. On October 8, 1876, after five years of marriage, Sophie had finally borne a healthy child, a daughter whom they named Lylah Leah. Her arrival gave urgency to Browne's need for a stable position.

Browne was ready. In these years, he became widely familiar with Middle America, intimately so with the communities of Evansville and Peoria where he had lived. He preached and published advanced ideas, often at odds with mainstream Jewry. Fortified by his understanding that science could be compatible with religion, he advocated both Darwinism and biblical criticism which were bitterly opposed by most rabbis as well as by the Christian clergy. His approach to ecumenism included stripping both Judaism and Christianity of their popularizing but extraneous embellishments, and explaining the crucifixion from the standpoint of the Judas gospel.

During his brief but highly successful tenure in Peoria, Browne broadened his reputation as a public orator and "ambassador to the gentiles," established himself as a fighter for ecumenism and against agnosticism, furthered his activity as a journalist, and gained friends in the highest levels of government including the president himself.

Storm clouds began to rise in the distance, however. While still supported by Wise and embraced as a member of his family, Wise's widowhood and remarriage, as well as his son Leo's return, initiated changes in his relationship with Browne. As a delegate to the opening conference of the Union of American Hebrew Congregations in 1873, Browne fostered regulations that, while needed, were unpopular with the lay leaders whose support Wise required in order to reach his goal of establishing a seminary to train rabbis in America. Though unsuccessful, these proposals signaled Browne's growing divergence from his teacher's opinion on some issues, seeds of independence that questioned the former acolyte's future reliability as an automatic supporter of the master's views. These were dangerous waters for a young rabbi.

V - GATE CITY AND THE SOUTH'S FIRST JEWISH NEWSPAPER

In Atlanta, Browne's abilities were quickly acknowledged and appreciated by the general community as well as within the Hebrew Benevolent Congregation. He embarked with apparent success on a new enterprise, the South's first Jewish newspaper, which even today provides the reader with a colorful and telling source for the study of the lives of Southern Jews from 1877 to 1881. His close relationship with Wise came to an end, arguably due to competition for newspaper circulation. Browne subsequently lost the paper. A false rumour then smeared his character, leading to the loss of his pulpit and other employment opportunities. The incident marked a distinct turning point in his career as well as another long period of dissension and change for the congregation.

Details of synagogue operation, press coverage, social and family life, development of Reform Judaism in America, and the far reaching effect of petty peeves and bullish pride portray an experience that parallels other Jewish communities and their leaders in nineteenth century America. On July 18, 1877, the *Atlanta Constitution* announced:

> *The Jewish Synagogue has just called Dr. E. B. M. Browne, who lectured here last season, and is well remembered by our citizens, to take charge of the church. Dr. Browne is a gentleman of fine culture, of strong vigorous mental constitution, and of blameless character. He will prove to be a proper head of the large and influential Jewish population in this city. He will take charge of the church about the 1st of September. The church building, a handsome and commodious one,*

will be finished by the time Dr. Browne comes to take charge. As is usual with this thrifty and clear-headed people, the church will be paid for when it is finished.

As we shall see, the closing statement was slightly inaccurate.

Congregation and Community

Browne arrived in Atlanta on the heels of an incident in which the New York banker Joseph Seligman and his family had been refused accommodations at the Grand Union Hotel in Saratoga Springs, New York. This incident was the first widely publicized act of discrimination against Jews at a luxury resort hotel, and marked the rise of what John Higham characterizes as an era of social and intellectual antisemitism. The story filled long front-page columns in the Atlanta Constitution, where a progressive young reporter, Henry W. Grady, soon became editor and partial owner, and by the mid-1880s the foremost spokesman for the New South creed. Grady brought the city forward to what promoters later characterized as "a city too busy to hate." Whether he and Browne ever met is unknown, but Grady's beneficial influence was quickly felt especially by the local Jewish community unnerved by the new expression of antisemitism in New York.[1]

Atlanta's Jews then numbered 525 within a total population of 35,000. About half of the Jews belonged to the ten-year-old Gemilath Chesed Kehillah Kodesh, or Hebrew Benevolent Congregation, subsequently known as The Temple. This small but highly visible Jewish population drew a disproportionate amount of positive public interest. As the Atlanta Constitution opined in 1870, "Among her most orderly, enterprising and public-spirited citizens, the Israelites of Atlanta may be justly classed. Some of them are ranked among our oldest and most respected business men. In our cosmopolitan city, but little of that general prejudice against Jews is ever demonstrated."[2]

In 1875, reporting on the cornerstone laying ceremony for the city's first synagogue at the corner of Forsyth and Garnett Street, the Atlanta Daily News had proclaimed:

> . . . *nothing is so indicative of a city's prosperity as to see an influx of Jews who come with the intention of living with you, and especially as they buy property and build among you, because they are a thrifty and progressive people who never fail to build up a town they settle in; and again because they make good citizens, pay their obligations promptly, never refuse to pay their taxes and are law-abiding . . . The solemnity and good order which prevails during the worship in their synagogue is worthy of imitation by many of us Gentile Christians.*[3]

After Browne's election, work resumed on the synagogue. The community—Jews and gentiles alike—gathered for its dedication on Friday, August 31, 1877. The elegant Moorish- style brick and stone structure boasted doors and bima (pulpit platform) of heavy walnut, jewel-like stained glass windows, plush carpets, and eight chandeliers that were "very handsome and of the latest patent." Pillars of galvanized iron "in perfect imitation of red marble" upheld its interior arches along the sides of the sanctuary and bore inscriptions from the Psalms in gold leaf. No specified balcony for the women existed because the congregation had already introduced family seating. A gallery was provided for the choir directly above the entrance.[4]

Newspapers described the dedication as "one of the most impressive scenes that ever occurred in Atlanta." Due to widespread interest in the building the congregation had sent invitations to some three hundred dignitaries and others who were not members. Fully an hour before festivities were scheduled to begin, a standing room only crowd braved the exhausting heat of the late summer afternoon which, according to reports, had been made tolerable indoors by good ventilation. The ceremony, standard for such occasions, began at 3:45 PM with a fifteen minute musical prelude performed by a string band. At four o'clock the procession began, led by President Levi Cohen, in formal attire, alongside the new rabbi. Browne wore a billowing black academic robe, white stock tie, narrow knee-length tallit (prayer shawl, in this case abbreviated symbolic version) and six-inch high cushion shaped hat, traditional among English rabbis.

According to custom, the board of trustees and the building committee immediately followed them, after which two of the oldest men in the congregation carried the Torahs. Then marched fifteen young girls dressed in white, their leader bearing a velvet cushion upon which rested the key to the building.

When all had ascended the bima and the key presented to building committee chairman Joseph T. Eichberg the choir sang an appropriate selection, after which Eichberg handed the key to Cohen. In accepting Cohen reviewed the congregation's history, including the fact that only fifty-five members could afford to contribute to the building, which left a small debt that would soon be paid. He also thanked the many Christians who had contributed, as well as the ladies of the congregation who by sponsoring a fair had raised $3000 and purchased carpeting for the synagogue.

Following Cohen's acceptance, Eichberg opened the ark and the organ emitted solemn chords while the elders set the sacred scrolls in their places within the ark. Browne read a relevant portion from Scripture after which the choir sang the hymn "Praise the Lord." Only then did Browne deliver his dedicatory sermon and begin the regular Friday evening service.[5]

Browne based his sermon on Genesis 28:17, the passage in which Jacob awakens from his dream and exclaims, "How awe inspiring is this place! This is none other than the house of God, and that is the gate of heaven." With the stated intention of defining modern Judaism and how it differs from Christianity, Browne developed a theme that he had used years before, in Quincy, Illinois, emphasizing the importance that Reform placed on rationality and ecumenism. He argued that all religions have three stages: the mythical or legendary, which reflects people's initial attempts to understand creation and is conscientiously followed by future generations; the theological, beginning with the establishment of a group as spiritual guide to think and pray for others; and the third—which he did not name—when individual reason motivates people to think for themselves. According to the Reform rabbi, this final stage differentiates Judaism from Christianity by the tenet that reason is the only mediator between God and man universally. "The sooner a religion discards the belief in a mediating prophet," he said:

> the sooner it abandons the idea of its own superiority above its neighbours in its own conception, and in the eyes of God, the nearer we are to truth; the less we maintain that our church is the only "house of God," the more it will become the dwelling of our Lord. Judaism, I mean pure Judaism, the Judaism of Deuteronomy, is an exception to the rule of passing these stages. We have no theological system. True, we had for the time being priests and prophets, but they were the teachers of our people and nothing else.[6]

In a lengthy, lyrical metaphor about nature, Browne spoke of watching "the wild play of the billows breaking their fury against the rocky cliff," and asked rhetorically if it were nothing more than "the sport of chance." He followed with another question, tracing billows to tide, tide to storms, storms to the rotation of the earth and influences of the moon, then to the planets, comets and fixed stars, finally declaring that all "are only so many steps in the ladder which will bring you, by virtue of those angelic messengers of reason, in communion with God . . . returning again to you in the very same steps, bringing along the godly blessings of satisfaction to the inquiring soul. . . ."

Browne concluded with a return to his text, recalling the rabbinic tradition that every good deed became an angel and declaring that Jacob's angels on the ladder were his own good deeds ascending to heaven and returning to him. Everyone has such a ladder near at hand, Browne said, admonishing his listeners to look for them in Nature, "the great and only 'house of God.'" Since the entire universe was a house built by God, he maintained, it was impossible for humans to build one, but only to build gates to heaven in which they could erect ladders for the angels of good deeds to ascend. "Happy then that you have not called this the church of God," he told his listeners, "but the congregation of the Sons of Benevolence. It is only one of the gates to heaven."[7]

In his reference to the Judaism of Deuteronomy, typical of Reform belief, Browne indicated his rejection of laws later added by rabbinic tradition. As the synagogue's design and the ceremonies surrounding its dedication were deliberately planned to reflect the melding of Jewish distinctiveness with American custom and environment, so did the rabbis gear their sermons to express unique aspects of Judaism while addressing the commonalty of Judaism with Christianity. All of it was a conscious effort to make their upwardly mobile congregants feel good about themselves and gain ever greater acceptance within society.

The congregation was not disappointed. The following day, the Atlanta Constitution reported the sermon as "a profound and admirable discourse, full of original ideas and characterized by a broad liberality which Christian churches would do well to imitate." Such use of hyperbole by reviewers was standard in the newspapers of that era. So was the effort on the part of rabbis to preach ecumenism. This required keeping a delicate balance between one's own belief and accepting the validity of others.[8]

Browne may well have equated the gates of heaven with the Gate City of the South, for Atlanta, impressed from the start by his oratorical skill and long list of academic degrees, quickly opened its arms to him and his family. He followed three other rabbis who briefly served the Atlanta congregation, each sharing some of his attributes. They typified the range of backgrounds and experience that rabbis then brought to the American hinterland.

David Burgheim, who came to Atlanta as its first rabbi in 1869, was like Browne in that he was a scholar, linguist, and avid student of early Christianity. He opened a secular school, the English German Academy, which historians believed to have been the immediate predecessor of the Atlanta Public Schools. During this period before the wide-scale advent of public education, many rabbis organized English-German-Hebrew academies—a reflection of the tripartite identity of their community—to supplement their pulpit incomes.

Burghein came to Atlanta from Nashville, and returned there after one year leaving Benjamin Aaron Bonnheim, whom he had hired to run his school, to serve as rabbi. Bonnheim remained for two more years, after which he moved to various cities, including Baltimore where he served as superintendent and resident physician at the Hebrew Hospital and Asylum. Like Browne, he had studied medicine and received his degree after coming to America.

Atlanta's next rabbi was Lithuanian-born Henry Gersoni, a linguist, orator, author, and at times the editor of a newspaper. He allegedly converted to Catholicism in Europe but recanted after coming to America. Later denounced by Wise for his "venomous sarcasm" and opposition to the UAHC, Gersoni was best remembered in Atlanta for his admirable social qualities and cantorial skills. He too, like his predecessors, departed after two years.[9]

Although lack of funds had been a primary factor in Gersoni's departure, Browne was not discouraged by the meagre offer of $1500 a year as compared to the $2500 that he had earned elsewhere. He and Sophie liked the South, she had close relatives in Atlanta, and the young couple longed for a permanent home. They settled first in temporary quarters at 46 East Hunter Street, uncomfortably close to the noise and soot of the railroad terminal, but satisfactory for the time being. After only three months, they announced their intention to remain in Atlanta and began planning a house of their own at 182 Forsyth Street, a lot next to the Temple which the congregation had purchased for a parsonage. It was a comfortable distance from the railroad and on the "Haas block," so-called because several branches of that prominent family built their homes there. Among them were Sophie's cousins, newlyweds Aaron and Frances (Fannie) Rich Haas.[10]

The Haas family was well established in Atlanta, Jacob having been the city's first Jewish resident when he arrived in 1844. His brother Herman came later with his wife and children, one of whom was Aaron. Their story bespeaks the comfortable position that Jews enjoyed in the general community, one that easily transferred to the Brownes.

Aaron Haas, long one of Atlanta's most respected citizens, had emigrated from Europe as a child with his mother, sister of Sophie's father, Moses Weil. They lived with the Weils in Evansville for two years while Aaron's father, Herman, who had preceded them to America in order to earn money to bring them over, continued peddling until he could afford to take them south to Atlanta where his brother Jacob had arranged a partnership for him in a dry goods store. Soon Herman moved his family to Newnan, Georgia, some forty miles south, where he opened a wholesale grocery business. He later returned to Atlanta, went to Philadelphia to be within a larger Jewish community, and returned again to Atlanta after the Civil War. His son Aaron remained in Atlanta and gained fame as a twice captured war hero who ran the Union blockade to sell Southern cotton, the Confederates' only source of income.

Aaron subsequently served as an alderman and in 1875 as the city's first mayor pro tempore. He taught Sunday school in his bachelor quarters—a single room above his office—was among the founders of the congregation in 1867, and represented it at the UAHC convention in Philadelphia the summer of 1877. That same summer he married Fannie Rich, sister of the men whose dry goods business became Rich's, the South's largest department store. He currently headed the Gate City Lodge of B'nai B'rith, into which he promptly enrolled his cousin, the new rabbi.[11]

Browne, permanently settled, serving a young, vibrant and growing congregation, seemingly had all factors in place to make his impact on American Judaism. One of his first actions at the Temple was to reorganize its religious school, dividing it into four classes that met both on Saturdays and Sundays. The faculty consisted of himself, two other men and three women, one of whom was Sophie, fulfilling a role often expected of the rabbi's wife. Of their thirty-eight students, fourteen were in high school. A large proportion of these were girls, which surprised Browne because it was unusual in those days for girls to continue their education to that level. He publicly commended the congregation for this commitment to learning.

As he had done in Evansville, Browne encouraged the formation of a "Young Israel's Literary Association." He also conducted a private, afternoon

Hebrew school for boys at the synagogue, which the board had suggested as a means of supplementing his salary. He abandoned it after one year because of difficulty collecting tuition, after which the congregation continued it under board direction, supported by special dues.[12]

When Browne arrived the congregation had already initiated the ceremony of confirmation for girls and boys together at age fourteen, a custom early adopted by Reform as a recognition of gender equality in affirming Judaism when adolescents come of age. It still retained bar mitzvah for boys, as did most Reform congregations at that time, but also like the majority of others, discontinued the ceremony in the 1890s due to the influence of rabbis trained in radical Reform. The Temple reinstated bar mitzvah and added bat mitzvah for girls in 1973. As the Atlanta Constitution explained:

> The Israelites of Atlanta, have never divided upon the question of orthodoxy and reformation. They are extremists on neither side. While many of the prayers and customs, if not applicable to the present age and the present conditions of the descendants of Jacob, are omitted . . . , they do not go as far in ignoring ancient traditional usages as do the extreme reformers in many other places. . . . [13]

This statement expressed Browne's beliefs. He led the congregation into mild reforms but rejected the more radical ones that were later instituted by his successor, David Marx. In Atlanta, as in most other cities, the changes developed gradually, instituted according to the wishes of the congregation's leaders-- rabbi, president or both. Such positions and the opinions of those who held them in most communities underwent frequent reversals until the 1890s when rabbis trained in Reform at the Hebrew Union College became available. By 1877, the Temple had already enhanced its services with organ music and a mixed choir (a submission to modern tastes long permitted in many European synagogues) but tabled a motion that allowed men to remove their hats during religious services. Like most of his congregants, Browne abandoned the prohibition against riding on the Sabbath, but he strongly opposed holding services on Sunday, a practice being touted by some Reform congregations, to be discussed in the following chapter. As the Atlanta Constitution in effect stated and Reform advocated, he approved those rituals that seemed meaningful, but abandoned the "external [i.e., halachic] additions" to the Decalogue "suited to the dark ages in which the law-giver lived, but . . . outlived by growing civilization. . . ."[14]

If the trustees ever discussed ideology at their meetings, they failed to record it. Reflecting the limitation of their interest, minutes indicate that they dealt only with practical issues such as assignment of pews, assessment of dues, decorum during the worship service, and regulation of duties for synagogue functionaries. For example, they voted to enforce a rule requiring the choir to have "at least two rehearsals a month." Another ruling required the rabbi to ask permission before leaving the city for any purpose, regardless of how long he would be away, whether for two days to dedicate a synagogue in a nearby town or for a two-month vacation in Europe. This pattern obtained in other congregations as well. It identified a tension that existed in most congregations over competition for control, and reflected the degree of subjugation imposed on their rabbis. The absence of theological discussion probably also indicated a desire to keep debate on this highly controversial subject at a minimum by avoiding it whenever possible and declining to record it when it occurred.[15]

Atlanta's Temple was one of eight congregations in Georgia serving a total of 309 families in Athens, Augusta, Savannah, Albany, Columbus,

Rome, and Macon. Whereas the historic Savannah congregation, third in the nation, had been founded in 1733, almost simultaneously with the colony of Georgia itself, those of Augusta, Macon and Columbus had also preceded Atlanta, having been established in the 1850s, prior to the Civil War. Rome, Albany and Athens followed much later, in the 1870s. All suffered at times from economic recession—hence fluctuations in dues-paying membership—and all endured periods without a rabbi.[16]

Although affiliated with Wise's UAHC at its inception, typical of many congregations, the Temple waffled in and out of membership until the 1890s. This was possibly due to economic factors in the same fashion that individual members sometimes dropped off the congregation's list temporarily during business hardships. It could also have been caused by dissension when control passed from more traditional leadership to more Reform, or vice versa. Because Browne had not yet been installed as the Temple's rabbi when the UAHC convened in 1877, the congregation sent Haas as its delegate to that convention. Browne participated at the meeting nonetheless as a delegate representing Congregation Ohaveh Sholem of Summit, Mississippi. He served on several committees and delivered the closing prayer, and in the next two years attended the UAHC conventions representing Atlanta. For reasons unknown, the Temple refused a request from the Athens congregation for him to represent them also, and—possibly due to financial considerations—directed him not to invite the UAHC to meet in Atlanta the following year.[17]

While it is not known if these denials were caused by personal pique or other issues, it is certain that the Jewish communities of Georgia bonded for charitable purposes and that the Atlanta congregation proudly permitted its eloquent rabbi to lecture publicly for worthy causes. As he had done in Evansville for the first Hebrew Orphan's Home, built by B'nai B'rith in Cleveland, he now lectured to benefit another that the order was in the process of building in Atlanta. One of the first in the nation, the Atlanta Home served indigent or abandoned children throughout the Southeast for almost half a century, closing only when foster care supplanted the use of such institutions. Although B'nai B'rith recognized as early as 1903 that placement in private homes was preferable to group care and took steps to implement the change at that time, it continued to support existing facilities as long as they were needed.[18]

Browne's interests and those of his congregation were not limited to Jewish causes. He toured the South in 1878 to raise money for sufferers in one of America's devastating yellow fever epidemics which was especially virulent along the Mississippi valley, from Memphis to New Orleans. The disease took more than 4,000 lives in the Crescent City alone.

On another tour that year, Browne lectured to benefit sufferers of the potato famine in Ireland. Some twenty years after the most devastating famine struck there in the 1850s, the Irish were again starving due to drought combined with unfavorable trade policies imposed by Great Britain. Browne raised money in the American South to help them, waiving his customary fee of $150 when lecturing for benefits, so all of the proceeds could be sent to the designated charity. Although tickets cost only twenty-five cents and were free for the clergy, these events usually netted significant amounts. Beneficiaries thanked him in various ways, one of which was an attempt on the part of B'nai B'rith members in Navasota, Texas, to name their lodge in his honour. This did not come about because of B'nai B'rith's standing regulation forbidding its lodges to be named for living members of the order.[19]

With his abundance of energy, Browne managed these travels and more without neglecting participation in local affairs. Temple members had long been prominently involved in Atlanta's cultural growth. Some helped establish the Young Men's Library Association, forerunner of the Atlanta

Public Library. David Mayer, a founder of the public school system in 1869 and member of its Board until his death in 1890, made certain that Jewish children were excused on the High Holy Days, a privilege that did not yet apply in many American cities, including New York. Browne, too, took an active interest in the public schools and shortly after his arrival was appointed one of the city's six examiners for high schools.[20]

Georgia Governor Alfred Colquitt quickly recognized the rabbi's potential, especially his intellectual credentials having served as professor of medical jurisprudence and diseases of the mind at the Evansville Medical College. With that in mind, Colquitt appointed him the state's sole delegate for a "World Congress of Social Science," scheduled to convene the following summer in Stockholm. Noting the intensified worldwide concern with temperance, the conference president invited Browne to lecture on "Jews, Temperance and Crime, or How the Chosen People Keep Sober and Out of Mischief." Browne planned to leave for Sweden on July 29, and stop off on the way in Paris to attend a meeting of the Jewish Ecumenical Council convened there by the Alliance Israelite Universelle.[21]

As it happened, Browne did not make it to either conference. In June, 1878, Sophie gave birth to their second child, a boy, whom they named Jesse Logan in honor of a family friend, Congressman John A. Logan, Republican of Illinois, who advocated public education. Sophie developed severe postpartum depression, causing her husband to cancel his summer travel. Whatever disappointment he felt in missing the trip was amply overcome by the joy of beholding his newborn son. Upon Sophie's recovery, even after suffering two illnesses himself including a winter bout with typhoid fever that almost killed him, Browne appeared to be happily settled and functioning at top speed.

Apparently the congregation appreciated his services, especially in regard to his community outreach. Responding to "many inquiries of Christians as to whether they can attend. . . ." he publicized the fact that he conducted services and delivered his sermons in English. The Daily Constitution reported in 1878 that his Rosh Hashanah Eve service was well attended "not only by members of the Jewish church, but also by a number of Christian friends," and that his sermon was "very appropriate . . . a very able one."

This truly bespoke success in Atlanta. Southern Jews, perhaps even more than their mid-western counterparts, valued above all else their rabbis' talents as ambassadors to the gentiles. In this respect Browne evoked the pride they felt in the city-wide recognition and achievements of lay leaders like David Mayer and Aaron Haas, ethnic brokers who preceded him, and later spokesmen such as Joseph Hirsch and Victor Kreigshaber. This was a role that the rabbi enjoyed, and one for which he was well prepared.[22]

The Jewish South

Unfortunately, Browne's aptitude for diplomacy did not extend to relationships with the leaders of Reform Judaism. His affiliation with Wise began to split shortly after he arrived in Atlanta when the younger rabbi began weekly publication of the Jewish South, the first newspaper ever addressed specifically to Southern Jewry.

Having observed how his mentor used the American Israelite and Die Deborah to propagate his ideas and influence, Browne perceived the possibility of doing likewise, focusing on Jewish interests throughout the South. The need arose, he believed, because most Jewish journals other than Wise's were "chiefly local in circulation and tendency," therefore little known beyond their respective areas. Wise's American Israelite, the only paper serving Jews in the middle states, "endeavoured to cover too large a territory, which naturally placed affairs nearer home ahead of those from the far South. . . ." Believing that "the interests of Southern Judaism and the dignity of the South call loudly for a mouth piece worthy to represent them," on October 14, 1877, barely two months after arriving in Atlanta, Browne produced his first issue of the Jewish South.[23]

Initial publishers of the paper were the brothers J. R. and W. B. Seals, Christians who said that they were alerted to the need, "by many of our Hebrew friends," and would have undertaken the publication two years earlier had they found a competent editor. They assumed full responsibility for business matters, with Browne as editor-in-chief, leaving all else to him as as he wished. He wanted no part in financial affairs, even advising subscribers to send payments directly to the publishers rather than to him. His reporters were Henry Powers of Nashville and Elias Haimon of Atlanta, proprietor of the Southern Agricultural Works. He was able to recruit Charles Wessolowsky, a former state senator from Albany, Georgia, as assistant editor.[24]

Browne envisioned the Jewish South as an instrument by which "to drain the swamp of ignorance in which breed the diseases of hatred and bigotry," promoting education and brotherhood among Jews while providing information about them for non-Jews. Believing that Jews and Christians, especially in the South, would welcome the chance to learn more about each other at an affordable price, he proclaimed across the newspaper's masthead, "The Largest and Cheapest Jewish Journal in the World," set the subscription rate at $2.00 a year (rather than the $4 or $5 charged by Wise and publishers of other Jewish weeklies), and specifically invited Christians to subscribe, gearing much of his copy to their interests. He promised Jewish readers that the paper would remain independent, uninvolved in "the combative liturgical and theological arguments" of American Jewry.[25]

Ads cost $1.50 an inch for a single entry and $30 for the year. Christians as well as Jews from as far away as New York, Cincinnati, Chicago, and St. Louis, bought them to tout area hotels, railroads, plantations in Florida (from $2,500 to $15,000,) Jewish books, tea, toupees, pianos, scuppernong wine, the study of French dentistry, and a brownstone in Manhattan. The Southern Educational Institute for Boys advertised Judaic studies as well as preparation for college at a bargain rate of $400 compared to the $1000 charged by northern schools. Notices of marriages, births, betrothals, deaths, welfare needs such as a job for a young Jewish girl with "a good Jewish family," were published free of charge as were those of congregations seeking rabbis or rabbis seeking congregations. As other rabbi-publishers did, Browne promoted his own lectures, Sabbath services and books. Advertisements for his 420 page translation of The Book Jashar appeared regularly, with a gradual reduction in price from $5 per copy, to "buy four copies and get one free," and finally to $2.50 each.[26]

The Jewish South covered essentially the same subjects as other Jewish weeklies, but in a format that suggests a more popular appeal. Because, like others, Browne sought to educate both Jewishly and secularly, he also published literary offerings—serialized novels, familiar quotations by such authors as Jonathon Swift and Washington Irving, poetry (often contributed by readers) as well as an introduction to the Hebrew language with translations of Hebrew poetry, including some by Judah Halevy. He featured a chess column, a "Boys and Girls" department, and to attract those inclined toward material pursuits rather than intellectual ones, a section entitled "All About Diamonds." Under the title "All Sorts" he published literary trivia, theatre commentary, occasional humor such as "A few words to the ladies from a rooster-pecked wife," and fashion notes to keep readers in the rural South au courant with life in the more sophisticated world of big cities. When he and Sophie celebrated their seventh wedding anniversary, he joked about it in "All Sorts," referring to their marriage as "the Seven Years' War."[27]

As Wise did, Browne published outstanding sermons by other rabbis. The Jewish South differed, however, in that it occasionally carried sermons of Christian ministers. In later issues Browne published a series entitled "Our Christian Brethren—what they are saying and doing for their religion— Know thy neighbours as thyself," informing readers about different Protestant denominations. However, not all Jewish readers appreciated this degree of attention to Christian beliefs and interests, as one indicated in a long, scathing criticism. With antisemitism on the rise, rabbis were challenged to maintain a delicate balance between ecumenical outreach and Jewish cohesion.[28]

Browne published opinion pieces and, as one who abjured card playing himself, no doubt especially welcomed articles from Max Meyerhardt, a Rome, Georgia, attorney who criticized card playing. The editor freely expounded his own views, a very strong one being that Jews should take part in government. In "The American Hebrew in Politics," Browne questioned why so few American Jews engaged in that arena, compared to their European counterparts who, despite living in countries with virulent antisemitism participated in proportionately far greater numbers. He credited the fact that in England, France and Germany, Jewish talents were recognized without regard to religion, noting that in Britain, Queen Victoria appointed Jews to visible positions. In America initial appointments were made by lesser officials, which made it more difficult for Jews to get ahead, therefore less appealing to attempt. It was true that some Jews had risen to high offices in emancipated Western Europe, but there they had been settled and acculturated for centuries, whereas in America they were largely immigrant or first generation, still struggling to gain a foothold and become Americanized. Presumably Browne's purpose was not to chastise his fellow Jews, but to goad them into pushing for government recognition. As always, he challenged America to live up to its promise of equal opportunity.[29]

Social notes announced Jewish visitors to Atlanta and locals traveling elsewhere, including merchants on buying trips to New York. When Emmanuel Rich, one of the brothers who founded Rich's Department Store, married Bertha Sartorius in June, 1878, an item mentioned that the ceremony, scheduled for 5:00 PM, was "the shortest affair on record, at the special request of the groom," and that guests grumbled at being invited "to witness wedding rites performed with nothing to witness, going even so far as to blame the minister. . . ."[30]

The blame was not misplaced. Browne, scheduled to speak at the dedication of the synagogue in Selma, Alabama, two days hence, had no way to get there more quickly than an overnight and all day journey by train that left Atlanta at 5:10 PM. He persuaded the station master to delay the train's departure until he could conduct the wedding and come aboard. As reported elsewhere in the paper, "At 5:10 PM Wednesday, or rather later, the train having been detained by order of the railroad officials to accommodate the Doctor after performing the ceremony at Mr. Rich's wedding, Dr. Browne left for Selma. . . ."[31]

A Selma resident reported the synagogue dedication, including Browne's sermon, which began with a metaphor that he had probably used before and would use again as appropriate for the dedication of a synagogue in a building that had formerly housed a church. Making the point that the "business" of the building had not changed, he referred to its previous occupants' Son and Holy Ghost as partners who retired, leaving their Father solely in charge. In essence the sermon reflected ecumenism more seriously, strongly promoting the values of Reform. He referred to the thousand-fold laws and directions added to the Decalogue, emphasizing that they had been given for a reason but noting that they were wrappings, external additions "suited for the dark age in which the law-giver lived," but outgrown by civilization, which required them to "give way to the light." Christianity as an outgrowth of Judaism, he said, accepted the law without wrappings, with only dogma, without which it would contain only the Decalogue and become Judaism. He equated the customs added to Mosaic law by the Talmudic rabbis with the evening star, which shines brightly at night but disappears in daylight. To appreciate those customs, he declared, one must return to the dark ages where they were born.[32]

Browne's visit to Selma increased his awareness of the need to bring Jews together from the dozens of small, isolated towns scattered across the Southern states, to provide the tools by which they could develop a sense of community. To this end he engaged Joseph Menko as assistant editor for local news, thus freeing Wessolowsky to visit the region's far flung towns and villages, meeting and writing about their Jewish inhabitants. The former legislator made two trips, in 1878 and 1879, stopping in sixty-two cities and towns as far west as Dallas and as far north as St. Louis. Not only did he encourage people to subscribe to the paper and to submit their local news and opinions, he also urged them to organize congregations under the aegis of the UAHC and to establish B'nai B'rith lodges. Wise sent a reporter on a similar assignment, but with less travel, unable to match Wessolowsky's extensive stops and detailed reporting.[33]

As a result of Wessolowsky's travels, the Jewish South received more contributed material than other Jewish papers. It fostered the immigrants' need to fit in with items of typical American interest such as a 5-0 baseball victory of the Natchez Press Club over the Milwaukee Lager Beers. It nurtured a sense of Jewish peoplehood, linking minuscule communities to each other with such news as the formation of a B'nai B'rith lodge in Halletsville, Texas; activities of the Ladies' Aid Society in Pine Bluff,

Arkansas; and bar mitzvah announcements which sometimes listed the name of every boy who attended the event and quoted the entire speech of the celebrant. Response to the heimish (Jewish folksy) outreach of the paper is evident in a report from one Louisiana community in the throes of a yellow fever epidemic. It read, "Plasquimine yehudim all doing well."[34]

The Jewish South brought news from the wider Jewish world, which Wise did also but with more emphasis on news from London and less on happenings in Africa and the Middle East. Browne's international news included such items as notice of a new congregation in South Africa ("Jews Flourishing Everywhere, Even in Cape Diamond Fields,") reports of knighthood being conferred upon seven Italian rabbis, Jewish soldiers in the Netherlands being given leave on the High Holy Days (adding proudly that the Atlanta School Board had already done this for its Jewish children), and claiming that the Zulus' language contains many Hebrew idioms. Reflecting consistent Jewish interest in the Holy Land, he reported plans for a railroad between Jaffa and Jerusalem, the opening of a school for needy children on Mt. Zion by Palestine's Portuguese synagogue, and other news of the Middle East.[35]

A story captioned "Are We to Have Peace in Israel?" was not an item of international news, however, although it may well seem so to twenty-first century readers. Rather, it referred to the theological warfare within Am Yisrael, the Jewish people, throughout America. Another article, published during Passover and captioned "Israel Declaration of Independence," equated the current problems of American Jewry with some encountered by the Israelites in Exodus.[36]

As others did, Browne used his paper to promote Jewish education. He continued to campaign for the UAHC to implement religious instruction within congregations and provide circuit-riding rabbis for those unable to afford full time rabbis, and published lessons and prayers to assist individuals wishing to establish religious schools. As an example for an opening prayer he suggested that students thank the Almighty for ". . . . Thy indispensable assistance for the labours of our teachers. May their instructions be received by willing hearts, so that the mind will easily accept what Israel confesses to be divine truth . . . " declining to state specifically what that truth might be so as to avoid offending his non-Jewish readers. To close a class session he advised teachers to express their appreciation "for the privilege of having imparted Thy word and Thy will to the children of Israel." He provided a catechism for young children, first addressing their comprehension of the word "religion" and its interpretation within Judaism, recognizing pluralism as always.

Only after establishing this base for understanding did Browne initiate the study of Biblical history, which he began by defining the patriarchs and their surroundings as illustrated by this portion of Noah and the Flood:

> *Q. How long did the waters prevail on the earth?*
> *A. One hundred and fifty days, and the ark rested on the mountains of Ararat.*
> *Q. Where are the mountains of Ararat?*
> *A. In Armenia, a province of Asiatic Turkey.*[37]

Despite his promise of neutrality in the theological warfare between American Jews, Browne did not hesitate to criticize Jewish practices that he considered to be counter-progressive. In a series titled "The Iron Mask of the XIX Century: The American Jewish Pulpit—Its Shame and Its Glory," he attacked both the rabid traditionalists whom he accused of answering innovations with violence, and ultra liberals who advocated the more subtle but in his opinion equally harmful lack of regulation. He saw danger in the radical path ultimately leading to total disappearance of Jewish practice, which he recognized as an integral part of Judaism, an issue that he believed should be addressed by the UAHC.

Elaborating on his remarks in a previous interview elsewhere, Browne declared that the disrespectful attitude of Jews toward their rabbis (compared to the reverence of Christians for their ministers) was not the fault of the congregants because in America their rabbis were rarely well trained or capable of serving as spiritual leaders. He advocated greater regulation in order to attract more qualified students to Wise's newly established Hebrew Union College. As things were, he wrote, when a congregation of average pretensions wanted a minister, "They advertise for one that has to be a teacher, a reader, a lecturer in German and English, a Shochet (and Mohel preferred) who shall also be able to instruct a choir, and besides, that man must be a 'gentleman.'" The typical applicant for such a position, he declared, was a self-styled "Reverend" who had just failed in business, and "having no other mode of making a living, he says to himself, 'I can read Hebrew. . . .'" Many congregations either believed that this qualified an applicant or were so desperate for a rabbi that they suppressed their doubts about the one available.[38]

To goad the UAHC into launching a widespread examination of its policies in the hope of effecting these goals, Browne reprinted the plea that he had made at its 1874 conference in which he proposed resolutions to improve conditions for qualified rabbis and weed out the unqualified. Although regulations were eventually adopted, his proposals were rejected at the time, perhaps because the fledgling Union was not yet prepared to deal with such controversial matters. American Jews, remembering the tight control over their lives imposed by the Orthodoxy of Europe, still resisted any ruling that hinted at the possibility of its return.[39]

Browne took leaves of absence from the paper on several occasions for personal reasons, the first having been during his first winter in Atlanta when he suffered the near fatal attack of typhoid fever. He was ill again that spring. Another time he excused himself to work on "an important literary commitment." After Sophie's post-partum depression in 1878, his newspaper reported that he had taken leave due to "the sanitary condition" of his family, undoubtedly referring to emotional illness rather than domestic hygiene. Canceling his trip to Stockholm, however, did not mean that the preparation of his lecture for it had been in vain. The increasingly militant temperance movement urging government-mandated prohibition made his subject "Jews, Temperance and Crime, or How the Chosen People Keep Sober and Out of Mischief" a popular one for public lectures in America. More importantly, by offering a proven alternative—personal temperance as opposed to government-mandated prohibition—the subject served as an acceptable response on behalf of Jews and others who deplored such legislation but feared popular reaction if they openly opposed it. To research the subject, Browne asked his readers (assuring them anonymity, of course) to relate their own experiences with "crime, drunkenness, divorces and pauperism among Israelites." Regrettably, he did not publish the results.[40]

Although Browne appeared to be doing well with his newspaper and his congregation, seeds of trouble sprouted in both areas. His relationship with Wise showed cracks as soon as the Jewish South began regular publication. A gross indiscretion by Browne many months later probably deepened the fault but did not cause it as some historians believed.

In July 1878, when Wise's daughter Helen eloped with James Malony, a non-Jewish friend of her brother Leo, Browne made the tactless faux pas of publishing the announcement in his newspaper. Because of Wise's prominence and well known opposition to intermarriage, "Helen's folly," as it was called, caused him deep embarrassment and fuelled gossip that newspapers quickly spread throughout the country. Browne copied the bare facts from the Cincinnati Enquirer, and added: [41]

> *We deplore the hasty step taken by Mr. James Malony and Miss Helen Wise. Mr. Malony is our "class-mate," we were his successor as President of the Philomanian Literary Society connected with the "Ohio Farmer's College," at College Hill, and we count him amongst our bosom friends. For twelve long years our friendship has been unbroken, and, if anything, every year added strength to our attachment. Miss Helen Wise, we have seen grow up from childhood, we have always treated and loved her like a sister, and it is very painful to us to hear that two such dear friends of ours could be guilty of such a hasty step. Mr. Malony is one of the noblest young men in Ohio. Miss Helen is one of the brightest intellects, and it is especially painful to us to be compelled to deplore the sad event of their union, consummated against the voice of religious parents, against the voice of reason and their own future. Dr. Wise knows we share his grief.*

This incident highlights the great dilemma confronting acculturated Jews of that era who moved comfortably in gentile society. Leo Wise had not only introduced Malony to his sister, but helped conceal their developing romance from his parents. Helen confided her feelings to Browne when she visited him and Sophie in Peoria three years earlier, even showing him Maloney's letters. Knowing Wise's outspoken objection to intermarriage, Browne promptly informed him, suggesting that he send Helen on an extended visit somewhere to discourage the relationship. Wise agreed, but failed to act. Eventually he reconciled with his daughter and her husband, but only after much bitterness and hurt.[42]

When Browne realized that he had blundered by publishing the announcement, he apologized to Wise, saying "it scarcely occurred to me possible for you to pass by with silence an event of such notoriety. Had you stopped me the matter would never have appeared in our columns." Continuing in the same familial tone, he asked Wise for news of Hebrew Union College so as to promote it in a forthcoming issue, and only in conclusion did he express suspicion that something other than his announcement of the wedding had caused Wise's displeasure. "Our relations of late," Browne wrote, "especially since my having started this paper, have been made so cold and distant . . . that it is a matter of delicacy with me to inquire into matters which greatly interest me in connection with you and yours."[43]

Browne should have been alerted to this possibility by a letter he received from a reader in January, 1878, less than a month after beginning his regular weekly publication of the Jewish South. From Bayou Sara, Louisiana, the writer questioned why Browne had not responded to Wise's "abuse"of him in the Israelite. "I know of no one in our neighbourhood who is personally acquainted with you," he stated before referring to the scathing criticism long aimed at Browne by Wise's opponents:

> . . . but there has been so much of foul-mouthed malignity (I must say
> for your credit nothing to touch your integrity save general scolding) in the
> New York papers, and so much high-sounding praise in the Israelite . . .
> for the last ten years that we formed an ideal Dr. Brown, a man of tall
> stature, somewhere near 60, bold and defiant. A friend of yours from
> Natchez undeceived us, in telling us you were a young man of medium

size, but he said you were actually "independent and fearless." Is there anything against reason if we expected your red-hot leader in answer to the not overly kind and generous leader in the American Israelite, as a reception to your first number? I must confess that the sense of propriety was shocked in many of our people to see such rude treatment of the man whom Dr. Wise, for the last ten years, and even last winter, praised to the sky. Why, even the ordinary journalistic civility was denied you, and the name of the editor was altogether ignored. People understood the "madness" of the American Israelite; they know that you were unjustly assailed; they have heard of your independence and hot logic; they have seen sufficient weakness in the "North and South" leader to warrant a crushing rebuke—but lo and behold you are silent. You turned the volley of dirty abuse away with a smile, inviting the Israelite's editor and correspondent to furnish a new name for your paper since you deem it your duty to please them in all particulars. I heard some say "Brown is a coward!"[44]

Browne graciously replied that Wise could not be held responsible because he had been out of town at the time. In his absence his son Leo edited the American Israelite. Then, possibly while Leo was still in charge, the Israelite carried a long sarcastic article datelined Florence, Alabama, in which the writer criticized Browne and the Jewish South for containing too much of interest to Christians and too little for Jews. On February 4, another person from Florence wrote to Browne denying responsibility for it. "The communication in the American Israelite of last week, abusing the Jewish South has not been written by any one in our place," he wrote. "It is a fabrication gotten up in the Israelite office to injure your paper. I repeat it, no one in Florence, Ala., has written the foolish article referred to. We know better than that. I dare the Israelite to refute me."[45]

Again Browne withheld retaliation.

While subsequent letters to the editor of the Jewish South criticizing the UAHC for ignoring the problems of small congregations probably annoyed Wise, the source of his anger lay not in the content of Browne's publication but in the very existence of it. The master's former acolyte and spokesman was becoming too independent, perhaps even competitive. Furthermore, Wise had made Leo his assistant, his deputy in charge during increasingly frequent absences from Cincinnati. Leo could now repay Browne for refusing to send him the abortion-inducing drug for his pregnant girlfriend three years before. Until then Browne had stood beside Leo, helping him to reconcile with his father after multiple episodes of bad behavior. Now and for the rest of his life Leo held a position that enabled him to retaliate.[46]

Given I. M. Wise's reputation as a man of "very envious and jealous disposition . . . [who] cannot endure that anyone shall stand near him" it is likely that Browne's competition displeased him. As noted by Rabbi David Philipson, one of Wise's first ordainees and a devoted disciple, the teacher was a man great in many ways, but one who "must rule . . . [who] would gladly excommunicate all whom he cannot subdue, even his own pupil."[47]

Is it possible that such an upstart journal as the Jewish South posed a threat to the long established and esteemed American Israelite? Initial subscribers to the Jewish South numbered approximately 250. Browne's later claim of a 15,000 circulation, while probably exaggerated because only an estimated 30,000 Jews were living in the South, could possibly be valid due to the fact that he had many subscribers outside the South and many who were not Jewish. Based on letters addressed to the editor from readers in 177 towns across the 13 Southern states from Virginia to Texas, it is reasonable to posit that Browne's influence through this vehicle could be seen as a potential threat to Wise's previously unchallenged dominance of Jewish opinion south and west of the Alleghenies. Even discounting Browne's claim to have stolen all of the American Israelite's Southern readers, the numbers indicated a circulation large enough and wide enough to have been perceived as serious competition. The Jewish South was Wise's only rival in a vast territory with growing Jewish communities. Cincinnati, home of the American Israelite, was a transportation hub where newspapers could be quickly distributed cross-country. So was Atlanta. Browne's location gave him advantages rivaled in the South only by the Crescent City.[48]

Notwithstanding increased circulation and what appears to have been no dearth of advertisers, after one year the Jewish South was rumored to have financial problems. Possibly caused by poor management, its lack of operating income may also have been due to Browne's initial announcement inviting people to "read it for a month or two" before subscribing; i.e., the paper may have had greater circulation than paid subscribers. In late 1878, the Seals brothers transferred their ownership to Herman Jacobs of New Orleans, who had been an original financial supporter. Representing a stock association, Jacobs moved the business office to New Orleans, home of the largest Jewish population in the South and central to the paper's area of circulation which reached into Texas and Arkansas. Although Browne continued from Atlanta as publisher, the paper underwent subtle changes. It concentrated more on Jewish news and reduced its folksy tone, both responses catering to a changing readership.[49]

In May, 1879, Rabbi Joseph Hayim Mendes Chumaceiro of New Orleans, a sometime contributor to both Wise's and Browne's papers, asked to buy a partnership in the Jewish South. Agreeing, Browne drew up a contract that designated Chumaceiro as Managing Editor, responsible for business but with no involvement in content or editorial decisions. Browne took the contract to New Orleans to be signed but had to leave before copies could be made for participants who were not present at the meeting. For them, Browne signed three blank legal forms in addition to the original, and left them with Chumaceiro for completion. When receiving his copy a few days later, he filed it automatically without looking at it.[50]

After some weeks of smooth operation, Chumaciero began to lift articles from an old English book, "The Festivals of the Lord," and publish them as editorials written by Browne. He ignored Browne's orders to stop. Jacobs reported that Chumaceiro became insolent, saying that Browne was no longer in charge. One day Jacobs entered the office unexpectedly and noticed Browne's signature on a blank sheet of paper. Chumaceiro whisked it away, but not before Jacobs realized its significance. Chumaceiro had altered the contract to give himself control.[51]

When Browne learned of this he looked at his copy, saw that his signature was missing, realized what had happened, and rushed to New Orleans to confront Chumaceiro. Chumaceiro offered to buy him out for $6,400, four hundred of which would be in the form of a note. Browne considered the note worthless and the total less than a third of what he thought the Jewish South was worth, but he had no choice. He had to accept.[52]

Still determined to publish, Browne asked another rabbinic colleague, Jacob Voorsanger of Houston, to join him as co-editor of a new paper to be called the Jewish American. Voorsanger, who immigrated from Amsterdam in 1872, had worked as a reporter for Wise's German language paper, Die Deborah, as Chumaceiro had done, and like him had served several congregations in the East to which Wise probably recommended him. Browne, based on his confidence in Voorsanger, bought another printing office "at great expense," reasoning that he dared the risk because of his confidence in his new partner and the partner's proximity to New Orleans.

Supported by friends in Cincinnati and New York, including an elderly Georgia Civil War hero, Major Raphael J. Moses, Browne again began publication in Atlanta. The new enterprise lasted less than a year due to yet another misfortune.[53]

Voorsanger promptly proved that he was no friend. In the last extant issue of the Jewish South, August 5, 1881, he and Chumaceiro announced that henceforth they would be its editors, and Voorsanger continued to published it in Houston until 1883. According to Browne, the co-conspirators soon "gave each other the lie and called one another the vilest names in the Israelite, and finally Wise bought the Jewish South and killed it."

Browne believed that this had been Wise's plan all along. He suspected that Wise had engineered Chumaceiro's appointment to the New Orleans pulpit for that purpose, positioning him to become involved with the Jewish South in order to further its demise. Paranoid though the theory appears, it evolved from Browne's long, close observation of his opponent. Wise's greatest admirers acknowledged him to be a clever and unrelenting manipulator.[54]

The False Rumor

Meanwhile, Browne suffered another disaster, apparently unrelated to the newspaper. As later implied, some members of the congregation may have had personal reasons to seek his departure. Possibly, although there is no evidence to substantiate it, he may have alienated some members in 1880 when he addressed the first graduating class of Clark College (now Clark Atlanta University), a school for African American women founded by the Freedman's Aid Society of the Methodist Episcopal Church. Whatever the cause, the ensuing finale of Browne's rabbinate in Atlanta constituted a devastating experience for him and for Sophie.[55]

A major element in the saga of Browne's sorrows was the fact that, early in 1880, he injured his foot, which kept him on crutches for most of the year and curtailed his activities to some degree. Despite the disability he proceeded with a scheduled summer visit to his family in Hungary, spending his days aboard the S.S. Silesia stretched out on a settee in the liner's club room. A group of fellow passengers kept him company and, for entertainment, composed a souvenir journal of the voyage that they planned to have published when the ship docked in Hamburg. Subscribers paid five cents per copy. Upon learning that English type was not available in that city, the writers asked Browne, who would be the first to return home, to publish it from his own printing office of the Jewish South, giving him the $29.85 that they had collected from subscribers to cover his cost. By the time he reached Atlanta, he was in so much pain from his injured foot that he could not immediately attend to the printing. After a brief delay, he sent it to someone else to print for a cost of sixty-one dollars, paying the difference out of his own pocket.[56]

In January 1881, he was still in too much pain to attend the annual meeting of the congregation at which time it was customary to vote upon renewing the rabbi's contract. When the contract came up for discussion, Jacob Elsas, the Temple's wealthiest member and an erstwhile friend of the Brownes from Cincinnati, stated that he objected to having a minister who embezzled money---seventy-five dollars said to have been collected for the souvenir journal. Max Franklin, another prominent member, said he knew of it also. According to a report, "No one would believe it, but Mr. Elsas said . . . two of the most honourable and responsible men in the city told him so, and were ready to prove it."

Elsas, Franklin, Jacob Fleischel, William Teitlebaum and Aaron Haas were appointed "to look into the strange charges" and the meeting was adjourned, postponing for two weeks the decision on re-electing the rabbi. Browne, upon hearing the news, immediately displayed the journal and the receipted bill for its printing.

Elsas and Franklin apologized, but Browne refused to accept their apologies until they revealed the names of the two "honorable men" who originated the slander. Otherwise, he said, he would have to sue in order to clear his name. They refused, possibly because they believed that he was bluffing, for they knew that he had just built two houses in Atlanta and announced that he planned to stay for life, which he could not do if he sued two such powerful leaders of the community.[57]

Browne was not bluffing. Against the advice of his attorney, he filed suit and resigned his position at the Temple. "Great excitement followed," a witness recalled, "and the telegraph carried the news that Rabbi Browne had been discharged for embezzlement . . . "[58]

Browne's attorney warned him that the expense would be prohibitive because the litigation was likely to drag on for years. Browne persisted nevertheless, seeking $20,000 in damages and announcing that he would give to charity whatever financial gain he received from the case. In order to clear his name quickly so as to get another position, he also brought his charges to B'nai B'rith, one function of which then was to arbitrate disputes between its members, thus avoiding embarrassment by keeping such matters out of the courts and unseen by the general public. Decisions were announced to the Jewish communities through B'nai B'rith's network of lodges.

The local lodge of B'nai B'rith supported Elsas, possibly in order to force Browne to drop his public litigation. When Browne refused to retreat, the lodge acquitted Elsas and Franklin and charged Browne with leaving the room without permission and swearing at the members, even threatening to expel him unless he dropped his suit. Browne appealed his case up the ladder, from one B'nai B'rith jurisdiction to another. This resulted in what he described as frivolous demurrers to gain time and force him to yield. He did not. When offered a compromise, he refused, and upon discovering that his lawyer, a prominent Civil War general, had been bribed to make a settlement, fired him and hired another. Finally, the highest B'nai B'rith court upheld his charge so the case could be tried. Browne won, which required the lodge to reinstate him. Elsas apologized in writing and paid all court expenses. Browne accepted reluctantly, according to Isaac Frisch, his nephew, only to please Sophie.[59]

The litigation lasted for five years, and only after two more years did Browne learn the identity of the two "honorable" men who initiated the slander against him. One was the new president of the congregation, Samuel Weil (no relation to Sophie) a judge who was Elsas's attorney and reportedly advised him not to fear Browne's suit because he would throw it out of court. Frisch, who lived with the Brownes in Atlanta during much of this period, believed that Weil, an embittered man who married an elderly Irish Catholic woman, hated the rabbi for preaching against intermarriage.[60]

The other reported initiator of the slander was a Hungarian physician, Dr. Henry Bak, whom Browne had helped settle in Atlanta, and according to the testimony, even "bought his wife a silk dress to introduce her in society . . . "[61]

It was also expected of a Jew to use the services of a Jewish physician, and so Browne did. After many months of unsuccessful treatment on his foot by the newly arrived Dr. Bak, Atlanta's only Jewish doctor at the time, Browne turned to the city's leading surgeon, Dr. Willis Westmorland. Possibly this offended Bak.

Lifelong enmities are incurred by such incidents even today, and were quite typical of nineteenth century relationships between local bigwigs and their rabbis. While overdeveloped pride and shortness of temper probably triggered Browne's problems with congregants, such experiences were not unique to him. A notable example was that of Wise himself, who left his congregation in Albany, New York, after engaging in a fist fight with his president on the bima of their synagogue.[62]

Whatever the cause of the doctor's pique, the prominent Atlanta physician Dr. Westmorland also failed to heal Browne's foot. By the time of the congregational meeting at which the trouble began, Browne had made arrangements to consult Dr. Lewis Sayre, a noted New York specialist, and had accepted an invitation to stop off in Washington enroute, to lecture on the Talmud at Mount Vernon Place Methodist Episcopal Church. There, despite his disability and questionable employment, he gave a performance acclaimed by the Washington Star as "more humorous than Mark Twain." The National Republican judged it "a most interesting and eloquent exposition of the philosophical and literary gems of the Talmud, revealing beauties which gentile eyes have seldom gazed upon." President Chester Arthur had written personally to Dr. W. P. Harrison, pastor of the church and chaplain to the House of Representatives, regretting his inability to attend.[63]

Before leaving for New York, Browne had been asked by Howard Williams, publisher of the Sunday Gazette, a local weekly, for information about the trouble between himself and the congregation. Browne replied that there was no trouble, but promised to give Williams the full story in time for his next issue. Unwilling to wait, Williams sent a reporter, whom Browne turned away with the following message for his publisher:

> *I deem it judicious again to warn you against the publication of*
> *statements on the alleged dismissal of mine unless you can upon inquiry*
> *give the names of your informers to the public. From the points your*
> *reporter gave me I judge that you have not seen men of both sides, such*

as Messrs. Aaron and Jacob Haas, A. Rosenfeld, Joseph Hirsch, Levy

Cohen, Emanuel and Isaac Steinheimer, Menko Bros., and I think it

proper for you to get the statements of those men also if you are resolved

to publish the statements of those sent me by [the reporter]. [64]

All of the men named had been founders of the congregation and continued to be deeply involved in its proceedings.[65]

Ignoring Browne's response, Williams immediately devoted ten column inches to the rumour under the caption, "BROTHER BROWNE RECEIVES HIS DISMISSAL FROM THE CONGREGATION, The Capers That Led To It, etc." After adding the equally scurrilous statement that the rabbi had faked his infirmity in order to collect insurance, Williams ended with a one-inch contradictory paragraph headed "This We Do Not Believe," in which he noted that Browne had been suffering for months "and is now scarcely able to walk without the aid of his crutches." Apparently Williams valued circulation above consistency.[66]

Major newspapers from New York to New Orleans copied the story or adapted it without checking facts, and largely ignoring Williams' final ameliorating paragraph. Wise's American Israelite copied the story from the Cincinnati Enquirer on January 28, and refused Browne's request for a correction. As the libel continued to appear in newspapers, Browne engaged Isaiah Williams, a popular New York attorney, to file suit against those who refused to retract it. He specified the New York Times, the Evening Post, and the Express, papers in which he had seen the story, and told Williams to add any other paper in which the attorney could locate it.[67]

He also advised Williams to associate with "one of the most prominent lawyers" naming an example of someone whom he did not consider "that kind of an attorney" and whose name he did not want to appear even on a complaint to the Messenger, published by B'nai B'rith. He then identified several attorneys whom he favored, informing Williams:

> *From the financial point of view they can make the cases pay. The Times is a big concern and there is not a shadow of truth in the libel . . . Let the Times be sued for a million dollars . . . Certainly $500,000 at least should be the damages against the Times if we claim $100,000 from the Messenger." Now then, go to work at once . . . Write out your complaints and send them down here so I can swear and subscribe . . . and I will send you letters to parties who will sign all my bonds by return mail provided you get a great attorney or two associated, and send me the contract as to your contingent damages, which I am sure will be enormous considering the cases and my character.* [68]

In a postscript, Browne reminded Williams to place his ad in the March 27th New York Herald. On that day, the Temple's Board of Trustees, at Elsas' request, passed a resolution declaring that newspaper reports attributing Browne's dismissal to charges affecting his character were contrary to fact, and that the rabbi had withdrawn his candidacy voluntarily. The Board sent copies to him and to the Atlanta Constitution. Browne returned his copy with the statement:

> *. . . had you rebuked the slander three months ago, you would have done justice to yourselves, to Judaism and to my family, saving this community at the time a good deal of disgrace; but now, after a delay of THREE LONG MONTHS, so far from disarming suspicion, your action only gives public opinion the assurance that the actions against me must have been true, or else you should not have required three long months of*

deliberation to refute them. In truth, your resolutions, at this late hour,
have the appearance, and are actually looked upon by the public, as a
WHITEWASH of the thinnest kind..[69]

Continuing with a sixteen point outline of his case, Browne observed that his opponents, their relatives and business partners were trustees of the Temple, and their attorney, Samuel Weil, was its president, which effectively stacked the cards against him in any appeal he might make to the congregation. He noted that he had been "charitable" to the two newspapers that consented to retract the libel, repeated his vow to give any money that he received from the case to charity, and announced his intention to bring the matter before the council of the UAHC at its next meeting.[70]

The American Israelite published his letter with a disclaimer stating that it had "neither libeled Mr. Browne nor offered a retraction," but had merely copied the article from the Cincinnati Enquirer. If the rabbi felt himself aggrieved, the note added, the editor would give him an opportunity to explain.[71]

Browne then asked help from Herman M. Moos, a Cincinnati friend who had once been a part owner and editor of the Israelite. Moos obtained Leo Wise's written agreement to make a correction. It never appeared. When yet another false allegation appeared in the American Israelite, Browne wanted to sue, but Moos dissuaded him by insisting that "Dr. Wise says it is Leo's doing and he cannot help it." This was not the only occasion on which Wise used that excuse to avoid being sued for libels published under Leo's supervision.[72]

Reflecting sensitivity to public relations, Temple records and releases to the press do not mention Browne's resignation, but state only that the committee for annual reelection of the rabbi decided by a four to three vote not to reelect him. The reasons given were that the congregation had not made progress under his leadership and that he did not teach the children. Without disclosing the identity of the committee members, it noted that a minority report declared that these conditions were not entirely the fault of the rabbi.[73]

The affair took a terrible toll on Browne and his family. Sophie suffered a nervous breakdown, and he, for the first time in his career, found himself with no offers of a pulpit. He responded to ads from congregations in Vicksburg, Mississippi, and Portland, Oregon, but received no response. So desperate was his situation that he accepted an offer from the Atlanta & Piedmont Railroad to edit its bulletin. Even that assignment was cancelled when its owners learned of the scandal.[74]

High ranking friends tried to assist. Georgia's Senator and former Governor Joseph E. Brown, and Congressman Alexander Stephens, as well as Senator John A. Logan of Illinois asked President James A. Garfield to grant the rabbi a diplomatic post. Garfield agreed and indicated that he would recommend Browne for the consulship in Jerusalem if it became available, otherwise Port Said or Alexandria, and would send his name to the Senate as soon as a current filibuster ended. The filibuster continued longer than expected, during which time someone showed the president newspaper reports about the scandal, causing him to withhold the recommendation. Browne, still hopeful, obtained an appointment to visit Garfield in the White House to appeal in person. The appointment never took place. It was scheduled for July 2, the day that Garfield was assassinated.[75]

Finally it appeared that Browne's luck had changed. The trustees of Baltimore's Floyd Street Temple invited him to become their rabbi. Assuring him that the requirement of ratification by full membership was a mere formality, they urged him to prepare immediately for the move. He did so, alerting Sophie and placing their two Atlanta houses on the market, selling them at a substantial loss. When news of the scandal reached Baltimore the trustees rescinded their invitation.[76]

Now Browne's situation was so precipitous that he grasped at any possibility of work and finally consented to a long standing proposal from Reverend L. W. Scott, a Protestant minister who was president of a Texas college, to debate him on Judaism versus Christianity. Scott had invited him repeatedly over the past three years, and Browne had published some of their correspondence in the Jewish South to elicit comments. At first readers favored the debates and he made tentative arrangements to go, but when a learned Jewish friend in Sherman, Texas, who knew the reverend personally, presented irrefutable arguments against it, Browne had changed his mind and declined. Now the need to support his family overrode other considerations and out of necessity alone he accepted Scott's offer.[77]

As Browne recalled, publicity had already gone out, the debates were "eagerly looked for by the Jews and Gentiles in Texas particularly," and all was in order, "even the opera house engaged in Texarkana," when suddenly Rev. Scott cancelled the tour. People had learned of the scandal, Scott explained, "and the rabbi's reputation had become so bad that it is no honour for him to debate with me."[78]

The ultimate blow came when Browne's publishers, after copious advertising and the receipt of some four hundred subscriptions, stopped production on his two volumes of Talmud translation and commentary. Georgia statesmen Alexander H. Stephens and Joseph E. Brown, Senator John A. Logan of Illinois, and the late President James A. Garfield had been among the subscribers.[79]

Finally, Browne received a call from what he described as "a broken-down little obscure congregation without even a house of worship of their own," in New York City. Sadly but with relief, he and Sophie left Atlanta. They retained close contacts there, and enduring friendships throughout the state. He had given the Temple the longest and most prestigious leadership that it would have until 1895 with the arrival of David Marx, its first rabbi born and educated in America. Browne, although foreign born, brought scholarship and culture to the position, as well as a level of Americanization to which most Temple members aspired and admired above all else. He founded the South's first Jewish newspaper, through which he publicized Atlanta Jewry to beneficial effect over a widespread area, not only to other Jews but to non-Jews in the highest echelons of government and religious society. He delivered in abundance the ambassadorial gifts that his congregants so highly prized.[80]

What went wrong? His frequent absences from the city, absences from duty due to illness, and pursuit of other interests undoubtedly diverted his attention from congregational matters. Whereas rabbis and other public figures could offset many personal grievances through social contact at dinners and card games, Browne did not play cards and avoided parties, not only denying his opportunities to dispel criticism, but leaving a vacuum in which it could grow. His potential as ethnic broker, obvious in the beginning, could not be realized in so short a tenure. Despite his close family ties, civic recognition and initial honeymoon offered by the trustees, he nonetheless veered off course at some point. Arguably he brought downfall on himself through his characteristic demons of impatience, indiscretion, hubris, disregard for detail, and excessively rigid pride. More than any other single factor, his fall from favor with Wise radically changed the course of his future, leaving him in a virtual no-man's-land of the American rabbinate. Wise's enemies continued to view Browne as an enemy, while Wise's friends would henceforth march in lockstep with their leader and turn their backs on

Browne. In 1881, at thirty-five years of age, his rabbinic career had peaked; he stood alone.

Browne was not the only maverick rabbi of his day. There were others who possessed similarly erratic characteristics and experienced equally brief tenures in multiple pulpits. Congregations themselves were in a state of flux, still trying to define their objectives as proponents of Judaism in America. The Temple exemplified this by its choice of the next three rabbis after Browne. For the first two, Jacob S. Jacobson and Leo Reich, they asked recommendation from the traditionalist leader Dr. Marcus Jastrow, Wise's most bitter opponent. Rabbi Reich, veering further from Reform, convinced the congregation to change its prayer book from Wise's Minhag America to the more traditional Minhag Jastrow.[81]

In 1895, under the caption "His Election Postponed. Rabbi Reich was Not Included Among the Church Officers Named Sunday," the Atlanta Constitution announced Reich's departure. "A change of rules was adopted by the Hebrew congregation at the synagogue last Sunday," it added, "and the congregation now belongs to the ranks of reformed [sic] Judaism."

Indeed it did. Reich had been notified by the Board that it intended to recommend reducing holiday observance to one day, permitting men to uncover their heads in synagogue if they wished to do so, using the new Union Prayer Book published by the UAHC, and forbidding the rabbi to continue wearing a robe, hat and prayer shawl when officiating at services. If these measures were unacceptable to Reich, he was invited to leave. The measures passed, and David Marx, recently ordained by Wise, replaced Reich, thus ending the congregation's sectarian seesaw. The radicals prevailed by a vote of seventy-one to three, and for the Temple, the age of indecision was over. [82]

VI - NEW YORK
Pulpit, Press and Politics

This was a decade of significant change in American Judaism, with Reform defining itself in its Pittsburgh Platform of 1885 and the Conservative movement establishing its Jewish Theological Seminary in 1887. Browne, banished to the sidelines of organized Judaism, had no part in either of these historic events but played a significant role in several others for which he was highly publicized, reviled by some, and long remembered.

Again misfortune turned to opportunity for the resilient rabbi. Despite being shunned by New York's Reform leadership and reduced in status because of his small, unprestigious congregation, Browne found the city congenial and ideally suited for fully engaging his diverse talents. He championed causes of the underprivileged, using his legal training to oppose injustice wherever he detected it, and again established a newspaper which brought him into public circles and ultimately into politics. Having strengthened his relationship with Ulysses S. Grant, he served as a pall bearer for the former president, and because the funeral occurred on a Saturday used the occasion to demonstrate against current attempts to change the Jewish Sabbath to Sunday. This delighted orthodox Jews but further alienated New York's Jewish leaders, whom Browne continued to confront—usually with Phyrric success—on issues affecting Jews and immigrants.

The 1880s was also a decade of significant change in America as a whole, and nowhere did this impact the people more than in New York City. Even before the great immigration the metropolis housed 80,000 Jews, one third of America's Jewish population. When the Brownes arrived in 1881, mass immigration and the labor disputes that ultimately helped transform the Gilded Age into the Progressive Age had already begun to disturb beneficiaries of the status quo. Successful German Jews, following patterns they had known in Europe, accepted responsibility for their impoverished brethren and retained a nervous look-out for anti-Semitic reaction on the part of Christians. Temple Emanu-El, wealthiest of American synagogues, viewed itself as arbiter of public relations and dispenser of welfare for all of the city's Jews. Its rabbi, Gustav Gottheil, with his most affluent supporters— primarily Jesse Seligman and Jacob H. Schiff—acted as public spokesmen on all matters involving Jews and Judaism.[1]

European customs were not readily forgotten, and congregations were by no means uniform in their beliefs or practices. Even among the reformers controversy existed regarding ritual, synagogue funding, assignment of pews (a matter of prestige) and control. Lingering memories of authoritarian state-appointed rabbis in Europe sometimes affected congregants' treatment of their newly independent rabbis in America. Here the president, not the rabbi, was sovereign.[2]

Pulpit

Browne's Congregation Gates of Hope was not one of the city's four or five leading synagogues. When he arrived the ten year old congregation consisted of seventy upwardly mobile German-speaking immigrants, largely from Austro-Hungary. Successful enough to have moved uptown to Yorkville, they still worshipped in rented quarters, unable to afford a sanctuary of their own. Anticipating the day when an increased membership would permit them to buy a synagogue, they expected Browne's reputation as an orator to make that happen. He did not disappoint them. Within a year Gates of Hope doubled its membership and in March, 1883, moved into its own sanctuary in a renovated church on 86th Street between Park Avenue and Lexington.[3]

The Brownes settled into a brownstone walking distance away, at 152

East 93rd Street. Sophie found the city especially congenial, one reason being that she again had close relatives nearby. Her mother's sister and brother-in-law, Clara and Emil Brentano, had recently come to New York in the wake of their sons' huge success as proprietors of Brentano's bookstore. Sophie's brother, Jesse Weil, an importer of fine fabrics, frequently visited enroute to or from business in Europe, bringing her style sketches and materials that enabled her to dress elegantly on a rabbi's budget. With Lylah entered in public school and a reliable nanny for young Jesse, Sophie dedicated much of her time to assisting her husband wherever possible. Initially, she helped establish a Ladies Benevolent Society for the synagogue and served as its treasurer.[4]

In New York as elsewhere in America, the dedication of a synagogue attracted public interest. The New York Sunday Herald published Browne's entire ceremonial sermon, "The Evolution of Religion," which the congregation recorded in a commemorative booklet. The message, as usual on such occasions, expressed deep devotion to America and to universalism, sentiments resonating strongly with most newcomers, especially with Jews because of their historical suffering from discrimination elsewhere. As in his early attempts at poetry, Browne drew imagery from nature, science, world literature, and history. Examples of his sharp wit and variations of cadence are noticeable even on the printed page. According to reports, listeners responded with frequent "peals of laughter and plaudits."[5]

Browne also pleased his congregation by preaching in German on Saturday morning for the older members, who knew little English, and in English on Friday nights for the younger set, most of whom had grown up in America, understood English and sought to improve their fluency. Those services attracted gentiles as well, since public lectures provided a popular form of entertainment and there was no admission charge to attend a synagogue. As a result, seven hundred worshippers overflowed into the Gates of Hope vestry rooms, rendering its new sanctuary short of space only four weeks after opening.[6]

As the controversy over prayer books epitomized by Wise and Einhorn continued, that argument soon surfaced within Gates of Hope. Some members objected to the liturgy currently used, arranged by the late Rabbi Leo Merzbacher of Temple Emanu-El. Their reason was that it contained a hymn by Felix Adler, founder of the Ethical Culture movement, which most Jews considered a denial of Judaism, a sin second only to conversion. Some even called its founder "the infidel ex-Jew Adler." Browne advocated a standard ritual for all congregations and had urged the UAHC to produce one almost a decade earlier. He was ruled out of order, possibly because Wise wanted to encourage continued sales of his Minhag America. Nevertheless, Browne conceded to his congregants' request for a new book and composed Prayers of Israel, arranged for The American Reform Services in The Temple Gates of Hope.

Almost entirely in Hebrew, the 160 page abbreviated Hebrew liturgy for Shabbat, Festivals and Holy Days, with the Haftorah of Jonah for Yom Kippur, included only a few memorial prayers in German—some in rhyme—and one important instruction in English which read: "The Congregation, without exception, *must* rise and resume seats when the Rabbi and *presiding* Officers do so." Emphasized by those original italics, it reflected the importance that Reform Jews placed on decorum. Not surprisingly the two members who initiated use of the Mersbacher prayer book, Henry Rosenblatt and Max Zenn, resented Browne's introduction of the new one and nursed their resentment into ongoing opposition.[7]

Browne did well in his early years at Congregation Gates of Hope and solidified his support, though not without incurring some animosity.

Simultaneously, his activism outside the synagogue attracted attention, gaining him both friends and enemies. He eagerly embraced the challenges without questioning their possible consequences.

Immigration was then New York's foremost problem. Europeans, many of them Jews, were entering the United States in numbers unprecedented, unforeseen and unmanageable. Some 14,000 Jews arrived in the two years between 1881 and 1883 alone. Overcrowding at the inadequate Castle Garden reception station virtually invited exploitation. Criminals, including pimps who highjacked women into white slavery, could not be controlled by the government and relief agencies. In an effort to protect the newcomers, Browne went daily to Castle Garden to meet them and try to help. As often as possible Sophie went with him, watching especially for Jewish women travelling alone. She frequently brought them home, providing temporary work and shelter while helping settle them safely in a more permanent situation. Daughter Lylah later recalled that she never knew whom she would encounter in her kitchen when she returned from school each day.[8]

Browne quickly concluded that agents of *tzedakah*—Jewish welfare—were mishandling the immigrants. Like the government itself, Jewish philanthropists did their best to help but could not provide the skills and oversight necessary to care properly for such a massive influx of penniless strangers, most of whom spoke no English and were ignorant of their new environment. Also inadequate was the long established system of immigrant relief provided by the Board of Delegates of American Israelites, recently merged with the Union of American Hebrew Congregations and now joined by the Hebrew Sheltering Society. The small but effective Hebrew Emigrant Aid Society (HEAS, 1882-1884), a makeshift organization of twenty-four Polish congregations, helped somewhat, but was also powerless to do a thorough job.[9]

Neither HEAS nor the later, successful Hebrew Immigrant Aid Society (HIAS) was in operation when Browne arrived. HEAS soon began, but lacked sufficient funds to care for the immigrants, and begged its European affiliate, the Alliance Israelite Universelle, to stop sending them. At the same time Moritz Ellinger, an official of both HEAS and B'nai B'rith who headed the firm "Ellinger, Karsheadt, Birnbaum & Co., Importers and Jobbers in Russian Jews," travelled abroad to recruit immigrants. Publicly, HEAS urged American Jews to give liberally, "not to carry out any grand plan of colonization . . . but to save [the immigrants] from actual starvation and ourselves from reproach."

Most American Jews agreed with the self-protective philosophy of HEAS, Wise even declaring that European Jewry should take care of itself instead of flooding America with paupers. Ellinger wrote, "America is not a poorhouse (or) an asylum for the paupers of Europe. (European Jewry) may ask us what they are to do with the sick, aged and infirm. (My) reply would be 'That is your business; we take care of our own sick, aged and infirm, and ask assistance of no one."[10]

It became apparent to Browne that those were the prevailing sentiments among the men responsible for settling immigrants. As he explained to the Alliance in 1881, American Jews habitually contributed to sporadic overseas emergencies such as the 1876 relief for Algerian Jews, but as patriotic Americans they were unwilling to commit themselves to a continuing need for sending money outside the United States. He and a few rabbis from other areas across the country tried to help by establishing regional branches of Alliance, for which he offered to represent the organization on a speaking tour. Nothing came of it. Later, Rabbi Henry Illowizi formed a short-lived branch of Alliance in Louisiana in an attempt to settle Jews there.[11]

In Browne's opinion, the immigrants had been "so shamefully

managed" by the Hebrew Aid organization "that humanity appealed . . . for interference." Outraged by the news that girls were sold "for immoral purposes," he turned to the philanthropists themselves "whose great names were the only guarantee to European Committees in London, Amsterdam, Berlin, Paris, Vienna, etc., for the judicious distribution of the contributed money and the fraternal treatment of the strangers." Because the European Jewish press was blaming these charitable men for mistreating their fellow Jews, Browne assumed that they would appreciate being exonerated by having the true culprits identified.[12]

To the contrary, the moguls were embarrassed by the news that many of the friends and relatives they employed to distribute their largesse had in fact misused it. Although Browne had emphasized that the contributors themselves were "noble and generous," and had thought that he "slighted nobody except Ellinger & Co," he did indeed offend the de facto leaders of New York Jewry. They told him, in effect, to mind his own business, and that the press "would not heed" whatever information he provided. In his words, "the Jewish papers belonged to the Committee . . . the dailies were 'instructed' . . . [and] even modest, noble Mr. Jacob H. Schiff . . . did not want to be convinced that the twenty thousand dollars he gave for the Ward's Island Shelter was perverted for the most inhuman and immoral purposes."

Browne's friends told him that so many persons with questionable records were connected with HEAS and the men who funded it, that no one would admit having hired them. They believed that Moritz Ellinger, the HEAS officer and recruiter of immigrants, had then set a trap for him.[13]

Press

Browne responded by starting his own newspaper, the Jewish Herald. Within a week he published the story, announcing it on street corners in

New York and on the desks of Jewish journalists throughout Europe. As a consequence, he noted, "The moneys from the European Committees were stopped, the Emigrant Aid Association died and was buried without a friend to 'omit flowers.'"[14]

In his next two issues Browne reported that some $60,000 raised for the refugees had disappeared, and identified the alleged thieves. At the Schiff Shelter on Ward's Island where immigrants were housed pending settlement, he found evidence indicating extortion, robbery, even prostitution in the case of a young girl sent to a brothel in Pittsburgh. He then went to Washington, met with President Chester A. Arthur and Secretary of the Treasury Charles J. Folger, convinced them to provide a government transport for refugees desiring to return to Europe, and was appointed by the president to escort them.[15]

Two days later, a melee erupted at the Ward's Island Shelter, turning public opinion against the immigrants and causing Washington to cancel the transport. The incident became known as "the tzimmes riot" because it was precipitated by a serving of that traditional Jewish festive dish at a Sabbath dinner. As reported, upon requesting an "extra allowance of some stewed prunes and apples" and being refused, a frustrated newcomer seized the ladle and struck the uncooperative orderly on the head with it. Henry Blank, a HEAS employee who as superintendent had previously been known to antagonize his charges, called the police and joined them, wielding a club to enforce his authority. Browne, who had already gone to press with his Jewish Herald announcing President Arthur's offer, published an extra to report the riot and cancellation of transport.[16]

The New York Tribune characterized the tzimmes story sympathetically "for the poor Hebrews who have been kept in idleness," some 700 of them, in "rude sheds at the best," being fed "with rigid economy" from "large dishes," (possibly pails). It noted that HEAS employees had previously been accused of "dealing with the men and women under their care in the most offensive ways," as well as brandishing clubs and pistols "when there was no disorder or cause for intimidation." The Tribune also mentioned that Blank and his assistant had named Browne as one of the "meddlers" from the city who stirred up discontent. The paper did credit HEAS with trying to find jobs for the newcomers, but noted its lack of success in doing so.[17]

Copies of Browne's Jewish Herald, are extant only from February 1883 through August 1884, but the import of earlier issues is preserved in a memoir that Browne wrote only a few years later. The Jewish Herald was an English language weekly with a section in German, sold on the streets and available for "cash only." Like the Jewish South in Atlanta, it covered a wide range of subjects, but differed by adapting to its New York readership with less personal, social news and more emphasis on Jewish communal issues and political opinion as seen in other New York-based Anglo-Jewish papers such as Einhorn and Adler's Jewish Messenger and B'nai B'rith's Menorah.[18]

By expressing his political views in print as well as from the pulpit, Browne drew the attention of non-Jewish editors and politicians, some of whom became staunch friends. His support of Senator Charles J. Folger in the Republican's 1882 bid for the White House probably gained him his instant access to President Arthur, although the president knew of the rabbi from his acclaimed lecture in Washington the year before. On the downside, Browne's support of Folger may have riled some Jews by suggesting that he opposed Folger's then adversary, the popular Henry Ward Beecher, eminent Congregationalist preacher and editor, greatly admired by Jews for his stand against racial prejudice. Beecher left the Republican party in 1882, citing dishonesty in the nominating process and urging Folger therefore to decline the nomination.

Browne did not shrink from expressing his opinion, even criticizing influential friends, Jews and Christians alike, if he believed that circumstances warranted it. When the Sun's publisher Charles A. Dana, his friend who, like Beecher, evidenced friendship for Jews, published a series of anti-Semitic articles on travels through the south by reporter Frank Wilkeson, Browne denounced the stories as libelous, though softening his criticism by referring to the "unDanalike spirit" of Wilkeson. Dana stopped Wilkeson's slander, published a mild apology along with letters from offended readers, and remained friendly with the rabbi.[19]

Although Browne continued jousting with Wise as customary in the Jewish press, he also applauded his former mentor on opinions they shared, such as Wise's advice to newly ordained rabbis that they should marry before assuming a pulpit. Less congenial on personal matters, when Wise scheduled a lecture in New York during the litigation for libel that Browne initiated against him, Browne publicly warned him against coming to the city. Wise ignored the threat and came, whereupon Browne reported gleefully that his lecture "did not draw crowds as expected."[20]

At times Browne criticized Wise indirectly by quoting such colleagues as the revered Bernhard Felsenthal of Chicago, who declared that some of Wise's "decided notions . . . " were "very crooked and perverted ones." Browne also quoted the Jewish Record's censure of Wise for having said that not all of the dietary laws had been mandated by Moses as well as its opinion that Moses "has been stripped by Dr. Wise of much of his authority." When the Jewish Messenger criticized Wise for heading too many organizations, suggesting that "the next president of HUC should spare us further humiliation," Browne agreed, noting, "distemper of the pen is a fatal disease for presidents of religious institutions."[21]

When the infamous dinner known as the trefa banquet (non-kosher, serving shellfish, forbidden by Jewish dietary laws) caused representatives of traditional congregations to leave the Union, Browne asked sarcastically "What had the 'Council' in Cincinnati done besides insulting Orthodox Judaism?" The occasion, celebrating the tenth anniversary of the UAHC and first ordination of rabbis at the Hebrew Union College, included guests from a wide range of Jewish observance. It so incensed representatives of tradition-leaning congregations that they initiated establishment of the Conservative Movement with the Jewish Theological Seminary as an alternative to HUC. Debate continues over whether the dietary gaffe was intentional and if so, who approved the menu. Wise first denied personal responsibility, then stonewalled to justify it. In either case, it ended his dream of unifying American Judaism.[22]

Shortly after 1884, Browne ceased publication of the weekly Jewish Herald, and in 1886, signed on as editor-in-chief of Kasriel Hirsch Sarasohn's new paper, the Jewish Daily News. That journal, also known as the Tageblatt and published in Yiddish, concentrated on circulation among the immigrants and endured well into the next century. Here as elsewhere Browne continued to touch and to influence New York's "downtown" Jews for as long as he remained in the city, and to some extent thereafter as we shall see in subsequent chapters.

Grant and the Sunday Sabbath

The Sunday Sabbath debate loomed large at that time. Strict enforcement of Sunday closing laws, one of the means by which Christians addressed their own decreasing attendance at church services, posed great difficulty for Jews. In a time when the six day work week was not only the rule but an economic necessity, Sunday laws made it virtually impossible for the vast majority of Jews to observe Shabbat. This especially left young adults who had not lived under the strict rules imposed in Europe increasingly vulnerable to diligent efforts at conversions by Christian missionaries. Rabbis viewed the situation as a threat to the very existence of Judaism in America.[23]

The Reform movement, developed partially in response to widespread non-observance in Europe and America, sought to address the problem by tailoring its ritual to current interests and needs. It initiated family seating, shortened prayers, insisted upon decorum during the service, instituted professional choirs and organ music, substituted the vernacular for much of the Hebrew, which few people understood, and in many cases changed the Sabbath Eve ritual from brief sundown prayers to a longer, more inclusive service featuring a weekly sermon and scheduled at a later hour, after dinner. Wise had inaugurated the practice in Cincinnati as early as 1869. In 1886, with the passage of a Saturday half-holiday closing bill in New York, which Browne was widely credited for having authored, Shabbat afternoon became another option for observance. At least one congregation adopted it but without lasting success.[24]

A more popular response to the situation was the Sunday Sabbath movement, which both Browne and Wise opposed. Wise called it "a bare-faced and downright hypocrisy and lie," and declared, "You can desecrate the Sabbath, but you cannot consecrate the Sunday."[25]

Nevertheless, the idea of observing Shabbat on Sunday gained support from some congregations, the first and most successful being Chicago's Temple Sinai which initiated it in 1874. Others eventually followed, but without Sinai's success—a phenomenon widely attributed to the brilliant oratory of its rabbi, Emil G. Hirsch. Browne, like Hirsch, also filled his pews by delivering outstanding sermons, and like Wise had been among the first to confront non-attendance successfully by initiating the late Friday evening service, so he had no reason to change. When a prominent opponent declared that late Friday services had failed, Browne responded, "This will be cheerful news, no doubt, for those who think [that] 'Sunday Sabbath' is the only way to save Judaism."[26]

The Sunday Sabbath concept evoked acrimonious debate throughout America. Even a decade earlier, young members of Browne's congregation in Evansville had argued the subject as an intellectual exercise. More recently a youth group in Memphis, Tennessee, confronted it in debate with the decision affirming change, and the audience enthusiastically approved. In Rochester, New York, where a leading radical Reform rabbi opposed it, the newspaper Jewish Tidings led a forceful campaign in its favor, declaring, "To a just and merciful God, it matters little on what day His worshippers see fit to bow before Him." In another city the rabbi predicted that observing the Sabbath on Sunday would bring about "the downfall of our sacred landmarks, the melancholy knell for the burial of our divine institutions."[27]

Both critics and advocates contended that rabbis who favored Sunday services did so because it gave them an additional weekly opportunity to preach. Later studies confirmed this, and showed that Sunday services succeeded where the rabbi was a good speaker, as in the case of Chicago's Sinai. Due to the popularity of lectures as entertainment, congregations with eloquent rabbis who held services on both days drew even larger crowds on Saturday than on Sunday, whereas poor speakers remained as unsuccessful on Sunday as on any other day. New York's Temple Emanu-El eventually established Sunday services, but when Rabbi Gustav Gottheil had originally requested permission to do so, the trustees refused, influenced according to one observer, by Browne's "powerful sermons against it."[28]

Browne chanced upon a unique way to publicize his position. His acquaintance with former president Ulysses S. Grant and former secretary of state Hamilton Fish blossomed into friendship when he moved to New

York where both of them also lived. Fish later noted that the president had "personally introduced the Doctor . . . in such high terms that I could not help becoming interested in him as a scholar, and bold defender of right and justice. . . . " Browne met them on a number of occasions, often with his close friend Bishop John Newman, who was pastor to the Grants. During the president's terminal illness, Browne sometimes accompanied Newman on visits to the family.[29]

When Grant died, in August, 1885, his family invited Browne to serve in the elaborate state funeral as an honorary pall bearer representing the Jewish citizens of America. Browne recognized the invitation not only as an unprecedented honor for Jews but also a unique opportunity to demonstrate for religious observance because the ceremonies were to be held on Saturday. In his words, he "saw the Sabbath of Israel as it is now threatened by the Sunday transfer mania, and decided to set a public example in American Judaism. . . . "[30]

On the afternoon of Saturday, August 8, 1885, onlookers crowded the sidewalks from City Hall to Riverside Park. More affluent viewers paid as much as $30 to rent space in windows and on balconies to watch the procession. Sophie and nine-year-old daughter Lylah observed it from grandstand seats at the Fifth Avenue Hotel, erected to accommodate dignitaries and families of the fourteen honorary pall bearers, all but one of whom rode in carriages of state. The rabbi demonstrated his Jewishness by walking.[31]

It was no secret that Major General W. S. Hancock, in charge of arrangements, had originally refused Browne's request thus to deviate from the norm. Upon receiving Hancock's edict, Browne telegraphed Colonel Fred Grant, the President's son, "since I cannot honor your sainted father and my religion both, I would have to forego the honor. . . ." He then left the city for the family's summer retreat in Bath, Long Island.

The next day Browne received the following message from General Hancock: "The family of General Grant express their hope that you may be present at the funeral. By referring to Colonel H. C. Hodges, USA, at the Fifth Avenue Hotel, you will be provided with transportation and a suitable position."

The implication that Browne used transportation on Shabbat to reach the ceremony and return home from it in no way contradicted his purpose. Reform Judaism did not recognize the injunction against riding on the Sabbath, so his personal mode of transportation was immaterial. Not so in the public procession, however, where he represented Jews of all persuasions, not only his own.[32]

Since it was customary that the highest public honors for Jewish clergy be accorded to the rabbi of Temple Emanu-El, the episode could only have exacerbated that congregation's annoyance with Browne. As the Daily Graphic expressed it, his refusal to ride on the Sabbath was "contrary to their progressive views."[33]

In contrast to the reaction of Temple Emanu-El, Christians and Orthodox Jews highly praised Browne's demonstration. Some Christian ministers even joined him, taking turns to walk alongside him for segments of his 7.5 mile trek from the Battery to Riverside Park. The Daily Graphic applauded his action in telling hyperbole. "While we are writing this," it proclaimed, "Rabbi Browne is 'footing it' to Riverside in honor of the Jewish Sabbath, and every time he sets foot upon the pavement he tramples upon the hearts of his opponents who tried to transfer the Jewish Sabbath to Sunday."[34]

The Graphic also announced that the rabbi:

> . . . mingles largely with the best families of Christians; he speaks
> extemporaneously and is very polite and accessible to reporters, unlike
> some of his prudish brethren. The six leading Jewish Rabbis [Gottheil,
> Kaufman Kohler, Henry Jacobs, Adolph Huebsch, Henry Pereira
> Mendes, Frederick de Sola Mendes] and their congregations combined
> against him. The wealthiest held a meeting about him and sent a
> committee of its trustees to his Congregation, but they were bowed out.
> They oppose everything, if ever so proper, if it originates with Browne.

Browne had indeed provoked leaders of Temple Emanu-El. Having
already riled them to the point of sending a delegation to Temple Gates of
Hope in an effort to muzzle him, his demonstration at Grant's funeral placed
him firmly in the category of "dangerous dissident" for these leaders of
established German Jewry.[35]

It was not so with the newer immigrants. However excoriated by nervous
uptown coreligionists, Browne's action was deeply appreciated by traditional
newcomers downtown. On the day after Thanksgiving, 1885, a delegation of
Orthodox Jews came to Temple Gates of Hope to express their appreciation
for Browne's courage in publicly demonstrating his respect for them and
for the ancient laws of Judaism. The much revered Chief Rabbi Abraham
J. Ash, representing ten "downtown" congregations, presented him with an
illuminated manuscript and a gold medal that depicted him wearing the pall
bearer's badge. Below his image was inscribed, "City Hall Riverside;'" and
above, in enamelled Hebrew, "Boruch mkadesh Hashabos," [blessed be he
who sanctified the Sabbath]. For decades after, on anniversaries of Grant's
funeral and announcements of Browne's lectures, newspapers throughout the
country copied that picture and its story.[36]

Browne's triumph, however, did not go unblemished by opposition. When Christian ministers, distressed about neglect of their own Sabbath, invited him as one of the "powerful hitters . . . the 'walker' and the champion 'talker' on the Sabbath question" to present the Jewish point of view in a public discussion at the elite Nineteenth Century Club, the New York Mail and Express reported that "some of the Fifth Avenue Israelites [were offended] to see Rabbi Browne, an outsider, selected for the Jewish side over Rabbi Gottheil, one of the Vice-Presidents of the club and a Fifth Avenue preacher." Pressure from Temple Emanu-El subsequently forced the organizers to rescind Browne's invitation and substitute Gottheil in his place.

Clearly New York's German Jewish aristocracy could not tolerate honors historically belonging to one of their own being bestowed upon a maverick upstart. Browne's notoriety now became more than a blow to their pride. It bespoke a disturbance of still waters that they viewed as a possible threat to Jewish security. Right or wrong, he gave them more reason to worry.[37]

Politics

Concomitant with his other activities, Browne became a political activist, his claim that he never "meddled with politics" truthful only in the sense that he never sought political office. In other respects he became very much involved. Critics accused him of espousing unpopular issues to gain publicity for himself, yet many of his actions affirm his claim that he preferred to work behind the scenes, managing and promoting politicians whose platforms reflected his values. Although he often did seek publicity, evidence suggests that he did so for a cause rather than for himself personally and frequently asked not to be identified. He denied having a hidden agenda. "Jewish politicians and rabbis," he said, ". . . cannot understand how a man will give his time and money without selfish aims as a prelude for a political nomination."[38]

The genesis of Browne's political activism and that for which he worked longer against the most vituperative opposition was, surprisingly, legislation permitting Jewish children to be excused from public schools without penalty on the two most important religious holidays, Rosh Hashana and Yom Kippur, the Jewish New Year and the Day of Atonement. When he first came to New York, he petitioned the city for such a ruling on behalf of its estimated thirty to forty thousand Jewish students, at the same time asking that Catholic students be excused on Good Friday. The Superintendent of Public Schools did not respond.[39]

Perceiving that downtown Jews comprised a silent majority of his coreligionists, and aware that it was an election year, Browne retaliated by threatening to "carry the question into politics and enlist 25,000 Hebrew votes" for the Mayor who would side with him. Leaders at Temple Emanu-El vehemently opposed the action. Gottheil, expressing full satisfaction with "things as they are," told the press, "I regret that any one man should make himself in such a manner the spokesman of the Hebrew citizens of New York. We do not desire that this should be made a public question. The Hebrews do not combine for political purposes."[40]

Browne consulted the chief rabbis of Europe: Nathan Marcus Adler of Britain, Lazare Isidor of France, Azriel H. Hildesheimer of Germany, Adolph J. Jellinek of Austria and Meyer Kaiserling of Hungary, plus the chief rabbis of Morocco and Jerusalem, and I.M. Wise of Cincinnati, a group generally acknowledged to be "the greatest rabbis in the world." All sustained his position. He also sought the opinion of school superintendents in every large city across America, who likewise agreed, and noted that in their jurisdictions Jewish children were already fully excused on their most important religious holidays. With these testaments in hand, Browne appealed directly to the board of education and the state assembly in Albany. As a result, in October, 1886, every school principal in the state was ordered to excuse Jewish students without penalty on Yom Kippur. As reported in the New York Herald:

> The "closing feast" of the Hebrew autumn holidays fell yesterday, and .
> . . it was a veritable red letter day in the history of American Judaism
> because of its being the first holiday on which Hebrew children were
> permitted to be absent from the [New York] public schools without loss
> in their standing. In order to bring about that grand achievement Rabbi
> Browne, of the Temple Gates of Hope, has been fighting ungrudgingly
> for three years against the opposition by the radical rabbis of this city
> who maintained that it was not against the Mosaic law to send children
> to school on the Day of Atonement, one of them going so far as to
> announce that he would send his own children to school on that day.[41]

The children themselves thanked Browne with a handsome gold medal inscribed "Our rights to observe our holidays without loss of marks."[42]

Browne again aggravated the vocal Jewish hierarchy by fostering the so-called "Saturday Half-Holiday" bill, another New York State ruling. As Colonel Elliot F. Shepard, son-in-law of William H. Vanderbilt, and an outspoken supporter of rights for African Americans, noted approvingly in his newspaper, the New York Mail and Express, the rabbi had labored for "the early closing of the retail clerks and the Sunday closing of the hatters . . . although those measures secured him the animosity of the many manufacturers and dealers amongst his own people." Browne, credited with authorship of the bill and largely responsible for its passage, admitted to having partly selfish motives. His goal: "to secure the Jewish Sabbath for the

Jew, starting first with one half and then trying for the other half."

New York Governor David B. Hill agreed, even favoring a full holiday on Saturday and concurring that "the American working man, like the American school boy, can accomplish in five days as much as the European in six, and we could then observe two days of rest, the Jewish Sabbath and the Christian Sunday."[43]

No sooner was this issue settled than another disagreement arose between Browne and the Jewish leadership. Legislation known as the "Hebrew Marriage" bill came before the state assembly, sponsored by a Jewish politician, Jacob Aaron Cantor. Its ostensible purpose was to prevent "the systematic trade in marriage . . . carried on by some rabbis of the Hebrew Church . . . by confining the right to perform the marriage ceremony to the rabbis of incorporated congregations."

Browne contended that no such abuses existed, and that the underlying purpose of the proposed law was to increase congregational membership. An anonymous letter in the Jewish Messenger endorsed that view, identifying "the Jewish Ministers' Association" (rabbis of the most important congregations, known as the Big Six) as motivators of the action, and observing that "our brethren downtown appear to be highly agitated about a bugbear which is very harmless and in the end will produce results which were not to be foreseen by our liberal rabbis."[44]

The bill prevented rabbis and *chazanim* (cantors) who were not employed by congregations from officiating at weddings. Predicting passage, the writer maintained that any group could easily and inexpensively circumvent the rule by chartering a congregation, which would result in a proliferation of small synagogues and hurt the existing ones, "while the ministers that moved in the matter will hardly be benefited by it."[45]

Again Browne conducted his own investigation and again produced a lengthy document for use in arguing his case, this time before the New York Senate Judiciary Committee. The bill passed despite his efforts, but in amended form allowing "priests of every denomination" to officiate at weddings.[46]

It may have been that these activities were in part responsible for the signal honor that Browne received soon thereafter by being invited to offer an opening prayer in the United States Senate. The only other Jew to have invoked God's blessing on the upper house of America's governing body had been his mentor, Wise, on the eve of the Civil War. On May 27, 1884, Browne proudly stood in the senate chamber of the national Capitol as the second Jew in history to pray in that place for the welfare of our nation.[47]

Unfortunately his message did not survive. Newspapers did comment, however, on his lecture the previous evening at Washington's Metropolitan Church. There he said that if the Talmud were translated into English, "it would open up new channels of thought for the learned men of today, for without the Talmud it is impossible to give a correct conception of the Jews as a people." As noted in the Washington National Republican, the minister of the church read a letter from President Arthur regretting his inability to attend. The Washington Post declared the lecture a "thoughtful, scholarly production" commanding close attention.[48]

It soon became apparent that Browne leaned toward Republican partisanship. In a letter written while he was in Europe during the summer of 1884, an election year, he indicated his concern for labor rights and open immigration, reporting that newspaper editorials advised against workers immigrating to America for jobs and better pay. Anticipating that Democrat Grover Cleveland would soon become president, Europeans reasoned that Congress would then pass tariff legislation favorable to European markets, which would enable European workers to earn as much at home as they could earn in America. Browne warned: "Let this be the best argument for the [Republican] ticket. Blaine's [Republican] success means American workingmen protected and prosperous, whilst his defeat means 'the prosperity of Europe' as an outlet for its pauper labor and a decrease of our immigration." In addition to his advocacy for American labor and trade, Browne joined the widespread Jewish effort to keep immigration open for all who suffered poverty and persecution in Europe.[49]

Opposition to free trade and overriding concern for public education brought Browne into the camp of former Secretary of State James G. Blaine, then running as the Republican nominee in the 1884 presidential campaign. At a rally Browne spoke extemporaneously on Blaine's behalf, explaining that he endorsed the candidate because "Jews value education, and the Republican Party is the party of education. . . ." He quipped that the Bureau of Education "is not the Bureau of Internal Revenue, but of eternal revenue." As a result, the two men became friends.[50]

Shortly after the election, the Union League Club asked Browne to head a three-man committee to lobby Congress for passage of the Blair bill, which called for temporary support of public schools in states unable to afford it. After carefully preparing his presentation, Browne brought the draft to Blaine for advice. The defeated candidate praised it, reiterating his appreciation for Browne's help during the campaign and citing an article in the Tribune that called Browne's speech "a masterpiece of strategic oratory." Blaine declared that it should have been the only speech delivered at the rally, and that he would have become president and included Browne "amongst those nearest to me in the affairs of our nation" if the rabbi's comments had been circulated as zealously as the oft-quoted gaffe about rum, Romanism and rebellion.[51]

In the 1880s, the majority of New York's uptown Jews were Democrats notwithstanding that party's tainted association with Tammany Hall and the fact that wealthy Jews like the Seligmans and their rabbi belonged to the Republican-oriented Nineteenth Century Club. Few Jews engaged actively in politics, and their rabbis especially shunned political activism so as not to be accused of abrogating the separation of church and state. Browne claimed to be an independent—"as much of a Democrat as I am of a Republican"— but was drawn to the Republicans by their platform. After being criticized by Wise and others, especially in the South, for having forsaken the Democrats, Browne explained to an audience in Charleston, South Carolina:[52]

> *Since I delivered my speech by the side of James G. Blaine in the Fifth Avenue Hotel Preachers' Meeting, I have been assailed by the press and people of the South for having left my former associates for the Republican camp. The American Israelite spoke with special bitterness about it. Let me therefore assure this audience that I was indeed what that paper says, a wild Bourbon, before coming to New York. I love the South and the Southern people with the sincerest of affections, and I pride myself that as minister of the Atlanta Temple and editor of the Jewish South I was instrumental in giving our present Congress the brightest of its Southern members, that noble-souled Representative Nathaniel J. Hammond. . . . Yet was I no party follower and no politician, but I stood by Hammond because [he was] a friend of religious liberty and public education. When however, the Blair bill was passed by the Senate, I became less angry with my then political opponents, and when Congress hesitated to accept the proffered aid to educate the illiterates of the Southern States, I abandoned my life-long political associates and went over to the Republicans. . . .[53]*

Regarding his partisan sentiments, Browne made an amusing as well as prescient observation in a sermon during the 1886 session of the New York State Assembly. Grover Cleveland, then governor, and Theodore Roosevelt, then a Republican state assemblyman, had endorsed a certain bill that Browne favored, and at the same time Assemblyman Albert Daggett introduced a discriminatory Christian-oriented bill, obviously not to Browne's liking. Referring to the three, Browne quipped, "Governor Cleveland should receive the presidential nomination of his party, Mr. Roosevelt should be our next Governor, and Mr. Daggett . . . should be sent to the political morgue." He predicted accurately. Although another decade passed before Roosevelt became Governor, Grover Cleveland did go to the White House in the next election and Daggett was defeated, and plunged into obscurity after that one term.[54]

Browne's growing fascination with politics soon led to problems. In 1886, he contradicted his claim of never meddling by announcing to Republican Party Chairman, Elihu Root that he knew of a good Republican who could be elected over the Tammany incumbent in the upcoming New York City mayoral election. Without revealing the man's name, he invited Root to visit him and discuss the matter. It is not known if their meeting ever occurred or who Browne intended to name, but his subsequent action suggests that he supported the candidacy of Henry George, whose philosophy and Single Tax theory he greatly admired.[55]

As expected, Democrat Abraham Hewitt won the mayoral election, but George surprised many by scoring second, ahead of Republican Theodore Roosevelt, with between 5,000 and 15,000 Jewish votes. This was significant because in previous elections a large proportion of Jews voted for Tammany Democrats. According to analysts, many Jewish workers voted for the first time in the 1886 election in order to support George and the United Labor

Party, and at that time initiated the influential role of Jews in New York City politics.[56]

Supporting George's championship of labor and his philosophy of landownership by the government positioned Browne among those whom the Jewish Tidings called "rabid agitators" who "want to take from the man who has acquired property all that he possesses to divide among his neighbors. . . ." Unruffled, Browne did not flinch when he learned that the propertied Jews to whom the Tidings referred opposed George so strongly that the paper, reflecting the views of its patrons, recommended firing a Rochester rabbi who favored George's Single Tax Theory. Its stated reason was, "Such theories compromise [our] religion and bring them [sic] into disrepute with all fair-minded people."[57]

At a June, 1887, rally of the United States Labor Party in Union Square honoring the British Member of Parliament William O'Brien, Browne told the crowd of 100,000 people, "The power of Labor, guided by law, is the power of God. . . . .The 'overalls' are the grandest uniform upon the face of the earth." The New York Jewish Daily News reported it, calling him, "Rabbi Browne, the poor man's friend," to which Henry George added "champion of the toiling masses."[58]

Also in 1887, Browne and Bishop John P. Newman, who had become his closest friend, led a state-wide campaign in New York for Colonel Fredrick Grant, son of the late president, as New York Secretary of State on the Republican ticket. They acted independently, eschewing the party machine, because they believed that to be "a gang of professional politicians . . . [who] sacrifice the party for their own selfish ends." Browne visited every synagogue and B'nai B'rith lodge in the state, recruiting prominent men and women, "amongst the best element of our people such as worked *without* pay. . . ." Grant lost, but Browne's work proved valuable by introducing him to Jewish voters throughout the state. The campaign whet his appetite for more.[59]

In 1888, Republican Benjamin Harrison stood in danger of losing his home state of Indiana in his bid for the presidency because of Alvin P. Hovey, currently a senator running for governor on the same ticket. Hovey, a war hero, self educated attorney, jurist, and advocate of public education, had written a letter containing anti-Semitic remarks during the Civil War that had been used in a former campaign to discredit him with Jewish voters and was being revived in the current contest. Previously Moses Weil, Browne's father-in-law and an active Indiana Republican, had asked Hovey to explain, to which Hovey had replied, "Twenty-five years ago, the Jew was unknown, had no social position, no business nor political standing and I did so regard him, but now we see what the Jew is, we had Jewish Governors, Senators, Ambassadors, Merchant Princes . . . and I really regret having used such language even in the heated passion of war time. . . ."[60]

Presumably this mollified Indiana's Jewish voters, for Hovey won his seat in the Senate. When Wise in his American Israelite again publicized the slur in 1888 to defeat Hovey, Weil perceived that the publicity could threaten others on the ticket, including Harrison, whereupon he appealed to his son-in-law for help. Browne asked Hovey to publicize the apology, reminding him that Weil and the Jews were largely responsible for his election to the Senate. Hovey failed to reply. Browne then warned Harrison that his home state of Indiana was "more doubtful than New Jersey because the Jews are against Hovey, and the American Israelite with Rabbi Wise the strongest man in the pulpit [is] against you." He added that the senator is "a dead weight hanging to your neck, and he will drown you."

Senator Matthew S. Quay, chairman of the Republican Committee, asked Browne to save Harrison by joining the campaign. Browne's friends, notably former Secretary of State Hamilton Fish, publisher Elliot Shepherd, and Bishop Newman, persuaded him to accept, which he did with one caveat: he abjured financial compensation, asking instead that Harrison, if successful, appoint a Jew to his cabinet. Quay agreed on condition that Harrison consented. Realizing that no one could openly commit to such a promise, Browne advised Harrison that it was unnecessary to respond in writing because he could read between the lines.

Recognizing Browne's popularity with immigrants, Quay asked him to secure the Jewish vote in New York as well as in Indiana, and if possible to neutralize Wise's opposition in Ohio. Beginning in August, unusually early for campaigns in those days, Browne mobilized the Hebrew American Republican League, a coalition of twenty-three workingmen's clubs that he had organized the previous year for Fred Grant's campaign in New York. He then recruited friends in Ohio and Indiana, notably rabbis, advising them to work quietly because, as he later explained to Harrison, "Jews don't like their rabbis to become politicians. . . ." He also told Harrison that rabbis "can do much more in another way," which apparently they did in Indiana where Jews were considered to be the swing vote. If so, Browne arguably saved Harrison the embarrassment of defeat in his own home state.

In Ohio, although the American Israelite had already carried articles against the Republicans, Browne hoped to lure Wise by telling him that Harrison, if elected, would appoint a Jew to the cabinet, and he–Browne– could designate who that would be. If Wise supported Harrison, Browne intended to name him for Secretary of the Interior. Unimpressed, Wise replied:

> *The Republicans know full well that they will not have the opportunity of selecting a Cabinet, hence their promise which otherwise they would not make. The Republican party is not friendly to the Jews and it is surprising that a Browne does not see these facts and allows himself to be deceived by hollow and dishonest promises. It is however very probable*

that President Cleveland who honored us in his first term with a Jewish

Ambassador will distinguish us in his second term by a Hebrew in his

Cabinet.[61]

Quay sent a similar message to Wise, composed by Browne. Leo Wise
responded, making it clear that "under no consideration" could his father
support the Republican nominee.

Browne then turned to another influential Cincinnatian, State Senator
Henry Mack, to "undo Wise's work." Mack, who had chaired building
committees for the Cincinnati Public Library and Wise's beautiful Plum
Street Temple, was currently in Bad Nassau, Germany, undergoing medical
treatment. Browne managed to reach him with the same incentive that he
had offered Wise. Mack accepted, and against doctor's orders, immediately
returned home.[62]

After determining the exact date that Mack's ship was due to arrive,
Browne booked New York's Grand Opera House for the following day, wrote
a speech on the tariff question for Mack to deliver there, and arranged for a
government tug to meet the senator's ship in the harbor, bringing him and his
wife to town undetected. The morning after they arrived, Mack awakened
too ill to appear. Undeterred, Browne had himself made up to impersonate
the senator and delivered the speech himself.[63]

Two days later, Mack and Browne set out on a speaking tour, first
addressing a mass meeting in Albany's Drislane Hall. Browne reported its
success to Harrison, noting that "all the Hebrews and particularly every
prominent one, came . . . even the Democrats."[emphasis in original] The
two campaigners then proceeded to Indiana for "at least six speeches," only
to learn that no advance arrangements had been made. Still undaunted,
Browne had Mack's speech printed and distributed throughout the state. He

was so confident of the Jewish vote that he predicted the winning Republican majority of 2,000 to 3,000 votes despite the prevailing view that Democrats would win Indiana by at least 5,000.[64]

Meanwhile, Browne learned that the New York Democrats planned to run State Senator Cantor, author of the objectionable Jewish Marriage bill, as lieutenant governor with the popular incumbent Democrat, Governor David Hill. Fearing an all-Democratic win in New York, Browne hurried back to the city, called a meeting of the downtown rabbis, and persuaded them to pass resolutions detrimental to Cantor. Browne delivered them to an influential Democrat, ensuring that the campaign leaders would see them and drop Cantor from the list in order to gain the "downtown" Jewish vote.[65]

Browne's Hebrew American Republican League launched its campaign in New York with a mass meeting on the square where East Broadway meets Canal, Essex, and Division Streets. It endorsed the Republican platform with a huge banner featuring its name and its goals: "Protection to American Homes" and "Free Education, Free Worship, Free Ballot, But No Free Trade." It was credited with bringing in more than half of the Seventh Ward's 16,000 Republican votes, most of which had previously gone to Tammany Democrats. Considering the prevalence of patronage in the political system, this gave the Hebrew American Republican League reason to expect tangible symbols of appreciation for its service.[66]

After the election, the league reorganized as a permanent body "upon the lines of religion, sociability, education, charity and politics," with activities to include "Divine services, lectures, entertainments, free physician and medicine, free legal advice, arbitration, and defense. . . ." plus insurance and a free loan facility. Members recalled that Chairman Quay, speaking for the Republican Party, had offered these amenities along with office space and job patronage.[67]

Ten days after Harrison's victory, with appointments being announced and as yet no mention of a Jew, Browne wrote a very long letter to the president-elect detailing disjointedly and with great repetition his reason for asking patronage in return for his work:

Strictly Private
New York November 16th, 1888

My dear General Harrison:

I have allowed ten days for the felicitations of the enthusiastic thousands of your friends and admirers and now I come to tender you my hearty congratulations. May the God of our common ancestor Abraham, Isaac and Jacob strengthen you to carry the great burden soon to rest upon your shoulders, as I hope during the next eight years to come.

And now I must approach a subject that has disturbed my mind ever since the election regarding my position in the campaign.

Browne then restated his purpose for joining the campaign and for his caveat that, if elected, Harrison would appoint a Jew to his cabinet. Chairman Quay was the only other person aware of it. Browne reminded Harrison that in his letter of October 9th:

you justified my expectation in reference to Senator Quay's promise by saying that whilst you had accepted the nomination "without any promise or entanglement . . . if I should be elected I will not only be willing but shall regard it as a duty to listen to the suggestions of my republican friends and give them such weight as they seem to be entitled to." Knowing fully well that Senator Quay's "suggestions" are of such weight and being convinced myself that the Jews of New York and Indiana have secured you these two states, it is plain to me that all things considered the success of our party should accord the Hebrews of the United States the recognition the Germans received in Carl Schurz.[68]

Considering the difficulties faced by the president-elect and the apparent influence of others in his cabinet selections, Browne offered to release Harrison and Quay from their implied promises but requested a mandatory explanation for his volunteers. He explained his caveat, again noting his friendship with Bishop Newman, their campaign for Fred Grant, and Newman's having convinced him to work for Harrison "though he knew that I hated to think of politics. . . ."

Claiming to be "the only Jewish minister on the Republican side," and that all the [New York city] rabbis were "with the petty Jewish politicians-- most of whom are democrats -- to create troubles in my congregation," he had reasoned that the Jewish vote "rightly handled could carry every doubtful state" and hoped that an "appeal to my people's pride by a promise of high political recognition" would do the trick. He reminded Harrison that Cleveland had "catered to the taste of the Hebrews particularly in this state [New York]" and did it correctly "by ignoring the Jewish politicians generally despised by the Jews and appointing men of learning and prominent business men." As a result Jews believed that the Democrats, having appointed three Jewish senators and an ambassador, were their true friends whereas the Republicans "in their long reign never recognized us, excepting some petty offices given to petty politicians. . . ."

Browne next described his relationship with Wise, including his appeal with the promise of an appointment, and his belief that he could counteract Wise's methods because he understood them. He then detailed his gambit with Senator Mack, emphasizing that he did it entirely with promises, at no cost to the campaign other than for his own travelling expenses and the price of Encyclopedia Britannica for "your Rabbi Messing [of Indianapolis, Harrison's home] my right hand man in Indiana." In New York the vote proved easier because of the Hebrew American Republican League, men who worked generally "without drawing one cent from the R.N.C.," even as reimbursement for travelling expenses. This being so, Browne continued:

> . . . all things considered, I could say now 'My dear Gen. Harrison, I
> have worked for three long months . . .; have organized the Hebrews in
> two states which gave you victory and honor; have given you the power
> of the only Jewish daily in the land, have traveled throughout these
> states for four weeks incessantly when my congregation needed me at
> home, did all that without one cent, upon the one condition that I select
> you a Hebrew for your cabinet, a mere 'promise' which really had no
> value when given, now I have fulfilled my promises and I insist upon the
> agreement made by the party of the second part.

Browne then admitted the unseemliness of such arm-twisting, and declared his admiration for Harrison in ecumenical terms approaching adulation. The source of his devotion, he revealed, was Harrison's background as the son and grandson of seriously religious forebears dedicated to public education. He told Harrison:

> There is a spiritual surrounding above you which made me look upon
> you since your nomination, as upon the religious son of religious sires

*called by the Lord as his 'Messiah' to reinstate the party of Education
and to be the victor in this the "campaign of the restoration." You are
to me the 'true Christian' which is the same as the 'true Jew' from my
standpoint, and as such I reverence and love you and therefore cannot
allow the least uneasiness to rest upon you through my claims, hence I
come to say to you I release you and Senator Quay if you so desire it you
are absolutely free, politically as well as morally. All I would want in
that case is some plausible excuse to give to my people who have acted
upon my assurance in this campaign, as that I do not lose the confidence
which in 24 years of my public life I have secured for my utterances. . . .
There will be another election in four years and Jews are long lived as a
rule and their memory is very good.*

*In order to consult about this very important matter I hold myself ready
to come to Indianapolis at any time you will appoint and I wish to
come and go in all silence unbeknown to anybody. I shall prefer to come
for any Tuesday or Wednesday so that I can be back on my Sabbath ,
my assistant being a green foreigner and I having been away for so may
Sabbaths during the Campaign that I don't like to be absent myself again.*

*This letter does not accord in either form or diction as I should have
written it to the President-elect but if it lack great wealth of reverence
and appearance and contents it boasts a wealth of reverence and
affection for you and a grateful spirit towards Him who has led you to
victory, Jehovah our Father and our Lord.*

*Yours in Truth ethereal,
Edward B M Browne*[69]

A strange letter indeed, one that raises suspicion about Browne's grasp of reality and certainly invites the opinion that he displayed an inexplicable degree of naiveté. Harrison did not respond, nor did Browne accept the discouragement that this omission should have conveyed.

No Jew won appointment to the United States Cabinet until eighteen years later when Theodore Roosevelt nominated Oscar Strauss for Secretary of Commerce and Labor. That choice undoubtedly pleased Browne, for notwithstanding his view of Strauss's 1888 ambassadorship to Turkey as Democratic patronage, in 1906 he asked Republican Senator William Sherman to help facilitate Strauss' confirmation in case any difficulty should arise in Congress due to anti-Semitism or the fact that Strauss was a Democrat. Sherman replied assuring the rabbi that no hurdle of either sort would hinder Strauss' appointment, although "We would prefer that he was a Republican, as one would think a gentleman of his position ought to be. . ."[70]

Browne had strayed far from the customary rabbinic orbit. Although Wise, too, travelled from pulpit to press to politics, the elder rabbi did so with far more success and staying power. Browne soon dissipated his initial success through unfortunate decisions, misplaced pride, and uncontrolled temper. In this case his judgment may have been clouded by his simultaneous involvement in two additional high profile controversies besides his normal work as a congregational rabbi and part-time journalist. As shall be seen, he defied discretion and hurtled headlong into irremediable defeat.

VII - NEW YORK
Crime and Punishment

The heedless rabbi became embroiled in two very different issues that intertwined simultaneously with the Harrison campaign and ultimately led to his downfall. Both had political overtones that were arguably exacerbated by his tendency toward flagrant behavior and use of unorthodox methods. Ironically, the first and most damaging of these was a *pikuach nefesh*, the saving of a soul, in this case saving the life of an innocent man.

Browne's defense of Adolph Reich, a Hungarian immigrant falsely accused and convicted for murder, is documented in a brief he prepared and presented to New York Governor David Hill as a plea for stay of execution. It poignantly exposes miscarriages of justice suffered by the most vulnerable of citizens, here specifically by immigrants from Eastern Europe, ignorant of the language and customs of America. In Reich's case as in untold others, partisan politics and corruption among officiants of local law enforcement abrogated the right of a wrongfully accused defendant to receive justice. The entire text is too long for inclusion here; however, in order to provide a deeper understanding of the anguish suffered by many immigrants in the late 19th and early 20th centuries, portions of it are included as an addendum. Here, in essence, is Browne's story:

A delegation of Hungarian immigrants came to Browne's home in June, 1887, seeking help for their friend Adolph Reich, then on trial for the murder of his wife. They brought their appeal to Browne because he was reputed to be only "uptown" rabbi (i.e., assumed to have both savvy and clout) willing to assist the poor free-of-charge. In his words, he was apparently regarded as "the Attorney-General of the Human Race and the District Attorney of the down-town Jews . . ." and instead of bringing him their religious disputes, as they did to other rabbis, they came "with their quarrels, fights, and similar troubles, to arbitrate and prevent a lawsuit, or to defend or bail out a poor fellow who has been arrested for selling prayer books on Sunday, running his sewing machine on the Lord's Day, or for some disregard to the whimsical orders of the policeman on the beat who terrorizes these strangers as a rule. . . ."

Samuel Neuman, spokesman for the group, explained that, although there was sufficient evidence to prove Reich's innocence, after having observed the first day's proceedings they suspected the court-appointed defender, C. F. Kinsley, of not sincerely seeking an acquittal. They wanted Browne to come to court with them and advise them as to what they should do.

Browne had read lurid reports of the crime in which newspapers repeatedly referred to Reich as "the wife-murderer." Also, he recalled having met the victim when she came to his home with another woman several months before, seeking his intervention in a quarrel with her husband. He remembered Mrs. Reich as a woman "of coquetish, bold bearing, over-dressed, and what amongst the ordinary class of Hungarians would be called 'good looking'"[1]

Upon arrival at the courthouse Browne met Kinsley, the defense attorney, who immediately aroused his suspicions by telling him that Reich had a fool-proof alibi and then quickly asking about expected payment from the Jewish community. When court reconvened, witnesses confirmed Browne's impression of Mrs. Reich, testifying that she was a woman of strong physique and weak character. They also disclosed that she had numerous lovers, including the family's boarder, Samuel Gross, a witness for the prosecution who appeared to Browne to be lying. Another witness, a woman whom Browne recognized as the one who had come to his home with Mrs. Reich, also aroused his suspicions. All testimony confirmed that the victim was much stronger than her husband and that she "received visitors in her rooms at all times of day and night."[2]

While the court was in recess, Browne met the accused and spoke with him in Magyar (Hungarian). Reich, a frail man in his seventies, did not understand English and had no idea of what was transpiring in the courtroom. Upon interrogating him, Browne soon learned that the only existing evidence that could possibly be used against him was a small amount of blood on his undershirt—a few drops only—which Reich said came from his wife's nose bleed the night before and witnesses could testify to having seen prior to the murder. Reich also told Browne that Kinsley, his defender, had urged him to plead guilty by reason of self defense but that he had refused to do so, even after Kinsley told him that it was his only chance for acquittal. Despite his client's refusal, however, Kinsley had sent a coach to the jail to teach Reich how to demonstrate the killing when ordered to do so in court. Reich continued to refuse the plea of self defense, declaring that he would rather die than live with the stigma of having killed his wife.[3]

In order to reassure himself of Reich's innocence, Browne concocted a ruse, telling Reich that scientists could distinguish whether blood stains came from the nose or the throat. This elicited such a joyous response from the prisoner that Browne was convinced of his innocence. He was likewise convinced that Reich needed another attorney, one who understood the cultural differences between Hungarian peasants and American urbanites, and could clarify them for the court when necessary. He offered to assist Kinsley, pro bono, but Kinsley refused. The attorney, who was later reported to have abandoned an assigned case due to the client's inability to pay, again asked about payment from the Jewish community for defending Reich.[4]

During the lunch recess, Reich's friends took Browne to a shop owned by another of the Hungarians with whom they had set a trap for one of the witnesses, a man known in the neighborhood as a tramp and a beggar. They wanted Browne to see and hear for himself as the shopkeeper tricked the man into revealing that he had been offered payment in return for testimony damaging to the defendant. Witnessing this, Browne became ever more determined to procure proper legal defense for Adolph Reich.

That afternoon when court adjourned for the weekend, the rabbi wrote to four leading Jewish philanthropists, including Jacob Schiff, asking for help with the case. At his synagogue in the evening, Browne took up a collection for Reich's defense. He spoke of charity in his Shabbat sermon, highlighting the case and concluding dramatically by swearing to Reich's innocence before the open ark.

On Saturday, Kinsley visited Reich in prison and reiterated his decision to change the plea to guilty by reason of self defense. Now deeply alarmed, Reich sent a message to Browne imploring him to convince Kinsley otherwise. Browne pleaded with Kinsley to desist, noting that the change was unnecessary, that it countermanded the client's wishes, and that it would damage his case by being introduced at the last minute.[5]

That same day Browne received a $50 check from Schiff with a note saying that he had referred the matter to the trustees of Temple Emanu-El, and that they had engaged Adolph L. Sanger to defend Reich at the expense of the congregation.

Sanger, though still relatively young—about the same age as Browne— was a distinguished legal advocate already known as an eloquent orator, president of the New York City Board of Aldermen, a commissioner of the Board of Education and subsequently its president, past president of the Board of Delegates of American Israelites, future Grand Lodge president of B'nai B'rith, and member of the board of the Union of American Hebrew

Congregations. Such heavy artillery for the defense of an unknown Jewish immigrant was not as surprising as it might seem, for the privileged few generally felt it their duty to protect the community from public stigma, and the unprecedented disgrace of a Jew being convicted for murder had to be avoided at all costs. The philanthropists, though grateful to Browne for having alerted them to such imminent danger, nonetheless considered him a publicity seeker and wanted to avoid his participation in order to stifle future publicity as much as possible. They needed a discreet person of high stature at the helm.

After reviewing the case with Browne on Sunday, Sanger appeared in court on Monday and, as Browne had done, begged Kinsley not to change the plea. Kinsley ignored Sanger's advice as he had ignored Browne's, likewise refusing to let him onto the case to assist in the trial. Kinsley then stood before the jury, and moments before the trial ended, announced the defendant's change of plea. This caused an audible surprise throughout the courtroom, for apparently no one had expected such a reversal at that time or understood the logic behind it.

Although unrecorded by the court reporter, Browne noted flagrant bias on the part of Judge Frederick Smyth in his charge to the jury. As predicted, the jury voted guilty. It did, however, recommend clemency. Judge Smyth denied clemency and sentenced Reich to be hanged in forty-one days.[6]

Horrified, the Hungarians, led by Samuel Neuman, engaged Browne's help to organize an appeal for retrial based upon misrepresentation of the case during trial. One result of their meetings was the emergence of an organization, the Hungarian Society for the Protection of the Imprisoned, "to help out prisoners who are friendless and poor and have before them the ordeal of facing a judge and jury." Between forty and fifty men signed up. Although its history is unknown, the society probably served as a precedent for Browne when, two decades later (described in Chapter XII) he inspired the establishment of a legal aid organization for needy immigrants, which he served as public defender for the rest of his life.[7]

In Browne's opinion, two powerful groups obstructed justice for Reich, exerting all possible effort to prevent a retrial. The German Jewish leadership, intent upon stopping the harmful publicity as quickly as possible, quietly sought a pardon. Reich rejected the pardon because it would be based on the plea of self defense, and therefore constituted admission of guilt. Law enforcement officials opposed a retrial, according to Browne, because of the possibility that a retrial might reveal misconduct which could cost them their jobs and do further damage to their already questionable collective reputation. These and other factors caused Reich's execution to be postponed until the following year—an election year—when city officials and politicians of both parties would press their personal causes on New York Governor David Hill, a Democrat striving to protect his own interests in hotly contested state campaigns.[8]

Despite concerted efforts to thwart it, the appeal produced a retrial in early October, 1888. Reich was represented by Alex Rosenthal, a young attorney who, while serving in the United States Embassy in Paris, had been introduced to Browne by Lazare Isidor, Grand Rabbi of France. Despite Rosenthal's valiant appeal, he failed to reverse the original decision. Again Reich was sentenced to death by hanging, with execution now set for November 30.[9]

On November 12, Browne appeared before Governor Hill to present his brief for Reich's defense. After hearing it, the governor told Browne that his argument was "quite reasonable, but the fact is, the woman has been killed; well then, who did the killing?"

Browne replied, "sufficient is it unto me in the success of the showing that Reich was not the man," and then added. "but since Your Excellency wishes me to do so, I shall gladly name the murderer. . . ." He identified Gross, the boarder, and proceeded in making a convincing case against him using the official court record itself to verify his statements. By the same means, Browne also incriminated Judge Smyth and others for unethical misconduct during the investigation, the coroner's inquest, and the trial.

On November 26, 1888, Governor Hill held a public hearing on the application for commutation of Reich's death sentence. Many people attended including Browne, Rosenthal, Sanger and one Joseph Grosner, who represented "a society of 5,000 Hungarians." Attorney William F. Howe, pleading for the defense, submitted a petition for commutation reportedly signed by 85,000 citizens of New York.[10]

Kinsley claimed not to have been present when Reich pleaded guilty by reason of self defense. When the governor asked if it were true that he had advised his client to change his plea, Kinsley "colored up" and challenged the governor's authority to question him. Further testimony by Herman Roth, Reich's interpreter in the original trial, confirmed Browne's suspicion of Kinsley's duplicity.[11]

Governor Hill granted Reich a stay of execution for two months in order to study the case himself. Those who believed Reich to be guilty or for other reasons welcomed closure, used the time to foster publicity that kept public opinion against the prisoner, presumably in the hope that it would frighten him into admitting guilt by reason of self defense, thus leading to a rapid conclusion. After depicting him as a murderer, they portrayed him as a perjurer because he had originally pleaded not guilty. Someone forged a letter of confession and planted it in his cell to be "discovered" after his execution, appearing to have been left intentionally by Reich himself. It was, of course, found and dutifully delivered to a newspaper. Reich notified Browne and attorney Alex Rosenthal, who immediately rushed to the newspaper office and identified the letter as a forgery. The editor refused to retract it, insisting that the coroner had verified the letter as genuine. Rosenthal then obtained and published affidavits from Reich and others, reaffirming Reich's statement that he had not killed his wife nor had he ever stated that he had done so except when his attorney tricked him into changing his plea in court.[12]

Browne reported that further tampering ensued when two of his witnesses appeared at the coroner's office, as they had been instructed to do, to receive money for their transportation to Albany for the hearing. They were met not by the coroner, but by Julius Schwartz, a leader of the Hungarian Immigrant's Association, editor of the newspaper Hungaria and—perhaps not incidentally—one of those whom Browne had cited in the immigration scandal of 1882. Schwartz took the witnesses to the office of former coroner Moritz Ellinger, whom Browne had specifically identified in his accusation of fraud among the functionaries responsible for settling the immigrants. According to the witnesses, Ellinger had handed them affidavits to sign affirming that Reich had killed his wife in self defense. When they refused to sign, they were told that there was no need for them to go to Albany because the judge who ruled on the case would be there to ensure that Reich's life be spared by the plea of self defense. Six months later, a newspaper reported that Schwartz had absconded to Kansas where he had been arrested for forgery.[13]

Despite further attempts to prevent Browne's witnesses from appearing in Albany, they arrived as summoned and testified to the accuracy of his claims. So did the eminent Adolph Sanger. Because Sanger's reputation alone ensured the weight of his testimony, the presiding prosecutor tried to avoid putting him on the stand. Sanger foiled him by volunteering. In Browne's Machiavellian view, the prosecutor's attitude emanated from the machinations of party politics. Both the prosecutor and Sanger were

Tammanites, as were all of the officials involved, but they belonged to a faction in competition with the one led by Sanger. Browne believed that they wanted to suppress Sanger's testimony in order to deny him credit for Reich's commutation, thereby protecting their own status with the electorate. Right or wrong, this explanation implied sympathy for Reich among the masses.[14]

Subsequently, Browne discovered still more questionable behavior. Samuel Neuman had gone, with power of attorney, to collect money and jewelry belonging to the dead woman, and was denied access to it. Browne learned that the valuables had already been removed from custody in the name of Samuel Gross, the boarder, who claimed to be nearest of kin. The property clerk had released them on his behalf to two Irish vagabonds who had been accepted as bondsmen after introducing themselves as the owners of well known businesses and offering him a total of $3500. Reich's son David reported seeing the jewelry in the hands of defense attorney Kinsley. Its final disposition remained unknown. Gross later asked Browne for money to buy passage back to Europe. Not surprisingly, Browne refused.[15]

On the eve of Reich's scheduled execution, Governor Hill declared that a miscarriage of justice had occurred, and commuted the sentence to life imprisonment. Browne, grateful that the man's life was spared, but remaining unsatisfied until complete justice was achieved, pursued the case with each subsequent governor until he finally, after fifteen years, succeeded in obtaining an exoneration with full pardon for the aged prisoner. Success notwithstanding, the case of Adolph Reich placed a cloud on Browne's mind and reputation, affecting his effectiveness for the rest of his life.

Congregation

While concentrating on campaigns outside of his congregation, Browne either overlooked or purposely ignored one that was developing within it.

The issue, when it first arose in early 1887, ostensibly had nothing to do with the rabbi, but concerned the sale of pews.

Synagogue seating was significant in those days because it implied status and control. It was a common practice for dues to be set too high for lower income members to afford, thus denying them the right to vote. Although a few congregations had already suppressed this manifestation of elitism before 1918 when the Central Conference of American Rabbis addressed it in its first social justice platform, the Declaration of Principles, others continued for decades, ignoring the Principles and fostering the undesirable reputation of Reform as a "rich man's institution."[16]

Congregation Gates of Hope, unlike most synagogues in the 1880s, had no membership in the usual sense, but endeavored to operate more democratically by renting its pews annually and allowing voting rights to anyone who paid the current rental fee of $40. As this placed everyone on equal footing without regard to financial status, it eventually drew complaints from the elite. Some preferred to buy their pews outright in order to maintain their seating permanently, thus keeping their position at status quo. Henry Rosenblatt and Max Zenn, the men who had introduced the previously used prayer book and objected to having it supplanted by Browne's new one, repeatedly led the dissenters in unsuccessful efforts to change the system. They finally succeeded by means of a coup in which a president was elected who favored the permanent sale of pews. When the new leader changed the congregation's rules permitting pews to be sold on a permanent basis, the fifteen purchasers became a voting majority, disenfranchising more than a hundred members who rented as previously required. This changed the congregation's concept as well as its leadership, significantly altering the power of Browne's friends and supporters.

This congregational brouhaha had occurred a few months before Reich's trial began, during the period in which newspapers continually referred to the indicted man as "the wife-murderer," virtually convicting him without benefit of trial. When Browne spoke in his defense on Shabbat, declaring Reich innocent before the open ark, the congregation's former dissenters, now its controlling power, seized the moment as an opportunity to discredit the rabbi. Browne's friends only fanned the flames by begging him to be silent. Their well meant effort to protect him from himself so infuriated him that, by his own admission, he insulted them publicly, thus losing the friendship of some who still had the power to vote. Not surprisingly, growing numbers of his original supporters moved into the ranks of Rosenblatt and Zenn.

Thus the battle over pews gradually morphed into a battle over Browne. His opponents accused him of perjury for having sworn to Reich's innocence when supposedly—since the plea was then changed to guilty by reason of self-defense—Reich had lied by first claiming to be innocent. Although probably not sustainable in a court of law, the charge went unchallenged in the court of public opinion. It enabled Browne's opponents to brand him as a perjurer and therefore unfit to serve as a rabbi. The dissenters, sufficiently increased in number by those whom the rabbi had insulted, soon comprised a majority under the new voting rules and moved to dismiss him. In July, 1887, while Browne struggled to save Reich's life, he lost his position at Congregation Gates of Hope.

The news pleased Browne's detractors throughout the country. Wise gloated over it in the American Israelite, while the New York Times, still owned by Jones, whom Browne had sued for libel along with Wise in 1881, announced the dismissal in an eight inch column headed "SQUELCHING RABBI BROWNE." The article declared that Browne's "suspension" resulted from an investigation by three members of the congregation confirming charges of "conduct unbecoming a minister," and added:

That this erratic minister should have reached the end of his tether is
no surprise to any who have been familiar with his character or lack
of character. He has been a seeker after notoriety for years, and his
officiousness and ridiculous methods had at last disgusted even the few
friends that he had left. Long after he was repudiated by respectable
Jews, who were grieved that one who presumed to be a teacher and who
called himself 'The Modern Maccabbee' and the 'Jewish Beecher' was
permitted to bring odium on those of the Jewish faith. His latest and
most peculiarly offensive public act was to appear as a defender of and
apologist for Adolph Reich, the wife murderer, now under sentence of
death.[17]

The allegations were obviously spiteful and largely untrue. Browne may
have been referred to by others as a modern Maccabbee or Jewish Beecher,
whether in adulation or to promote his lectures, but, despite his penchant
for bragging, there is no evidence that he ever glorified himself with those
metaphors. He did enjoy being called "the poor man's friend," a title
bestowed by an admiring newspaper reporter and repeated famously by the
"White Knight," former Secretary of State and presidential candidate, James
G. Blaine.

The Times continued its defamation of Browne, maintaining that Judge
Smyth rebuked him for divulging a confession made in clerical confidence
by testifying about his conversation with Mrs. Reich. It also asserted that
he was "unceremoniously thrown out of court by the verdict, as he is now
thrown out of his congregation by his people, who have found out what
a charlatan and notoriety seeking individual he is. . . ." Not satisfied with
those slanderous statements, it derided him for having made "a great deal of

talk about 'upholding the Jewish law'" by walking in Grant's funeral, while ignoring the Orthodox prohibition against attending a funeral on Saturday; and reported that he reacted angrily when the president of his congregation told him "to have no more to say" about the Reich case. In conclusion it reminded readers of Browne's libel suit against the Times.[18]

Two weeks later, the Atlanta Constitution copied the story, sandwiching it between a rehash of Browne's problems in that city and a complimentary review of his achievements in New York. It noted that the New York newspapers frequently printed his sermons in full, that his opinion was often sought on both religious and secular questions, and that his eulogy for Grant outshone all others including that of his dear friend Bishop Newman. "But alas!" it concluded, "His relentless Nemesis has caught up with him. The rabbi is again in trouble."[19]

The Atlanta paper revealed that Browne had been charged with "conduct unbecoming a minister" not only by testifying for Reich but also for the apparently unpardonable sin—referring to his advocacy of social justice for laborers and taxpayers—of "participating in the labor meetings of Henry George and Dr. McGlynn." (McGlynn was a Catholic priest temporarily excommunicated for supporting George in defiance of his archbishop's orders.) The paper also reported—inaccurately—that Browne took out an injunction to prevent his dismissal, which only delayed it briefly while the legal requirement ran its course. "He must go," the Constitution declared, and then added the more friendly conclusion, "but . . . he cannot be considered an unfortunate man, for as soon as he loses one good situation his tact and talent find another for him."[20]

Unfortunately, the Constitution erred in assessing the rabbi's tact.

The Times misstated Browne's loss of friends within Gates of Hope. Although he had surely lost a crucial majority of current voters, friends who remained credited him with the success and growth that their congregation enjoyed during his tenure there. Not he, but one of his friends, took out the reported injunction to delay his departure, while others, including the brothers Morris and Herman Herrman, wealthy junk dealers, left Gates of Hope to organize a free synagogue for him, which they named Mount Sinai Temple. The Herrmans first offered $210,000 cash to buy the Gospel Tabernacle on Madison Avenue at the corner of 45th Street and renovate it as their synagogue. According to one report, the offer was rejected. Mount Sinai Temple first held services at 140 East 72nd Street. The congregation still hoped to buy the Gospel Tabernacle but soon abandoned the idea because the neighborhood appeared to be unsuitable for a "conservative" congregation.

This use of the word "conservative" hints at another possible reason for the turmoil within Congregation Gates of Hope. Some of Browne's detractors, in addition to disapproving his outspokenness in regard to Reich, may also have opposed his resistence to the brand of Reform then being propagated by most of the elitist German Jewish congregations. He had not brought Gates of Hope into Wise's Union of American Reform Congregations, possibly because he saw the Union dominated by laymen and clergymen whom he considered "sweinfleisch rabbis," those who discarded dietary laws and most other religious mandates of Judaism. As in the case of the Temple in Atlanta and elsewhere, where the change of rabbis reflected changing views of Judaism on the part of lay leaders, subsequent mergers of Gates of Hope with other New York congregations indicated changes of philosophy as well as the more frequent reason of economic necessity. Gates of Hope, after several mergers with other congregations, ultimately became the prestigious, Conservative bastion, Park Avenue Synagogue.

Browne's friends, when they abandoned their plan to buy the tabernacle, decided upon five available lots at 160 East 112th Street in Harlem, and Sophie's father, Moses Weil, loaned them $1000 to use for construction. Shortly after they received the building plans, someone bought a large church nearby to be renovated as a synagogue on behalf of another congregation. Since Harlem's Jewish population was not yet large enough to sustain an additional house of worship, Browne's group retreated. Mount Sinai Temple then rented a Baptist church on 112th Street for temporary use and directed its architect to draw plans for remodeling some unfinished buildings on 88th Street.[21]

City authorities delayed approving those plans, and then claimed to have lost them, requiring Mount Sinai's trustees to extend their lease of the Baptist church. When they tried to do so, authorities told them to vacate immediately as the church had just been sold.[22]

It was then that the eminent Adolph Sanger, who had befriended Browne as a result of the Reich case, gave him the hard facts as he saw them. As a member of the Jewish elite who constantly interfaced with politicians, Sanger was in a position to know wherefrom he spoke. He declared that the misplacement of architectural plans and other misfortunes thwarting Mount Sinai's search for a home were not accidental, and were due to continue as long as the rabbi remained in New York. As Sanger later wrote referring to Browne, "with all his pluck . . . [he is] only one man without money or backing, whereas his enemies are legion and omnipotent."

Browne took his advice and tendered his resignation, but not before finding a temporary home for his congregation, a church suitable for renovation at 149 East 72nd Street.[23]

Leaving New York

On January 18, 1889, at the close of Browne's final Friday evening service at Mount Sinai Temple, the congregation's president announced that, despite the rabbi having forbidden the planning of any public demonstration, "the delegates of ten thousand Hebrews, working men from down town, are here to express their sentiments. . . ."

At that point, a delegation from the Hebrew American Republican League entered the sanctuary, led by the chairman of its Presentation Committee, Bernard Wolff. Wolff opened a scroll of resolutions which he read to the assembly. One item announced the committee's intention to publish a commemorative book for Browne, for which purpose a professional stenographer had been brought to record the proceedings.[24]

Then Alexander S. Rosenthal, having become president of the League after associating with Browne on the Reich case, came forward to announce that the League had elected Browne Honorary President and Chaplain-in-Chief for life, a tribute for doing "what no other Hebrew has ever done in this country before . . . [that he saved] the honor of Judaism . . . and our proud tradition that no Hebrew has ever been executed in the state of New York." He said that he had seen Browne regularly on the lower East Side, "in the humble Courts . . . where the poor and needy seek redress or protection. . . ." but rarely find anyone to help them.[25]

Rosenthal mentioned the canard that Browne's opponents had published accusing him of perjury, even spreading rumors that he was Reich's nephew and embezzled a fortune collected for Reich's defense. (In reality, Browne had received only fifty dollars from Jacob Schiff, which he returned.) The attorney then reported that Reich's son David, who had come from California to support his father, had "hardly rested himself" from his journey before being accosted on the street by the president of Browne's former congregation and Moritz Ellinger, the former coroner and recruiter of Russian Jews. Rosenthal, revealed that Ellinger tried to make David Reich sign a petition for Browne's arrest on charges of having misappropriated the defense fund, and threatened him when he refused to sign.[26]

In conclusion, Rosenthal noted that he had published affidavits from Reich and others in order to prove that attempts were made to prevent witnesses from testifying at the commutation hearing, and forcing them to swear "to the contrary of what is the truth, in order to defeat Dr. Browne, even at the sacrifice of a human life."

Then, on behalf of the League and twenty-three other Jewish organizations, Rosenthal presented Browne with a gold medal inscribed, "To Rev. Dr. Browne for saving the life of Adolph Reich, Chol Yisrael arevim zeh l'zeh" (All Jews are responsible for each other) in Hebrew characters. He also handed the rabbi a check partially reimbursing him for his expenses in defending Reich. Browne gratefully accepted the medal, but refused the check.[27]

A succession of others rose to praise Browne, among them Reverend J. G. B. Heath, minister of the Protestant Episcopal Church and Chaplain of the Tombs prison where Reich had been held. Heath said that he, too, had been convinced of Reich's innocence. After explaining his reasons and emphasizing the culpability of those whom Browne had so identified, Heath reminded his audience that the rabbi, in his unwavering pursuit of justice, was not a lawyer working for a large fee, nor a politician seeking office, money and fame, but "a quiet, modest preacher . . . a diligent, ambitious student of science, literature, history, theology and reform."[28]

The final tribute came from Reich's son, who on behalf of his family presented Browne with a gold-headed cane inscribed for the occasion. Apologizing for having unwittingly participated in the campaign against Browne, David Reich asked him to accept the gift as a token of gratitude not only for saving his father's life, but even more importantly, "for saving his honor, which is much dearer to him yet."[29]

In acknowledging the tribute, Browne revealed his anguish over what had transpired. "I lost my temple, acquired by six years of hard work," he said, "I lost my name, gained after twenty-three years of an intrepid public life, my wife almost crazed by the false reports in the press, anonymous letters, etc., my children often almost ashamed to acknowledge me as their father. Today I am repaid by you for those two years of agony."[30]

Browne asked that publication of the commemorative book be postponed lest it interfere with his continuing efforts to free Reich. Although the publication was never completed, the book's galley largely survived, providing a record of Browne's experiences in New York as seen by others as well as his own colorful narrative and opinions which he had written almost immediately after the incidents had occurred. He also related much about his difficulties in Atlanta and with Wise.[31]

In his introduction to the commemorative book, Chairman Wolff wrote that, before he met Browne, he had been prejudiced against him by people who themselves did not know him personally and could not cite anything against him other than his defense of Reich. They praised his oratory but denounced him based solely on the word of Jewish notables. The "great men" of the city had driven Browne away, Wolff said; so that "The rich Jewish people and their rabbis will be happy," but not the poor immigrants whom he defended in court and treated for their illnesses, even bringing them medicines, all without charge. According to Wolff, Browne had cured hundreds of cases of epilepsy, and even discovered a new remedy for it. The fact that this was not publicized and up to that point unknown even by Browne's friends, contradicts the contentions that he sought notoriety for himself.[32]

While it was surely true that Browne had highly placed enemies, he also had admiring friends in high places. Unfortunately, most had their own reasons for not attending the public demonstration. Sanger, in declining his invitation to speak at the farewell ceremony, made a candid admission which probably paralleled the true feelings of others who did not attend. He wrote:

Your second invitation to speak at Mount Sinai Temple is at hand, but I shall not be present. That I "more than anybody else" should raise my voice on that occasion I admit, but circumstances favor my silence. Prudence is not cowardice. Personally no one respects Dr. Browne more than I do. I have met him in "the ring" on the B'nai B'rith Statue of Religious Liberty ten years ago and he knocked me out completely. It hurt me at the time, but thinking over the matter calmly I reached the conclusion that he was right and although all the members of the Statue Committee are his bitter enemies to this day, I am, and ever since have been, his true friend. Dr. Browne will confirm my statement. Dr. Browne is not the man to be liked by people who believe in policy and we may say of him: "Every man has his fault, and honesty is his."
My position constrains me to use policy, and yet, if I could speak as I would like to, my going to Albany as Reich's witness, which meant "Browne's Witness" might convince you I did not act like a man of policy in this case.

As counsel in the case on appeal, I suggested the grounds which Dr. Browne argued before the Governor, but Kinsley and his supporters, Rev. Dr. [Aaron] Wise, Mr. Julius Schwartz, etc., overruled me simply because it would have given Dr. Browne satisfaction and prominence.

Again I beg you to excuse me. My laudation of Dr. Browne publicly would do him no good and might do me harm. Dr. Browne will understand and agree with me.[33]

Prominent Christian friends, understandably as reluctant as Sanger to involve themselves in "Jewish politics" by attending the reception, also praised Browne in writing. One of them was Col. Elliot F. Sheppard, William H. Vanderbilt's son-in-law, the newspaper editor known for having championed justice for African Americans. When invited to speak he sent a letter of regrets in which he made some telling observations about the Jewish community. He noted that the city's "six leading Rabbis and their congregations" had combined to oppose everything, "if ever so proper, if it originates with Browne," and then declared:

> *I knew the rabbi for several years and we meet often. I always found in him a model gentleman socially, a true friend of the people publicly, and what endears him to most perhaps, a sincere defender of the Sabbath and of religion. His refusal to ride during President Grant's funeral has done more for the Sabbath and for religion than thousands of sermons. The orthodox Jews of this city showed their appreciation by publicly honoring him and the reformed [sic] Jews showed their temper by denouncing him for that noble act. The Spanish Portuguese Hebrews, the highest type of American Jews, speak of Rabbi Browne very kindly. The foreign [i.e. German] Jews, who grew rich in this country persecute him, and his most ardent enemies are amongst the reformed Jews.*[34]

Among other notables who appreciated Browne and agreed with his views on Reich but feared to show it publicly, was Rev. Dr. Howard Crosby, head of the Christian Union and pastor of the 4th Avenue Presbyterian Church. He declined to speak at the testimonial, but wrote that he was honored by hearing Browne referred to as the Jewish Crosby. "Dr. Browne does more good than I," he said. "I am at the head of a powerful organization, and pastor of a great church to aid and support me, but the Rabbi has only his own energy and enthusiasm to rely upon."

Crosby quoted the esteemed Orthodox Chief Rabbi Abraham J. Ash, Maggid of Beth HaMidrash Hagodol, who told him that Browne was the best Jewish orator in town and "the only conservative who fights the reformers." He then commented on the source of animosity toward Browne:

I know Rabbi Browne intimately, and am sufficiently familiar

with Hebrew affairs to appreciate the difficulties of his task, with

appearances and the leading Hebrews against him. Rabbi Browne

has bitter enemies amongst his own people and particularly among the

reform element of the pulpit. Since the crucifixion of Christ, no man

has suffered at the hands of his own brethren for doing them good like

Mr. Browne these eight years in this city. . . . There is also a little bit

of jealousy in the case, . . . and I could well imagine how ordinary

ministers of wealthy congregations feel when such a brilliant rabbi of

a small Synagogue secures all public attentions they always had thrown

upon themselves. But far beyond that is Rabbi Browne's merit in broad

charity and unselfish philanthropy which he extends to Jew and Gentile

alike. . . . If Rabbi Browne meets with prejudice anywhere amongst

Christian people, it is due to the efforts of his Jewish brethren who make

it their business to slander him. They have tried hard to influence me

against him, but I know the man and love him for his virtues and his

merits. Rabbi Browne is the stoned prophet of our western Jerusalem,

and judging by the great size of the stones and the gigantic (social)

stature of those hurling them, the Rabbi must be a great and true prophet.[35]

Was Browne a stoned prophet? He was certainly one who spoke forth in the spirit of the Biblical prophets from the cutting edge of contemporary thought, and sometimes beyond it. As Reverend Crosby used the phrase "stoned prophet" in its Christian connotation, however, Browne did not qualify, for he was neither a messiah according to the Jewish definition nor was he entirely blameless as Jesus of Nazareth is believed to have been. He was a man with high regard for his own ability, remarkable capacity for perseverance, and very little patience with what he perceived as insincerity, duplicity or rudeness in others.

Although Browne resigned his pulpit for the sake of his congregation, he did not immediately leave New York. Still clinging to his faith in President-elect Harrison and Senator Quay despite their apparent disinclination to return his friendship, the rabbi asked for a diplomatic appointment to Turkey, a mission recently established by outgoing President Grover Cleveland and generally understood to be a Jewish post. On Inauguration Day, March 20, aware that he was probably destroying any chance of remaining employed in New York, Browne joined Harrison's Inaugural Parade at the head of a hundred members of his Hebrew American Republican League. Still Harrison and the Republican administration ignored him.[36]

Likewise unanswered were complaints from the League's officers to Senator Quay for reneging on promises to them. When local Republicans asked Browne to run for a suddenly vacated Congressional seat which he could easily win with their votes, League members displayed their resentment and refused to back him unless Quay fulfilled his commitment. Browne could not win without the League. He reported this to Harrison, emphasizing the obvious benefit to the Party of having another Republican in Congress. It did no good, and he declined to run.

Finally, in autumn 1889, Browne departed the city where he had given his utmost and found the greatest opportunity to pursue his interests as well as exercise his abilities and use his expansive energy to its fullest. He had accomplished much and lost much. Whether stoned prophet or publicity seeker, the question haunted him throughout his life and obscured his legacy. He had no difficulty getting other pulpits, but never again would find one so suitable for the work he most enjoyed as that "broken-down little obscure congregation" in New York.

RABBI BROWNE.
Champion of Religious Liberty
In our Public Schools.

H. BOGARDUS,
872 Broadway.

VIII - INTERMEZZO

As the final decade of the nineteenth century opened, America expanded its outlook in many directions. The addition of new railroads, western states, college football and long distance telephone service were among those providing positive reasons for exuberance. Beneath the fragrance of prosperity for many Americans, however, there lurked a fetid stench of corruption and exploitation for others. Anti-trust legislation was enacted to curb exploitation by big business, as the Pendleton Act had been meant to do when it established the Civil Service in 1883 to eliminate government patronage. Neither succeeded beyond the effectiveness of a fly swatter.

At forty-four years of age, Browne was past his prime by nineteenth century standards, and facing the downward slope of his career. New York had been his longest tenure and by far his most challenging. Despite disappointment in having to leave, he remained hopeful, still seeking some favorable gesture from the Harrison administration. Meanwhile, he accepted other pulpits and began to focus more on national and international issues, especially the increasing brutalization of Jews in Eastern Europe. In addition, he renewed his quest for the establishment of a permanent Jewish military chaplaincy. This longtime interest in the chaplaincy now intensified into an obsession.

Browne went first to Toledo, but was soon lured away from the comparatively provincial life there by being called to a prestigious congregation in Chicago. Although successful there and recognized with an honorary position in the forthcoming international Columbian Exposition, he remained in Chicago little more than a year, explaining his decision to leave as necessary for the health of his family. It had been a harsh winter in the Windy City.

In the beginning, Browne still clung to the illusion that Harrison might make good in some way on the Republican party's commitments to him and the volunteers that he recruited for the campaign, especially members of the Hebrew American Republican League. Having applied for the appointment to Turkey before leaving New York, he now recognized competition from Benjamin Peixotto, a prominent Jewish attorney, diplomat and lobbyist, who like himself had been active in helping Harrison win New York. Peixotto, however, unlike Browne, had campaigned openly, backed by local Jewish politicians and aided by long standing friendships with movers and shakers like the banker Jesse Seligman.

Browne reported to the president that Peixotto had offered to help him get another position if he withdrew his candidacy for Turkey, which he refused to do. The rabbi then went to Washington to discuss the matter with Harrison, and for the first time was denied access. Having been warmly welcomed at the White House on previous visits, he attributed this sudden change to the president having been prejudiced against him by some influential person—in his opinion, Seligman. (Considering the volume of his correspondence with Harrison it is more likely that White House officials simply tired of dealing with him.) He finally gained a few minutes in the oval office, but to no avail. Harrison appointed Solomon Hirsch of Oregon, a non-career diplomat who had not sought the position.[1]

What followed was a long series of letters from Browne to Harrison and to Harrison's personal secretary, Elijah W. Halford. Largely repetitious and increasingly inappropriate, they reveal the side of Browne's character that had consistently counteracted his virtues in efforts to achieve his goals.

In September, believing that his most recent letter to Harrison had not been delivered, Browne wrote candidly to Halford claiming to be no politician and asking not to be treated as one. "There is no need to ward me off by evasive answers and delays . . . ," he declared.[2]

In response to a reply from Halford on behalf of the president saying that Harrison could not attend to the rabbi's request [for minor patronage jobs] until he had conferred with the Secretary of State, Browne noted that the president did not need to consult with the Secretary of State to confer an office such as "Inspector of Boilers." He then launched an abject supplication to be treated "in a Christian spirit, for I am now homeless, made so through my services in the campaign. I ask the President for bread. . . . The President can feed my family with one of the crumbs that fall from the table of his great patronage. . . . Others who have done nothing for him are rewarded, and it is not meet to take the children's bread and to cast it to the dogs."

The exaggeration is bewildering, even in light of nineteenth century hyperbole and Browne's penchant for melodrama. He followed with a repetition of reasons for the president's obligation to him; he had been the only Republican rabbi in New York City, a campaign worker without pay, an organizer "virtually saving New York State [for the Republicans] and gaining victory with the Jewish clubs," editor of the only (Republican) Jewish daily, and responsible for the Jewish vote in Indiana, thus "saving Harrison's honor" by preventing his defeat in his home state. In conclusion, Browne asked to be informed if "for some freak of political perversion" unfathomable to himself, "the ethics of political gratitude to the undeserving forbid the reward due the deserving . . . so I do not waste my time and my hope, and quit working in vain."[3]

Two weeks later, having received no reply, Browne wrote to Halford again with an enclosure to the president, which he begged the secretary to deliver. He referenced the party's offer to run him for the unfinished term of the late Samuel S. Fox, Democratic congressman from New York, and the League's refusal to endorse him unless the administration made good on its campaign promises. In closing, he quoted Harrison's letter of November 27, 1888, stating that he would gladly consult "at the proper time [with you] and any of your friends . . . and will give them all the friendliest access to me. . . ." He also noted that he had already visited Washington three times for that purpose and that now the time had come "to grant me a speedy access and hearing."

Browne added that he had been told his letters were not delivered to the president, which might explain why White House officials treated him "like a tramp . . . [but] if I am to be ignored . . . kindly let me be so informed and I shall stop annoying you . . . no evasive answers are required. . . . I hold myself ready to visit Washington at your bidding."[4]

Still the White House did not reply.

In March, 1890, a full year after Harrison's inauguration, Browne once more reminded him of his promised "access" and "kindest hearing." He understood the president's inability to see him, he wrote, because "Of course you had to overcome great internal differences in the selection of men for the leading offices," and then suggested that since "those party wrangles" had by that time been settled, perhaps the president could deal with "smaller matters, concerning myself."

Unlike the Browne's previous requests, this one targeted a specific appointment: chaplain to Congress. He had heard that the administration's nominee, a Catholic priest from Ohio, would be rejected, and was confident of congressional approval for himself. Pointedly reminding the president that Jews knew about the help that he and Senator Mack had given the Republicans in the recent campaign and were generally unhappy with the party, he announced that after waiting eight months for an appointment to see Harrison, he had left the New York congregation [Sinai] that he served only "as a temporary occupation." He had accepted a call to Toledo, "a pulpit quite prominent though not very remunerative," he declared, only because his family needed a home, a temporary measure until, "after having settled the prominent vacancies, you would find time to remember and give if not a 'reward' at least a 'pension' to one who lost his usefulness in the fight for your success." Now after four months in Toledo, he was "anxiously awaiting the time" when he could have an interview.[5]

Returning to his point about Jewish dissatisfaction with the Republicans and how Isaac M. Wise was hurting the party through his newspapers, Browne cited an editorial that Wise had written "to show the Hebrews what they get from a Republican administration." In it Wise reminded readers that although former President Cleveland established the Turkish Mission as a Jewish Mission, "the present administration . . . has decided that no Hebrew need apply, and those that did apply have been snubbed." Apparently neither Wise nor Browne yet knew that Harrison had already appointed Hirsch, a Jew, to the Constantinople post.

Browne urged action "to disarm the enemies of the Republican Party in the Jewish press and do me justice . . . something not very remunerative as an office but satisfactory to me because of its life term. . . ." A chaplaincy in the army or navy would ensure Harrison his legacy with the Jews as the president who appointed the first Jewish chaplain "like President Cleveland who created the first Jewish Ambassador."[6]

The rabbi added that the appointment of a Jewish chaplain offered potential benefit to the armed forces by attracting young Jewish immigrants who had been forced to serve in the Russian military and were now eager to serve America. He noted that the Russian navy consisted largely of Jewish sailors who emigrated after escaping or being discharged, and estimated that in New York City alone there were thousands who would volunteer if a Jewish chaplaincy were established. Some of them had approached him in 1886 offering to enlist if their religious needs were met.

At that time, Browne wrote, he had responded by presenting a resolution to Senator John A. Logan of Illinois. Logan preferred to delay introducing it until1887 in order to help Republicans in the forthcoming campaign. More recently Browne had seen a published letter from General John M. Schofield to Senator Preston B. Plumb of Kansas highlighting the need to "improve the morals of the men by providing religious instruction for the army," and had forwarded his information to Schofield and Logan. He had enclosed a copy for the president in that letter to Halford.

Browne noted that three Jewish students were currently at West Point, and assured Harrison that a Jewish chaplaincy would attract to the service "the grandest sailors this country ever saw." He suggested that one Jewish chaplain in New York and another in San Francisco could travel wherever needed in respective sides of the country, and that the chaplain based in New York could serve Jewish cadets both at West Point and Annapolis by visiting each on appointed days. Adding that when previously asked to "see to the matter" he had ignored it because "no Jewish minister of some standing would accept a position with a salary of $1500," he explained that he now sought the job for himself because of his situation, "unfortunately damaged as I am by my political attempts."

In addition Browne noted that he could also teach subjects other than religion, and could get such a bill introduced in Congress with assurance of being passed. Since there was a vacancy "for which several hundreds of Christian ministers apply," he advised the president, "you might get out of the great opposition by appointing a Hebrew. . . . This should be satisfactory to me and restore the administration in the confidence of the Hebrews."

Finally concluding, Browne apologized for the length of his letter, declaring that it would be his last one on the subject, and repeating that he was only in Toledo as a sojourner:

(my home being still New York City legally). . . . Now all I crave is an answer which will tell me to give up all hope, in case it is so be determined, and I shall accept this congregation's offer to become their permanent Rabbi, a very undesirable charge. . .but I shall accept my degradation as a punishment for my meddling in politics before I studied the politicians' ways whereby a man not working with the machine, no matter how useful his work, cannot hope for a reward.[7]

Browne sent the same message to Halford, reminding him of past promises and enclosing the reply that he had received from his previous letter. He also noted that he doubted Halford had dictated it himself or was even aware of it, and did not believe that anyone had spoken to the president about it as stated.[8]

Halford evidently responded vaguely about an appointment with the president. Browne, having all but given up on the possibility of a government posting, replied that he expected to be in Washington on his way to New York for a meeting of the League, but saw no point in taking up the president's time to present his case, which "needs no arguing . . . [because] if the President wants to do something for me he can do it without my calling and if he has concluded to ignore my claims upon him then I would not [even] if I could, try to turn him in my favor by arguments and persuasion."[9]

Browne did not write to Harrison again until November 1891, and then in regard to his rough treatment by White House officials. Having been confirmed in his belief that Seligman was responsible for the sudden rejection, he informed the president:

I "carry no knives" about me and never strike a man in the back and shall not begin so with you. You have done me a great wrong, I claim. . . . If I had done for another man what I did for you in 1888, giving you three months without any remuneration and bringing success to your cause, then lost in your own state, I would receive not only one of the leading offices but would have been one of the most frequent guests at the White House.

You however have ignored all the appeals of the 23 New York Jewish mechanics who worked for you under my direction, and have treated me with contempt at the pleasure of Mr. Jesse Seligman.

Now then the time of reckoning will be soon at hand and I am marked to become one of a few decided men, formerly your friends, who resolved to prevent your nomination, and if they fail in that, your election.

I may not be in your eyes as big a man as Seligman but . . . I have a plan which will defeat you at the next convention and if not there at the polls in November. . . . I don't brag but come to give you due warning. I never heard your explanation why you failed to consult with me as you wrote me you would and to do what was agreed upon by yourself. For all I know Mr. Halford has never shown you my letters but disposed of them in a stereotyped, polite reply to me. I have never wronged any man and never passed judgement upon any man without a hearing. If you wish to see me for that purpose I shall come to see you in all silence and at a time specially appointed, between now and December 25th. The sooner the rather.

Failing to hear from you soon, I shall take for granted that you have

no time to devote to such silly letters like this and I shall accept it as a

challenge to your nomination in secret and your election publicly on the

stump.[10]

In conclusion Browne called attention to enclosures indicating that he was now a citizen of Chicago "and Chicago is a 'second New York' as to the Jews."[11]

Browne did not let go of the subject. On Thanksgiving Day after Harrison's defeat for a second term, he wrote:

Mr. President: A year ago today I apprised you of the combination

your best friends formed against your renomination and—failing

that—against your reelection. My prediction is fulfilled. You have been

ungrateful to the Hebrews who carried for you Indiana and New York,

not to speak of Senator Mack, myself and 23 other Jews who worked

for you without remuneration. The visitations of Providence have come

upon you in accordance with your merits. God is just! Compare your

entry in Washington with your exiting and learn how perfidy will change

a man's lot.

Yours for Truth and justice.

E.B.M. Browne.[12]

So ended Browne's correspondence with Benjamin Harrison. After five years and untold anguish, the rabbi finally faced his failure, a result of hubris mixed with blind trust in politicians whom he greatly admired, naiveté inexplicable in one otherwise so perceptive. His efforts and those of his recruits were not rewarded with patronage, a practise that continued openly and largely unabated despite the establishment of civil service in order to curtail it. Whether Seligman or others influenced Harrison against Browne as Browne believed is irrelevant. By his persistence and intemperate statements, the rabbi portrayed himself to the administration as a nuisance and a crackpot, thus dissipating his credibility and discouraging sympathy for his cause. He appears to have been unique among rabbis of his era in his method of pursuing political solutions to moral issues.

Meanwhile, the Browne family moved to 125 Michigan Street, Toledo, Ohio, only a few steps from the newly formed Shomer Emunim, known as the Toledo Hebrew Temple, at 132 Michigan Street. As Browne had told Harrison, he accepted the position on a temporary basis only, a point further indicated by the fact that he listed two addresses in the city directory, the second one being 348 LaSalle Avenue, Chicago. This may have been the office of his lecture booking agency.

Toledo was certainly no backwater, except in comparison to Chicago and New York. It boasted one of the largest Jewish communities in Ohio, as well as three congregations of which Shomer Emunim was the only Reform. Originally established in 1870 and disbanded a few years later, Shomer Emunim was reorganized in 1884. When Browne arrived in the fall of 1889, the congregation had just dedicated its first synagogue. The local newspaper noted that it had a membership of approximately 200, including "twenty-four of the wealthiest Hebrews in the city."[13]

Typical of most congregations, some members showed instant cordiality to the rabbi and his family, while others found fault. Senior citizen and longtime president Max Eppstein extended warm friendship to the Brownes, even taking responsibility for teenagers Lylah and Jesse only a few months after the family's arrival in Toledo, in January, 1890, when Sophie's father died suddenly requiring her and the rabbi to depart for Evansville on short notice. The following summer, less friendly members questioned the congregation's gift of partial support for a family trip to Europe that included work as well as a vacation for the rabbi. The ensuing controversy reportedly triggered a refusal of the newly elected president and vice president to join Browne on the bima during the High Holy Days. That they reconsidered and ultimately all went well was reportedly the result of a tongue-lashing by Eppstein, still a force in the congregation. Such incidents, apparently, are the stuff on which congregational memories often thrive.[14]

The Browne family spent that summer partly with grandmother Katje Braun in Hungary, and partly sightseeing elsewhere, including Vienna where they visited Fred Grant and his wife, Ida Honore Grant. The president's son, posted to Austria as United States Consul, had written to Browne the previous October, inviting the family to stay with him and Ida at the legation and mentioning, among other topics, an exchange of family photographs. He devoted the bulk of his letter to a glowing report on the situation of Jews in the Austro-Hungarian Empire, noting that they held influential positions in science, industry, journalism, and other fields, and were such an honor to the government that if he were the emperor, he would "make much of [his] title 'Koenig von Gerusalem,' [King of Jerusalem] for in my mind it is one of the most important of Franz Joseph's long list of titles." Browne's correspondence with leaders of European Jewry undoubtedly kept him informed, but his discussion of the situation with Fred Grant and later his visit to Grant in Vienna indicated a deepening concern and perhaps a premonition of future conflict.[15]

Browne's travels in Europe that summer probably involved work with one of the Jewish agencies trying to ameliorate the so-called "Jewish question" through a program of resettlement. Upon his return to Toledo a local reporter, believing that this was the case, asked him to comment on a recent newspaper article about it. He replied first that he had only just seen the piece, had not read it thoroughly, and would notify the reporter whenever he received any information about it. He then added, however, that he was somewhat familiar with the situation and was in a position to speak advisedly on the subject because he belonged to the organization mentioned in the article, presumably the Alliance Israelite Universelle. Explaining that the men named in the story were "of no influence," he told the reporter, "a good deal of this talk comes from the New York press. I know the press there. . . . They don't hesitate to put in anything whether it is true or not." Based upon his correspondence at that time with Zadok Kahn, chief rabbi of France, as well as previous correspondence with the Alliance, it is reasonable to assume that this was the organization to which he referred, and that his summer travels in Europe were partly in its behalf.[16]

The following year a Toledo reporter heard a rumor that Browne was moving to Chicago and asked him if this were true. Browne replied that he was thinking about it but had not decided. "Whilst our city is not a Chicago in size," he said, its beauty and the intelligence of its citizens are certainly equal to any city...Socially my people here belong to the elite of the city, and I do dearly love them all. I can say what hardly a Jewish minister in the United States can boast, there is not one amongst our members who is not dear to me; whilst with a number I am on most intimate terms. It is therefore not very easy for me to decide, and my congregation, I am very gratified to say, do not like to see me go.[17]

It was true that Browne had hesitated in accepting an offer from Chicago's Temple Emanuel in September, 1891. Understandably his family was reluctant to leave Toledo so soon after taking up residence there. They had made warm friends in the city and their two teenagers were happily settled in its high school. Nevertheless, when Emanuel offered to pay $3000 a year, an unusually large salary at that time for a rabbi outside of New York City, Browne accepted. He departed Toledo shortly after the High Holydays.

Sophie and the children remained in Toledo through the school year so that Lylah, a senior, could graduate with her classmates at the end of June. The decision was a good one. Lylah was elected class valedictorian, and her valedictory essay, entitled Shakespeare's Fools, was published in full in the Toledo Bee. Her rabbi father, meanwhile, commuted between the two cities as well as elsewhere to pursue his many interests, frequently to New York for meetings of the Hebrew American Republican League.[18]

Its brevity notwithstanding, the Brownes' stay in Toledo was apparently pleasant, both for the family and for the community. Browne had stated at the outset that he considered his tenure there a temporary measure born of necessity, so it was not entirely a surprise for the congregation that he decided to move on. Sophie and the children retained pleasant memories of the city, as he did, and friends remained to welcome him again for another brief stay in the future.

Temple Emanuel of Chicago, founded in 1880, was one of the last German congregations to begin in the Orthodox tradition. By the end of the eighties its one hundred members had embraced moderate Reform, using Wise's prayer book, Minhag America. They worshiped in their own synagogue, a former church at 280 Franklin Street (now North Franklin) on the west side of the street, just south of the Chicago River.[19]

Browne was the congregation's second rabbi. Three months after his arrival, the Chicago Herald reported that, when the "handful of members of Emanuel Congregation" called Browne to its pulpit with an increase in its normal salary due to his fame as an orator, it was thought that the financial commitment would be too great for the congregation to sustain. His popularity, however, according to the Chicago Herald, quickly "demonstrated the wisdom of those who brought him to the city...Emanuel Church has advanced under his influence until the present place of worship at 280 North Franklin Street is too small and a new church must be built."

In those days of religious revival, it was not unusual for non-Jews to contribute to the building of synagogues, or for Jews to assist in the building of churches. The Herald invited public participation in financing Emanuel's larger facility with the assurance that no collections would be taken at the rabbi's lectures, and the congregation subsequently built the addition on a lot adjoining its North Franklin site.[20]

From the time that Browne returned to the Midwest he was again sought by Christians for public lectures. His most popular ones were those on the Talmud in which he argued against the theories propounded by "The Great Agnostic," Robert Ingersoll. During the summer of 1891, while still in Toledo, he made an extended cross-country tour, spending twenty-three days in San Francisco alone. His lectures there included at least two for which he did not accept a fee, one of them at the Taylor Street Synagogue for the United Hebrew Charities and another at the Howard Street Methodist Episcopal Church to benefit "the Wornout Ministers of the California Conference."[21]

With customary hyperbole, the San Francisco Chronicle reported that the church ". . . was ringing with plaudits for two long hours." Although other newspapers as well as clergymen and the general public received Browne with equal enthusiasm, one prominent San Francisco rabbi, Jacob Voorsanger of Temple Emanuel, disagreed. Once a trusted friend, but then a participant in Browne's loss of his Atlanta newspaper, Voorsanger apparently bad-mouthed him to a local Methodist minister who reported it to Bishop John P. Newman, a known admirer of Browne. Newman informed Browne with the comment, "Dear Brother . . . I am constrained to believe that you are misrepresented, and at the bottom of the whole thing was Jewish hatred towards one whose liberality has excited jealousy."

While the bishop was probably accurate in his assessment, especially as it pertained to New York, it is also likely that the enmity of rabbis elsewhere could be attributed to causes other than jeaslousy. In the case of Voorsanger it probably involved their conflict over the Jewish South, presumably an early skirmish in the war between Browne and Wise which continued throughout the remainder of Wise's life and beyond. Arguably that contention affected Browne's relationship even with successful rabbis like Voorsanger, who aspired to leadership in Wise's Union of American Hebrew Congregations and his newly established Central Conference of American Rabbis.[22]

That summer Browne also lectured in Omaha and Lincoln, Nebraska, and in Minneapolis, where he spoke in one of the churches on "The Talmud–Its Ethics and Literary Beauties." With religious leaders still concerned over diminishing observance of the Sabbath, the Minneapolis Tribune in an admiring review recalled the rabbi's walk in President Grant's funeral procession to demonstrate respect for the Jewish Sabbath. The Tribune added that recently the Lord Mayor of London, Sir Henry Isaacs, also Jewish, after learning of Browne's example decided to walk rather than ride as scheduled in a Saturday procession.[23]

Both in Lincoln and in Minneapolis, Ingersoll's philosophy was a dominant interest. The Great Agnostic, asserting that Jesus never existed, attempted to justify his statement by pointing out that Tacitus and other early historians never mentioned him. Browne identified the fallacy in that logic by referencing James G. Blaine's memoir, **Twenty Years in Congress**, in which the author gave extensive coverage to the slavery issue without mentioning the celebrated abolitionist preacher Henry Ward Beecher. Does that negate the existence of Beecher? Browne countered. [24]

The Lincoln Nebraska State Journal concluded that, after hearing Browne, "it could be easily understood why the bold and eloquent Colonel Ingersoll is afraid to meet him." It devoted some thirteen column inches to a resume of the lecture, which even heavily expurgated, seemed prohibitively complex for a public audience composed largely of Christian laymen untutored in Talmud. The audience, crowding the auditorium, side rooms and stairs of the Lincoln YMCA, listened attentively to a history of the Mishnah [part of the Talmud] from its formulation "to the earliest days of Israel in the desert." Browne, with flowery metaphor, explained it as an accumulation:

a successive and natural growth of the tree of knowledge, the seed of which being planted with fingers divine on the heights of Sinai, sprouting into sunlight . . . under the eyes of Moses, matured into the tree of eternal life by the prayers of our priests and the admonitions of our prophets, moistened and fertilized into its gigantic proportions by the tears of our martyrs and the brains of our jurists; every succeeding generation added a new limb to the combined production of God and man. Thus, rooted in the lofty peak of Horeb, the divine seed of truth never ceased in its natural development, but assimilating the legal precedents laid down at its feet by our purest hearts and minds, according to their constructions of the Mosaic law in its bearing upon the disputes and questions at issue before them, we find it 1,500 years later perfected into a civil code, which, like a star upon the face of night, outshines the codes of Persia, Greece and Rome in its intrinsic merit of law and equity while in system and symmetry . . . having providentially steered clear of the imperfections besetting the Roman code, and possessing by far not so many contradictions and redundancies as the digest, even after Tribonian's vigorous pruning knife had been applied thereto in revision and cleansing; and that, in spite of the fact that the Mishna was for seventeen centuries as a 'lex non scripta' (an unwritten law), existing only in the memory of our people.[25]

Enough? It was barely the beginning. Browne continued outlining the Talmud in a division of four cardinal points, comparing each to a familiar parallel in Greek mythology. "The heavy points," declared his gushing reviewer, "are filled with powerful speaking and interjected with flashes of sacred humor that sends a ripple of smiles or a burst of laughter through the audience." Then, almost as a retraction, the reporter primly assured his readers that the "moral drawn from the humorous passage reasserts itself and the audience returns to the reverential behavior of pupils in the presence of their teacher."

The writer's praise reflected Browne's understanding of his audience, the general popularity of classic literature, and the teachings of Christianity. It especially noted the fact that Browne compared "the beauties of the gospel with the Talmud, and literary gems from the Rabbis with gems of Schiller and Goethe." These references were Browne's weapons in combating anti-Semitism, his tools for promoting ecumenism. Although he was not alone among the rabbis in the use of these techniques, he still had oratorical advantage over most of his American colleagues, who like him were foreign born but did not share his fluency in English. A few could challenge him, however, and there would soon be more. The earliest crop of native born rabbis to be trained in America had just completed their studies at the Hebrew Union College and taken positions in congregations across the country. Browne's approach to ecumenism through his knowledge of Christianity had gained him a reputation with Christians as a learned Jew who could relate to their point of view. This asset, however, came at the cost of offending many Jews who feared his unorthodox methods and pronouncements which they perceived as compromise and deliberate rejection of unpleasant truths. They had not yet attained the sense of security in a Christian environment that future generations would take for granted.[26]

Resuming his travels on the lecture circuit brought Browne into contact with more politicians, one of whom was John M. Thurston, an active Republican who was general solicitor for the Union Pacific Railroad in Omaha. Thurston wrote to the rabbi that he had wanted to meet him at his lecture in Omaha in order to hear his views on Republican issues, and offered to cooperate with him for the success of the party.[27]

The Nebraskan soon revealed the true purpose of his letter, which was to explain one of his remarks that was perceived as anti-Semitic, and obtain Browne's exoneration for it. Thurston claimed to have been misquoted when he referred to importers besieging the Ways and Means Committee in Washington to protest proposed tariff legislation. He admitted saying that:

almost without exception they were aliens to our civilization, representatives of the money changers of the old world, here for no other purpose than to put money in their purses, with scarcely an American name among them, and concluding I declared that they were the Shylocks of the business world, whose only solicitude on the tariff question was for the "haluf [sic] a dollar."

Thurston furthermore maintained that this was nothing "which would have been seized upon by any one of any nationality, except some person who was actively engaged in an effort to advance the cause of the Democratic party." He added that, although "a narrow-minded prejudiced man might seize upon these expressions and treat them as directed against the Jewish race," he trusted that Browne would understand them, and noted that the term "Shylock" was no longer limited to Jews as in Shakespeare, but "has become a term of general reproach as against the grasping avaricious money makers of the entire world."

Conceding that he may have been injudicious in using the term "haluf a dollar," Thurston observed that the leading actor in a prominent American play had coined the expression, so he "never dreamed that any intelligent American Jew would object to its use." In conclusion, the Nebraskan wrote that he counted "the leading Jews of this city" among his very best friends and informed Browne of the situation in order to relieve him "from any idea that I have causelessly or intentionally aimed any thrust at the race of people, unfortunate in the history of many ages, but illustrious in antiquity and respected in the United States at the present time."[28]

This was not Browne's first encounter with a well intentioned Christian who fancied himself free of anti-Semitism. His immediate response to Thurston is undocumented, but it is well substantiated that the two became lasting friends and that the future senator from Nebraska later aligned himself with Browne on more than one key political issue. Hopefully the rabbi set him straight on what is offensive to Jews.

Thurston wrote to Browne again in December, 1892, after Browne moved to Chicago, suggesting that, in view of the rabbi's influence with the Jewish rank and file, he should make himself available to the Illinois Republican League and the Republican National Committee in Illinois. Thurston then commiserated over the impending death of James G. Blaine, deploring the state of the nation and probably echoing Browne's own view in observing that "the dead level of mediocrity casts no tidal wave upon the shores of time. Statesmen now busy themselves with the price of calico and crockery, and the rights of men are relegated to the waste paper basket."[29]

This reference indicates the bond that drew the two men together. There is no evidence that Browne followed Thurston's suggestion to connect with the Republican establishment in Illinois, although he did stay in touch with political friends like Thurston. As the years pass it becomes increasingly apparent that the rabbi's primary interest lay in helping his fellow Jews, American and worldwide. He remained an activist, and although he worked on many projects as leader of his Hebrew American Republican League in New York, he did so essentially as a loner.

Browne's appearances during the winter after moving to Chicago included a highly acclaimed presentation to the Methodist Conference of Illinois, and his perennially popular talk on the Talmud which he delivered at the Chicago YMCA. Not surprisingly, the latter was reported as "one of the most scholarly and greatest efforts . . . brilliant and sparkling with wit, pathos, anecdotes and beautiful thoughts, marvelously dressed...the master effort of a master mind."[30]

By midsummer 1892, the Browne family was reunited in rented quarters at 517 Dearborn Avenue, on the Southeast corner of what is now North Dearborn Street and Grand Avenue, presumably a duplex, since the Chicago Blue Book listed another couple at the same address. The Brownes were also listed as having a summer residence at Long Branch, New Jersey, where President Grant had spent his summers. Their "receiving day" according to the directory was Tuesday evenings, although their formal calling cards state that the "Rev. Dr. and Mrs. Browne" were at home on Saturday evenings. [31]

This reflection of Gilded Age etiquette was illuminated by a note from Ida Honore Grant introducing the Brownes to her sister Bertha in Chicago.

Mrs. Grant informed her sister that the Brownes had settled in the city "to remain there for some time [and] their acquaintance will prove mutually agreeable." She enclosed the dainty card in one of her husband's letters to the rabbi, but apparently it was never delivered and possibly Sophie never even saw it. Perhaps Browne withheld it because he realized how unlikely it was that the introduction would lead to any social relationship. The well intentioned Ida had apparently not considered that the Brownes were unsuited—both financially and by virtue of being Jewish—for socializing with her sister. Bertha Honore Palmer was the wife of billionaire builder Potter Palmer and the glittering doyenne of Chicago's high society.[32]

While the Brownes did not attempt to engage the Palmers socially, they may have met in connection with Chicago's World Columbian Exposition. As president of the Board of Lady Managers, Bertha Palmer had approached Hannah G. Solomon about organizing a Jewish section for the women's exhibit at the fair. This led Solomon, along with Sadie American, to convene the Jewish Women's Congress out of which came the National Council of Jewish Women. The fact that Sophie belonged to NCJW from its earliest days did not necessarily indicate that she was involved at its inception, but her husband's honorary position at the fair as well as rabbi of one of Chicago's most prestigious congregations suggests that they may have attended related events and made passing acquaintance with the Palmers.[33]

Little is known about Browne's brief stay in Chicago other than the fact that he served as a vice president of the United States Government Educational Congress at the fair, an honor apparently not implying any memorable activity since he left no note describing participation. The rabbi was hardly settled in Chicago when, corresponding about the Jewish problem in Eastern Europe with his friend Zadok Kahn, Grand Rabbi of France, he inquired about moving to Paris. Kahn discouraged it, citing the city's high cost of living and the fact that Paris had no English or German speaking congregation for Browne to serve. Even though both Brownes spoke French fluently, it is unlikely that the rabbi would have been able to achieve the level of eloquence in that language that he had in English and thereby earn a living on the lecture platform. Meanwhile, he also applied for admittance to the Cook County Bar and took offices as an attorney-at-law in suite 1013-1016 of Chicago's Teutonic Building. By October, 1893, when he was admitted to its bar, he had already left the city.[34]

Browne explained his reason for departure as being necessary for his family's health. Sophie and the children needed to escape the "Chicago catarrh," he said. While it seems implausible to have given up a well-paying pulpit in the North for a struggling one in the deep South, a reading of conditions in Chicago the winter of 1892-93 provides a strong case for leaving. The weather was brutal. Temperatures sometimes registered twenty degrees below zero, blizzards caused residents to remain indoors and roofs to collapse, crime was rampant, and frequent failure of sanitation facilities made life in the city malodorous as well as dangerous and frigid. When Browne received an offer from Temple B'nai Israel of Columbus, Georgia, the warm Georgia sun trumped all other considerations. He later revealed a hidden purpose, however, an altruistic idea concerning the rescue of persecuted Jews from Eastern Europe that could conceivably become a financial bonanza for all.

Initially Browne accepted the Columbus position as part time only. Intending it merely as a winter refuge, a respite from the Windy City for half the year, he agreed to a salary of little more than half of what he earned at Emanuel. Soon, however, he relinquished the Chicago pulpit to settle full time in Columbus and held that position longer than any other in his career.[35]

Browne's few years in Toledo and Chicago were an interlude between two major tenures, the demands of which contrasted sharply with each other.

While politics remained important to him, he no longer engaged actively on the local level as in New York but focused increasingly on fighting anti-Semitism in America and relieving the terrible plight of Jews in Eastern Europe. It was a turning point also in the life of his family, with son and daughter entering adulthood and Sophie, as well as Browne himself, facing the challenges of middle age. Like an intermezzo in music, this was a period of change, a relatively light connector between two movements of much darker content.

IX - FAMILY, FOREIGN AFFAIRS, AND FRUSTRATION

Browne did not permit his separation from the centers of Jewish life to deflect his attention from Jewish issues, whether in the American political arena or in European based efforts to relieve Jewish suffering worldwide. He traveled in Europe and the Middle East as head of a commission of European rabbis investigating archaeological sites used for anti-Semitic propaganda, met with Ottoman Sultan Abdul Hamid in Constantinople and with Pope Leo XIII at the Vatican, worked with Chief Rabbi of France Zadok Kahn to settle persecuted Russian Jews in Florida, and pressed President William McKinley to establish a Jewish chaplaincy for the military, especially after America entered war with Spain. These were years of development for Browne's family, highlighted by Lylah's marriage and Sophie's public recognition as a speaker and organizer. Although she found some difficulty in adjusting to life in the deep South, Sophie prevailed and sank roots there for her family's future.

Columbus was nothing like Atlanta, where the Brownes had experienced southern living once before. Built on a bluff above the northernmost navigable point of the Chattahoochee River, the city grew from an Indian trading post to a shipping center for nearby cotton plantations, attracting Jewish settlers even before its incorporation in 1828. In the 1850s, mill owners from Massachusetts relocated textile factories there and it became an industrial center. During the Civil War the presence of an ironworks factory enabled Columbus to become a shipyard for the Confederate navy. Affluent residents built a magnificent entertainment facility, the Springer Opera House, which attracted the world's leading actors, orators and musicians as they traveled between engagements in New York and New Orleans, and where Browne lectured about Jesus' crucifixion in 1877.[1]

Seeking relief from a surge of anti-Semitism during the Civil War, some Jews moved to Columbus from the small Georgia towns of Talbotton and Thomasville. Among them were the Strauss brothers, former owners of a retail business on the main street of Talbotton. One remained in Columbus where he developed the prosperous Archer Hosiery factory. The other, Lazarus Strauss, continued on to New York where he bought Macy's Department Store and sired sons who became renowned in philanthropy and for their service to American government.[2]

Twenty Jewish families organized Temple B'nai Israel in 1854. Twelve years later the men established a B'nai B'rith lodge. By 1887 the congregation was sufficiently affluent to cease worshiping in a renovated house and construct the city's first synagogue, a stately neo-Gothic structure on the corner of Tenth Street and Fourth Avenue. In 1893, four years after the departure of their sixth rabbi, members invited Browne to become their seventh. The local newspaper had announced that he had taken a year's leave from his Chicago congregation because of sickness in his family, and that "if his family are benefitted" by their stay in Columbus he would then resign his position in Chicago and make Columbus his permanent home.[3]

Upon Browne's initial appearance in his new pulpit, January 5, 1894, the Columbus Enquirer announced that "the noted Chicago rabbi . . . delivered his first lecture to his new charge last night at the synagogue. Columbus warmly welcomes the distinguished rabbi and his family."[4]

It was a warm welcome indeed, but not without challenge. Unlike Atlanta, as Georgia's bustling state capital rebuilt after the war, Columbus remained untouched, its antebellum homes elegantly intact. It was Deep South, languid and laid back literally as well as figuratively, its houses and sidewalks set back from the dusty, largely unpaved residential avenues by wide plots of green lawn bisected by paved paths from walkway to street. For much of the year ladies usually endured the warm afternoons outside on their verandas rocking in their painted wicker chairs, fanning themselves, sipping lemonade, and chatting with passersby who stopped to greet them, often en route to shops on the main business street a few blocks away. Sophie expressed surprise to see them wearing sunbonnets on city streets.[5]

Nowhere did Sophie notice the regional difference more than in the operation of her Victorian style home on Twelfth Street. In Georgia, unlike New York and the Midwest, she found no steady stream of Jewish girls just off the boat from Europe seeking household employment. Here in Jim Crow country domestics were mostly illiterate former slaves or their children, vastly different from their northern counterparts in temperament, training and work habits. Although in Atlanta the family employed at least one African American, a man with some basic education, Sophie was unprepared to deal with helpers such as she found in Columbus, and she never became fully comfortable with them. Nor did she trust their cleanliness, as a consequence of which she did not leave the cooking to them as many Southern Jewish women did. She operated her kitchen in person even in advancing years, grinding meat herself, filling cheesecloth bags to make her cottage cheese, and hanging hens from the rafters of her back porch until the time came for her to pluck them.[6]

The rabbi's duties were routine, differing little from his previous ones. He conducted services as usual at 8:00 PM on Fridays and 10:00 AM on Saturdays, performed occasional weddings and funerals, and celebrated annual confirmations—his first class in Columbus consisting of eleven girls and seven boys. He was not required to train the boys for bar mitzvah, because the congregation, composed of German Jews committed to reforms, had already abandoned that ceremony in favor of the gender inclusive confirmation.[7]

A major problem for long tenures among rabbis soon manifested itself at B'nai Israel. No sooner had Browne agreed to serve the congregation full time for the pitiable annual sum of $1650 than the 1893 depression rendered it impossible to support even that amount. Nor could members meet the mortgage payments on their synagogue building. When the board notified Browne that it was necessary to terminate his position after the current term, he offered to remain for substantially less salary and to give a public lecture to raise money for the mortgage. B'nai Israel's Ladies Aid Society sponsored the event, reserving the Springer Opera House where the sale of 1,000 tickets at 50 cents each promised to bring significant budget relief. Unfortunately, sales did not meet expectations and the venue had to be changed to the more modest space of the temple's sanctuary.[8]

The ladies also raised funds by organizing bazaars and bake sales. At Sophie's suggestion they sponsored coffee parties in members' homes at 25 cents per person. These helped somewhat, but hardly enough to pay the mortgage. One of the women proposed that they seek assistance from the widow of the late French philanthropist Baron Maurice de Hirsch. Since none of them had ever met the baroness they laughed at her suggestion, but the intrepid member persisted nonetheless. She wrote to de Hirsch's widow asking for the money and offered to memorialize the baron within the synagogue in whatever way the baroness wished in return. The baroness responded with a generous bank draft of some 200 francs, enough to retire B'nai Israel's mortgage. Consequently, each year the congregation still recites kaddish, the mourners' prayer, for both the baron and his wife on the anniversaries of their deaths, and a plaque bearing their names is mounted on the memorial wall alongside the names of deceased members.[9]

Such congregational activities hardly sufficed to utilize fully the time and energy of an "Alphabet" Browne. Always interested in partisan politics, he maintained correspondence on the subject with friends, much of it with Fred Grant and Sen. John M. Thurston, Republican of Nebraska. Focusing on the next presidential campaign, Browne urged Grant to run for high office, which Grant declined, avowing that he was "contented to live the quiet life" and did not seek advancement. With Thurston, Browne discussed the 1896 election, agreeing that the Republicans should nominate William McKinley, and offering to oppose any attempt at reelecting Harrison because of the latter's "unprecedented abuse of the power of federal patronage."[10]

Harrison's denial of reward to Browne and his campaign volunteers in no way suggested reluctance on the part of that administration to distribute patronage. The minimum one quarter of federal jobs guaranteed by the Pendleton Act to be filled on merit left many thousand more places to be passed out by party machines to insure rubber stamp loyalty. One suspects that it was less anti-Semitism than Browne's fierce independence (and by association that of his recruits) that caused the administration to ignore him.[11]

Alex Rosenthal, the New York attorney who helped defend Reich and headed the Hebrew American Republican League, had been appointed United States Consul in Leghorn, Italy, by the previous administration. In April, 1895, he wrote Browne a long, newsy letter sprinkled with expressions in Hungarian, German, Italian and French, in which he glowingly described the city as the most perfect post in the entire consular service. Rosenthal noted that the city was home to "seven thousand Hebrews . . . some of whom are millionaires and play very important roles as bankers, lawyers, physicians, engineers, etc." Although still a staunch Republican, he acknowledged his gratitude to President Grover Cleveland, a Democrat, for giving him the job. Declaring that he was unhappy with the current administration, he expressed his wish for political office in a future one which he hoped would be Republican. He also mentioned, in regard to Browne's ongoing efforts to free Adolph Reich, that the Governor of New York State and the Mayor of New York City still held the rabbi in high regard.[12]

The remainder of Rosenthal's letter concerned a proposed visit by Browne scheduled for the following summer, at which time he planned to stop in Italy on his way to Jerusalem. The Georgia rabbi had been invited by chief rabbis of Europe to join them on a fact-finding mission to obtain evidence with which to counter a virulent new spate of anti-Semitism appearing in the European press. Journalists attributed their information to reports from archaeologists on expeditions in the Holy Land who purportedly discovered secret documents proving the culpability of Jews in the death of Jesus. Because of Browne's expertise in early Christianity, the rabbis asked him to head their delegation.

Anti-Semitism reasserted itself throughout Western Europe in the wake of the Dreyfus trial. In 1894, Captain Alfred Dreyfus, a French Jew, was accused of treason, convicted, and sentenced to life imprisonment. Ultimately proven innocent, it was only after years of incarceration on Devil's Island and outraged protests from such world figures as French author Emile Zola that Dreyfus gained his freedom, and even then at a terrible price for European Jewry. The publicity generated by the struggle for justice stoked embers of hatred even in countries where anti-Semitism had long lain dormant, supposedly expunged especially in liberal, fraternal, egalitarian France. In such an atmosphere manipulation of archaeological bulletins from the Holy Land threatened serious consequence and called for authoritative response. As Browne explained to the Chicago Times-Herald:

Antisemitism [sic] has been spreading in Europe for some time, and the
instigators of that spirit have utilized every means to slander our people
by perverting and misquoting Talmudic sources. Having exhausted that
measure they have spread the report that the Jews of Jerusalem had
secret archives concerning Jesus and his experience during the thirty three
years of his life, and have charged that the most abominable things are
contained in those archives. They claim to have possessed themselves
of those archives, and several books full of these 'traditions' have been
published, some of the trash having reached this country.

The Jews of Jerusalem and of Europe are tired of being slandered and
have resolved to let the world know what those traditions really consist of.
A well-known gentleman, whose name will be disclosed later, no doubt,
had offered to defray all expenses for such an inquiry. It is difficult to
foretell what the commission will find. There must be traditions in the
mouths of the Jewish people, and possibly documents, but what those
"secret archives" are I know not. The antisemitic [sic] press of Europe
has certainly never seen them.[13]

Browne planned to meet Moritz Kayserling, Chief Rabbi of Hungary, in Budapest, and travel with him to Jerusalem where they were to be joined by Rabbis Adolph Jellinek of Austria, Meyer Kaiserling of Hungary, Moses Ehrenreich of Italy and Zadok Kahn of France. Theirs were the leading Jewish voices in western and central Europe, men to whom traditional Jews turned for guidance in all matters concerning the spiritual aspect of their lives, personally and communally.

Unfortunately, Browne had to postpone his trip until the following year because Sophie again became ill. The nature of her problem is unknown, but it was serious enough to require her to spend much of the summer at Mount Sinai Hospital in New York and for Browne once again to cancel a planned mission abroad in order to remain at her side. It is not known if the other rabbis began their investigation that year or waited until Browne could join them a year later.[14]

The following summer Browne did travel to Europe and the Middle East. Noting that the trip was necessitated by "unfinished circumstance," he asked his congregation for an extended leave, promising to return by the end of July. Sophie, Lylah and Jesse accompanied him as far as Hungary to visit his family, then toured Germany, France and England while he proceeded on to Jerusalem for his mission with the other rabbis. On the way, he stopped in Constantinople to obtain an order from Sultan Abdul Hamid requiring all military and civil officials of the Ottoman Empire to extend him courtesy and protection. This enabled the delegation of rabbis to be escorted by a cadre of twenty-five Ottoman soldiers for thirty-three days as they crossed the desert following "the march of Moses and Israel." In and around Jerusalem they visited the holy sites, and in Aleppo toured the fortress of David.

Browne returned via Athens, then part of the Ottoman Empire. While there, he wrote to Rosenthal commenting on the headlines in European newspapers emphasizing the government's anti-Christian aggression in Armenia. He believed that the European powers, watching as the sultan approached bankruptcy and greedily awaiting his downfall, purposely exacerbated cultural and religious differences between his Muslim forces and Armenia's predominantly Christian constituencies in order to motivate violence. He said that his sources were "the highest authorities among impartial and unprejudiced Jews, Christians and Armenians." Contrary to international opinion, he defended the sultan's position and accused former British prime minister William E. Gladstone of inflaming the situation with "bloody shirt" oratory, saying that Gladstone would not have championed such a view "had he heard the truth as I did."

In explaining his point of view, Browne noted that he had observed such techniques when he lived in the South during Reconstruction, and equated the Armenian situation to "Southern outrages after the war, when so many innocent Negroes were so frequently killed. . . ." He contended that in America most instances were provoked by carpetbaggers who came south as "friends of the colored man," incited the former slaves to commit acts of violence, and "when the Southerners in veritable defense, killed one of their assailants," thereby setting in motion the Southern "outrage mill and the 'bloody shirt' orator did his work for political purposes." In Browne's opinion European governments similarly provoked Armenian Christians to strike Turkish Muslims, and then cried "outrage" when the Turks retaliated.

Contrary to strong opinion in the United States, especially among religious Christians, he proposed that:

> . . . *if the European monarchs decide on dividing Turkey among themselves, they might act like upright men and notify the Sultan to move over to Asia. But let them not provoke disturbances and sacrifice the poor Armenian Christians in order to have Mr. Gladstone's "bloody shirt" oratory call England to arms. At all events, we Americans, who know what the "bloody shirt" was, should keep our peace and not join Europe in that ignoble policy.*[15]

Much of the letter was published in the New York Herald. Through its Commercial Cable Company it also dispatched the following views on Crete to Europe and America:

> *We have the words of no less an authority than Rabbi Browne, who left*
> *here some months ago on a mission to Jerusalem, to the effect that the*
> *troubles in Armenia were started by European Christians, who instigated*
> *the Armenians against the Mohammedans, thus enabling Europe to*
> *raise the cry of Armenian outrages and inspiring Mr. Gladstone to his*
> *"bloody shirt" oratory and calling England to arms— the Cross against*
> *the Crescent. The same thing has been tried in Crete and has failed.*[16]

Here as elsewhere Browne's views differed widely from accepted opinion. They were undoubtedly influenced by his contacts with Turkish Jews, deeply grateful to the government for having welcomed their ancestors after their expulsion from Spain in 1492, and appreciative of the status quo as were other protected minorities enjoying satisfactory conditions. It is likely that he met and spoke with Armenians when he and the other rabbis visited the fortress of David in Aleppo. The infamous genocidal slaughter known as the Armenian Massacre had not yet occurred.. (This took place in 1915, when Europe was embroiled in the first World War.) Persecution of Armenians by government edict, however, had been worsening for decades, occasionally erupting into violence, and the bloodiest incident of that era occurred the summer that Browne was there. Although true to some extent, his comparison of the Armenians to former slaves in the American South during Reconstruction indicated a myopic view of the Armenian Turkish conflict. Similar incitements did occur, but were incidental to the long brewing complex relationship that ultimately led to brutal genocide.[17]

It is unlikely that Browne was totally ignorant of that backdrop. The question arises, therefore, as to why he took a stand against the preponderance of world opinion condemning Abdul Hamid for his treatment of the Armenians. Browne must have known that the publicity would do him no good personally and might turn Christian friends against him due to their missionary-inspired bonds with Armenia. The only plausible answer seems to be that he wanted to propitiate the sultan for the sake of Jews within the Ottoman Empire. They, too, like the Armenian Christians, were infidels in the Muslim world, living there safely and comfortably only at the pleasure of the sovereign. Should they lose his protection they would be as much at risk of persecution as any other infidel community. Browne's contacts with Jews throughout his travels in the Ottoman Empire that summer may have alerted him to a potential shift in the winds of Jewish security.

Sultan Abdul Hamid expressed his appreciation for the rabbi's support with an invitation to visit his court, known as the Sublime Porte. The Ottoman ambassador to Italy delivered the invitation in Rome, where Browne had been invited for an audience with Pope Leo XIII. His Holiness, long admired as an intellectual and a modernist, received the rabbi in his private quarters and engaged him for over an hour in a discussion of "Catholicism, Judaism and Americanism." The pontiff's concern for education, social justice, ecumenism, labor rights, early acceptance of Darwin's theory, and especially his actions reversing the excommunication of Father Edward McGlynn (for supporting Henry George) presumably fed a stimulating conversation. Browne subsequently shared the essence of that dialogue with American audiences via public lectures which he stipulated were "for charitable purposes only."[18]

His experience that summer alerted Browne to the machinations of the European powers, provided further insights to the situation plus confidence in assessing it, and intensified his determination to rescue Jews from Czarist tyranny. To that end, immediately upon his return to America, he enlisted his friend Senator John Thurston of Nebraska to help him obtain a government position abroad. Thurston recommended Browne to President McKinley with the observation that, among other qualifications, the rabbi "stands high in the estimation of the people where he has lived, and . . . is splendidly equipped for successful service, especially in the diplomatic line." The senator added that he was sure the appointment "would be a strong one, and would do much to ensure the continued allegiance of an important element in the Republican Party. . . ."[19]

Browne apparently never received the offer, but he persisted in efforts to relieve the suffering of his co-religionists, details of which are discussed in the following chapter. Meanwhile, America's war with Spain had preempted his attention. In 1898, as the United States geared for battle, he approached President William McKinley, as he had done with Harrison, to present his case for a Jewish chaplaincy from the standpoint of its recruitment advantage.[20]

American Jews, especially newcomers from Russia, welcomed the opportunity to prove their patriotism. Even before the nation formally entered hostilities, Jews in Baltimore, New York, Chicago and San Francisco organized their own military companies and trained for service. Jewish farmers in Woodbine, New Jersey, volunteered "almost to a man." Some 250 others from New York's East Side applied for enlistment. The carpentry class of New York's Baron de Hirsch Trade School offered a company of 70 Jews who had been Hussars in the Russian army. Some of their enthusiasm was thought to be vaguely attributable to a desire for avenging their forebears' expulsion from Spain in 1492. [21]

Reporting in the (London) Jewish Chronicle, I. M. Wise noted that Ohio Jews had initiated or spearheaded an exclusively Jewish nationwide effort to present the government with a warship. Symbolically identifying himself as one of "our Russian Jewish brethren in the United States," he applauded that magnificent effort with a poignant expression of the fervent patriotism felt by all Jews and especially those most recently arrived in America:

> *We . . . can appreciate the privilege which the citizenship of the country*
> *of our adoption confers upon us more than any other class of citizens.*
> *Coming as we do from a land where the holiest rights of mankind . . .*
> *are trampled upon, we feel most keenly the liberty which we enjoy under*
> *the glorious stars and stripes.*

Wise evidently spoke as representative of all American Jews as he continued the dispatch with these words:

> *Most of us have come since 1882 when the change in the policy of the*
> *Russian Government deprived us of even the meager privileges which*
> *we still enjoyed. . . . We have left the country of our birth because we*
> *hate tyranny; we have come over to these shores because we love freedom.*
> *Let us give a lasting testimony of these sentiments at this period of a*
> *momentous struggle between tyranny and freedom.*

> *Organize in all the cities of the Union . . . that we shall be able to*
> *present to the United States Government a war-ship [sic] which,*
> *flying the flag of freedom, shall be a lasting testimonial to this country,*
> *showing how her adopted children value the high privilege of living under*
> *the protection of the stars and stripes.*[22]

According to the dispatch, the project for American Jews to finance a warship for the U.S. government began in Ohio and soon spread across the country with its appeal most telling among the recent immigrants from Russia. Because of the horrific conditions they had suffered there, these newcomers were even more eager than earlier arrivals to display their gratitude to America. For that purpose in May, 1898, they organized The American Patriotic League of Russian Jews.[23]

Since Wise had been an American since mid-century and had never suffered Czarist persecution, attributing the statement to him appears at first to be in error. It could be considered valid, however, in the opinion of this writer because it reflects his need and that of his Reform constituents to be seen along with the large numbers of Russian Jews in their display of patriotism. For the vast majority it was a first experience of their nation at war, and while Wise strongly objected to the formation of a Jewish regiment he lost no opportunity to publicize individual acts of patriotism by Jews. One notable example was the announcement by some of Cincinnati's business owners that they intended to continue the salaries of any employees who signed up for military service. An estimated 4,000 American Jews served in the Spanish American War.[24]

Women as well as men hastened to prove their patriotism. On August 1, 1898, only weeks after the United States entered the war, the New York Section of the National Council of Jewish Women, among others, offered its services as auxiliaries to the Red Cross.

In Columbus, the 4th Congressional District of Georgia asked Sophie Browne to head the women's auxiliary of the Army and Navy League for Muscogee County. In that capacity she organized local women to serve the fighting men and their families. It was their duty to solicit contributions, distribute alms to the needy, and generally to promote "the comfort and health" of the Georgia State Volunteers in the regimental hospitals before the men went to the front.[25]

Browne, while insisting that he no longer sought the post for himself, recognized that there was no national organization to meet the spiritual needs of the Jewish servicemen away from home, and continued his campaign for a Jewish chaplaincy by repeatedly applying for such an appointment "in case no younger rabbi should seek the place." This drew sarcasm from some elements of the Jewish press, most notably from Wise, who during the Civil War had led a movement to amend the provision limiting the chaplaincy to Christians. Now in a long, vitriolic editorial, he belittled Browne for urging the appointment of a Jewish chaplain to serve in the current war. Only a month later he led the CCAR in a resolution asking President McKinley to appoint one, however, agreeing with Browne's objective while opposing Browne. Atlanta's Jewish Sentiment and Echo duly noted the hypocrisy.[26]

Continuing his campaign, Browne directed an appeal to the Secretary of War, and upon being rebuffed, appealed to the commission charged with investigating the conduct of the War Department. He was told that the probable reason for denial was that he had failed to mention a Jewish regiment to which a Jewish chaplain might be assigned. He then applied to the Navy for an appointment and was told that there was no vacancy in its chaplain corps, nor would one appear until June, 1901, unless the prescribed limit were changed by an act of Congress.

Browne then approached Admiral George Dewey and was again rejected, this time with a puzzling non-sequitur in which Dewey stated that he did not remember anyone of the Jewish faith associated with him in the Civil War. "But," the admiral added, "there were a number of Jews in the squadron under my command during the late war with Spain, and they, in common with the men of all other creeds in that squadron, performed their duty in the best possible manner."[27]

Browne finally gained honorary recognition as a defender of his country when Governor Allen D. Candler of Georgia, in 1899, appointed him to serve with the rank of colonel on the military staff for the State of Georgia.[28]

Browne did not hesitate to criticize President McKinley for his reluctance to appoint a Jewish chaplain. In one sermon he predicted that McKinley's failure to provide religious guidance for the many Jewish volunteers in the war with Spain would cause Republicans to lose the Jewish vote in the next election. He blamed McKinley's Jewish advisor, Cincinnati businessman and communal leader Bernhard Bettman, for having misinformed the President when he allegedly told him that Wise controlled the Jewish vote. The "so-called leading Jews," Browne insisted, no longer spoke for the masses. "The new Russian citizens who are faithful to their sacred religion," he declared, did not take orders from the radical reform leaders as to whom they should elect. Then, still the staunch Republican, he expressed regret that the President— "my dear friend"—might lose the Jewish vote in the next election. The Atlanta Journal published that sermon on its front page over a portrait of Browne captioned in 14-point type proclaiming "Rabbi Browne, of Columbus, Ga., Republican, Denounces McKinley."[29]

In the following months, Browne continued to criticize the president for refusing to establish a Jewish chaplaincy, repeating his offer to serve if no better applicant was found. His attack elicited publicity on the political aspect of his pronouncements, which he hastened to deny. "This is a family quarrel between McKinley and myself," he wrote to the editor of the Columbus Enquirer-Sun as the campaign for the president's reelection began. "I have a theological difference with the president . . . " he noted, repeating his willingness to serve as chaplain "provided no other rabbi younger than myself" could be found. He noted that Wise had ignored the resolution of the Central Conference of American Rabbis the previous year asking the president to appoint two Jewish chaplains, and since Wise's death on March 26, 1900, effectively buried the resolution, that left Browne to struggle alone in the quest for a Jewish chaplaincy. "This led the press and public to believe I shall fight Mr. McKinley 'on the stump,'" he continued:

> *But my issue with the president is not political, as stated. I feel, as a*
> *Jew, that my people as Jews were insulted and this is the only cause I*
> *am defending, as will most likely every true Jew in the land who has not*
> *been "influenced."*

> *As to my having given out that I would stump for Mr. Bryan, and that I*
> *"issued a manifesto" to my "following" it is very amusing. I am a "has*
> *been" as they say, a "back number," lost in this quiet city from public*
> *view, from public activity these seven years. But I am not a back number*
> *when my religion is assaulted and may have something to say on that*
> *subject, most likely after the election rather than before.*

The rabbi concluded his letter to the editor with a hint of his humor so
fondly remembered by his family:

> *A friend asked me what territory I would stump, and whether the*
> *laboring classes like in New York in the South are my following. I*
> *answered that I would stump the District of Columbia, and was*
> *positive every vote in the district will follow my direction.*

> *The gentleman seems not to have grasped the joke. . . .* [30]

So disenchanted did Browne become with McKinley that he flirted with
the idea of changing parties and working to elect the Democrat William
Jennings Bryan. Although he gave Bryan some assistance indirectly through
friends in New York, in the end he remained a loyal Republican and

apologized to McKinley "for having troubled you about Jewish chaplains, having ascertained that several of our 'Jewish (?) Politicians,' personal enemies of mine, have induced you to listen to them." He admitted to having scheduled a three weeks speaking tour with Bryan, but concluded that it would be foolish to leave his party and wrong "to work against you who are simply the innocent tool of a few Jewish Bankers of the Panama Canal Syndicate [i.e., Seligman], and other Jewish politicians. . . ." Acknowledging that the President had acted in good faith, Browne said that he would hold the politicians to whom he alluded responsible "for the wrong done to our Jewish soldiers."[31]

Browne's championship of a Jewish chaplaincy for the American military now began to show signs of becoming an obsession. In retrospect we may see seeds of it sown in 1871 when he applied for a chaplaincy at West Point. At that time he had written to President Grant that he sought the position because "no Jewish minister has yet been given a single office while the Christian clergy is very well represented . . .," a statement that begged questioning in view of his bright promise as a rabbi and his newly-earned law degree. Two decades later, hindsight may suggest that he had been motivated by determination to test America's promise of equality for Jews at every point where he detected an absence of it. In the intervening years he had seen many other manifestations of inequality, often more obvious and more damaging than that of the military. His return to the subject when Harrison became President had not been without self-seeking overtones, for he really had needed a job, but it was also driven by concern for young Russian Jewish immigrants seeking employment, which in the military, as an additional benefit, would project an image of Jews as both brave and patriotic. In 1898 with America at war and anti-immigration sentiment rapidly rising, this motive became more significant.

Meanwhile, family events required Browne's attention at home. On November 16, 1897, daughter Lylah married David Simon Goldberg, an attractive bachelor from Macon, Georgia, who worked in the Columbus general store of his brother-in-law, Max Simons, and later opened his own business selling toys and furniture. The wedding attracted much notice, not only because of the Brownes' position but also because it featured a double ceremony. The Goldbergs shared festivities with the groom's sister, Yetta Goldberg, and her fiance, Ben Gerson.

The festivities reflected the moderate affluence of the Jewish community as well as the customs of the time and place. On the evening before their wedding, the couples were honored at a dinner dance, specified as a "german, [sic]" a popular entertainment featuring the style and music of middle Europe played by Mike Rose's Italian Band. It was held at the city's Jewish social club, the Harmony Circle, with the honorees, their attendants, chaperones and visiting friends—some thirty-nine in all—celebrating "until a late hour."[32]

The double ceremonies took place at the Rankin House Hotel, with Browne officiating. The first, uniting Yetta and Ben, began at 12:30, followed at one o'clock by the marriage of Lylah and Dave. Each couple was attended by four bridesmaids and four ushers. The brides carried bouquets of sweetheart roses and carnations, and neither bride wore a traditional wedding gown. Lylah, who appeared in bright green velvet, was escorted down the aisle by her uncle, Aaron Weil.

There is no mention of non-Jews attending the ceremony as they had done in Evansville a generation before, which may have been due to budgetary considerations or possibly to the rise of social discrimination. Prejudice had already manifested itself in Georgia by the resignation of non-Jews from Atlanta's Concordia Club which then reorganized as the all-Jewish

Standard Club. In Columbus, the Harmony Club had developed in response to similar circumstance as did German Jewish clubs elsewhere.[33]

Following the ceremonies, the four newlyweds joined family and attendants at a private luncheon, then received friends—Christian as well as Jewish—at an afternoon reception, again with music by the Italian band. They departed for their respective honeymoons on the afternoon train north, Lylah and Dave heading to Baltimore. When they returned, they lived at the Rankin House Hotel, and Dave, a caring and dutiful son-in-law, became active in synagogue affairs.[34]

As the century came to a close, Browne planned another literary project, a history of American Judaism. He published a description of it in Souvenir, an eight-page paper distributed by Atlanta's Universalist Church, to promote lectures that he was scheduled to give there to benefit its building fund. Such interchange between Protestant and Jewish clergy, triggered by the interreligious assemblies at Chicago's Columbian Exposition, had been developed initially by the more liberal denominations such as Unitarian and Universalist. In Atlanta, it led directly—within the year—to Rabbi David Marx's establishment of the Unity Club, one of the nation's first ministerial associations promoting Jewish-Christian solidarity.[35]

In the Universalist Souvenir, Browne described his forthcoming book as "a grand volume" of 825 pages, "profusely illustrated" with some 250 pictures of "Jewish public men in pulpit, press and politics; science, art, etc., but containing profiles of many Christians also." These included Georgia Governor Allen D. Candler with his three Jewish staff colonels, one of whom was Browne. His captions for the three sections of the book indicated his awareness of the impact being made by America's most recent Jewish immigrants. They were "Portuguese Judaism—The Past; German Judaism—The Present; and Russian Judaism—The Future." Among the historical subjects to be covered were "Lincoln and Grant and the Jews," "Cleveland and the Jews," and "McKinley and the Jews."[36]

There is no indication that the volume ever went to press. The article, apparently written by Browne himself, declared that such a comprehensive study was needed among both Christians and Jews because of "the most nauseating stuff of fulsome flattery and distorted ideals . . . " in recently published articles, "making every great man a Jew and flattering Jews to disgust." This may have been a reference to Mark Twain's 1898 series "Concerning the Jews" in Harper's Magazine. The Universalist publication quoted Browne's longtime friend, Methodist Bishop John P. Newman, as having said that the rabbi was the only man qualified to write such a book, both because of his previous close relationship with Wise, and also because "no other man would dare write it" since many of those mentioned were still alive.[37]

Assuming that Browne authored the article, he displayed a surprising degree of candor by writing "Browne is the most unpopular man in American Judaism, we are told." He did not leave the comment there, however. The next paragraph states, "Unpopularity means independence, independence means self-reliance in character, courage and ability, and knowledge of what one is talking about, characteristics that call forth occasionally envy, jealousy and animosity." This reveals a bravado that suggests defensiveness, a response aimed at his detractors with a flourish of superiority reminiscent of that which probably fueled much of his difficulty in his former positions.[38]

The series of Browne's lectures advertised in the paper took place on three successive evenings, each featuring a different popular subject. They were "The Talmud, Its Ethics and Literary Beauties," "The Crucifixion and the Jews: or Did the Jews Actually Crucify Jesus of Nazareth?" and "The Jews and Temperance: or How the Chosen People Keep Sober and Straight." He began with his dissertation on the Talmud and followed on the second night with the Crucifixion, which drew a larger audience. On the third night by popular demand he repeated his Talmud lecture in lieu of the one that had been announced.[39]

In an extensive coverage of these events, the Atlanta Journal began by describing the difference in Browne's dress and demeanor on each of the first two evenings. For his lecture on the Talmud, he wore "faultless full dress swallow-tail coat and white necktie, on his face a pleasant smile, his diction full of flowers and humor, to help the audience enjoy the heavy chunks of learning wrapped up in aphorism and metaphor." By contrast, when he spoke about the crucifixion, he wore a Prince Albert and black cravat, his countenance on that occasion being "serious in the extreme," like that of a lawyer arguing "before the audience who were his jury, the indictment public opinion . . . has found against his people."[40]

Browne's version of the crucifixion, which the Atlanta journalist found extraordinary, began with a fictitious legal example set in 19th Century America, paralleled by a similar case under Roman rule in Judea. There, the rabbi explained, false messiahs constantly arose in attempts to liberate the people, and were crucified when this failed to occur. "The captive nation cried in bitterness for the Messiah that would save it," he said, noting that the nation was already torn in fragments, many of which Jesus had been able to reconcile.[40]

Much of his lecture as quoted in the paper echoed earlier versions, strikingly enhanced by subsequent experience. The reviewer found "especially attractive," the rabbi's reference to great masterpieces of art depicting the crucifixion that he had studied in his travels "from the Golden Gate in Jerusalem to the Golden Gate in San Francisco," all of them "intended to harm the Jews." The lecture, according to the critic, was a "splendid tribute to Christianity, no less than Judaism," that should be heard to be appreciated for "no synopsis can do it justice."

In closing, the article reported that Browne had been greeted by many old friends who had not seen him in the nearly twenty years since he went to New York. "He left here a young man of thirty. He comes back now a YOUNG man of fifty, but he has changed very little except in learning and eloquence, which seem to grow on him with years."[41]

That assessment was only skin deep. Actually, Browne had changed profoundly during those twenty years. Frustration and a measure of bitterness had set in, along with hints of paranoia and megalomania. Although he moved through the country and across the Atlantic as nimbly as if he were living in the jet age, his effectiveness was severely circumscribed by the fact that he was based in a city far from the centers of Jewish activity. Columbus, Georgia, was not New York or Chicago. He had no enthusiasm for his commitment as its rabbi.

Portraits of the family taken in 1896 and 1901 reveal marked changes in appearance during those six eventful years. This was less so with Browne than with the others, although he was certainly no longer the dapper young Napoleon of his 1869 portrait. At age fifty, he seemed to be of slightly stocky build and full face, with fashionably drooping mustache, shaven chin and hardly noticeable hairline recession. He stands beside his seated wife, his arm through hers, both of them facing straight ahead thoughtfully, she in billowing black taffeta and lace, and so somber an expression as to suggest sadness. Behind them stands Lylah, a serious but comely twenty-year-old in pince nez glasses and white shirtwaist, holding the hand of her handsome, eighteen-year-old brother Jesse, who stares blankly in the opposite direction from the others. With his lips slightly parted as if on the verge of speaking, his image begs the question of whether it signifies defiance or uncertainty. It could have been both. He was the adored only son of a man too brilliant and too complex to have been profitably emulated as a viable role model.[41]

The second portrait shows the family increased by the addition of Lylah's husband, Dave, and their new baby, Carolyn. Jesse, still somber but confidant, stands behind his mother who is seated proudly holding her infant granddaughter. Lylah, no longer wearing eye glasses, her dark hair softly upswept in Gibson Girl style, occupies center stage between her brother and her husband, who stands behind the seated rabbi. All seem happier and more relaxed than in their photograph of six years before. Except for Jesse, each appears to be suppressing a smile.[42]

Each of them, including Jesse, had reason to smile, for they were embarking on new phases of their lives. The recent past had been years of growth for the family, though hardly so for Browne himself. Whereas for Sophie and for Lylah especially the period had been one of opening and setting a course for the future, for Browne it was more like treading water, even floundering to find and grasp a rope that could anchor him to a cause. Lecturing, writing and providing spiritual leadership to a small Jewish community far away from the center of action was not enough to consume his abundant energy. Clinging to the fringes of political action was unsatisfactory and accomplished nothing. Even his extraordinary encounters with the Ottoman Sultan, with Pope Leo XIII, and traveling in the Holy Land did not yield the sense of satisfaction that less ephemeral incidents might have done. His passion for justice, now channeled into obsession for establishing a Jewish chaplaincy, and the urgent need to rescue Jews from Eastern Europe remained unfulfilled.

This might be considered a turning point, perhaps even the major one in his career. Before turning, however, this account must detail a hugely significant facet of the rabbi's life and the future of Jews everywhere that occurred in the interim between sittings for those two portraits.

X - ZION ON THE CHATTAHOOCHEE

Theodor Herzl, an assimilated Jewish journalist from Vienna, while in Paris reporting on the Dreyfus trial, conceived the idea of an autonomous Jewish state in the Holy Land as a solution to anti-Semitism. The dream of return to Zion (Jerusalem) was not new. Throughout the two millennia of Jewish exile, individual Jews had resettled there or arranged to be buried there when they died. During the current century philanthropists supported Jewish settlements in that desecrated, sparsely populated piece of the Ottoman Empire as an escape from persecution and poverty in Eastern Europe. What was new about Herzl's plan was its political ingredient. It was to be a national homeland for the Jewish people. To this end Herzl, with the help of the renowned Jewish writer Max Nordau, called Jews from all lands to a Zionist Congress to be held in August, 1897, in Basel, Switzerland.

Before Herzl's Congress, the known organizations fostering Jewish colonization in the United States had not yet been launched. The first of these, the Industrial Removal Act, began only in 1901 and was engaged not in bringing oppressed Jews out of Europe but in decentralizing the settlement of those who arrived in order to relieve the over-crowded, unsanitary tenements of the East Coast. The Galveston Plan (1907) was among several others that alleviated the problem somewhat but ultimately failed. American Jews were eager to help their unfortunate brothers and sisters leave Europe, but due to the growing anti-immigrant sentiment in America, most preferred to steer them to lands other than their own.[1]

As word of the impending Congress reached America, acculturated Reform Jews opposed it bitterly. Fiercely patriotic Americans, they feared the establishment of a political Jewish entity as an excuse for anti-Semites to accuse them of dual loyalty. Rabbis, Orthodox and Reform alike, rejected the movement for religious reasons as well because it contradicted the Jewish tradition that Israel could be resurrected only by the Messiah, who had not yet arrived. Many treated news of the Congress with derision. In the opinion of Isaac Mayer Wise, "The men at the head of that pseudo-congress, except perhaps Max Nordau, are harmless zealots, most of them standing with one foot in the sixteenth century."[2]

In his presidential address to the Central Conference of American Rabbis in July, 1897, Wise referred to Zionists as those "who revive among certain classes of people the political, national sentiment of olden times, and turn the mission of Israel from the province of religion and humanity to the narrow political and national field, where Judaism loses its universal and sanctified ground and historical significance."[3]

Some went so far as to call the Congress "a fata morgana, a momentary inebriation of morbid minds, and a prostitution of Israel's holy cause to a madman's dance of unsound politicians."[4]

Notable exceptions to this attitude among Reform rabbis were Bernard Felsenthal in Chicago and Gustav Gottheil, of Temple Emanu-El in New York. Both were old, approaching retirement, and further limited in their ability to participate by the fact that they served strongly anti-Zionist congregations. Felsenthal, who openly endorsed Herzl's plan from the beginning, refrained from attending the Congress only because his health did not permit him to travel. There is some question as to whether Gottheil attended. Richard Gottheil, his son and biographer, maintains that the rabbi did go, but earlier accounts of the latter's interest in Zionism do not mention this, while the younger Gottheil's attendance at subsequent Zionist congresses is well documented. Among the younger Reform rabbis, Max Heller of New Orleans had not yet embraced Zionism in 1897 but later stood virtually alone in supporting it.[5]

Browne, who upheld the traditional hope of return to Zion and had
been deeply engaged in finding safe haven elsewhere for Jews needing to
leave Europe, espoused Herzl's plan only shortly before the first Congress
convened and corresponded heavily with him for the next seven months.
Eager for an engaging challenge, he solicited Herzl for an active role while
offering him advice about attracting Americans to Zionism. Much of what
he wrote suggests a strong desire to leave Columbus, and his perception that
organizing Zionism in America offered a satisfying opportunity for doing
so. He undoubtedly detected a possibility to propel himself into mainstream
Jewish life again, reestablishing his influence as spokesman for a Jewish cause,
utilizing his abilities as orator, publicist and advocate for the needy. Most
importantly, the work would require him to be based in a city more central to
the pulse of America and American Jewry than his serenely dormant place
on the banks of the Chattahoochee.

Herzl sought support for his plan among influential Jews in western
Europe, his first priority being the establishment of a Jewish bank by which
to purchase land in Palestine from the near bankrupt Ottoman Empire.
Browne first heard of him during the summer of 1896, while visiting Zadok
Kahn in Paris on his return from Jerusalem. Herzl had called at Kahn's
home while the two rabbis were away, and left his card. Browne decided
not to pursue an introduction because, as he recalled, Kahn commented,
"C'et Herzl est un original" (that Herzl is a crank) "who wants to become
a messiah." In London, Arthur Cohen, a community leader and Member
of Parliament, told Browne that Herzl's Zionist idea was ridiculed there.
Furthermore, Browne learned that Zionism's chief proponent in Britain was
the sensational author Israel Zangwill, who was frowned upon by observant
Jews for having married a gentile and espoused assimilationist ideas, therefore
"not considered the fit person to represent a cause of Judaism, any more than

Herzl." Nevertheless, Browne conceded, "Herzl made headway against all expectation."[6]

At that time, Browne and Kahn were collaborating on an idea to settle Jewish immigrants in America according to a plan that Browne had long cherished. He later revealed that his motivation for moving to Columbus in 1893 was largely based on an idea for settling immigrants nearby after learning that the "great water power of the Chattahoochee" had been harnessed to run giant cotton mills. When a spokesman for Columbus' Eagle and Phenix Mills told him that hundreds of such mills could be operated along the river, he envisioned a Jewish farm settlement nearby supplying raw material for the mills. "I put myself in communication with the Jewish Colonization Association of London and the Baron Hirsch Fund at Paris," he recalled, and through Kahn, who was honorary president of the Hirsch Fund, which was an associate of the British group headed by Alfred Cohen, proposed his plan to those organizations. Perceiving that the two groups had millions of dollars to spend for the benefit of Russian and Rumanian Jews, he projected that ten million invested in farming cotton could produce enough to run the proposed mills, "and give employment to a hundred thousand hands." The idea, he understood, was "considered with great favor."[7]

Meanwhile, Florida real estate tycoon Henry B. Plant was developing land along the Gulf Coast near the mouth of the Chattahoochee. Browne went to Tampa in 1895 "for a conference with the Plant system," and obtained an offer of lands for settlement in Florida. "I look upon this work not as a matter of 'charity', but 'business,'" Browne declared. "The Hirsch millions invested here will pay a good dividend..."[8]

Having secured the sites and the funding, Browne engaged a Hungarian steamship line to transport the proposed settlers from the Italian port of Fiume to Savannah, Georgia, and arranged with the Southern Railroad for their transfer from there to the designated land in Florida. Although Baron de Hirsch died suddenly after agreeing to fund the venture, Kahn was able to make good on the promise of Hirsch money to build houses and factories for processing the raw materials and to provide the necessary agricultural tools and instruction.[9]

These plans never came to fruition. The reason—according to Browne—was that after he and Kahn had everything in place, "unexpectedly Dr. Herzl sprang his Zionism scheme and spoiled all our plans." A year later, Browne noted, "the Russian [and] Roumanian Jews who were anxious to come to America, with one great sigh exclaimed, 'on to Zion to the land of our fathers.' I had the land, the means, the railroads, the steamer line, but could not get the Russian Jews who preferred starvation in Zion rather than opulence in the US."[10]

Browne's version of what happened, even if accurate, could have had little impact on the flow of Jewish immigrants to America during those years. Nevertheless, his failure to lure them to Florida convinced him that "regardless of the rich-reform Jews who control the press and create public opinion, the Jews at large [i.e., the Jewish masses] are for Zionism." The fact that he wrote this years later in defense of Zionism suggests that it may have been influenced by subsequent development as well as by his tendency to dramatize. In 1897, prior to the first Zionist Congress, he had not yet embraced Herzl's brand of political Zionism. His priority was that of most westernized Jews: expediency, i.e., the immediate need for relief.

According to his recollection, Browne's initial connection with Herzl and political Zionism was through Berthold Frankel, former president of Browne's New York congregation. Frankel had joined a small group of Zionists in downtown New York, mostly Yiddish speaking immigrants from Eastern Europe. Their leader was Michael Singer, a Hungarian newcomer who published a Yiddish newspaper, Toleranz. Frankel's wife, who shared the popular opinion that Herzl and his friends were crazy anarchists, implored her husband to stop associating with the Zionists and cancel his plans to attend the Congress. Frankel did as she wished, and asked Browne to take his place at the Congress.[11]

Before agreeing to Frankel's request, Browne wanted to learn more about Herzl's movement, so he attended a meeting of the Zionist group in New York. He was not encouraged by the experience. The members, he recalled, were all "workers and others unknown in the city," who spoke only Yiddish and collected only $2.15 for their cause. Their leader, Michael Singer, tried to impress Browne by claiming that millions had already been raised in England and that Grand Rabbi Zadok Kahn would participate in the Congress, neither of which was true.[12]

Nevertheless, Browne decided to go to Basel, but only with accreditation by Herzl as an independent delegate, not as representative of the obviously ineffective group in New York. Singer, not planning to attend, volunteered to contact Herzl on Browne's behalf, which he did but with questionable content. After describing the rabbi as "an energetic man from the State of Georgia" who came to offer his services, Singer wrote, "the man is a hustler. He would like to be invited to the Zionist Congress." The publisher then asked Herzl to send a subvention for his newspaper.[13]

Not anticipating that Browne would actually attend the congress, Singer informed him, "I wrote to Dr. Theodor Herzl to invite you to the Zionist Congress in Basel. Dr. Herzl will do this with pleasure, but time is too short to really bring this off. The names of the New Yorker friends of Zionism are herewith enclosed so that the American Jews are represented. Naturally, I will keep you informed in detail about the Congress."[14]

Unaware of the deception, Browne nevertheless contacted Herzl independently to insure a favorable introduction. Using lecture bureau letterhead that displayed his endorsements from prominent Christian clergymen, he wrote in German, candidly detailing his views about the attitude of American Jewish leaders toward Zionism, his personal assessment of those leaders (especially rabbis Wise and Gottheil) and the means of establishing support for political Zionism in America. He believed that American Christians were ready to embrace Zionism and that Herzl must tour America in order to sell it. "Quite honestly," Browne wrote:

The [Zionist] movement did not matter to me until now, but after the 'Reform' rabbis (unfortunately) came out publicly against Zionism, I agreed with the opinion of Mr. Fraenkel that it was my duty to stand up to the old enemies of Judaism in this country. . . I promised Mr. Fraenkel and also Dr. Singer to represent Zionism in America at the Congress in Basel, when you send me right away an invitation, for (due to certain reasons) I was not selected by the "New York Zionists." Unfortunately, the "Reform" Jews, (although really not Jews at all), are the public representatives of American Jewry, and from them one can expect nothing but opposition. But I have the advantage to overcome them, for I am considered by the Gentiles in the highest circles as the true representative of Judaism, and have lectured during the last three years in every one of the outstanding churches about "the relationship of Judaism to Christianity."

Now, if something really will click in Basel, I can raise millions of dollars from gentiles in America for the founding of a "Jewish State." Yesterday I talked about this with four Protestant ministers. They saw in the "restoration" the fulfillment of the prophecy of a "second coming

of Christ," and I plan a tour throughout the country as soon as I return
from Europe, in order to win the Christian community for our cause.
When I succeed in that, even the Reform Jews will join us, for they ape
everything that the Christians do.[15]

The comment was basically true. Many traditionists even today do not
acknowledge that Reform Jews are Jews. Browne's accusation stemmed both
from an attempt to describe the situation to Herzl, and his own increasingly
voiced perception that American Jewry was represented publicly by elites
whose adherence to radical Reform had stripped them of their Jewishness.
His constant exaggeration, off-putting to readers unaccustomed to nineteenth
century expression, was nonetheless rooted in reality and in this instance
motivated by his eagerness to establish credentials for the role he sought in
promoting Zionism [16].

Likewise, while Browne probably overestimated the amount that
religious Christians were willing to spend for the cause, he based his
opinion on thirty years' experience with them. He also knew that since
the seventeenth century there had been groups of Zionists among British
Protestants who believed that the return of Jews to their ancient homeland
was prerequisite to the return of the Messiah. In nineteenth century America
the evangelical movement regenerated interest in the subject and some
Christian groups offered Herzl their support.[17]

Browne wrote a second letter shortly after the first, again using his
lecture letterhead fully adorned with endorsements and telling Herzl that he
did so "in order to show you what the largest American newspaper and the
two greatest spiritual leaders in (Christian) America think of us."

Having heard a rumor that William Randolph Hearst's new,
sensationalist New York Journal had hired Max Nordau to report on the

Congress, Browne warned Herzl, "Persuade Mr. Nordau to give up this plan immediately, for he does not know the conditions in this country, and a single misguided word can here (where the rich Jews control the journal) spoil all our plans. . ." He added, "I'm coming to Basel at my own expense. . .although I'm not rich, and have no time to lose, knowing what I am doing for the sake of Zion; for that same reason I do not want the correspondence of Mr. Nordau to be negated."

To support his claim of friendship with prominent Christians, Browne enclosed a newspaper article about his role as a pall bearer in Grant's funeral, along with letters from the recently deceased Rabbis Adolph Jellinek of Vienna and Lazare Isidor of France to indicate his rank among Jewish intellectuals, stressing that they be returned. He also noted that he had already discussed Herzl's plan with four Protestant ministers and Senator John Sherman of Ohio, brother of the noted Civil War general, William Tecumseh Sherman, "who very much likes the idea of a Jewish State."[18]

In conclusion, Browne apologized for his less-than-perfect German, saying "German is not easy for me to write but I hope that you will understand me well." Future correspondence suggests that he was not well understood.[19]

Only after making the above arrangements did Browne request his congregation's permission to leave. He announced that he had been "honored with the distinction of a delegate to the Zionist Congress in Basel, for the purpose of establishing a Jewish State in Palestine," which would take him away from the end of the current week until September 15th, virtually a month. "Under ordinary circumstances," he said, he would not have gone to Basel, "but the cause is so good and far-reaching, that I am sure you will agree with me that it is worthy of a sacrifice to act in the solution of the terrible problem as to what shall become of our poor Jewish Brethren who are now being persecuted in other lands more than in Russia."[20]

Here Browne referred to Austro-Hungary as well as to Rumania. Emperor Franz Joseph had recently knuckled under to Austrian anti-Semites by confirming Karl Lueger as mayor of Vienna after refusing to do so in three previous elections won by Lueger through blatantly anti-Semitic campaigns. In a later era, Adolph Hitler would acknowledge Lueger as his inspiration.

Notwithstanding the urgency of his cause, Browne miscalculated his congregation's response. These established Jews, like the majority of their counterparts throughout America, while assisting their persecuted brethren with contributions for succor and colonization, did not look with favor on the image of their rabbi publicly endorsing a Jewish state. The trustees refused his request to attend the congress. For them, America was the Promised Land. The only Zion they acknowledged was that which their forebears established on the red clay banks of the Chattahoochee.

Less than a week after Browne wrote Herzl asking to be appointed as a delegate to the congress, he had to write again saying that he could not attend. "Several hours prior to my leaving for New York on the 19th. . ." he wrote, "I received a direction from my congregation that I do not have the permission. . . to go." Explaining that his situation "is such that I cannot resign my position, for my only daughter is to be married on November 9," he noted that, "fortunately, her marriage makes me a free man and I am putting myself totally in the service of the Congress, both here as in Europe or Palestine."

Expounding on his qualifications for the role he proposed to fill, Browne boasted that he was acknowledged to be a man of "rare energy, endurance, courage and eloquence," who knew "how to manage and organize the people" and in 1882 was the only one to whose word the 14,000 Russian immigrants listened. He promised to send newspapers "which paint exactly the picture of American Reform," specifying particularly a laudatory one by the recently deceased Dr. Howard Crosby, preeminent Presbyterian minister, author, orientalist and chancellor of New York University. It showed, in Browne's words, "what American Reform Jews and American Reform rabbis really are."[21]

Next, Browne noted that he was about to send the same information to Zadok Kahn for delivery in Basel in case this letter did not reach Herzl in Vienna, and did so, sending another to the Congress itself. In both, he detailed in English what he intended to say had he gone to Basel, which was essentially what he had initially written to Herzl. He added, however, as his "painful duty . . .certain features of American Judaism:"[22]

1. The American Jew (the foreigner and not the native Portuguese) becomes a Reformer as soon as he becomes rich, or can make people believe him rich.

2. The American Reform Jews are avowed opponents of Zionism and so are their Rabbis and Editors who speak. . . .of the Congress. . .[as] the usual meeting place of Socialists and anarchists. The Central Conference of American Reform Rabbis (a name whose size is not at all a measure to the numbers of Rabbis in attendance, there having been only 29 present) have decided to send you a unanimous protest. . .[23]

In referring to American Jews as "foreigner" and "native Portuguese" Browne drew the distinction between German Jews, the majority of whom were foreign-born and still relatively insecure, and the earlier arrivals, mostly of Iberian descent who were completely acculturated. Many of these, second or third generation Americans, were children of conversos, secret Jews who had converted to Christianity in the sixteenth century to avoid execution or exile. Thus accustomed to nondiscrimination, they felt more secure in America than the Germans who, however successful, still tended to harbor thinly veneered angst about their acceptance by Christians. Browne's mention of the protest referred to a resolution passed by the CCAR in 1897 stating, "we totally disapprove of any attempt for the establishment of a Jewish state. Such attempts show a misunderstanding of Israel's mission, which from the narrow political and national field has been expanded to the promotion among the whole human race of the broad and universalistic religion first proclaimed by the Jewish prophets. . ." It characterized Zionism as anti-American and unfeasible because "those who would be willing to expatriate themselves, . . .are. . .only the poorest classes of Jews."[24]

Browne continued by explaining that in America:

> the Reform Jews, i.e., the rich Jews. . . control everything Jewish, and no cause, however noble, can succeed unless headed by one of them. All things you call Jewish in Europe, including any memory of Israel as a state or nation, are not only ignored but have become entirely unknown with Reform Judaism here. The Jewish press would turn the secular press and public opinion against Zionism, ridiculing the opinion of the poor. Regardless of their numbers, the poverty of attendants at a Zionist meeting, and the "unfashionableness" of its venue, will forfeit the sanctity of any cause.[25]

Despite Browne's penchant for exaggeration, this evaluation was essentially true. The "young Turks," rabbis like David Marx of Atlanta, born and educated in America, were beginning to occupy major pulpits and influence their own generation of congregants in the radical philosophy of Classical Reform as enunciated in the UAHC's Pittsburgh Platform of 1885. More affluent and acculturated than their parents, patronizing and inhospitable to the observant new immigrants, they strongly encouraged "Americanization" i.e., looking, sounding, and acting as much as possible like their Christian neighbors.

Browne believed that the lack of help from affluent Jews would not be a problem for Herzl because "the noble sentiments of the American Christians" would initiate American support for Zionism. To prove his point and serve as a guide in judging what he was about to propose, he enclosed an article from a major journal that quoted similar statements by two prominent New York clergymen who echoed his own view of American Reform Jews and Judaism.[26]

America, Browne informed the Congress, is a religious country where Christians venerate the historic aspect of Judaism and "the true Jew." He cited Reverend Crosby's letter as proof that the best society in America was religious and that the "Judenfrage" (Jewish problem) derived from those "very rich reformed Jews." He had been fortunate enough to "be thrown into the best society of Americans," he said, "where the rich Reform Jew can not dream of entering."[27]

Again, Browne's egotism smudged valid information with self-serving exaggeration. As seen in earlier chapters, since his student days in Cincinnati he had had friends in the top echelons of Christian society, clergy and politics. While he was by no means the only Jew for whom this was true, he did have justification for claiming acceptance by leading Christians, whereas wealthy Reform Jews like Theodore Seligman were being rejected for membership in exclusive clubs and refused reservations at resort hotels. He was likewise justified in expecting the powerful Christian press to follow its clergy in respect to Zionism which, if endorsed, would mean that "even the rich reformer and his rabbi will come with offers of assistance, because reform Judaism means aping Christian fashionable society. . ."[28]

Believing with good cause that prominent Protestants would open their churches to him, Browne offered to tour the country lecturing on Zionism and contribute his proceeds therefrom. He did not want to be responsible for the money, so he proposed that the local committee of each church forward the proceeds directly to a New York committee for deposit. Despite his low opinion of Michael Singer and the conviction that "his zeal and energy are great and far out of proportion to his means socially, financially and in knowledge of men and affairs American," Browne recognized the publisher's efforts on behalf of Zionism and suggested including him on the tour. He also asked to be on the executive committee representing America if the Congress endorsed the plan, and to engage Singer as his secretary. Singer should receive an adequate salary, he said. Since his own needs were less, he might not ask as much for himself, but surely no more, although he customarily earned $150 or more for a lecture. It was true that Browne did not currently need money, for he still held his position in Columbus and family inheritance probably supplemented whatever he earned.[29]

After dramatically reiterating his willingness to devote himself to Zionism, Browne predicted that if the Congress established an organization, "the hands of the new Jewish State would find more takers in this country than elsewhere." He suggested that initially he might be more useful abroad than in America, and declared that he could obey orders like a soldier, speak the required language "whether it be Russian, German, Polish, Hungarian or Hebrew." He even volunteered Sophie's time and effort, describing her as "a noble woman with equal zeal for the cause of humanity, who for ten years in New York made herself beloved by the poor and needy, an angel of beauty, love, kindliness and charity," and noted that she could help the women and children while he worked with the men. The two would ask no pay [i.e., wages, as distinct from living expenses] "save the reward which our poor oppressed people's happiness will give us under the blessing of God."[30]

Browne also mentioned his connection with Sultan Abdul Hamid, and the possibility of gaining his favor toward concessions in Palestine.

He concluded by refuting a derogatory statement in which American Reform leaders claimed that no organization of Russian Jews could succeed alone. Perceiving the difference between a group such as Singer's that focused on persuading others, and one focused on its own development, Browne demonstrated that the latter could succeed by describing the achievement of immigrants in "a city called Brownsville [Brooklyn] near New York:"

> Currently a part of greater New York, [it has] about 20,000 inhabitants, all Russian. . .a model of prosperity, clean lives and above all morality [that] grew up by itself, one Russian tailor, cloakmaker &&& [sic]one after another from the crowded city of New York. They need not thank the rich Jews for any assistance.
>
> Now if one Brownsville was such a success, why not 100 such cities, especially when organized into a state, superintended by the unselfish solicitude of men like you, protected by their own laws, ruled by their own superiors, living upon their own land, the land of our Fathers, of our triumphs and of our sorrows, of our hopes and promises prophetic? Be the land ever so sterile, our poor and downtrodden brethren—like the Mormons in this country did with the alkali deserts of Utah—they will change that desert into a flower garden. They will irrigate the sterile lands with their tears of joy, they will clear the miasmas of the atmosphere by their fervent prayers to Jehovah, they will

cast the spectra of rainbows athwart the leaden skies by their trust and

hope in the blessings of heaven. Let us do our utmost to bring about

that glorious restoration of Palestine to the dispersed of Judah and

let our motto be henceforth: IM ESHKACHESH YRUSHALEM

TISHCHACH YEMINI [If I forget thee, oh Jerusalem] until the

daughters of Judah will once more lay hands on the harps suspended

by their mothers upon the willows of Babylon's stream and those who

"sowed in tears shall harvest in joy" chanting the songs of Zion.[31]

Leaving no stone unturned, Browne then wrote to Max Nordau, co-convener of the Congress, introducing himself and basically repeating what he had written in the preceding letters. Apropos the possibility of getting help from Abdul Hamid, he noted that his dispatches concerning the Turkish situation had been widely circulated in Paris editions of the New York Herald.[32]

In a postscript he mentioned that he expected to be in Vienna the following summer, then broached the subject of Gustav Gottheil, his old nemesis in New York, asking if Gottheil had contacted Nordau and asserting that the New York rabbi was a spy for Wise. Gottheil had kept private his sympathy for Zionism because it was contrary to the sentiments of his congregation. In rabbinic circles it was said that Gottheil, then vice president of the Central Conference of American Rabbis, expected to become its president upon Wise's retirement which Wise had announced for the following year. Browne, with increasingly Machiavellian logic, posited that Gottheil had suddenly embraced Zionism openly in order to propitiate Wise by infiltrating the movement like a Trojan horse. As Browne's later correspondence with Herzl attests, he misjudged the situation.[33]

Before the Congress adjourned, Browne sent Herzl a short note enclosing one of many newspaper articles about his aborted trip to Basel and saying that these had generated letters from many people throughout the country, including gentiles, to whom he could not respond until he received a report on the Congress. "Going by what Dr. Wise and his gang write," he informed Herzl, "you are out of your mind." He then offered to send Herzl "the biography of this Wise, from the time when his permit as a shochet [kosher ritual slaughterer] was withdrawn, until today."

In closing, Browne wrote, "If we cannot get to Palestine, we could have beautiful Florida at our disposal. . ."[34]

The next day Browne sent Herzl a post card asking him to submit to the Congress the letter he had sent to Kahn for delivery in the event that Kahn did not attend.[35]

A few days later Browne wrote again saying "I burn with impatience to hear from you," and gave the following data on Wise:

It seems that Wise from Cincinnati, (the Bohemian shochet who forty-five years ago had to leave Radnitz because they removed his butcher permit). . .in his last sermon in his temple (the most beautiful one in America unfortunately) talked about Browne and the Zionists, and called them a bunch of anarchists. Next Saturday I will reply to Wise and the newspaper will print my whole talk.[36]

Browne then proposed that Herzl come to America with Nordau if possible, in November or December. "We must kill the negative plans of the rich Jews and rabbis," he wrote, noting that he could give the lectures himself as originally suggested, but "if you give a hundred talks here, I could better follow it up. I can guarantee for each presentation $200 to $250, so that you could in three and a half months earn 20-25000 guilders in addition to your good work." Presumably these earnings referred to voluntary collections rather than set fees which rarely generated such large amounts.[37]

Repeatedly cautioning secrecy to ensure surprise, Browne assured Herzl that he could easily get publicity for the tour, and asked him to cable his agreement simply "Browne, Columbus, Georgia, satisfactory," adding his expected month of arrival if possible. He needed two months to make advance arrangements, which he planned to do personally in the largest cities as well as to organize a reception "by the greatest Christians" to welcome Herzl upon his arrival in New York.

A week later, as the Congress adjourned, Browne wrote again, this time to say that Gottheil had just released an article in the New York Herald in which he "suddenly confronts Zionism." Describing the New York rabbi as "a Pole who has promoted himself in England to rabbi and Doctor," Browne reminded Herzl of Gottheil's high position in the association that called Herzl and Nordau "strange anarchists who publicize Zionism out of self-interest," and warned that Gottheil's "sudden change of heart is a trap they would like to prepare for you." He noted that it was Gottheil whom Rabbis Isidor and Jellinek had sharply criticized in the Hebrew publication that he had previously sent to Herzl, and predicted little good to come from Gottheil's helping Singer, "unfortunately a very poor man" whom any financial attention could easily blind. Browne cautioned Herzl "not under any circumstance to smuggle Gottheil into Zionism. Only after good reports came from Basel . .. did he have a good word for Zionism."

In closing, Browne repeated his conviction that Zionism did not need the rich Jews because "the rich Christians will do everything for us...especially if you and Dr. Nordau plan to come here later this winter."[38]

It was not without reason that Browne wrote disparagingly about wealthy Jews. In this context he referred primarily to the top echelon, the New

Yorkers, upon whom Herzl focused hoping to win them so as to establish a Jewish bank and purchase Palestine. These were the men who opposed Browne from his earliest days in the city when he insulted them by exposing exploitation of Jewish immigrants, and continued to oppose him as he espoused causes which they did not approve.

Apparently Herzl replied, but without commenting on Browne's assessment of American Jewry or the urgency for immediate action on behalf of Zionism. One can only guess whether Herzl determined these points unworthy of comment or, besieged by reams of contradictory advice, he simply overlooked them. Whatever the reason, his lack of attention infuriated Browne, who replied, "I know very well that you are presently very busy. . . Nonetheless, it is absolutely essential that the terrible lies that this fellow Wise prints against you, Nordau and Zionism be negated. Otherwise, the public will believe that he speaks the truth. . ."

Wise was indeed publishing derogatory statements about Zionism. After the Congress adjourned he denounced its leaders as politicians taking advantage of the people, calling it "a gathering of visionary and impractical dreamers who conceived and acted a romantic drama, and applauded it all by themselves." He portrayed the meeting as being "of no importance. . .a farce. . .a crazy antic of irresponsible men." Two months later he wrote:

Most of them [Zionists] may be classified as socialists, idle dreamers, who fancy they have discovered a panacea for Jewish ills, as they have already done for the world at large. . .At present they are harmless and will be as long as they confine themselves to talking and writing, but should they make any attempt to stimulate and assist emigration to Palestine with more than words, they will do infinite hurt, they will surely sacrifice the welfare, probably the lives, of those they send there.[39]

Browne responded by sending the article to Herzl and demanding to know immediately "In order to correct the misrepresentation," if Herzl really expected to buy Palestine from the Sultan and how much it would cost; if there was truth to the rumor that all the important rabbis and rich Jews in Europe, including the Rothschilds, opposed Herzl's plan; and if Chief Rabbis Moritz Kaiserling of Budapest and Moritz Gudemann of Vienna opposed it. Actually, neither Gudemann nor the Rothschilds endorsed the plan. Gudemann, a traditionalist long distinguished for his scholarship in Jewish culture, criticized Zionism for its tendency to stress Judaism's national character more than its religious one.[40]

Noting that Wise called him a liar for saying that Kahn favored Zionism, Browne told Herzl that he had just received a letter from Kahn confirming his support, and asked about the possibility of receiving help from the Hirsch Fund. Then he again advised Herzl to visit America, cautioning secrecy in order to proceed without preemptive interference, and promised to publicize the tour as soon as he received authorization.

Next, Browne stressed the urgent need for an inexpensive English weekly in New York, Washington and Cincinnati to counter the derogatory views expressed by Wise and others. He repeated his request to be made a member of the [yet unannounced] American Committee or otherwise empowered to form a publication committee, maintaining that Singer's "little German paper" had no influence, because "a person who is not known here, and in addition (unfortunately) lives in the slums, will damage even the best cause."

Offering to copy Herzl's Die Welt into an English paper if were sent to him, Browne asked for transcripts of the Congress' proceedings and yet again requested authorization as a member of the Executive Committee for America, with Singer as his secretary. He noted that "a so-called Dr Schloder from Baltimore and an attorney Rosenberg from New York that nobody knows here" were mentioned as delegates to the Congress, an announcement that "gives our enemies reason to ridicule us even more." Browne's suggestions did not pose competition with already established entities because Singer's newspapers had failed and his New York Zionists were not recognized as a committee for America. Although accounts of the first Zionist Congress do not mention the two men from Baltimore and New York, they may have attended without being listed as delegates.[41]

A week after posting his previous letter, Browne sent Herzl two almost identical memos in which he admitted his mistake in believing that Nordau represented an insignificant New York newspaper, and giving Nordau permission to quote him. He offered to supply Herzl with publishable material on request, and enclosed pages about the Reich case from the galley of his commemorative book, the publication of which he had postponed lest it hurt Reich's chances for full pardon. He also sent an article from the New York Herald about his connection with Sultan Abdul Hamid, reminding Herzl that he might be able to assist at the Divine Porte.[42]

Herzl's response must have again suggested that he paid little attention to what Browne wrote. Frustrated by the disconnect, Browne replied:

> *My time is very limited. Nonetheless I will write to you extensively since this letter will become [either] the basis of a great undertaking or the last one which I will dedicate to Zionism.*
>
> *Now to the matter of responding in detail to your latest letter. You say:*
>
> *1. You know me not, but believe I'm the right man.*
>
> *2. America is a very big arena.*
>
> *3. Should I first proceed, and prove what I have done prior to asking for a title?*

I will reply to this seriatim including the 4th point which says who is
Wise? Is he a rabbi?[43]

In response to the first issue, Browne repeated his reasons for espousing Zionism, his disappointing introduction to it at Singer's meeting and his personal qualifications for promoting it successfully in America. He also noted that Herzl's mention of not knowing him sufficiently suggested that Herzl had not read any of his enclosures. Regarding other Americans who might be authorized to speak for Zionism, Browne said that he had not known about "two obscure people, a Shochet Rev. Dr. from Baltimore and a 'Dr.' Winkeladvokat of New York" who would be his colleagues, but they should be given the courtesy of membership on the American committee because they attended the Congress as delegates. To emphasize his own qualifications, he quoted James G. Blaine's comment that "Rabbi Browne can work twenty-five hours a day."

Continuing, Browne reminded Herzl of his devotion to the movement, noting that Zionism was considered a bad word when he first espoused it, yet although he was not rich, he had unhesitatingly booked passage on the fast ship Bismarck at a cost of 1000 florins to attend the Congress. Despite having been denied permission to go, he was one of the three men accredited from America, so "it is not only thankfulness but justice that these three delegates be known as the rightful delegates of Zionism." Because the other two were not included in the committee despite being entitled by their presence at the Congress, Browne presumed that Herzl considered them unsuitable.

In response to Herzl's request to begin making propaganda, Browne noted that he had already sent a circular to contacts in all principal cities announcing Herzl's anticipated tour. He repeated the offer to resign his position in order to travel for Zionism, however emphasizing the ineffectiveness of doing so without official accreditation. "I don't need a title from Europe," he declared. "I am too old already for more self-importance, but I need to have a title in order to accomplish the work."

After reporting that Gottheil had finally endorsed Zionism, "but only after he has found out that the Congress in Basel would not be riddled by scandal as was prophesied," he responded to Herzl's inquiry, "who is Wise in Cincinnati? Is he a rabbi?" as follows:

> *I could as well ask you who is [Emperor] Franz Joseph in Vienna.*
> *. . .and who is [Pope] Leo XIII in Rome? Is he a Catholic priest?*
> *Wise. . . is the absolute autocrat of American Jewry, has the greatest*
> *congregation outside of New York and the largest Jewish newspapers*
> *[thereby becoming] ruler of the association of rabbis that issued the*
> *shameful resolution against Zionism.*

Browne was essentially correct in his description of Wise as the acknowledged leader of American Jewry. Outside of New York city, where exceptional wealth dominated via Temple Emanu-El, no other voice approached that of Isaac Mayer Wise as authoritative spokesman for American Jewry.

Proceeding with his history lesson, Browne told of Wise's early conflict with Einhorn [here seen in Chapter II], then explained that Wise and Gottheil "were arch enemies, until Dr. Einhorn (the leader of the anti-Wise people) died." After that, according to Browne, their friendship had continued with the understanding that Wise planned that year to retire as head of the rabbis' conference and promote Gottheil to take his place. Instead, the founder retained his presidency which, in Browne's interpretation, "made Gottheil furious and to infuriate Wise he suddenly

became a Zionist to the surprise of everybody. . .When I learned this I wrote
to you immediately asking you to wait for I wanted to examine the situation
and how the current position of Gottheil's is to be judged."

"Now take note," Browne warned, referring to his experience in New
York "that Gottheil and I are arch enemies. . .Gottheil does not believe it
possible that I would come close to him or will speak to him but from my last
letter you can see that this is my intention, and for the first time in my life will
I [not] act straightforwardly but as a diplomat."

Reasoning that Gottheil, although old and a poor speaker, might help
Zionism in New York because of his position, Browne suggested that Richard
Gottheil, the rabbi's son whom he called a nonentity, might be effective
"among the poorer classes in New York" and help neutralize Wise's attacks in
the rest of the country.[44]

Browne advised Herzl to appoint the elder Gottheil as president of
the American Zionists, with Rabbi Henry Pereira Mendes of New York's
historic Portuguese Congregation Shearith Israel as its first vice president;
Richard Gottheil as second; Rabbi Bernard Felsenthal of Chicago's Sinai
Congregation as third; the delegate Rosenbaum for general secretary; himself
chief organizer; and Singer with the delegate Scheffer as assistant organizers.
He recommended that Berthold Frankel, a respected New Yorker and devout
Zionist, contact them, reminding Herzl that to be successful it was essential
to know the field well, to be known by the people, to speak always in English
"so that the people as well as the press will listen," and to "think and feel
American."

Disclosing that he had already booked the best church in Cincinnati in
order to begin Herzl's tour with three lectures in Wise's home base, Browne
added that although Singer spoke only in German, read his speeches and was
a schnorrer [a beggar] he could nevertheless be useful as assistant on the tour.

"While I talked in a church to a large Christian public," Browne wrote, "he would speak to the. . .Jewish workers as in New York." Although Singer had initially agreed, he subsequently proposed making a tour on his own, which Browne believed to have been motivated by Gottheil and declared "out of the question." Be begged Herzl to forbid it, noting that Singer had asked him for money and was so needy that "a few dollars from Gottheil make him totally incapable of making a proper judgement. . ."

As usual, Browne included a postscript, this time advising Herzl that he had "stopped everything" and would speak at St. Paul's church in Cincinnati on the 22nd, 23rd and, 24th of the month. He intended to keep his position in Columbus until he received Herzl's authorization, but expected an immediate reply. Finally, he again offered "to create a state like Palestine in the United States, should Palestine not be available."

Herzl replied affirming Browne's slate for the American committee, but cautioned that his agreement did not mean recognizing the proposition as "definitive and exclusive." He could not appoint or replace anyone on his own because representatives from each country agreed separately on their suggestions, which were later ratified by the congress. No American had been elected to the action committee, he explained, because the American representatives made no suggestions.[45]

"You are entirely right," he told Browne, "when you want to end this unsatisfactory situation soon, because the growing tasks of our organization require also a good instrument in America." Admitting that he knew little about "the real circumstances in America," Herzl approved Browne's proposition as "well suited," insofar as he could judge, since it included those who were known to him from newspapers and meeting reports as pioneers of Zionism in America. He suggested strengthening the American bureau, "which already has an expanded field of activity internationally, including the most admired men of all Zionist factions."

Herzl approved the slate of officers proposed by Browne, omitting the position of treasurer for which he advised Browne to get "a well-respected, well-to-do and well known man. Maybe Mr. Frankel would be suitable." Herzl also mentioned Singer's agreement to Browne's lecture plan, emphasizing that he did not want "anyone who has struggled on behalf of Zionism [to] feel hurt or passed over." Browne's task, he wrote, "should be to create a firm union among all American Zionists. Only through unity can we advance: the dedication of individuals will hopefully lead them to subordinate themselves to the general interest." Browne should notify him as soon as he was organized, whereupon Herzl would send him regular announcements of the committee, with permission to copy "to the mentioned gentlemen," in hopes of hastening the much needed unity.

In closing, Herzl noted that the English Hovevei Zion [Friends of Zion] after refusing to send delegates to the Congress, had just agreed to join. One of many Zionist groups with differing philosophies and goals, Hovevei Zion disapproved of confrontational approaches, preferring to work quietly through modest labor. Herzl then reiterated the cornerstone of his plan, that the next task for American Zionists "is the founding of the Jewish Bank (see No. 25 of Die Welt)" in order to purchase an autonomous zone in Palestine from the bankrupt Ottoman Empire.[46]

The reference to the bank caused Browne to reply that Herzl must have read his letter "only cursorily" since he did not seem to understand the situation. Again he summarized his view of conditions for Zionism in America: no one of influence other than three elderly rabbis accept it; the one respected though not wealthy Zionist sympathizer was his friend Berthold Frankel, but Browne would not involve him before conferring with Gottheil; the only Zionists to be found in America were Polish and Russian workers in the industrial cities; and he had not discussed his plan with Singer since July because Singer had not responded to him for more than three months.[47]

It was true that no Zionist groups could be found in America outside of the cities named because the potential for organizing them existed only where there were large numbers of immigrant Jewish laborers. Even in New Orleans, where the dynamic Rabbi Max Heller would later espouse Zionism and courageously promote it despite the disapproval of his congregation, the movement did not yet have a voice or substantial advocates in 1897.

Browne indicated that he confided his plan to Singer originally so that Singer would repeat it to Gottheil, but he now believed that the New York rabbi was no longer interested. Due to the animosity between himself and Gottheil that had developed in the eighties, Browne assumed that it was he who had influenced Singer against him. When they first met, Singer had asked him for money to print a Zionist pamphlet, which Browne offered to do at his own expense, "but he (Singer) wanted only money. . .and since that time he is cool to me." Browne could forgive "a man who lives in poverty," he wrote, but did not contact Singer again, "for he cannot add much to the success of Zionism if Gottheil cannot secure the good reputation of Zionism, and I can secure its success."

Clearly status was crucial to getting sympathetic attention from the majority of American Jews, and Browne recognized his own inability to win them for Zionism without some token of recognition. Summarizing, he said that peace between himself and Gottheil was primary, and that Singer, "who is a Zionist but also a schnorrer, should admit that the success of Zionism will provide him with a good livelihood and he would without question be willing to travel with me across the country. . ." His refusal would damage "only himself and not Zionism. . ."

Meanwhile, Browne claimed, he himself had "made a sacrifice for

Zionism" in that he had stifled his pride to ask Gottheil's forgiveness for their past enmity. After explaining his reason for doing so, in his most melodramatic fashion he promised "unconditional obeisance, respect, etc. so that Zionism would have success because of us," reminding Herzl that Gottheil and Felsenthal were too old to succeed by themselves and that Singer was poor, unknown, and ridiculed by the Jewish press. "A person who is hungry and schnorrs," Browne declared, "despite all his talents, cannot succeed in this country."

In conclusion, Browne cited Herzl's own struggle for influence in Europe to help clarify the additional difficulty in America. "Gottheil and I would be able to overcome all that," he declared, "he in New York and I in the countryside." He asked Herzl to arrange the detente, predicting a fiasco otherwise "especially if persons who are unknown will be at the head, along with others who have no means of doing anything." He signed the letter, "Your honest Dr. Browne."

The following day, still doubtful that Herzl had grasped the full import of his message, Browne wrote again to emphasize that Zionists existed only among the poor in the large cities, and that Gottheil was old and known only in New York. He added that Gottheil's son, who (according to Browne) had become a professor only through political support, was not a speaker and had no influence. Mendes, although chazan [cantor] of the oldest Jewish Orthodox community, was active only among his own people, and Felsenthal from Chicago "is seventy-six years old and was never a speaker." To support Zionism against Wise's ridicule, Browne insisted, "one must have. . . a thunderous voice, and. . .travel through the country." Gottheil's name as president could be useful because of his position as rabbi of "the richest community in America with unlimited political influence," but neither he nor Mendes could be helpful outside of New York, and even there it was doubtful that Gottheil could convince influential Jews to accept Zionism. "Gottheil is no pioneer as you believe," Browne insisted, "but only a follower, and thus his enthusiasm will be lost very soon."[48]

Again Browne was overly candid but basically correct. Obviously he was biased against Richard Gottheil, who had not yet earned his reputation as scholar, author and effective Zionist, and whose influence came only from his father's position. Mendes was hardly known outside of New York and Felsenthal, recognized for his scholarship, could not travel abroad due to the frailty of old age.

Browne again warned about Singer's explosive temper, his "very sharp pen that has already killed two newspapers," and other negatives imposed by poverty, ignorance of the country and its people, reading his speeches in German, and the fact that he "considers honorability only to the extent that he can extract money from friends of Zionism." Responding to Singer's claim that he had sacrificed himself for Zionism, Browne reminded Herzl that in the ancient Temple only the best animals were accepted for sacrifice, therefore "a very poor man is a bad sacrifice." He himself, however, had made a great sacrifice for Zionism "before Basel did us the honor of supporting the idea."

Reports about large meetings of Zionists were much exaggerated, he said. In his opinion, Wise's attacks on him were intended to render him ineffective, which there was no need to do in the cases of Gottheil, Mendes and Felsenthal. Browne wrote that he forgave Gottheil "for the many injustices that he has done me since 1881," but maintained that the New York rabbi could never gain support for Zionism from his own community and that it was important for Herzl to consider both rabbis as equals. Still begging for recognition, Browne was nonetheless accurate in his assessment of Gottheil's chances for support from his congregation.

A week later, Browne acknowledged the return of one of the enclosures that he had sent at the beginning of their correspondence, thanking Herzl while again stressing the need to return the other items and enclosing a newspaper article typifying the American press coverage of Zionist affairs. He reiterated his views on Singer and Gottheil, who not surprisingly had declined his offer to collaborate. Browne attributed the rebuff to Gottheil's lack of support from his congregation. Noting that Singer had asked Gottheil to write for his paper, Browne reiterated his view that the rabbi's son would do little more for the movement than to attract "some attention from the so-called 'slum' Jews.'" Here Browne's snobbish expression and biased view of the Gottheils tends to obscure his accuracy. It was actually many years before Richard Gottheil, free of Singer's interference and valuably assisted by Stephen S. Wise—no relation to Isaac M— gained support from those of his own social stratum.

Repeating his prognosis of stagnation under present conditions, Browne advised Herzl to let Singer and young Gottheil do as they pleased "until they recognize their inability to do anything further." When they "will have given Zionism the death knell," he would organize some men of influence and begin. Again he suggested that Herzl tour America in order to "raise Zionism from the grave which Messrs. Singer & Co. are now preparing, and help it to be resurrected for eternal life." And again he offered to obtain "millions of acres of the best land here...should Palestine not be available," suggesting that Frankel and two others handle the finances since he himself was not a businessman. Browne reminded Herzl of the newspaper articles he had sent indicating possible support from Christians, and concluded with yet another warning of the harm that Singer could do, with assurance of his own ongoing readiness to serve, "but not as a second assistant to the current supporters of Zionism."

Singer also wrote two long letters to Herzl that week, bitter complaints about the leader's agreement with Browne on committee appointments. Calling Browne "an imposter and a swindler," Singer asserted that the Zionist leaders had, "to a certain extent, already been determined." They were rabbis Felsenthal and Mendes; "perhaps also Gottheil;" and Philip Klein, a relative newcomer who did not speak English but was soon to distinguish himself as a leader of American Orthodoxy.[49]

Zionist groups had indeed been established in some cities. The report of organizations in New York, Chicago and elsewhere in early November caused Wise to "study the personnel at the head of them very carefully" and reach the same conclusion as Browne regarding the members' social and economic status as well as their slim to zero chance of success.[50]

In a letter of which only the undated final portion survives, Browne noted the existence of a second American Zionist committee headed by Richard Gottheil and Stephen S. Wise, a newly ordained young rabbi from New York whose father, Aaron Wise, was a well known Orthodox rabbi, one of the city's "Big Six." Regarding Singer, whom Herzl mentioned in terms suggesting that he had already despaired of him, Browne responded:

Now he has become friends with a little Hungarian Jew whose name is Rabbi Klein. Klein is a very learned Jewish rabbi who knows so much about America as a Hottentot. The Central Committee's America has now two heads, Gottheil and another rabbi who form the elite, and Klein represents the slum Jews. I beg you not to appoint anyone, and you write to me that you cannot organize the American Committee. What will be the results? Klein, Singer and company are the representatives of the beggars that no one knows. Gottheil & Co are the rich aristocrats and while these are as I often explain of no use to Zionism, could they not damage? Whereas a central committee organized by Singer could be

despised and create its demise. And while my plans with you to travel next

year through the country 3 rabbis Wise, Drachman and Mendes . . . under

the chairmanship of Prof. Gottheil have now taken on Zionism and

left Singer hanging. In all haste, the following is my advice: obtain the

names of all the Zionist associations and write officially immediately

directly to the membership that the America Zionist directory will be

appointed in Vienna and nothing take place here.[51]

The rabbis that Browne named—Stephen Wise, Bernard Drachman and Henry Mendes—were indeed well respected and truly devoted to Zionism. Drachman, American-born and initially sponsored by Temple Emanu-El, was rabbi of the Orthodox Congregation Zichron Ephraim (now Park Avenue Synagogue) and became highly distinguished as dean of the Jewish Theological Seminary as well as a leader within other important institutions. Mendes, of the historic Portuguese Congregation Shearith Israel, was also active in numerous organizations both Jewish and general, and having been born and educated in England, had the advantage of speaking an elegant English, of vital importance for presenting Zionism in a favorable light. Stephen S. Wise was still relatively unknown, but not for long. He soon became the dominant voice in American Jewry.[52]

At the beginning of 1898, Browne reported to Herzl that the Gottheil-Singer collaboration had failed and again offered himself to Zionism when the situation was such that he could be effective. He again warned that Singer, who had twice rebuffed attempts to see him, had already failed with his third publication, the Zionist, and had again asked for money. Browne reported that San Francisco newspapers had quoted claims by Singer that he had done more for Zionism than Herzl and would himself solve the Jewish question in America. Asserting that those statements "have made Zionism ridiculous for the Christians," Browne assured Herzl that he would remedy the damage "as soon as Zionism is established. I have worked on this plan for the last six months and have everything in shape to start on the morrow when you are ready to come and ask the Christians everything that you hope from America." Adding that the United States could provide for ten million immigrants, he asked, "If Palestine is not available, where do you want to go with your Zionists?"and noted that he had already enlisted "some of our best men for this purpose."[53]

In the remainder of his letter Browne reiterated his dismay at the prospect of Singer being given a leadership position, his willingness to keep Singer as a secretary, his plan to visit Vienna in July, and his offer to make arrangements for Herzl's American tour if authorized to do so. Otherwise, he would "no longer wish to be associated with Zionism" and of necessity make public his reasons for it.[54]

Contrary to Browne's predictions and largely through the leadership of Stephen Wise, the New York Federation of Zionists became a reality by mid-January and by summer numbered 36 sections with a total of some 5,000 members.[55]

In February, still unaware of Stephen Wise's ability, Browne wrote to Herzl, "The bubble of the 'friends' of Zionism, Gottheil, Mendes et al, has finally burst. . .," though not precisely as he expected, for he was unaware that Gottheil Senior "wanted only that his son would be on top. . ." He was also surprised to learn that Herzl had dropped his interest in Singer.[56]

The final two letters of this correspondence suggest that Browne and Herzl had reached an extent of frustration with each other that precluded further discussion. In mid-March, Browne wrote again:

Dear Dr. Herzl

I find it important to tell you that I do not drink, I don't smoke, I don't gamble, I am not a gourmet, make no visits and receive no guests and work 18 hrs a day. Thus I do not need something to fill my time although my official responsibilities require my time only for 2 hours weekly and in addition I am able to do a lot. Now when I write to you I do it believing that my letters are very important. You are most likely bothered by people who love to write unnecessary letters and think it is honorable to do so, but it seems they have no time to contemplate carefully (although I explained everything quite clearly) what can be done here in America if one does it in a practical fashion, and what one can lose by impractical procedure.

My prophecy regarding Singer's doings have been borne out sufficiently for you to see that I know the circumstances exactly. Your Singer will ruin everything. You know him better than I do but I judge his activities. He has now killed the 3rd newspaper and from each venture has lost the money of others. I repeat, only through my plan and your visit here can America become a Zionist place. Until such time it is not necessary to do anything that might risk the future, and a dispute between 2 central committees has done much damage already and given the enemies of Zionism a weapon to fight with. I can make peace. I can resolve the dispute [between the two factions] and keep everything in readiness for our great "crusade" through the country, but I must be officially, or at least privately, enabled by you to do this. Your next letter will settle everything as far as my activities are concerned.

To end, there is:

1) We must have peace and only one central committee.

2. Your arrival in all quietness is a requirement.

3. *My letters must be found, and thanks for sending the Hamagid.*

Your Dr. Browne[57]

Eight days later, he wrote again asking Herzl to make yet another attempt to find the Jellinek letter sent at the beginning of August, 1897, offering a 20 FL reward, and noting that nothing had changed regarding Zionism. His predictions had become increasingly accurate, he said, and he was prepared "for the day when the crash will come."[58]

That the crash never came was due in large part to the leadership of Stephen S. Wise.

Although this concluded the initial correspondence between Browne and Herzl, other evidence indicates that it did not end their relationship. Fragments of letters to Max Nordau as well as other references tend to confirm Browne's claim that he maintained contact and renewed activity with Herzl. Browne told a reporter in 1904, "Herzl wrote me he would get the Vad 'El Arish', a wilderness belonging to Egypt. I met him in April, 1903, at Cairo, and found that desert couldn't be irrigated, the Khedive being willing to sell the desert but not the waters of the Nile. Herzl, however, stuck to this delusion until I made the facts known to the last Basel Congress, and Herzl settled upon Uganda, an equally undesirable country. . ."[59]

On June 3, 1904, one month before Herzl's death, Browne wrote to Nordau asking his opinion about something regarding committee appointments that he had discussed with Herzl in Cairo. Notes in the margin of that message refer to Herzl's November 1897 letter to Browne in which he confirmed Browne's recommendations for Zionist leadership in America, and suggest that Herzl never fully accepted Browne's assessment of American

Jewish philanthropists as unalterably opposed to political Zionism. Neither was Herzl convinced of that fact by Stephen Wise, who expressed the same view as Browne.[60]

Herzl never came to America. There is evidence that he accepted an invitation to do so and changed his mind after Simon Hilf, a devoted Zionist in Cincinnati who had been corresponding with him for more than a year, warned of the virulent opposition he would encounter from Reform Jews in America. Hilf called them assimilationists and believed, as Browne had first suggested regarding Gottheil, that those who professed adherence to Zionism actually opposed it, infiltrating the organization in order to make trouble.[61]

Browne again wrote to Nordau in 1905, requesting a complete report on the most recent Zionist Congress and offering, "I am ready if you and Professor [Otto] Warburg want to come here after Rosh Hashana." Browne's papers contain no further reference to Nordau or Warburg, a distinguished German scientist who served as president of the [international] Zionist Organization from 1911 to 1921.[62]

Stephen Wise and Richard Gottheil are today recognized as founders of Zionism in America. Numerous others are also remembered as early leaders: Harry Friedenwald, the Baltimore ophthalmologist who presided over the Zionist Federation of America from the time of Herzl's death until World War I, the young Rabbi Bernard Ehrenreich who many years later served and was greatly beloved by the largely anti-Zionist Congregation Kahl Montgomery despite his acknowledged lifelong devotion to Zionism, and the outspoken Zionist Rabbi Max Heller of New Orleans. Browne and Singer are forgotten.

In 1913, identified as a friend of Theodor Herzl, Browne spoke at Temple Beth El Jacob of Albany, New York, in a ceremony commemorating the ninth anniversary of Herzl's death. He predicted:

Zionism will yet triumph if we have proper leaders. What has happened once can happen again. Look back into Israel's history.

When the daughters of Judah strummed their harps by Babylon streams, the world considered Israel dead. When Belshazzar celebrated his 1,000-headed banquet, deriding Israel's God, Judaism was thought beyond resurrection, yet two years later Cyrus sent Israel back to reestablish its national home.

The success was due to the God-fearing, unselfish, self-sacrificing men like Daniel, Zerubbabel and Ezra. Such young men can spring up again in Judaism and Zion will be our glory again.[63]

As usual, Browne exaggerated and extrapolated, waxing poetic upon a basis of truth. Today his words invite dispute and beg questions: If Herzl had come to America, would Zionism have flourished sooner? If he or his immediate followers had succeeded in establishing Israel, would there have been a Holocaust? To what extent was Browne sincerely altruistic and to what extent self-seeking?

There are no certain answers. Browne's plan for promoting Zionism in America via Christians had practical merit not only as a boost for Zionism but also for the encouragement it could have provided American Jews who saw growing anti-Semitism in the current attempts to stifle immigration. As it happened, immigration was severely curbed.

Browne remained a staunch advocate for Zionism, continuing to promote it without having a hand in its development and without public recognition of his efforts. It was almost a century before most American Jews—certainly those of German Reform background—became convinced, as he had been, that love of Zion in no way contradicted loyalty and love for America.

Herzl was an assimilated Jew with little knowledge of Jews and Judaism and even less of their development in America. Considering the contentious personalities and conflicting messages with which he had to contend—not to mention the enormous egos, including his own—it is hardly surprising that he failed to comprehend, or even seriously consider, the involved and caustic details with which Browne bombarded him. They seemed to have been talking past each other, Herzl focusing on his immediate goal vis-a-vis America—to gain support for a Jewish bank—and Browne intent upon establishing Zionism in the hearts and minds of Americans. Neither really heard what the other was saying. Browne wanted relief; Herzl wanted a state. Neither lived to see his goals accomplished.

XI - TRAVELING WITH SOPHIE

Conditions in Europe worsened after the first Zionist Congress in 1897, making it ever more urgent to find a refuge for Russian and Rumanian Jews. The Turkish Empire, which spread from the Balkans across North Africa, in disarray and drowning in debt, nevertheless continued to deny approval of Herzl's scheme to reduce its financial burden in exchange for an autonomous Jewish state in Palestine. Nor was Herzl successful in persuading the European governments and Jewish philanthropists to provide money with which to do that. Browne, having embraced the new Zionism, anticipated accepting the audience which Sultan Abdul Hamid had offered because of the opportunity it provided to further the Zionist cause and help Herzl establish a more cordial relationship with the Ottoman court.[1]

While Browne was juggling his involvements with Zionism, ecumenism, politics, Talmudic scholarship and congregation, Sophie stepped outside traditional parameters of home and synagogue, gradually and imperceptibly to develop a career of her own. Traveling with her husband soon led her beyond Europe to North Africa and the Middle East, and her innate ability led her to public responsibilities at home in Georgia. Still the Victorian lady, she pushed the social envelope ever so gently to expand her possibilities and broaden the scope of other women she influenced.

Following her leadership of the Army and Navy League Auxiliary, Sophie taught classes in English literature to help foreign born women of her congregation improve their language skills. By 1900, as literary societies became acceptable "away from home" activities for Southern housewives, she took a cue from her Christian counterparts and organized a study group, naming it the Century Club in honor of the new century. The Jewish women held meetings twice monthly from October through May, with programs of music, theatrical presentations and lectures on assigned subjects prepared and presented by the members themselves. Sophie presided, closing each session with a discussion of current events. The club survives today, into its second century, having adapted to the needs of changing times and returned to its original mission as a book club. Sophie remained actively at its helm for twenty-five years despite prolonged absences required by the frequent moves of her peripatetic husband.[2]

In February 1901, an Atlanta newspaper announced that Browne had resigned his Columbus position in order to make an extended journey abroad. He did not actually depart until summer, 1902, but the date accurately marked the end of his tenure at Congregation B'nai Israel. Although he resided elsewhere intermittently after that, he considered Columbus his home, and Sophie continued to make an impact on the community while dutifully following him.[3]

Although Browne's career had deteriorated and he had declared himself retired, it was his work that motivated the travel. He wanted to complete investigations for the European Archaeological Commission and to expedite the rescue of Jews from Eastern Europe, an increasingly urgent need which was probably sponsored by the Paris based Alliance Israelite Universelle.

The Brownes left Columbus during the summer of 1902, accompanied by their daughter Lylah Goldberg, her husband Dave, and their year-old baby Carolyn. They traveled first to London and Paris, then sailed up the Rhine into Germany before entering Austro-Hungary, where they visited the beautiful capital Budapest as well as Browne's home town of Eperjies and nearby Kashau northeast of there. Then they toured Venice and Milan, proceeding east to Genoa where Browne investigated means of facilitating an exodus of Jews from Eastern Europe, consulting proprietors of Italian steamship lines about the transport of refugees from Romania to the Americas. One company proposed bringing them to the United States, another to Argentina.[4]

In October, the Goldbergs returned to America while Sophie and the rabbi took residence for the winter in Nice, at Villa St. Joseph, 16 Avenue Mirabeau. During their stay there, the Brownes signed over their power of attorney to their son-in-law, Dave, a procedure necessitated in part by pending litigation over a business initiative that Sophie had pioneered several years before. Browne then joined her in it to circumvent restrictions faced by women in what was still considered an exclusively male domain.

On their previous trip to Europe, Sophie had noticed the successful use of an innovative theft-proof box-and-bag combination for the collection of mail. It permitted letters to be dropped from the box directly into a bag without being seen or handled by the postman. Since mail theft was also prevalent in America, she brought back a sample hoping to sell the idea to the Postal Service for 15% of the profits. Browne accompanied her to Washington where she demonstrated it for the United States Postmaster, noting as an additional selling point that it not only prevented theft but also saved the government money by eliminating the need for overseers, thereby enabling one employee to do the work of twenty. She later acquired a patent on it.[5]

The government indicated interest but acted on it slowly, if at all. To facilitate its marketing, Browne brought in two men to join him and Sophie, applying for incorporation as the Combination Safety Mail Box and Bag Company. The partners persuaded the Brownes to order fifteen boxes for a test run, then denied all responsibility when the shipment arrived and the Post Office Department denied having authorized the order. Following several postponements of incorporation, the partners maneuvered themselves into control, bypassing the rabbi and Sophie.[6]

The Brownes appealed their case for several years without results, although they may have gained a small measure of satisfaction upon learning that one of their former partners had spent two years in jail for defrauding the United States government. Eventually Sophie transferred the patent to Dave, who then sold it for $4,000 to a group of four men, one of whom was Browne. The family apparently abandoned the project after two more years and its ultimate fate remains unknown.[7]

Continually attracted by new technology, Browne during his winter in France received a request to implement "the furnishing and installing at Columbus of a large number of water closets." The purveyor of the fixtures noted in a letter to Dave Goldberg that Browne considered their installation to be "a sanitary measure" needed by the city. The rabbi also referred this matter to his son-in-law, recommending that the writer contact Dave to work out the details. It is not known if the venture was responsible for solving the city's sanitation problems, but it further reflects Browne's fascination with technology. As with Sophie's mail bag project, it indicates the keen eye with which both Brownes observed innovative conveniences as they traveled.[8]

Soon after arriving in Nice, the Brownes departed temporarily for a brief visit to Cairo and Jerusalem. They did not state its purpose, although one may assume that it was for Browne to make advance arrangements for his meeting there in the spring with Theodor Herzl and the Khedive of Egypt. On the couple's return to Nice, local newspapers as well as the Paris edition of the New York Herald Tribune took note of it, mentioning—probably in error—that "*le distingue savant*," [famous scholar] and his wife were accompanied by his secretary. The presence of a personal employee seems unlikely because their financial means were not such as to afford one and Sophie did not mention an assistant in her regular, descriptive post cards to the family at home. It may be that a representative of the mission's yet-to-be-determined sponsor accompanied them on that portion of their journey.[9]

Back in France for the winter, the rabbi remained busy with his work while Sophie delighted in the beauty of Nice and its surroundings, especially the bright sunshine of the Cote d'Azur. Her fluency in French enabled her to make friends easily, with some of whom she retained correspondence long afterward. From all accounts she thoroughly enjoyed her time in France and expressed regret when it inevitably came to an end.

In late March, the Brownes bade farewell to Nice with a hasty departure for Marseilles from which they sailed via Naples to Alexandria. They continued to Cairo for Browne's scheduled rendezvous with Herzl and the Khedive of Egypt. The timing of their meeting suggests that it involved discussion about the possibility of Zionist settlement in El Arish, a sparsely settled undeveloped strip of land in the Sinai Peninsula which was currently administered jointly by Great Britain and Egypt. The plan, seriously considered by Herzl and others as a temporary measure, was ultimately taken off the table because the Egyptians feared that additional use of the Nile overflow for agricultural irrigation would threaten their own vital water supply.[10]

When the Brownes reached Egypt, they found its Jewish community in a high state of anxiety over a terrifying anti-Semitic incident that had just occurred in Port Said. Greek and Armenian Christians had attacked a wealthy Jewish merchant from Aden as he walked into town from the dock. Repeating the age-old blood libel accusing Jews of seeking Christian blood to prepare Passover matzah, they claimed that he lured a six-year-old Christian girl who was walking behind him to follow him so he could murder her for the blood. Although he insisted that he had never seen her and did not know that she was following him, they beat him mercilessly until he lost consciousness, then robbed him and spread the blood libel story to cover their crime.

The Greek Christian community believed the attackers' lie and became so agitated that local Jews feared a massacre. Jewish nobleman Baron Manasseh of Alexandria, upon hearing the news, alerted British authorities who sent troops to contain the uprising. The attackers were arrested and found guilty; and the girl admitted having been coached to support their story. Court testimony revealed that Greek and Armenian priests bore much of the blame because they had told their people that local Jews were mandated to supply blood for the matzoh.[11]

Browne reported the incident to the Associated Press with the headline "A Blood Accusation Nipped in the Bud," which was copied in European and American newspapers. The libel, rarely corrected so quickly or bloodlessly, was still frequently paralleled in Eastern Europe, the Middle East and North Africa. Within a week it would trigger the bloodiest massacre of them all.

Sophie feared that family members, upon learning of the Port Said incident, would worry that she and the rabbi were in danger, and became even more concerned when international headlines announced that Egypt had been placed under quarantine for an unspecified communicable disease. In reassuring the family at home that she and the rabbi were safe, she wrote that they were in no physical danger but the quarantine might delay their mail delivery. This and other reports, most of which she inscribed on picture post cards with instructions to save them for a collection, provide illuminating details of the couple's travels in Europe and the Holy Land.[12]

The Brownes left Egypt on April 11, sailing from Alexandria via Port Said to Jaffa, and then going by carriage overland to Jerusalem, a journey as emotional as it was tiring. Although Sophie rarely recorded emotions in her messages home, she reported then that "Papa almost wept" as they passed the mountains of Judea. In ascending to Jerusalem, ever a spiritual experience for Jews, the landscape augments imagination to produce an overwhelming sense of awe and historic connection. One seldom forgets a first arrival in Jerusalem.

The Brownes arrived in the Holy City on the eve of Passover. Sophie wrote that the city was very crowded in anticipation of the holiday, and that it was very expensive. As evidence of the latter, she saved her invoice from the Kaminitz Hotel certifying that she had to pay three francs merely to take a bath.

Frugal Sophie also deplored the need to pay a soldier in addition to their guide to escort them on their journey to Bethlehem, Hebron, and Jericho— cities between which they crossed bleak and dangerous desert—and along the Jordan River. Touring was uncomfortable and exhausting, she reported, because there were no tramways or railroads so they had to travel entirely by carriage, over bumpy roads fraught with unforeseen delays. She conceded, however, that these inconveniences were sometimes ameliorated by human courtesies, and praised the caretaker of Rachel's Tomb for unlocking it, thus permitting them to go inside despite having arrived after sun-down, its closing time.[13]

Although there is no record of how the Brownes celebrated Passover, it may be assumed that they did so in the company of resident Palestinian Jews. The rabbi's interest in Christianity added further meaning to his sojourn in Jerusalem at that time of year, for only a few days later he attended Easter services at the Church of the Holy Sepulcher. That was not a pleasant experience. "At this Easter celebration," he wrote:

The church itself is turned into a stable of unspeakable filth, the building being crowded for twenty-four hours previous, because the people are told by the clergy that about noon, fire will come from the grave of

Christ. Of course, by some contrivance, at the very time, flame does issue
from the sepulcher. Then comes the rush of these heathen Christians,
each one holding a candle in his hand and anxious to be the first to
light it on the holy fire. The scene baffles description when they rush
from the church with candles lighted, all singing hymns and swearing
vengeance on all other religious denominations. That mob is certainly fit
to massacre anyone not of its creed.[14]

Such was the superstition and hatred fostered by fanatic priests, especially in the Holy Land where competing branches of the Catholic Church vied to dominate sites sacred to all Christians and significant to world history. Imbued as he was with respect for Catholicism which his visit with Pope Leo XIII had enhanced, Browne was deeply shocked to experience first-hand the sort of depravity that historically ignited anti-Semitism among the masses.

Although he could not have known it then, on that very day as Browne watched Easter observances in Jerusalem, Jews were being massacred in the Russian-Rumanian city of Kishinev. The murderous rampage, one of the worst in recorded history, was ignited by the age-old blood libel against Jews, in its beginning not unlike the one recently foiled in Egypt. The Kishinev massacre appalled decent people throughout the world and set off a tidal wave of emigration from Eastern Europe. Its horror strengthened Browne's resolve, as it did for Jews everywhere, to find a refuge for their kinsmen who lived in fear and poverty. Browne's appointment to appear before the Sultan in Constantinople gave him a measure of hope that he could hasten that dream.[15]

Apparently this was his principal purpose in spending the year abroad. Sophie reported that it was unfortunate that they had had to leave Jerusalem on April 22 without his having completed his work of "following Christ from cradle . . . to grave." The deadline was necessary in order for him to reach Constantinople by April 29 for his presentation at the Sublime Porte.[16]

The rabbi reported that Sultan Abdul Hamid offered him lands for Zionist settlement in Mesopotamia, presented him with the Grand Cordon of the Osmanic Empire, and bestowed "signal honors" on Sophie. Browne declined the medal, believing it to be unpatriotic for an American to accept such an honor from a foreign country. Apparently Herzl and the Zionist Congress declined the offer of lands in Mesopotamia because the area was unsuitable for Jewish settlement.[17]

In addition to his audience with the Sultan, the rabbi lectured at the Literary Union of Constantinople and met with members of the Moslem, Christian and Jewish intelligentsia. They offered their views of conditions throughout the empire, presumably including candid assessment of possible threats to the Jews. The question remains unanswered as to whether Browne processed this information with the understanding that it came from the elite, the well-situated and well-educated of all three religious communities, and as such may have represented only one side of the complex reality as seen by other nations.

After spending several weeks at the Hotel Rubin in Constantinople, the Brownes departed the Ottoman capital and traveled by train to Sophia, the capital of Bulgaria. There Sophie joked about the city being her namesake. Without further comment on their time there, they proceeded to Hungary through Serbia. They were briefly detained by government officials when their train stopped in Serbia, an affront about which Browne complained to the American consul in Belgrade.

Having gotten no satisfaction from the consul, Browne pursued a year-long correspondence with the United States Department of State that concluded with the curt statement indicating that the case did not warrant government intervention. The rabbi failed to disclose any reason the Serbs may have given for detaining him, but in view of the treatment that Jews customarily received in Eastern Europe at that time, inherent anti-Semitism had probably been the cause. His reaction again demonstrates his bulldog determination that the American government address discrimination whenever it occurs, however trivial the incident may appear to be.[18]

In Budapest, the Brownes were joined by their son Jesse. The handsome young man, who for several years had been living and working in New York, was soon to be married to Fanny Mittledorfer, daughter of a prominent Richmond family. Possibly regarding the journey as his final bachelor fling, he departed Hungary after a brief stay and moved on to taste the delights of Berlin, Paris and London.

Sophie fell ill while in Hungary, presumably with a recurring stomach ailment, which forced her to stay there under a doctor's care throughout the summer. Browne remained by her side until August when he traveled north, possibly to attend the sixth Zionist Congress in Basel at the end of the month. On September 1st, he wrote to his family from Germany en route to Vienna, after which he rejoined Sophie in Budapest. They spent the Holy Days there, remaining until October. Then they visited Italy, making brief stops in Venice, Verona, Sorrento and Pompei, and embarked for America on the S.S. Cambroman at Naples on October 13.[19]

Suspicions arise indicating that their voyage was not altogether pleasant. In a letter to Lylah, Sophie hinted at the possibility of underlying marital discord, a condition that often may be suppressed until exposed by the stress of extended travel. She wrote that because she was ill when they reached Naples, she had asked her husband to check on their luggage to be sure that it had arrived in Naples and was loaded onto the ship, a task that she normally performed herself. He considered the caution unnecessary and refused to do it.

Their steamer trunks were not aboard the ship, and Sophie fretted throughout the voyage that they were irretrievably lost. In addition to clothing, her fine David Baer carrier with its elegantly decorated interior held numerous gifts and souvenirs, among them an elaborate brass quill and pen point holder from Turkey, a carved olive wood camel figurine inkwell from Egypt, and rosaries from the Holy Land to distribute among their Catholic friends in America. Fortunately the luggage was not lost. Sophie's trunk and much of its contents still survive.[20]

Sophie revealed another hint of marital tension, when telling Lylah that she wanted to go ashore while the S. S. Cambroman was docked in the Azores on the following day, she wrote, "Presume Papa will allow me to disembark, although he has already been there."

This suggests a degree of subservience on her part and indifference on his, even considering the mores of male dominance and protectiveness that obtained in 1903. It also questions the initial view of their union as one that promised balanced respect. Had her rise and his decline injected an element of envy in their relationship? Did she despair at the prospect of their future after so many moves, and sometimes fail to hide her feelings? Had a year and a half of travel, most of it in a cocoon of close quarters and unfamiliar environment, exacerbated existing tensions? Was the nine year difference in their ages beginning to take its toll? One can only guess, but the signs were clear.

In the same letter, Sophie told Lylah that she had been suffering with stomach pains and would probably stop in New York to see her physician there. In view of her several unidentifiable earlier illnesses, these shipboard complaints add to a suspicion that her health was affected by longtime marital stress. Considering Browne's personality and his peripatetic career, it is not unreasonable to suspect that tension between them grew as she developed into a progressive woman of the twentieth century while he faced the downward slope of what had been initially a meteoric success.[21]

Returning to Columbus in her prime after more than a year of foreign travel, Sophie used her newly acquired knowledge and experience to enhance the lives and broaden the vision of her community at home. For the next few years she led her Century Club women in the study of Shakespeare's plays and sonnets, then supervised their study of British and German history over another several more years. Eventually the group embraced community service through affiliation with the Columbus Federation of Women's Clubs, the Georgia Federation of Women's Clubs and the National Council of Jewish Women, suspending their study programs during the First World War to work with the Red Cross. Representing the Century Club on the boards of these affiliates, Sophie became active in public issues, primarily those affecting women, especially the woman's right to vote.[22]

Browne returned to Columbus jobless and no longer in his prime. There is no record of any specific accomplishment derived from his mission abroad, other than his renewed determination to pursue whatever means he perceived necessary that promised relief from anti-Semitism and opportunity for Jews to enjoy the full measure of first-class citizenship in America.

With the death of Isaac Mayer Wise in 1900 and the ascendancy of Rabbi Kaufman Kohler to the presidency of the Hebrew Union College in 1903, Reform Judaism in America veered ever further from its conservative beginnings. Originally it had retained ancient customs that still held meaning or could be made meaningful to modern life. Now this obtained only in Europe. In America most customs were abandoned and Hebrew, other than the *Shema* and the *Boruch hu*, was forgotten. Teaching increasingly focused on ethical issues and social justice as exemplified by the biblical prophets, soon rendering the name Prophetic Judaism synonymous with Reform.

The newly established movement of Conservative Judaism with its Jewish Theological Seminary was gaining adherents throughout the country. The rising generation of Jews from Eastern Europe sought to adapt their traditions to the realities of America without discarding them altogether. In ensuing years, Browne, more compatible with this path than with the current trend of Reform in which nearly all tradition was being discarded, served congregations that veered toward Conservatism although they had not yet joined that movement officially. With brief tenures in each congregation, he continued to make news as an orator and activist, a maverick intellectual stirring the waters for reforms in their broadest connotation, at every turn gaining staunch friends and admirers as well as bitter enemies. Sadly, each move was to a lower rung on the ladder of success.

XII - ROOSEVELT, TAFT AND TRAGEDY

Although a consummate reformer, Browne was not in tune with
the Reform movement. Since Wise's death in 1900, his disciples, their
congregations, and the organizations that he established had become
radicalized, ever more distanced from the early Reform that Browne
embraced. He and growing numbers of others looked to developing patterns
of worship based on the principles enunciated in Europe during their youth.
They believed that Judaism could adapt to conditions in America without
abandoning meaningful traditions merely for the sake of blending in with the
Christian majority. They understood that it was possible to be fully Jewish
and fully American simultaneously.

This concept congealed along with support for Zionism in a new branch
of Judaism, Conservatism, strengthened by young, Americanized rabbis
trained in New York's Jewish Theological Seminary. Founded in 1885,
JTS flourished only after Solomon Schechter came from England to be its
president in 1902. The Conservative movement itself, however, had already
gained adherents among the upwardly mobile Jews from Eastern Europe.
Whereas in 1880 the estimated Jewish population of America was 250,000
with only twelve out of two hundred congregations declaring themselves to
be other than Reform, there were now one million Jews in America with only
ninety-nine Reform congregations. This probably reflected less a diminution
of Reform than the fact that many congregations were previously open to
change but not to the extent fostered by the Reform Movement. Because
many of their members knew of Browne as an orator and defender of
immigrants, he became the rabbi of choice for a number of unaffiliated
congregations that leaned toward Conservatism.[1]

Ever more determined to convince the government of the need for a Jewish military chaplaincy, Browne grasped at politics to redress this as well as other perceived injustices. By this route he finally succeeded in obtaining a full pardon for Adolph Reich, although not without badgering those in power, specifically Theodore Roosevelt and William Howard Taft.

There is some indication that the rabbi resided briefly in Cleveland, Ohio, in 1901, where he temporarily served a Hungarian congregation before traveling abroad. He was then employed by the National Encyclopedia Company, a commercial venture in Cleveland that charged $35 each for biographical entries. Listed as editor, Browne documented examples of successful Jews in America and biographies of prominent non-Jews who notably interacted with them. These included Theodore Roosevelt, currently Vice President of the United States.[2]

This was not Browne's first contact with the irrepressible Teddy, nor would it be the last. Their initial friendship, presumably dating from Roosevelt's years in the New York state assembly, was confirmed by T. R. in 1888 when he introduced Browne to New York Governor David Hill for his appeal in the Reich case, identifying the rabbi as "my old social and political friend." Their relationship cooled when Roosevelt as governor refused Browne an appointment to plead for Reich's release, declaring that he had already devoted more time to the case than to any other that occurred prior to his administration. Now as Vice President, Roosevelt responded congenially to Browne's request for information.[3]

With perhaps a hint of defensiveness, Roosevelt noted several instances in which he had promoted Jews, "not because they were Jewish," but because he considered them best for the specific jobs to be filled. He also recalled that when it was his duty as New York City Police Commissioner to ensure the safety of a notorious European anti-Semite who came to lead a crusade against Jews in America, he had assigned a squad of forty Jewish policemen to guard him. ". . . it struck me," Roosevelt wrote, "that to have him protected by the very members of the race he was denouncing was the most effective answer to that denunciation." [4]

Roosevelt continued his correspondence with a characteristic burst of enthusiasm, asserting his friendship for Jews and offering advice on their welfare based on the popular belief that they belonged to a race short-changed on machismo. "I had rather prided myself on one point," he wrote, ". . . that it would be a particularly good thing for men of the Jewish race to develop that side of them which I might call the Maccabee or fighting Jewish type. I was confident that nothing would do more to put a stop to the unreasoning prejudice against them than to have it understood that not only were they successful and thrifty businessmen and high minded philanthropists, but also able to do their part in the rough, manly work which is no less necessary."[5]

The ostensibly renewed friendship did not last long. By 1904, Browne's earlier argument with Governor Roosevelt over the pardon had morphed into an obsession over President Roosevelt's denial of a Jewish chaplaincy. The absence of spiritual guidance became obvious during the Spanish American War when thousands of Jewish soldiers, sailors, and marines were serving their country abroad. Browne, although not alone among his colleagues in recognizing this, was one of the first to publicize it. They rewarded him with scorn and sarcasm. Possibly the president was like many other Americans who were, as historian John Higham observed, both pro- and anti-Jewish simultaneously. In any case, Browne now viewed Roosevelt's recalcitrance on Reich's pardon and the chaplaincy as evidence of anti-Semitism, and turned to political coercion as a means of accomplishing his goals.[6]

In September, 1901, Browne asked Thomas C. Platt, Republican

Party boss in New York, about the possibility of an assignment in the next presidential campaign. Platt replied that it was too early for him to know. By 1904, as the campaign geared up, Browne questioned his own support for Roosevelt in a second term because of the Jewish chaplaincy issue. Ever the optimist, Browne tried to appeal in person and when initially unsuccessful asked Roosevelt's close friend Elihu Root, then Secretary of War, to intercede for him. "The political situation is such," he wrote:

> that I must become either once more a friend of the President or his open opponent. . . . I can show that Roosevelt lied . . . in his pretended friendship to the Jews, that his "Russian Jews bloody shirt policy" is ridiculous, that he hates the Jews and has called a prominent New York Jewish lawyer a "dirty Jew-pop"—in short, I can blast him with every self respecting Jew and many Christians. . . . I have tried to reach R through several of his "friends" who knew of my means to harm him but those "friends" of his are not sincere and really want his defeat. You are a sincere friend . . . I therefore write to you. . . . I think the campaign of 1904 may depend upon your and General Clarkson's action in this matter.[7]

The letter found its way to the Oval Office where, predictably, it did not enhance Browne's chances for an appointment. In early September, 1904, Browne wrote to William Howard Taft, Root's successor as Secretary of War, introducing himself and suggesting "The election or defeat of Mr. Roosevelt may depend upon your giving close attention to these lines. . . . " He followed with voluminous documentation of his long service to the Republican Party, McKinley's refusal to appoint a Jewish chaplain during the Spanish-American War, and his own temptation to bolt from the party. The Democratic campaign, he wrote, had offered to pay him to support its candidate, the eloquent attorney, former congressman and perennial presidential candidate, William Jennings Bryan.

Browne also described his attempt in 1902 to coerce New York Governor Benjamin B. Odell to pardon Reich. Then, after summarizing candid complaints against Roosevelt, he stressed admiration for the president's achievements and expressed his desire to mend their relationship for the good of the party.[8]

There was actually a bit of logic in Browne's outrageous claim of power. Russian immigrants called him "our guardian angel." It was widely believed that as the city voted, so went the nation and, through his Hebrew American Republican League, he could still influence the large electorate of Jewish working men in New York. The influx of newcomers continued despite repeated attempts by Senator Henry Cabot Lodge and others to stem it by passage of anti-immigration laws.[9]

Browne informed Taft that he had consulted Republican king-makers Matthew Quay, Thomas C. Platt, and Mark Hanna about gaining the Jewish vote in New York, for which he wanted no pay except for Roosevelt to establish a Jewish chaplaincy and for Governor Odell to pardon Adolph Reich. Browne also wrote directly to Roosevelt requesting a Jewish chaplaincy "if only for one day." Here his logic is unclear. Perhaps he wanted to prove a point, or possibly to satisfy a long held personal ambition. Whatever his purpose, he failed to achieve it, for he received no answer from the president.[10]

He did, however, receive an answer from Platt, who reported that Governor Odell still refused to pardon Reich. This elicited from Browne a direct confrontation with Odell, reminding him that he had granted pardons "indiscriminately to less deserving prisoners than Reich," and threatening to campaign against him throughout New York State if he continued to withhold justice from an innocent man.[11]

This time Browne succeeded, for the race already appeared to be a close one. Contrasting the governor's grasp of reality with that of the president, he observed, "Odell, a man of sound mind, gave me on the 2 of July the pardon. . . . But Roosevelt is a stubborn man. . . ." The rabbi noted that Secretary of Commerce George Cortelyou, who wrote to him twice on the subject, "like a practical man, is evidently desirous to settle matters between Roosevelt and myself, but Roosevelt is stubborn and does not weigh the consequences."[12]

In Browne's opinion the president's indifference was caused by lobbyist Simon Wolf, a Washington attorney and a leader of B'nai B'rith who since the death of I. M. Wise in 1902 was looked upon by government officials as the voice of American Jewry. Characterizing him as one of the "court Jews," Browne maintained that Wolf spoke only for the elite, not for the majority of American Jews who by then, although primarily immigrants from Eastern Europe, were no longer voiceless greenhorns unable to speak for themselves. His contention that Wolf had no influence with them was largely correct. Furthermore, individual representation no longer prevailed. The newly established American Jewish Committee had supplanted the old "court Jew" system as the effective voice of American Jewry in government-related issues. Led by such highly respected men as attorney Louis Marshall and philanthropist Jacob Schiff, the AJC effectively employed low-key diplomacy to achieve its goals.[13]

It is possible that Cortelyou acted in response to Browne's threat of causing Roosevelt's defeat at the polls. The ninety percent of New York's Jews who were Orthodox could be turned against Roosevelt by revealing his refusal to appoint a chaplain for Jewish servicemen, and would surely vote him out if they suspected him of anti-Semitism. Furthermore,

Browne hinted at yet another arrow in his quiver for use against Roosevelt if necessary. While involved in Sophie's mail box project, he heard that the president had tried to protect some accused participants in a postal fraud. He told Taft that he had a letter documenting the incident, for which the Democrats offered to pay him, asking that he join their campaign to defeat the president. He refused, saying that he was "of course, still looking for a lucid interval in Roosevelt's mind."[14]

Browne assured Taft that he did not seek money or glory, but must "guard my name as the life-long defender of my people's rights," and suggested that Taft try to effect a reconciliation between himself and the president. In doing so, he cautioned, it would be best to imply that the initiative came not from himself, but from some of Taft's Jewish friends in Cincinnati. Although Taft's response is unknown, a rapprochement of sorts apparently occurred because Browne received a signed photograph of the president dated October 25, 1904.[15]

Whatever measure of reconciliation that gesture may have implied was extremely short-lived. Browne released flyers advertizing a Columbus lecture on October 11, in which he intended to blast Roosevelt with alleged anti-Semitism, bribery, pro-lynching sentiment, and even treason, the last incurred by permitting the escape of a European aristocrat purported to be a spy, "to please . . . a prince bearing gifts for Miss Alice," the president's glamorous debutante daughter, often called "Princess Alice."[16]

In an interview with the African American newspaper Southern Workman, Browne again criticized Roosevelt, bitingly but no more so than numerous other critics. It quoted the rabbi about a book that he was writing, the History of American Judaism, in which he called Roosevelt "The Savage in Kid Gloves" and "The Mad Mullah of the White House." Browne's publishers subsequently canceled their agreement, which he attributed to orders from the president. The accusation was not unreasonable in light of Roosevelt's character and practice as depicted by his eminent biographer, Edmond Morris.[17]

The Southern Workman also revealed that after Reich's release from prison, Browne wrote a play about the case for New York's Yiddish Theater. In it he included Roosevelt's refusal to exonerate Reich and reportedly cast himself in the role of the rabbi.[18]

However damaged by rash behavior, Browne maintained his pulpit appeal, continuing to receive and accept congregational positions despite his self-proclaimed financial independence and obvious lack of enthusiasm for synagogue work. He evidently enjoyed helping establish congregations for Jewish immigrants, especially his fellow Hungarians. These were liberals, reformers but not radically Reform, most of them later identifying as Conservative.[19]

Another reason that Browne continued as a pulpit rabbi may have been that he needed a constituency in order to validate status, a requisite for presidential recognition and influencing legislation. In this role he was virtually alone among rabbis. Although Wise remained an outspoken partisan throughout his life, helping Democrats mainly through his newspapers, few if any other rabbis of that time are known to have involved themselves in electoral politics beyond sermonizing their views on social issues. The new exponents of what had become known as Classical Reform such as Henry Berkowitz and Joseph Krauskopf of Philadelphia, Joseph Stolz of Chicago, David Marx of Atlanta and Max Heller of New Orleans, took leadership roles in local organizations devoted to civic betterment, notably those related to education, social welfare and brotherhood. Although Krauskopf won government recognition for his progressive achievements, no rabbi was known to have gone as far as Browne in coercing action.[20]

In 1905, on the heels of his politically manipulated success in freeing Reich, Browne returned to Toledo, not to his former pulpit but to the more traditional Vermont Avenue Synagogue. Here his known efforts focused on the courts, not the synagogue. He took up the gauntlet for two Ohio Jews, convicted of separate crimes and generally believed to be innocent. One of them, identified only as Weinberg, currently languished in the state penitentiary convicted for receiving stolen property. The other, Max Lisberger, was serving a life sentence for second-degree murder.[21]

Browne appealed to Ohio Governor Myron T. Herrick on behalf of both men, blaming anti-Semitic prejudice for having influenced the verdicts. Six months later, he attended a hearing of the Ohio Board of Pardons on the Weinberg case, along with two other Toledo men, both of whom had expected the accused to be released. Instead, the board sustained Weinberg's conviction and closed the case.[22]

Obtaining pardon for Max Lisberger was Browne's greater concern. As with Adolph Reich in New York, newspapers had glaringly referred to him as "Murderer" from the beginning, convincing readers that he was guilty even before the trial began. Lisberger testified that he had killed in self-defense, merely pushing his victim away without realizing that the man was attacking him with a knife. Browne doggedly pursued the case as he had done for Reich, lecturing to finance a new trial and to help support the prisoner's destitute wife and eight children. At a September hearing, according to the Toledo Blade, he gave an "impassioned address" before the Board of Pardons, charging that the trial had been affected by "a strong anti-Jew sentiment" locally.[23]

The prosecution maintained that Lisberger had been tried twice and given a fair hearing, making no attempt to plead self-defense. Browne countered that the second trial had been presided over by one of the "most

cruel" judges in the state, that many of Toledo's best lawyers had praised
the defense, and that the entire city was "dumbfounded" by the verdict and
sentence. When someone suggested that the judge might write a letter on
Lisberger's behalf, Browne replied that he had already requested it and had
been refused, adding, "I might as well have asked the devil for a blessing as to
have asked him for a good word for a Jew."[24]

A notation in Browne's papers indicates that his efforts were not in vain.
The defense launched an appeal based on newly discovered evidence. The
judge, while denying the motion for a new trial, asked the jurisdiction to
"entertain remedy of the accused," noting that Lisberger had been "unfairly
treated by witnesses for the state and that on account of some prejudice
against him he is a victim of a wicked conspiracy." Lisberger was freed on
May 14, 1908.[25]

Media sensationalism and anti-Semitism were not the only areas of
similarity between this case and Reich's. Here as in New York, the rabbi's
participation arguably impacted his tenure. Browne departed Toledo in 1906,
less than a year after he had arrived there. As in New York, the extent to
which his charitable action affected his position is unclear, but he is known to
have had at least one altercation with a member of Toledo's Vermont Avenue
Synagogue.[26]

These experiences in Toledo heightened Browne's awareness that indigent
Jewish immigrants unfamiliar with the ways of American courts were in need
of reliable, affordable legal aid, and would be best served by acculturated
Jewish brethren who spoke their native language. In some cities such ethnic-
oriented societies already existed for German-speaking immigrants, the first
having been established in Chicago during the previous century by Edward
Salomon, a practicing attorney who had also served as counsel for the
Prussian government. New York provided a legal aid society for all its needy

as early as 1876, and Rabbi Max Heller later founded a similar organization in New Orleans. Initially Browne sought government sponsorship for a national facility. Failing that, he turned to Jewish friends in New York who, in October 1907, combined to organize the American Jewish Seventy Elders. They elected J.P. Solomon, editor of the New York Hebrew Standard, as president and Browne as honorary president for life as well as public defender, a capacity in which he represented victims of perceived anti-Semitism, pro bono, for the next twenty years. Focusing primarily though not exclusively on the defense of needy Jews who ran afoul of the law, the group defined itself to be chartered not as a legal aid society but "a purely religious Secret Society like the SEVENTY ELDERS appointed by Moses 3300 years ago."[27]

The book of Exodus records that Moses chose seventy elders to assist him by adjudicating all but the most difficult disputes, leaving those cases for him to decide. Browne perceived that America needed a similar organization. The constantly increasing immigrant population rendered it impossible for existing legal aid societies to keep up with the overwhelming number of needy who applied, and rising anti-Semitism suggested that Jewish cases tended to be ignored or disposed of in a less-than-caring manner.[28]

Soon yet another manifestation of prejudice drew Browne's attention. The social anti-Semitism that first surfaced on the national scene by excluding Jews from fashionable summer resorts had grown and was gathering momentum in the press. Browne, again suffering from failing eyesight, was in New York during the summer of 1906 to undergo two operations at Mount Sinai Hospital and was invited to preach one Shabbat morning at Beth Tefilah, a synagogue at 107th Street and Lexington Avenue identified as his former congregation. There he addressed the current discrimination at fashionable resorts, being exacerbated by a spate of anti-Semitic newspaper comments about Jews on vacation.[29]

The World quoted Browne in detail under the over-all caption, "JEWS' WORST SIDE SHOWN AT RESORTS". It carried three sub-captions: "Best Left Home, Rabbi Browne Says, When the Summer Silly Season is On;" "His Religion Tends to Make the Jews Happy;" and "The Noted Preacher Explains Little Understood Phases of Jewish Life." While leaving no doubt about the prevalence of anti-Semitism, the reviewer's well-intended hyperbole may have obscured most of Browne's message.[30]

The rabbi began by noting that, because Judaism discourages total abstinence, celibacy and asceticism, "the Jew builds his club, which he visits with his family," considers vacation resorts as extensions of the clubs and behaves accordingly. Using the issue to criticize Radical Reform, he admitted that Jews had "undesirable elements, and in the watering places particularly so," but declared that the "true Jew— religious, intellectual and moral" was not to be found at summer resorts, and enjoined his "dear Christian brother" to remember that the Jew they see there:

> the "ham and eggs" rabbis, Sunday Sabbath rabbis, bare-headed Jews
> . . . [are] only a part of the Jew and that the worst part . . . for he has
> left at home his religion, his charity, his business and even his family life
> and takes along with him only his club. He is on a spree . . . yet he does
> not forget himself and become immoral.[31]

The same newspaper noted that, while Browne was minister of the Gates of Hope synagogue in the 1880s, he was "one of the trio—Henry George, Dr. [Edward] McGlynn and Rabbi Browne—who [sic] held the boards [public platforms] in New York at the time when George ran for Mayor for the first time." McGlynn was the priest excommunicated for endorsing George's theories which had by no means been forgotten then and remain largely unaccepted even now.

Although inconsistent with his urging Jews to become self-confident, Browne's hint of apologia may be understood in view of the prevalent anti-Semitism and anti-immigrant sentiment at that time. The surge of industrialization resulting from the Civil War had spurred a massive move to cities of the north and mid-west, mostly by poor, uneducated farm workers fleeing the South's devastated agrarian system. As this condition fostered the growth of existing social forces such as Populism and Protestant Evangelism, it also gave rise to new movements such as Progressivism, Social Darwinism and the Social Gospel. Overwhelming immigration of the 1880s added to the ferment, inundating cities with even more impoverished laborers and petty craftsmen, a large proportion of whom were Jews from Russia and its Eastern European satellites, among them intellectuals, equally poor yet highly educated. Some brought socialist ideas into the mix already bubbling with the likes of Henry George's single tax theory and William Jennings Bryan's advocacy of free coinage, national ownership of railroads and religious fundamentalism.[32]

Since the 1890s, rampant laissez faire policy had enabled large businesses to become giants, forming corporate monsters that reduced the ability of smaller businesses to stay afloat and arguably caused the economic panics of 1893 and 1907. So fragmented were the political discontents that eight separate parties ran nominees in the presidential election of 1908. While Republicans won with Taft, helped considerably by the incumbent Roosevelt, the Democrats emerged as a close second with Bryan who continued to dominate his party for the next four years. The Republicans ran on a platform of tariff revision, stricter enforcement of anti-trust legislation and land conservation, whereas Democrats in much stronger terms addressed tariff reforms and condemned monopolies. Urban Jews and other immigrants usually voted Democratic because, in city politics, that party catered to the poor and was perceived to be the friend of the underdog. Republicans, generally conservative, appealed more to middle and upper-income Americans, whose interests were well served by the status quo.

Browne himself was a Democrat during his first years in America but embraced the Republicans in the eighties because that party encouraged public education. Whereas his teacher and former mentor Wise had been a staunch Democrat, Browne's father-in-law, Moses Weil, was an active Republican. Wise may have been influenced by living in Cincinnati where political as well as geographical proximity to the South encouraged his views, but Weil who lived in Evansville, Indiana, also across the river from the former Dixieland, did not espouse his neighbors' views. Both men had emigrated from emancipated areas of western Europe and became successful, deeply patriotic American citizens. Their similar background and differing politics exemplify the range of political opinion that obtained among American Jews then as it does now.

Political ferment, overwhelming immigration, and intensified anti-Semitism combined to induce changes in the comfort level of Jews long integrated into American life. The emergence of rabbinical seminaries in America provided communities with religious leaders who could meet their Christian peers on equal footing and—most importantly—serve as ambassadors for their Jewish constituents. Capable young rabbis like Max Heller and David Marx became community brokers for Jewish interests on behalf of congregants who, their confidence shaken by resurgent anti-Semitism and economic change, were now increasingly reticent about speaking out as individuals. The atmosphere of openness that had welcomed Browne in the seventies and eighties had vanished. Now circumstances required a different approach to self-confident ecumenism, one to which he did not seamlessly adapt. Jewishness needed more explanation and Christian enthusiasm for it had waned.

On the High Holy Days 1906, again identified as rabbi of Temple Gates of Hope, Browne preached in favor of anti-trust legislation, a key tenet of the Roosevelt administration. Not permitting his pique over past issues to restrict his praise for the president's "apprehension of the necessity for muzzling the accumulators of unlimited wealth," he informed his listeners that neither the president's policy, nor Bryan's theory of national ownership and "Hearst-Stokes socialism," nor Henry George's single tax theory were new, for all had been tested in Jewish national life by the laws of Moses:

Moses foresaw the political-economical evils inevitable in every Commonwealth, hence he provided for the poor and needy by special laws, and while there ought not to have been a destitute class according to the division of the land, still, knowing the diversity of human nature, he says, "There will never be a lack of needy in the land." Moses provided also for panics. In the business world about every seventh year a panic sets in from unknown causes, hence Moses instituted the "year of release" every seventh year, which was a sort of national bankruptcy law wiping out all debts so that the bankrupt debtor could start again with a clean bill of commercial health. But although the land was divided up among the individual heads of families, it was owned by the nation after all, and Henry George's "single tax principle" was then already in force, as the tax was merely upon the land intended for the support of the Levites, the poor and the needy.[33]

Continuing his interpretation of Scripture as history, Browne noted that in ancient Palestine Jews had paid taxes amounting to approximately 20% of their income. "If we were to tax everybody's income as Moses did," he said, " there would be no needy in the United States." These were lessons seldom taught in synagogues during High Holy Day services, when most congregants preferred spiritual uplift to practical advice. Some may have interpreted it as preaching socialism, a policy unacceptable to many Americans then as now.[34]

The following April, Browne again drew crowds and fulfilled his wish to serve the needy when asked to address an audience of Christians at the Reformed Church, Convent Avenue and 49th Street, for the benefit of an impoverished elderly woman who had once been a leading philanthropist (her name withheld to ensure privacy). Sponsors advertized that his subject, "The Talmud and the Gospels; Their Ethics and Literary Beauties," was "bound to have a peculiar interest for ministers and Bible students of all religious denominations." In this and similar ways the rabbi followed his own path, independent of Jewish organizations and endorsement.[35]

Consistently seeking to gain points with the Republican party in the hope of convincing America's next president to establish a Jewish chaplaincy, Browne offered his services in New York for the presidential campaign of 1908. Ohio Senator (formerly Governor) Joseph B. Foraker told him that it did not seem likely that the party would have trouble winning, but would call on him if needed. Foraker added that there was not yet any indication that Taft would be nominated, for the district committees had not yet convened to select their delegates.[36]

A personal note by the politician suggested an interest in Jewish history. After trying unsuccessfully to get a copy of Browne's "History of Judaism in America," he assumed that it was not yet published and asked how to get one. Presumably Browne responded by admitting that he had not completed writing it.[37]

In another letter soon after Foraker, then chairman of the Senate

Committee on the Pacific Islands and Puerto Rico, told Browne that he had brought the question of a Jewish chaplaincy before the Committee on Military Affairs. The committee then asked the Secretary of War, William Howard Taft, how many Jewish soldiers were in the Army and in which units they served. Pending Taft's reply, Foraker could neither press the military committee on the subject nor predict its result.[38]

Taft was in no hurry to reply, for he was about to resign as Secretary of War in order to run for president. With elections imminent and a movement afoot for Republicans to choose the progressive Charles Evans Hughes, Browne sought patronage by asking elder statesman Stewart L. Woodford, a past acquaintance who now served as leader of the Progressives, to find a place for him in the forthcoming political process.[39]

Woodford replied with warmth and recognition but not with encouragement. He wrote that he remembered Browne well, "as a friend of General Grant and know how he trusted you," omitting any reference to a position. Regarding a suggestion by Browne about influencing the Jewish vote, possibly in reference to Woodford's own Catholic background, the statesman responded:

> *I do not wonder at your feeling after the horrible pogroms in Russia, but I do not wish to evoke religious feeling in a contest for nomination within our party. Your people and mine have suffered too horribly in the past from such passions when aroused and I must leave each man to act according to his own conscience and judgment, without any suggestion from me, looking towards the activity of any creed or sect. I write thus directly, because you and I knew each other in the old days when General Grant was our personal friend and I am sure you cannot and will not misunderstand me.[40]*

The correspondence revealed Browne's growing desperation, his need to regain a place in the larger world, to rejoin the activists and once again to experience the excitement of politics. It also revealed further evidence of his deterioration, his often questionable judgement, and his failure to draw support.

Still based in Columbus and predictably restless, Browne pursued a heavy political correspondence. As the landslide for Taft mounted that spring, Woodford, now head of the Hughes League of the United States, the purpose of which was to secure Hughes' nomination as Republican presidential candidate, wrote to Browne that friends of the New York governor and future Supreme Court justice had not yet "thrown up the sponge." They still intended to present Hughes at the convention, for they believed that Taft did not yet have within eighty votes of the number necessary for nomination. When Browne asked how to advise the Georgia delegation to vote, Woodford replied vehemently:

> If your Georgia friends have no higher purpose than to get on the band wagon, Secretary Taft certainly has more votes than anybody else at present and there ought to be good front seats on his wagon. If that is their higher purpose in our American public life tell them to get on quick. If they stand for conscience and for the strongest nomination that we can make, they had better stay off. But I am tired of this miserable attempt to get something out of politics all the time. If this spirit pervades all our people we are going to have a democratic victory next November.[41]

Browne was certainly guilty of wanting to get something out of politics. Whether due to his influence or not, the Georgia delegation attended the convention uninstructed. Frustrated and discouraged by his own joblessness,

Browne asked Woodford for an appointment as military chaplain for New York State. The politician replied that he did not believe state law permitted such a chaplaincy but would have one of his legal staff look into the matter. He perceived Browne's despair, however, and sought help for him through their mutual friend, the Jewish politician, elder statesman and philanthropist Edward Lauterbach.

Republican county committee chairman in the 1890s and currently founding president of the National Liberal Immigration League, Lauterbach responded directly to Browne that he found "nothing whatever that carries any salary with it that at this juncture would enable the governor to give you an appointment." Whatever could be done, Lauterbach said, must be handled by Woodford because he himself was "not entirely satisfied with the way in which political matters have proceeded during the last three months, and my dissatisfaction is well known." Seemingly, both friends understood that Browne's usefulness to the party had ended.[42]

Browne's situation worsened by summer,1908. Shortly before the Republican Convention in Chicago, Woodford wrote to him referring to having received the "painful words about yourself. . . ." He told Browne that he and Lauterbach had carefully culled the list of places where they wielded influence, but found nothing appropriate for him. "You are a thinker and naturally a leader among your people," Woodford added, gently softening the truth:

> *A merely subordinate place would (even if we could get such an [sic] one for you) is sure to soon become impossible. In the largest places I find no vacancy. I wanted to help you. I could not. I doubt if there is even a petty clerical place within Lauterbach's area he could get. I am sorry, but my respect for your ability and position compels prompt and entire*

frankness.

*So strong and learned a man as you must not and will not lie down,
overcome or crushed by misfortune. I know that you will pull yourself
together, make fight against misfortune, and win. My very best wishes
are with you and for you.*[43]

Bad as things were, Browne had by no means lost his fighting spirit. On
the contrary, the prospect of a new administration stirred his hopes and
strengthened his determination to see the Jewish chaplaincy established. To
that end he dispatched a series of lengthy letters to Taft immediately after
the national convention, again urging action on the chaplaincy in return
for campaign support. He reintroduced himself with much underlining, as
follows [emphasis in original]:[44]

*I am _Rabbi Browne_ and as it seems that Providence has put into my
hands the means of doing you more harm or more good than any one
citizen can in this campaign, I come to speak to you as a man to a man,
disregard your attitude towards me thus far—being aware that you had
to echo the sentiments of Mr. Roosevelt who is my personal enemy—up
to your nomination; but now you can not afford to ignore a man who has
in his powers to take away from you possibly your election.*[45]

Conceding that he may have sounded bombastic, Browne explained
the various items that he was enclosing, especially one that advertized his
forthcoming volume "The Immigrant and His Boy." The Democratic
Campaign Committee, he wrote, had made his publishers "a very acceptable
offer" to dedicate the book to its presidential nominee, William Jennings

Bryan, an honor that included picturing the honoree in the book's widely circulated prospectus along with other "prominent and useful citizens in the doubtful states." Browne noted that the publishers were urging him to approve Bryan for the dedication, but since his contract gave him full control, the choice was his and would rest upon Taft's attitude concerning the Jewish chaplaincy.

After listing his credentials as a committed Republican—a friend of every Republican president since Andrew Johnson, consultant to every Republican Campaign Committee since 1884 "as to the foreign and Jewish vote," and responsible for the Georgia delegation endorsing McKinley in 1896— Browne admitted having opposed Taft's nomination and denying him an instructed delegation from Georgia. Nevertheless he wanted the Republican standard bearer to win and, because he could cause loss of the Jewish vote, suggested that Taft welcome his help in exchange for a commitment on the Jewish chaplaincy. Browne added the comment that Taft was "not any too popular amongst the Russian Jews anyway."

Concluding, the rabbi mentioned his friendship with Taft's father in 1867 when together with Wise they were "pillars of the Free Religious Association started by the Unitarians." Browne also noted that he was enclosing a memo on the Jewish chaplaincy that he asked be read to Congress. Lastly, he proposed a meeting with Taft to clarify their understanding, assuring him that he wanted no remuneration for his services, not even reimbursement for traveling expenses.[46]

Less than two weeks later, Browne complained to Taft that he had not received an answer. Disclaiming any personal wish to decide on the book's dedication immediately, he blamed his publishers for continuing to press the matter. Because he presumed that Taft had to consult others, he volunteered to wait until the following Wednesday [two days] for a reply. If not notified by then, however, he must assume that the suggestion was of no interest and therefore "obey the wishes" of his publishers. To facilitate their meeting, Browne included instructions by which Taft could contact him in Norfolk, Virginia, where he would be preaching at Beth El Synagogue. "If I do not hear from you within five days." he stressed with underlining, "I shall make arrangements to take up the fight against you. . . . If you are willing to rectify the Jewish Chaplain mistake I am with you. . . . If you ignore this friendly letter I shall open fire on you in my pulpit on the Day of Atonement October 5th and in other pulpits until Election Day."[47]

Taft invited Browne to meet him in Cincinnati, but before he received Browne's letter. The rabbi answered, "I am very glad indeed, as [the letter] just came in time to prevent me from writing the editorial 'Why have we no Jewish Chaplains' for the New York Hebrew Standard as you see in an enclosure. . . ."[48]

Browne then suggested that Taft commit himself publicly to the establishment of a Jewish chaplaincy while still in his present position as Secretary of War. Offering to come to Cincinnati "at any time after Sunday noon," Browne volunteered a plan that he would launch "on next Saturday, September 26th when I preach the Jewish New Year's sermons." He explained that because the rebuilding of his New York synagogue, Temple Beth El, at 116th Street and Fifth Avenue, had been halted due to the death of its president, he would be in Norfolk to preach the Holy Day sermons but must be back in New York on September 25th. "Write me upon receipt of this," he advised, "and I will . . . be with you Tuesday morning." He also proposed that Taft invite Cincinnati businessman Moses E. Mack, "as noble a Jew as he is a Republican," to join them, and warned him to tell no one else of their plan. In a post-script he added that Lauterbach had just recalled him to New York "to map out the work on the Jewish vote" for Hughes who was running for reelection as governor since losing his bid for the presidential nomination. Happily, Lauterbach had found a use for Browne's services, if not nationally, at least within New York state, and if not a permanent job, at least for temporary work on the campaign.[49]

Not surprisingly, Browne received a telegram from Taft cancelling their appointment. Browne replied, "You may not remember the Gospel as I do," quoting from it "'He who is not with me is against me'" and then offering the following plan:

I will be either with *you or* against *you as things stand now. If you wish to right the wrong, do as follows: Ask your President to appoint me —without quibbling—as* Chaplain pro tem *just for the coming high Holydays, to look after the Jewish sailors and soldiers in New York and Norfolk...and you can announce as follows: In June, 1908, Rabbi Browne and Mr. Berthold Frankel of New York called on Judge Taft, then still Secretary of War, as a committee with a petition of 5,000 New York Hebrews to appoint a Jewish Chaplain at large for the Department of the East Jewish soldiers and sailors, presenting at the same time two editorials from the New York Hebrew Standard complaining that the Jewish soldiers and sailors in the Philippines were buried by a Catholic priest Chaplain, and a Catholic Chaplain had officiated in Manila to the Jewish soldiers on the* Day of Atonement *with a crucifix dangling down from his breast.*

Continuing with his plan, he suggested that Taft present the idea as his own, as follows:

Secretary Taft felt that this wrong must be righted as the Jewish soldiers had of course the same right to have a Jewish Chaplain. But there being

no vacancy, Secretary Taft promised to make temporary provision before
Congress meets to increase the number of Chaplains—for the Jewish
Holydays. During the excited days since the nomination of Judge Taft
the matter was neglected and Secretary Taft resigned without fulfilling
his promise to Dr. Browne and Mr. Frankel and the Committee, hence
Judge Taft asked his successor General Wright to do as he (Judge Taft)
had promised to do. Accordingly, Rev. Dr. Edward B. M. Browne
of New York has been appointed temporary Chaplain at large for the
Department of the East.

As soon as you do that and publish it you shall have my support. . . .
Failing to do as suggested, I shall have to preach against you from 25th
of September to 1st of November in New York and Norfolk.[50]

Incredible as this display of chutzpah appears, and unlikely as it was to
have produced Browne's desired result, his assumption of influence evidently
still contained some measure of credibility. Two days later, Meyer Koteen, an
official of the Norfolk synagogue, learned that the rabbi intended to preach
on "the Jewish Chaplain question" on Yom Kippur, and wrote to Taft in
alarm. "As a Jew," he declared:

I must share with Rabbi Browne the regrets that our Government
remains the only civilized Nation which denies the Jewish Soldiers and
Sailors the rights accorded the Protestant and Catholic Soldiers and
Sailors, but as a Republican, . . . I fear, from what I have heard within
the last few weeks, that Dr. Browne may say about you, as Secretary of
War, and his appeals to you for Jewish Chaplains, words which may
do you harm in the present campaign, hence I confidentially inform you

of said state of affairs. I cannot suggest anything, but forewarned is forearmed. I may however, find some way of preventing the discourse on the subject if you believe it will work a detriment to yourself in this present campaign.

Dr. Browne seems to be a staunch Republican himself, and therefore [I] cannot understand his motive in bringing forth this 'Jewish Chaplain Question' at this time. You may not know this gentleman, hence I may state that his views have a national influence amongst our people. Should you however believe that you could in no way be hurt by such utterances, I will let the matter drop, otherwise let me hear from you, and I shall use my influence to suppress the subject.[51]

Apparently Koteen held some influence with Browne, for the rabbi did withhold comments against Taft in his Yom Kippur sermon.

After the holidays Browne again wrote to Taft, this time simply asking, "Will you if elected President appoint Jewish Chaplains in our Army and Navy, a religious duty our Country owes to its Jewish defenders?"[52]

Continuing, Browne said that he was "willing to be kind" to Taft, considering that "Mr. Roosevelt's animosity prevented you from complying with my last letter," and stated that he would await an answer "here in Norfolk where I have organized the Russian Hebrews into a grand congregation. . . . " He added in a postscript that it seemed as though Taft had never seen his two earlier letters, and possibly his telegram and last letter as well.[53]

On the eve of Election Day, Browne wrote to Taft congratulating him in advance on what was certain to be a victory, but confessed that his heart was not with him due to Taft's failure to confirm that "in case you are elected you would do justice to me on the Jewish Chaplain question." Because of that, Browne said, he had accepted an invitation to speak with Bryan both in New York and Cincinnati, and noted that only because an old dear friend in Norfolk dissuaded him had he refrained from speaking against Taft at the services there. He also mentioned that, for the past two weeks, he had been working on the Jewish vote for governor of New York, where an unidentified friend of Governor Hughes provided him with $2500 to run a campaign against Nathan Straus.[54]

After the election Browne wrote again to Taft, now president-elect. He admitted being irritated that their meeting had been cancelled, then noted that he had been dissuaded from appearing with Bryan and insisted that it was not for personal motives that he would like to have Taft's good will. He again asked to meet with Taft, "Only for 30 minutes talk, in all silence if you are inclined to have me call before the end of November," he specified, noting that he and Sophie planned to leave for Nice, Tunis and Cairo on December 1st."[55]

We find no further mention of that proposed journey or of Browne's activities for the following months other than a post card from him and Sophie from Budapest dated August 21, 1908, saying that they planned to return in September. Nor do we find any hint of the trip's purpose, although an educated guess points to an assignment concerning Jewish welfare funded by a European-based Jewish philanthropic organization. What is certain is that Browne's powers were waning markedly and that he was unwilling to give up. He continued to work on his "History of Judaism in America," tracing the career of Isaac M. Wise from his beginnings in "old Bohemia eighty years ago," to his death in 1900. The writing then dealt with some of the professional politicians whose actions especially affected American Jews. Only an outline of its contents remains.[56]

Throughout these political maneuvers Browne continued to press the issue of a Jewish chaplaincy in whatever manner he could. Again serving Temple Gates of Hope for the High Holy Days, he offered religious services to Jews in the military. A Brooklyn newspaper noted that this congregation, currently located at 42 East 21st Street, welcomed Jewish service men and would reserve seats for them. Browne wrote to Fred Grant, now a major general heading the Department of the East on Governor's Island, asking that Jewish men under his command be given leave to attend synagogues on the High Holy Days. Grant replied welcoming him back to New York and noting that he encouraged his soldiers to attend services of their various faiths, but that year they would not return from maneuvers in time for the Jewish men to observe the High Holy Days there.[57]

By the following March, Browne was back in Georgia, renewing his efforts to assist immigrants. He organized the Immigrants' Defense Committee with headquarters in New York and Washington, and began work on a proposed publication, "The Immigrants' National Encyclopedia of Biography." Its sole purpose, as declared in its flyer, was to remove prejudices created by Congressional debate on the pending bill to limit immigration. The previous year's unprecedented influx of foreigners had resulted in passage of the Immigration Act of 1907, but did not end the debate because it stopped far short of satisfying its proponents who wanted more stringent limitation. Browne's volume, subtitled "The Immigrant and His Boy, What They Have Done For Our Country These Fifty Years Past," promised to contain biographies and pictures of immigrants and their children who had contributed significantly to the nation's greatness. It would also include "some of their true American friends" with a preface by New York congressman William Sulzer, reputedly the immigrants' most devoted advocate.[58]

In May, 1909, after trying unsuccessfully to obtain a New York state commissionership, Browne accepted a position as rabbi of Congregation Mishkan Tefila in Boston. Its leaders favored Conservatism, but became divided as a result of their former rabbi's partisanship, and without consulting authorities in any branch of Judaism chose Browne, still known as a Reform rabbi, because of his "remarkable oratorical ability." He received an enthusiastic welcome, a local newspaper describing his installation as "the most imposing Jewish event in Boston." It added, however, that Browne "boldly challenged 'the radical reformers,' which necessarily created some feelings."[59]

Here as elsewhere, the rabbi formed friendships with Christian clergymen, but criticized and frequently aroused enmity in his Jewish colleagues. Newspapers suggested that he made some enemies by declining to attend a meeting "where the Jewish leaders . . . organized themselves to elect Mr. Storrow." This seems curious, as the popular Boston Brahmin Democrat James Jackson Storrow stood for many of the same humanitarian causes as Browne, and also opposed Tammany type politicians such as the notorious "Honey Fitz" Fitzgerald, progenitor of the Kennedy clan. In addition to snubbing Storrow and the Jewish leaders who backed him, Browne further irritated some of his congregants by canceling an event scheduled at the synagogue which he believed to be a political rally rather than a committee meeting on education as announced. This, too, was curious in light of Browne's own political activism. Was it because those planning the meeting were ardent Democrats? Did Browne see it as an abrogation of the separation between Church and State? Neither possibility seems consistent with his previous record of sincerity and integrity, an observation that sadly suggests his increasing instability.[60]

Negatives such as these were initially offset by the fact that Browne's preaching regularly packed the sanctuary. At times he attracted more people than the space could accommodate. Bostonians called him "the Jewish Moody," comparing him to the famous Massachusetts born evangelist Dwight L. Moody, because, they said, "it was a Jewish revival to see such great crowds of Jews coming out from a temple."[61]

During that summer, Browne repeated his sermon against anti-Semitism at fashionable resorts, noting that thirty-three centuries had failed to change human nature and that hatred against Jews, "even in this enlightened United States" was due to "ignorance of our people's characteristics and selfish covetousness of Israel's power and success. . . ."[62]

Thus far the decline in Browne's fortunes had not seriously diminished his spirit or hampered his ability to preach. Now sudden tragedy struck with the force of an earthquake, plunging him and Sophie into an emotional abyss from which neither of them ever fully recovered. On September 3, 1909, their beloved son Jesse died of blood poisoning. Death came without warning, only three days after the handsome young man infected a slight blemish on his face by touching it.

Neither Jesse's bereaved parents nor his grieving bride ever came to terms with their loss. Married only four years, the young couple had lost their first baby, a girl, ten days after her birth earlier that year. Fanny Mitteldorfer Browne eventually remarried and bore a son. The marriage ended in divorce, and she raised her boy to love the Brownes as she did, considering them his true family. Likewise, the Brownes and Goldbergs continued to embrace their former in-law and her child.[63]

The loss of Jesse caused his father's powerful mind to deteriorate ever more obviously into patterns suggesting paranoia and megalomania. Sophie, whose principal achievements still lay ahead, never ceased to mourn her son, wearing black for the rest of her days and waking in the night to cry out for him.

Browne's intense grief undoubtedly hastened his departure from Boston. After little more than a year, Mishkan Tefila asked him to leave, which he contested on the grounds that he had been given a life contract. Although the contract was unwritten, he insisted on its validity and sued the congregation for $150,000, as well as suing the Boston Herald for slander based on its account of the proceedings. Both cases were dismissed. A Boston newspaper reported later that his departure "caused much discussion . . . the cause being unique in the history of the Jewish pulpit." Considering the Jewish reluctance to expose its internal disputes to public attention via court action, Browne's suit undoubtedly incited heated criticism and in all likelihood had no known precedent.[64]

Jesse's death climaxed a period of Browne's life that, from its beginning, seemed to signal impending tragedy. With his career in decline, his mind arguably so, he sought in vain to regain a place of influence such as he had once enjoyed. Even so, after losing two major pulpits and verbally assaulting two presidents, he maintained credibility in some quarters and succeeded in establishing an organization to provide legal aid pro bono to deserving Jews victimized by anti-Semitic discrimination. Surmounting all other issues, he upheld that of the military chaplaincy, each defeat only serving further to reinvigorate his zeal for the next round. In retrospect his dementia is obvious. That it was not fully recognized at the time remains a tribute to his innate talent and integrity. He continued on the same path, alternately illuminated with honors and success, for twenty more years.

Meanwhile, American Jewry organized to speak with broadened authority for the majority of its people. In 1906, German Jewish dignitaries in New York established the American Jewish Committee, the first organization in the United States devoted specifically to Jewish defense, preventing "the infraction" of civil and religious rights for Jews wherever they might be. It was later, in response to the virulent anti-Semitism exposed in the 1913 trial and subsequent lynching of Leo Frank in Georgia, that B'nai B'rith established its Anti-Defamation League Although primarily still elitist and oligarchic, these men combined their philanthropic activities with skillful diplomacy to successfully negotiate vitally important Jewish issues with government authorities. They lobbied for the United States to protest the wave of pogroms in Russia, to defeat bills requiring immigrants to undergo a literacy test, and in 1911 to abrogate an eighty-year-old treaty with Russia that led to discrimination against American Jews traveling in that country. AJC leaders themselves were not of the new twentieth century Jewish majority in America, but they served sincerely and effectively for those who were.[65]

XIII - WILSON AND THE WANING YEARS

Jesse's death accelerated the spiral of Browne's decline. Although still charismatic and eloquent, he increasingly displayed signs of mental instability and could not sustain a congregational position. Sophie, also crushed inconsolably by Jesse's death, grasped her roles as rabbi's wife and club woman as emotional lifeboats that enabled her to stay afloat. Somehow she did more than merely survive. While her husband's aura faded, hers brightened, beckoning her onto paths beyond the confines of home, synagogue, and local community.[1]

Leaving Boston, Browne turned once more to the lecture circuit, traveling across the continent to engagements on the West Coast and stopping en route to speak at Synagogue B'nai Amoona in St. Louis. He continued ever more fervently to pursue the establishment of a Jewish chaplaincy for the military and to prevent the passage of immigration laws intended to restrict the entrance of Jews and others from Eastern Europe. On two occasions he testified before Congress, once on behalf of a bill to insure the same rights for Jewish Americans traveling in Russia as those accorded to other Americans, and once on behalf of the Jewish chaplaincy. Remarkably, in view of his diminishing reputation, he was again invited to give opening prayers in both the House and Senate.[2]

By the start of the twentieth century, anti-Semitism was noticeably on the rise in America. Economic stress set off massive migration from rural areas to the cities, encouraging xenophobia and increasing social discrimination. Mass migration from eastern and southern Europe fanned embers of resentment into hatred, which sometimes led to racial and ethnic violence.[3]

Rabbinic leadership also underwent a major change as the new century unfolded. Whereas Reform addressed social justice with its immediate need primarily that of combating anti-Semitism, the newly minted Conservative movement concentrated on defining itself and building a strong Jewish commitment among the upwardly mobile sons and daughters of the East European immigrants. Both groups emerged as vocal factors in ethnic politics, soon to be regarded with much more attention than was warranted by their numbers alone. Browne's earlier approach to ecumenism required adaptation in order to address the current change of attitude toward Jews and foreigners.[4]

In spring, 1911, Browne held an Orthodox pulpit, that of the Summit Avenue Synagogue in Youngstown, Ohio. During his brief stay there he received wide coverage of two significant sermons, the subjects of which mirrored deep concerns of American Jews in the opening decades of the twentieth century.[5]

One of the sermons concerned anti-Semitism. Partially repeating his previous discourse on discrimination at summer resorts, he preached this time in response to news that a Mrs. Frank, sister of United States Senator Isidor Raynor, was evicted from an Atlantic City luxury hotel after the management learned that she was Jewish. Browne maintained that journalists encouraged such outrages by submitting contrived stories to substitute for real news when they had none. To fill space they publicized derogatory stereotypes such as reports of Jewish vacationers eating pork and shellfish, Jewish women ostentatiously bejeweled, and the number of "Jewish" noses seen on the boardwalk. Browne countered by reminding his congregation of laudatory reports from universities where Jewish students "carried off all the great honors and prizes," and noted that the current year brought even more kudos "due to the many Russian students. . . . " He begged Christians not to darken "the noble history of your fathers by prejudice against the Jews" because, being fair, "they looked with kindness on the chosen people who are relatives of your Saviour and the authors of the Holy Bible."[6]

In another notable sermon, Browne used Israel Zangwill's play, The Melting Pot, performed in Youngstown earlier that same week, to discuss the importance of religiosity in America and the hypocrisy with which politicians approached it. He criticized Jews who, encouraged by the melting pot philosophy, displayed indifference to their heritage and religion as the playwright was sometimes accused of doing. Zangwill, born to Russian Jewish immigrants, rose from a poverty-stricken childhood in a London ghetto to achieve great success, then married a strong-willed gentile aristocrat.

The play debuted in America three years before, opening in Washington to high praise from then President Theodore Roosevelt whose own beliefs it echoed. Its politically fraught title that introduced the now familiar phrase characterizing America as a bubbling cauldron of cultures undoubtedly contributed to the play's enormously successful first run throughout the country. Such popularity, despite receiving some negative reviews critical of its structure, suggests great appeal of the message contained in its title.[7]

Browne acknowledged that most Americans were sincerely religious, then noted the similarity between the playwright and his fictional hero. Next, instead of pursuing the current dilemma of American rabbis struggling to combat assimilation, he veered off onto "the easy religious views" of Presidents Taft and Roosevelt, criticizing them for insincerity in their display of religiosity, for merely pretending to be devout for political purposes. He gladly acknowledged, however, that politicians were routinely scrutinized to detect sincerity in their observance, seeing it as an indication that religion had not yet lost its value to most Americans. Noting that Judge Alfonso Taft, the president's father, had been widely criticized for his role in establishing the unpopular, Unitarian-sponsored, Free Religious Association, Browne suggested that President Taft was also a Unitarian, becoming an observant

Episcopalian after his nomination in order to overcome the impression that he shared his father's beliefs. In those days general prejudice against Unitarians was almost as widespread as that directed at Jews and Catholics.[8]

According to the rabbi, Roosevelt likewise was not a Christian. "He told me so himself in 1884," Browne said, further noting that as a candidate for governor of New York, Roosevelt became "a violent YMCA champion at the same time while affiliating with the Masons at Oyster Bay . . . " and upon becoming president, "immediately took a pew in the little Dutch Reformed Church at Washington, the existence of which . . . was unknown to him during the six or seven years in Washington before that time." Browne added that the Great Agnostic Robert Ingersoll, a man "most brilliant, capable and patriotic" as well as personally beloved, lost his race for governor of Illinois because he opposed religion. The rabbi erred, however, in his assessment of Roosevelt's religiosity, which is now well documented by respected biographers.[9]

Again referring to "The Melting Pot", Browne said that he opposed intermarriage not only for religious reasons, "but for the material happiness of our young people." He maintained that Zangwill's characters did not typify religiously-oriented Jews or Christians, citing the fact that the play's hero immigrated to America not for religious purposes but to escape the pogroms in Russia, and that the heroine, had she been reared an "ordinary Christian girl," would not have ended up in an East Side settlement house nor, "in a very unwomanlike fashion," proposed marriage without a thought for the man's religion or her own. Browne then remarked that Zangwill's wife also had "a seemingly faddish nature, not being much of a Christian."

Recalling that Zangwill opened his play in America on the night of Yom Kippur and "during the entire sacred day . . . busy with the preparation for the evening's performance," never visiting a synagogue, Browne declared him "not a Jew excepting for revenue only," the ugliest ever seen, and a Zionist only for personal advancement. He also condemned Zangwill for vying to become president of the Zionist Congress after Herzl died, proposing colonization "outside of Zion" in Uganda, and opposing the Zionists by forming his own International Territorial Organization. These final points may well have contributed to Browne's harsh judgement of the play. Actually, some rabbis agreed with Zangwill's bid to head the Zionists and his advocacy for the Uganda issue, but not on the subject of intermarriage which "The Melting Pot" so romantically endorsed. On opposing this they appeared unanimous.

It is possible that the publication of Browne's vituperative indictment of Roosevelt, Taft and Zangwill as well as the play and its message may have contributed to the brevity of his tenure in Youngstown. He departed that congregation prior to midsummer, 1912.[10]

The previous May a Boston newspaper had announced "NOTED RABBI TO RETURN HERE," stating that Browne's friends had "finally received his consent" to serve a new congregation organized when he left Mishkan Tefila, rather than going to a Hungarian congregation in Cleveland as expected. This was not so, however. He neither returned to Boston nor transferred to Cleveland.[11]

The same newspaper had also reported that "The Boston Jewish ladies rejoice at Mrs. Browne's return." It described her as "a great help to her husband . . . a great organizer, a leader socially and in Bible and literary classes . . . easily one of the most learned Jewesses in America, having mastered French and German languages and literature, which are to her like her own native English . . . and sincerely loved by all the ladies that meet her." It also mentioned that she had received honors from Sultan Abdul Hamid in Constantinople, and in Rome from prominent Jews associated with the Italian royal family.[12]

The references to Sophie's honors are accurate, but not the statement that she would return to Boston. She remained in their home at 309 Lincoln Avenue, Youngstown, instructing the Ladies' Bible Class of the Summit Avenue Synagogue until midsummer 1912. According to custom, her students expressed their appreciation with an affectionately inscribed gift of silver, in this case a pair of heavily weighted candlesticks shaped like Corinthian columns. Returning to Columbus, Georgia, where she lived for the rest of her life, Sophie resumed active leadership of the Century Club, spearheaded its affiliation with the Columbus Federation of Women's Clubs and subsequently with the Georgia Federation of Women's Clubs which ultimately led to her active support of women's suffrage.[13]

During World War I the Century Club and other women's organizations suspended their programmed activities to serve as auxiliaries of the Red Cross, and Sophie appeared on public platforms promoting the sale of Liberty Bonds. After the war she spoke from the stages of movie theaters between features to advocate for the United States Treasury Department's Thrift and Savings campaign. Further emboldened, she lobbied her senator, William J. Harris, for passage of the Sheppard-Towner bill on infant and maternity health care. In 1920, the Georgia Federation of Women's Clubs sent her to Washington as one of its two delegates to the Pan American Conference of Women, which featured women's suffrage.[14]

After leaving Youngstown, Browne conducted a two-week "New Year revival" during the High Holy Days at Temple B'nei Jeshurun in Milwaukee, where he also gave a public lecture to benefit a children's hospital being built by a local Jewish women's organization. A rumor surfaced to the effect that he was being considered to succeed the congregation's recently deceased rabbi, Victor Caro, but nothing came of it. Thereafter, despite occasional stints in his former New York synagogue, he considered himself retired as a congregational rabbi.[15]

Retirement, however, did not end Browne's professional life or suppress his political activism. During these years, and many ensuing ones, he continued to lobby for legislation that he favored. Increasingly discouraged about deteriorating morality and the abandonment of Jewish observance among the elite, he argued against government appointments of prominent but non-observant Jews as tokens. His suggestion to introduce a bill specifying and regulating such appointments was dismissed as unnecessary.[16]

Mostly Browne concentrated on the need for a Jewish chaplaincy and campaigned for it throughout 1912. His friend, Representative William Sulzer of New York, head of the Congressional Committee on Foreign Affairs, appeared eager to push such a bill through Congress quickly because he intended to run for governor and wanted to please Jewish voters. When Congress scheduled a hearing on the matter for April 25, Sulzer made sure that Browne would be called to testify.[17]

Browne did not want to testify because he feared his responses might damage Taft in his race to defeat Roosevelt for the Republican presidential nomination. To avoid appearing, the rabbi tried to get Taft's commitment on the chaplaincy prior to April 25, for which he appealed to Otto T. Bannard, a New York politician with close connections to the president, hoping for an immediate appointment. In a letter that sadly indicated increased paranoia, he identified New York banker Jesse Seligman [i.e., the "Jewish Republican Trust"] as the force responsible for all of his misfortunes. [18]

"You well know that all I wanted is to carry the Jewish Chaplain question," Browne wrote:

and you told me that the President had spoken to you on the subject and

agreed with me that the Jewish soldiers ought to have Jewish Chaplains.
. . . In the invitation for me to be present it says "You are the principal
speaker and will have unlimited time." Now in my speech I shall have
to discuss the history of the Jewish Chaplain Question during the
administrations of Roosevelt and Taft and other things which lead to
the disrespect shown the religion of the Jewish soldiers simply because
the multi-millionaire Jewish Republican Trust consisting of radical
reformed Jews secured Mr. Taft's ear and inspired him with indifference
to the right of the Jewish soldier.

I can tell you right now that my speech will place Mr. Taft, according to
many of his thoughtless and careless public deeds, into such a position
before the world that religious and sincere men will form their own
opinion about his availability, and if he succeeds to be nominated he will
be defeated at the election by what I am going to say. . . . I will give Mr.
Taft the last opportunity to meet him on that subject . . . and if, as you
told me, he agrees with my claims, he will do what is right and that he
will have to do by force after I argue the Bill. . . .

Finally, Browne promised—if Taft agreed—"to make the best of the President's voluntary justice to the Jewish soldiers, and the Jewish people will appreciate it."

Browne received no satisfactory answer. The hearing took place as planned, and he was required to appear. Also present, representing the Federation of Jewish Organizations of New York, were Nissim Behar, Nathan Krass, and Aaron D. Levy, their mission being to oppose establishment of a Jewish chaplaincy on the basis of adherence to the rule of church-state separation.

When called upon, Browne displayed his three medals from New York—the one for service to the Jewish school children, the one for observing the Sabbath while participating in Grant's funeral procession, and the one for saving the life of Adolph Reich. After handing them to the stenographer to record, he turned to one of three men from the New York Federation and declared:[19]

I believe my young friend said that religion and politics ought not to be mixed. He is right. But religion and politics, however, are the magnificent mixture, provided that religion has the majority vote and controls the political power. But whenever politics has the majority and controls religion for its own selfish purposes, then it becomes a dangerous explosion. . . .

Here Browne enunciated a major problem confronting religious leaders of all faiths who urged congregants to relate the ethical precepts of their religion to current realities of their lives. On public issues the scales inevitably tipped in one direction or another, which Browne believed should be that of morality as expounded by all of the great religions. In America then as now, it was easy to confuse that morality with the equally important mandate for church-state separation.

"Now, gentlemen," Browne continued, "when I came here . . . I came, first of all, after many misfortunes. . . . I was called to argue the Jewish immigration bill in July last. In 1896 I fought the bill of Senator Lodge to exclude Jewish immigrants; he did not word it that way, but he said certain immigrants should be able to read certain parts of the Constitution. . . ."

At that point the chairman interrupted, instructing him to keep to the subject under discussion.

Then a committee member asked Browne his name and to which denomination of Judaism he belonged. He replied "to the conservative portion of the Jews." The questioner then asked "Are you orthodox?" and he responded, "I am a conservative orthodox. Yes, sir. The orthodox Jews gave me this medal."

Questioner: What do you think about the proposed legislation?"

Browne: I am coming to it. I want to give you some of the history of this movement, because these gentlemen tell me that the President is going to give us a chaplain—

Questioner: We want to know about the proposed legislation.

Browne: Here is the History of American Judaism, my work. There is a chapter on the Jewish chaplain in this work.

Questioner: What is that volume you have?

Browne: The History of American Judaism.

Questioner: What page is it?

Browne: Page 51. This was set up and printed in 1900, after President McKinley refused to appoint a Jewish chaplain. I think this book would have been out now, but my friend, Theodore Roosevelt, has induced the publishers not to publish it, because I was chaplain of the Jews.

Questioner: What is that? A former President refused to do what?

Browne: Theodore Roosevelt; yes, he refused.

Questioner: He must have been pretty powerful.

Browne: Yes, he was very powerful then. When I came in here the gentleman to my right asked me, "Are you going to read all that?" I said, "No." But whenever I make a public speech I say things that make people say "That man is the biggest liar in creation," because I tell you things that seem incredible. . . . On that account I brought these

enormous documents to prove what I say, not to read them. But this
chapter I intended to read, because I was informed that there would be
an opposition committee.

The chairman then directed him to give an overview of the chapter, saying that it would be printed in full and available for anyone to read later. Browne began by recounting a discussion with Grant on the question of, "why the Jewish boys should not have Jewish chaplains," and added that in 1898 he had been told that "the Army scatters." He then rambled even more, saying that in 1903, when he came back from the Orient, "the late sainted Pope Leo XIII gave me an audience. I spent an hour with him in his chamber, and when I left he gave me his blessing. I respect the Catholics, but do you think the Catholic priest had the right to administer the last unction to a Jew who does not believe in it? Do you believe that on the greatest day of our calendar, when even the radical Jews do not raise a protest. . . ."

At this point, one of the New York delegates interrupted, objecting to the rabbi's "irresponsible statements. . . regarding the faults of others. . . ."

Browne: I simply want to show you that on the Day of Atonement
the Catholic chaplain officiated to the Jewish boys in the Philippines,
and he happened to have the crucifix hanging down from his breast. I
received letters from those boys saying, 'Do you think that is proper?'
And Archbishop [Michael] Corrigan [of New York] said, 'That is
not proper.' And Bishop [John P.] Newman said, 'That is not proper.'
And yet one of those gentlemen, Dr. [Gustav] Gottheil of New York, a
man who preaches on the subject, praised the Catholic priest's liberty,
officiating to God's soldiers.
Questioner: I judge then, from your remarks, without criticizing any

faith, that you say there is a necessity for the Jewish people in the Army to have a chaplain?

Browne: Yes, sir.

Questioner: Then you are in full accord with these other gentlemen?

Browne: They are in accord with me. [Laughter]

Questioner: Then that's the end of it.

Browne: Here I come to show them, and I hope to show you, that this is the very thing that the radical reformers have opposed as they have opposed me all along. And they are opposing me now, and they are sending warnings now. They have published in this week's papers, "Army Jewish chaplains will be in the Senate next week." But here they are opposed. "We don't want Jewish chaplains, because we are too liberal to claim Jewish chaplains."

Now, gentlemen, I don't want to speak on the subject, but President Taft is not going to appoint a Jewish chaplain, because he promised me on the 12th of February, through his friend Arthur T. Bannard, who is a friend of mine, that he is not going to appoint a Jewish chaplain.

Chairman: Please confine your remarks to the matter under consideration.

Browne: But I want to show you, Mr. Chairman, that the President is not going to approve it.

Questioner: But you probably don't know what you are talking about.

Chairman: No, Doctor, the committee wants to hear you; but we have an order here and you must confine your remarks to this bill under discussion.

Browne: But I have to show that the President will not give us a Jewish chaplain unless he is forced to do it by Congress. And I would suggest that you adopt an amendment to this bill providing for the appointment of two chaplains, to the effect that if there be any religion in the United

States which has no representation, that the President shall give one
appointment to that religion.
Chairman: That is the idea.

Now Browne's paranoia became more obvious as he spoke of Seligman and other New York bankers:

Browne: And those radical reformers, because they have the multimillions
of Wall Street, are now opposing me clandestinely behind my back.
Those people are what we call trustees, that the public can trust, so they
call them. They are: Jacob H. Schiff, who calls himself the Jewish J. P.
Morgan and the American Montefiore, the Guggenheims, the Seligmans,
the Sterns, the Strausses. They control American Judaism today without
having the right to it. They are the bosses.
Chairman: Doctor, are they opposing you?
Browne: They are opposing me as they have everything else—

At that point one of the New York delegates objected to Browne's "assaults upon reputable Jewish citizens," after which the chairman asked Browne if they were opposing the bill and directed him to omit personal remarks.

Browne: Well, I have to explain to you. Because they are telling me that
I am telling lies.
Chairman: Well, we won't let them say that.

Now Browne began to ramble widely, speaking of Reich, "a prisoner, an innocent, live prisoner, and he was to be hanged dead, and I saved him from the gallows," then something about a lecture he was to deliver, and the Democratic campaign having wanted him to give 30 lectures in the doubtful states in 1904. Asked if he had stumped against Roosevelt, he said he had not, and would show that T. R. had not wanted him to do so. Referring to the chapter in his book entitled "Roosevelt and the Jewish Soldiers," he asked rhetorically how Roosevelt could expect the Czar of Russia to recognize the rights of Russian Jews if he ignores the rights of American citizens "who are fighting the battles of Uncle Sam." In this respect Browne echoed the efforts of other rabbis and Jewish organizations that urged the government to abrogate its commercial treaty made with Russia in 1832. Americans of all faiths were incensed by the news of anti-Jewish pogroms in Russia and the treatment of American citizens visiting there. This disregard for the American passport, specifically aimed at American Jews, was particularly dangerous for naturalized Jewish citizens of Russian origin whom the Czar's government considered to be forever Russian and therefore open to the same inhumane discrimination as his resident subjects.[21]

When the chairman told Browne to conclude, Browne complied by regurgitating his opinion of Roosevelt, Taft, and Speaker Joseph Gurney Cannon. In his words, "the nonunitarianism of Taft, the false Christianity of Roosevelt, and the genuine blasphemy of Cannon have made the rising generation a heartless, soulless, Godless generation."

The chairman then assured committee members that they would receive a "clear and concise argument for the necessity of this legislation," and adjourned the session.

This pitifully embarrassing episode effectively ended Browne's campaign for a Jewish chaplaincy, although he corresponded over a period of years with House Minority Leader Champ Clark on that issue as well as on others. The rabbi had not been alone in asking the government to establish a Jewish chaplaincy in the previous century when America had entered the war with Spain. By April 1917, some 250,000 Jews including twenty-five rabbis had signed up for military service in World War I. Only then did representatives of seven Jewish religious organizations meet to develop and implement a unified approach to a national Jewish chaplaincy. Six months later Congress passed a bill authorizing the appointment of a Jewish Chaplain at Large for the United States Military. Thus Browne's purpose was finally achieved, but without him and without recognition of his persistent effort in its behalf.[22]

Although Browne still supported Republicans generally, as early as 1910 he favored Woodrow Wilson, a Democrat, for president. His increasing alarm over deterioration of religious observance in America, especially among the Jewish elite, led him to view Wilson, the son of a minister, as a man likely to lead the country in the spirit of its moral and ethical standards.[23]

In 1910, after addressing a group identified as the Jewish Educational Society at Harvard, Browne wrote to Wilson, then president of Princeton University, referring to their mutual kinship as scholars by addressing him "My dear Sir and Brother." He said that in a recent talk to the Harvard society he suggested Wilson for president of the United States, one who could reverse the deleterious examples set by Roosevelt, Taft, and Cannon. Browne charged that the first decade of the twentieth century produced a generation "careless, reckless, thoughtless, heartless, soul-less and Godless" due to "decayed religion and morals" inspired by "the pseudo Christianity of red-handed Roosevelt, the spurious Unitarianism of 'fairy-footed' Taft, and the genuine blasphemy of foul-mouthed Cannon," the only remedy for which was the election of a president with religious principles. He listed a few such men including Wilson, president of their rival school, at the mention of whose name the Harvard students cheered. "And they have nominated you for Governor," Browne concluded, "the stepping stone to my predictions."

However unusual that a rabbi should seek a president with Christian principals, Browne's position was no different than that of the well-meaning gentiles who use the term "good Christian gentleman" to compliment a Jew. His view of Wilson was shared by the majority of American Jews, who appreciated the professor's progressive ideas as expressed during his presidency at Princeton.[24]

Claiming that he could do more than any one to help Wilson win New Jersey by getting the bulk of its Jewish vote, Browne proposed that they meet, "and I shall show you how I am the 'specialist' on the subject and I never worked with selfish purposes, but for the good of the cause. Let me know at once how we can meet before Thursday noon."[25]

Although it is not known if the meeting took place, Browne continued to press Wilson to seek the presidency. A terse note from Browne to the then gubernatorial candidate the following July suggests that these efforts did not go smoothly. It read, "My dear Mr. Wilson, I wrote you last Thursday by request of prominent Jews whether you ever said 'Jews and Catholics make poor citizens' asking for immediate answer. By silence you simply jeopardize your election which now seems to be certain. If you don't answer me I shall take it that you cannot deny it." Evidently Wilson did not answer.[26]

After Wilson's presidential election in 1912, Browne first celebrated with his friend Sulzer who won the gubernatorial race in New York, and then focused on influencing the president-elect about cabinet appointments. He asked to visit Wilson with a committee of his Seventy Jewish Elders, hoping to convince him that whomever was chosen for high office to represent the Jews should be a "true" Jew, one who genuinely spoke for 90% of American Jewry rather than "an abject infidel representing wealthy Jewish politicians but not the Jewish religion."[27]

In December he wrote:

My Dear Dr. Wilson,

I am speaking to you now as colleagues academic, in reference to the Committee which called me from Georgia to present them to you last night. We were present on time before the banquet, but missed you. The Committee is very earnest, and consists of earnest men inspired by the "Seventy Elders" who virtually elected [New York Congressman] Mr. Sulzer by issuing "enclosure."[sic]

The Rule of a small minority, the 10 % of the old German Jews, has ceased and the newcomers, the Russian-Rumanian Jews, the 90%, will no more take dictations from Messrs. Schiff, Marshall, etc. The Seventy Elders are resolved not to allow persons who have rejected Judaism . . . to be the representatives of Jewish citizenship.

I am frank .. . to the bitter end, hence I am with the Seventy Elders and can pride myself on...[having] wrested the Jewish vote of New York from the grasp of Mr. [Oscar] Straus, having devoted five weeks exclusively to this campaign. . . .

Now my dear Doctor Wilson, as scholars . . . and as religious men, I would ask you to appoint a time when our Committee may call on you. I can convince you in five minutes that men like Messrs. Morganthau, Untermeyer and Brandeis—whatever their claims and merits—have no right to be in your cabinet as "Jews." The Seventy Elders and the Committee ask nothing for either themselves or others. Nor do they suggest . . . any other Jews. But if you decide to favor Judaism in selecting one for the Cabinet, they insist that your choice fall on a Jew and Hon.

Julius Harburger is the most desirable in their estimation.

Very respectfully,

EBM Browne

Here Browne, although obviously aware that the American Jewish Committee spoke for the American Jewish people, censured its leaders for their lack of "Jewishness." The criticism supports his premise that Judaism— openly and fully observed—is entirely compatible with full and complete recognition as an American, while yet maintaining that this will not have been achieved until visibly observant Jews are elevated to high government positions. Although the men whom he opposed as token Jews did not attempt to deny their Jewishness, they simply expressed it in other ways than those of Eastern European origin. His own relationship with Christians having been on a spiritual and intellectual level, he could not see—or seeing, could not accept—that the new generation of ethnic brokers related differently. Theirs was a more direct and practical approach.[28]

Browne wrote to Wilson again in January for the same purpose as before, seeking to visit with a committee of his Seventy Jewish Elders. "We don't say that a Jew should be in your Cabinet," he repeated, "but we do insist that if a Jew is to be selected he should be a genuine Jew of the people. . . ."[29]

Pushing his point even further, he wrote, "We the 90% have backed Governor Sulzer, a good Christian, by exposing the 'Jewishness' of his rival, Mr. Oscar S. Straus," bluntly noting that selection for the Cabinet of a man of the same stripe "will be remembered by a similar exposure." Browne then named several prominent men who qualified under his interpretation of a true Jew, and repeated that the Elders did not seek an appointment for any one of themselves, but only that appointed representatives of the Jewish people be persons who practiced more traditional Judaism.[30]

This statement may appear inconsistent because Browne had lobbied to ensure Straus' ambassadorial appointment in the 1880s, and he opposed Tammany which Harburger currently represented. It makes sense, however, in light of Browne's obsession with tokenism in government appointments. He did not condone it per se, but given the fact that tokenism was practised, he sought to change the process of selection to one whereby others than the assimilated elite would be considered. His goal was for the public to differentiate between those whose only connection to Judaism was hereditary and ethical, and those who lived openly as members of the Jewish community, devoted to Jewish causes and customs—a stand not inconsistent with his opinion of prominent gentiles who neglected their Christianity until political considerations sent them to church on Sunday. Exemplifying his concern was the tendency of prominent Jewish families like the Strausses to embrace Ethical Culture, a movement that rejected all visible signs of Judaism, retaining only its moral values.

In two letters addressed to Wilson's private secretary Joseph P. Tumulty, Browne seemed to reveal yet another inconsistency. He complained on behalf of "The New York Jewish Committee" that well-known Jews with questionable adherence to Judaism were being considered for cabinet and Supreme Court appointments. One was Louis D. Brandeis, who soon after became the first Jewish Justice of the Supreme Court, who was much admired for defending small business against giant corporations, aiding the cause of minimum wage against employers who opposed it, and helping to elect Woodrow Wilson as president—all of which were consistent with Browne's values but in no way defined Brandeis as Jewish. Although Brandeis later became one of the first assimilated American Jews to embrace Zionism, his interest in it was not widely known in 1913. It is unlikely that Browne knew anything about Brandeis's relationship to the Jewish community other than his activity in the American Jewish Committee, itself a predominantly elitist organization.[31]

Browne increasingly enunciated a philosophy of Judaism known as Reconstructionism that was being developed at the time by a young rabbi named Mordechai Kaplan. Kaplan's approach emphasized, among other defining features, the importance of community in Judaism. While so-called elitist Jews rarely abandoned all sense of community and responded generously to Jewish needs both at home and abroad, they seldom embraced it to any visible extent other than social exclusivity that mostly was forced upon them.[32]

Increasingly wary of discrimination, when the Navy planned to memorialize the victims of the 1876 shipwreck of the SS City of Vera Cruz, Browne reminded officials to honor its Jewish fatalities by inviting a rabbi to participate. It is not known if they heeded his suggestion.[33]

Despite his obviously growing dementia, the rabbi's reputation as an orator remained intact. It drew him to synagogues and lecture halls in various cities in New York including Poughkeepsie and Albany, where he memorialized Theodore Herzl in 1912. In 1913 he broke his leg in a street car accident, but returned to the lecture platform within a few months, in the wake of Wilson's election. There he addressed an interdenominational service in Carnegie Hall on "The Moral Lessons of the Campaign." The event's flyer advised prospective attendees to "Leave Politics at Home; Bring your own religion with you," and quoted Georgia Senator A. O. Bacon's reference to Browne as one of the two greatest pulpit orators, the other being the fundamentalist Secretary of State, William Jennings Bryan. Newspapers repeated Bacon's assessment, one of them even making the ironic suggestion that the rabbi substitute for Bryan when illness the forced golden-voiced Christian to cancel a scheduled lecture at Chautauqua. Georgia Representative W. C. Adamson sought to laud Browne still further by anointing him "the greatest Jew since Disraeli." It is doubtful that Browne, while acknowledging Disraeli's statesmanship, would have considered him a great Jew.[34]

In October 1915, Browne sustained an injury at a mass meeting in New York's Century Theater, sponsored by the American Committee for Armenian and Syrian Relief (later officially organized as Near East Relief), which aimed to alleviate suffering during World War I, focusing primarily on victims of the Armenian genocide. The rabbi was apparently attacked by a member of the Armenian or Syrian community, possibly in retaliation for defending the despised Sultan Abdul Hamid. He and his assailant were promptly evicted from the assembly room after which, despite counsel to the contrary, Browne sued for damages and lost.[35]

The prescient advice not taken came from Attorney Frank Moss, a Christian friend who had sought Browne's help in gaining Brooklyn's Jewish vote for his election as the county's District Attorney. Ever challenged by political engagement, Browne rallied support through his American Jewish Seventy Elders. He also applied for membership in the [Brooklyn] Kings County Bar and later sought appointment as probation officer in the Brooklyn Court of General Sessions. There is no evidence that he succeeded in either. Although these actions appear to deny suspected dementia, neither do they project the image of an effective public figure.[36]

On at least four occasions representing the Seventy Elders, Browne appealed successfully for Jews whose treatment by enforcers of justice appeared unjust. The first occurred in 1914 when a group of Brooklyn Jews sought help for David Sharfstein, a boy committed to reform school. The Elders believed that he was innocent and had been railroaded by a prejudiced district attorney. With assistance from Attorney Moss, Browne petitioned New York Governor Martin H. Glynn for a hearing and obtained Sharfstein's release. The experience motivated Browne to create a plan whereby services of this nature could be improved. Moss encouraged him and helped introduce it to the Legal Aid Society, but to no avail.[37]

The case of twenty-two year old Louis Berkowitz proved more difficult. Berkowitz, a house painter turned soldier sentenced to five years at hard labor for insubordination, suffered from a periodically disabling chronic bladder condition for which he had undergone treatment over a period of years. In the army at Camp Upton, he was suddenly stricken one day while on kitchen duty. Unable to continue peeling potatoes, he returned to barracks in extreme pain, too sick to rise from his bunk even when confronted by his commanding officer, who thereupon ordered his arrest and court-marshal.[38]

When the case came to the Seventy Elders, Browne took charge, questioning the soldier's family members, their physician, and specialists who had treated him. He had them sign affidavits to confirm Berkowitz's condition, then interviewed Jewish conscripts at Camp Upton. They told him that the camp physician customarily showed contempt for Jewish soldiers and had seen Berkowitz hospitalized several times for the same chronic condition but refused to treat him, reporting that he faked illness to avoid work. Browne went to Washington to appeal the conviction before Secretary of War Newton D. Baker, but failed to get action. He returned, again demanding that Berkowitz be released or granted a retrial, but beyond that no more is known.[39]

To continue helping immigrants, Browne sought—but apparently did not receive—an appointment as Welfare Director for Ellis Island. He continued to intercede where needed as public defender for the Seventy Elders. In this capacity he appealed in 1920 to the Secretary of War on behalf of an imprisoned conscientious objector, Meyer Bernstein. Here again the result is unknown. In another case, however, Browne is credited with notable success. A certain Mr. Jacobs had been pronounced "a dangerous lunatic" apparently without justification, and confined to a facility for the mentally deranged. According to a gracious note of thanks from banker and philanthropist Jacob H. Schiff, Browne was responsible for freeing Jacobs and thereby helping to crush the notorious state prison ring that allegedly sent him to the asylum.[40]

In 1921, Browne appealed on behalf of Ethel Szabac, who had been refused admission to the United States because of the 1917 immigration literacy law banning entry of persons unable to read in any of the accepted languages. She was literate in Yiddish, but this was still considered a jargon, not yet legally recognized as a language. Although Browne had once described it as a jargon, he now argued that Yiddish was truly a language by accepted definition and should be recognized. Actually, he had little hope of amending any law favorable to persecuted Jews at his time when anti-Semitism and anti-immigration sentiment had peaked, resulting in the Johnson-Reed Immigration Act of 1924.[41]

For more than a decade, Browne's correspondence had revealed desperation. He appeared as an eager outsider, excluded from the action yet undeterred from pursuing any possible break in the invisible wall surrounding the action. Continuing to see himself as advocate for the underdog, he offered his services at random without empowerment or invitation. One very early, exceedingly naive example surfaced when he wrote to Thomas A. Edison in 1913, volunteering himself as Shylock for a Kinetophone recording of "The Merchant of Venice." Edison declined the offer.[42]

Ever the enthusiastic scientist, in 1920 Browne offered the government his design for an airplane. Georgia Congressman W. C. Wright recommended it to the War Department but the agency showed no interest.[43]

Browne often flailed quixotically at issues with prominent people. He accused Louis Marshall of bringing charges against General John Pershing for mistreating Jewish soldiers overseas—highly unlikely due to the reputation of both men and Pershing's record of appreciating the valor of Jews under his command. Browne scolded President Wilson for ignoring that and other perceived or imaginary manifestations of anti-Semitism. Justified in protesting the infamous publications of Henry Ford, he also solicited Mrs. Ford for contribution to a hospital in Jerusalem, as he did First Lady Florence Harding to establish a female orphanage there. He invited philanthropist and social worker Sophie Irene Loeb to speak at a rally of Jewish youth and requested her help for a young woman in distress. He asked Clark Howell, publisher of the Atlanta Constitution, for his photograph in order to promote him for public office (Howell declined.) He likewise urged William Jennings Bryan and Postmaster-General Harry S. New to run for public office, and offered campaign assistance to Senators Oscar W. Underwood and Robert M. LaFollette. He volunteered to help newly appointed Assistant Attorney General Albert Ottinger. He discussed with chef Oscar of the Waldorf Astoria hotel a proposed dinner to honor President Grant's descendants. He offered charity collection boxes from Jerusalem to President and Mrs. Coolidge and, having involved himself in Coolidge's presidential campaign without authorization, was arrested on the complaint that he bombarded them with too many letters.[44]

Remarkably, despite all such erratic behavior, Browne still had friends and admirers among men of influence. In 1917 and 1918 he again received invitations to give opening prayers in Congress. Identified as rabbi of New York's Mount Morris Park Synagogue, on December 13, 1917, three decades after his first such honor, Browne again invoked God's blessing on the House of Representatives. With America eight months into the first World War, the words he spoke on Capitol Hill resounded as strikingly similar to those attributed to another rabbi who spoke on another hill in Galilee:[45]

Father, who art in Heaven, hallowed be Thy name. Thy kingdom came with the dawn of creation, and being established upon principles eternal and universal, its laws enforce themselves alike in all climes and in all ages. Therefore Thy will must be done amongst the celestials in Heaven even as it is done amongst Thy mortal children on earth. Thou has endowed nature with productive energies, subservient to man's will, whereby Thou givest us this day our daily bread. By imparting to us Thy divine spirit, Thou hast enabled us to enact just laws which guard human society, so that human passions may not lead us into temptation but divine grace deliver us from all evil.

For the purpose of enacting just laws for our great Nation, there are here assembled its representative sons, and I pray that as Thou wast with Moses on the peak of Moab, so here in this modern Sinai Thou canst send Thy shekinah [divine spirit] upon every one of the Representatives present, so that while they represent the will of the people they will represent the will of Thee, who art our Father and our Lord.

And we pray, oh God, our special blessing upon the President of the United States, our olive-branch President, who is waging an olive-branch war in order to bring about an olive-branch peace amongst all the nations of the earth. Open Thy religious magnanimity to forgive those who trespass against us even as Thou forgivest our trespasses against Thee. And thus give us the power and the will to bring mankind to Thy feet as children of God and to democratize every human being in justice and in equality. We thank Thee, oh Lord, that You have selected our

Nation as the chosen people of these days to bring about the peace which

the bewildered world now wants. But let us not be vainglorious at the

high position assigned us, bearing in mind that whatsoever we are in

greatness, in influence, in power, we are so only through Thee. For Thine

is the kingdom, and the power, and the glory, forever and ever. Amen.

It was unusual but not unique for a rabbi to employ Christological terminology when addressing a Christian audience. By so doing he immediately evoked core emotions of his listeners, enabling him to tell the frequently contentious and often self-seeking congressmen to act as their religion dictated—for the good of the people—and to appreciate Wilson's hard fought, though fruitless, effort to achieve peace in Europe without sending Americans into battle. At a time when anti-Semitism highlighted the prevailing belief that Jews applied the term "chosen people" to themselves, Browne wisely used it to signify all Americans, fortifying the image of Jews as the patriotic citizens that indeed they were. House members apparently received his words with appreciation, for he was soon invited for a second time to give an opening prayer in the Senate.[46]

On August 30, 1918, Browne once more mounted the steps of the United States Capitol to deliver virtually the same opening prayer to the Senate that he had previously intoned in the House. With America now feeling the pain of war casualties, he added a plea for "Thy special guidance for our own patriotic boys who are now ready to lay down their lives for the cause of justice and humanity, each of them being a 'lamb of God that taketh away the sins of the world.' And bless also the patriotic mothers who have sent out those boys in order to sacrifice themselves for their country and for humanity."[47]

Fervently patriotic as most foreign-born Americans were, Browne offered his services to the Red Cross when the United States entered the war, but yearned to do more. His prayers reflect deep love of country and the practice of democracy, as well as his trust in God and President Wilson. With Americans dying on the killing fields of Europe, he no longer quibbled about the degree of Jewishness evidenced by his government's high ranking Jews.

Except during the war years, the Seventy Elders regularly sponsored annual memorial services for President Ulysses S. Grant, and at the same time remembered Theodor Herzl. Other appropriate representatives, frequently women and non-Jews, appeared on the program with Browne who, as principal speaker, eulogized those two great leaders whom he had known as friends. In 1919 the ceremony focused on Jewish soldiers and sailors returning home, and he invited them to observe the forthcoming High Holy Days at several Brooklyn theaters free of charge, thanks to the Seventy Elders.[48]

The printed program that year carried the "Zionist's Prayer," a poetic elegy to Theodor Herzl written by "an ardent admirer" with the pseudonym "Gamliel," referring to the leader of the ancient Sanhedrin and presumably to the current leader of the Seventy Elders. The following year much of the program was printed in Yiddish, perhaps in order to appeal to the greater number of immigrants expected to attend. It included the same Zionist prayer, this time with a note indicating that it was originally dedicated to Browne, "Public Defender of the Seventy Elders, who chaperoned Dr. Herzl on his last trip to the Sultan of Turkey and the Khedive of Egypt in April, 1903."[49]

The program also noted that Browne, the oldest minister in the American pulpit in terms of years in service, continued to preach every Friday evening at 7:30 PM at the Cooper Union Free Synagogue. Remaining active, and to a remarkable degree credible despite his indications of failure, in 1925, at the age of eighty, he headed a committee on behalf of the Seventy Elders dedicated to repudiating the Ku Klux Klan.[50]

As old age did little to hamper Browne's constant traveling and outspokenness, his peripatetic lifestyle increasingly caused his family distress. On at least one occasion Sophie sent their granddaughter Carolyn to New York to bring him home.[51]

Finally, well into his eighties, Browne acceded to his family's pleas and settled down with Sophie in the Columbus home of their daughter and son-in-law, Lylah and Dave Goldberg. He frequently visited granddaughter Carolyn in Atlanta, delighting in her company and that of her young child, his great-granddaughter, who retains one vivid memory of their time together. It occurred when the little girl was about four years old. He was playing with her, letting her jump repeatedly from a low ledge alongside the front porch steps, and catching her in his arms, a delight well known to little children and their indulgent elders. At one point, after several jumps, he did not catch her, deliberately letting her fall the short distance to the ground knowing that she would not be hurt. He picked her up, hugged her lovingly, and then admonished, "Let this be a lesson. Never trust a Hungarian—even if he is your own great-grandfather."[52]

He had not lost his sense of humor. Nor did he lose his enthusiasm for old friends, although few were left to remember him. Fred Grant was gone, but his daughter Julia survived and remembered the rabbi. She had married a European nobleman and lived in Europe for many years as Princess Cantacuzene. Upon returning to America she learned that her father's and grandfather's old friend still lived, and wrote to him. In a warm, nostalgic note she recalled scenes from her childhood when she sat with him at the feet of her revered grandfather, the president. It was a kindness that greatly brightened the old rabbi's final days.[53]

Edward Benjamin Morris Browne died quietly in his sleep on October 24, 1929. He was buried in Atlanta's Crestlawn Cemetery with minimal ceremony, attended only by his surviving family and a few of their friends. Since the Temple's then current rabbi, David Marx, was out of the city at the time, the service was conducted by Nathan Saltzman, a trustee of the congregation that Browne had served half a century before.[54]

Sophie remained active and well informed, immersing herself in news of the greater world by scrupulously scouring copies of the New York Times which reached Columbus by train four days after publication. She survived Browne by seven years, the last four confined to a wheelchair as the result of a broken hip. At her death in 1936, she was buried beside her husband, heading a plot in which they are now surrounded by the next two generations of their family.[55]

Upon learning of Browne's death, the distinguished Rabbi Bernard Drachman of New York's Park East Synagogue (Congregation Zichron Ephraim), leader of the Union of Orthodox Rabbis and a founder of the originally Orthodox Jewish Theological Seminary, consoled the bereaved family with a warm and thoughtful tribute. Even though their loved one, he wrote, "had attained a ripe old age and the closing years of his life were clouded with sorrow and lack of appreciation, it is still a painful thought that that brilliant mind and eloquent tongue, and that pure heart, so true to the cause of his people and his faith, are stilled forever. . . . The Jewish Community should know what Dr. Browne was, and what he did for his co-religionists."[56]

Ensuring that such a man not leave the world unnoticed, Drachman wrote a moving obituary for both the New York and Jewish press. He remembered Browne as a man "of rare gifts and splendid qualities of heart and mind . . ."

who had been strangely neglected by his Jewish brethren, and was

deserving of far greater recognition and better treatment than he received

during the closing years of a long life unswervingly devoted to the glory

of Israel and Israel's God . . . he was a great-hearted Jew, imbued with

an intense love for his people and its faith and who strove to serve them

and every noble and humane cause to the utmost extent of his splendid

ability...He was a man of generous impulses and a most charitable

disposition who rendered great assistance to many in need. Despite certain

idiosyncrasies which occasionally brought him into trouble, he was

certainly a splendid champion of the Jewish cause and it is greatly to be

deplored that he did not enjoy the happy and carefree old age to which his

exceptional talents and meritorious services so richly entitled him.[57]

Rabbi Drachman said it well, generously recalling the good that Browne did, the positive aspects of a complex character that defied fulfillment. The tribute was especially meaningful coming from Drachman. Not only was he one of the most prominent rabbis in the country, but one who evolved as a leader of American Orthodoxy from origins in the German Reform community, having received his initial Jewish education at Temple Emanu-El, mentored by Gustav Gottheil. Instead of becoming Gottheil's assistant as planned, in 1887 Drachman began his rabbinic career in New York at a traditional congregation, from which he resigned after members initiated the reform of mixed seating. He probably met Browne during the late 1880s. In subsequent years they corresponded regarding work of the Jewish Sabbath Alliance of America, Inc., which Drachman founded. Known especially for his efforts to reestablish and maintain Sabbath observance, in this as in his move from Reform to modernized Orthodoxy, Drachman followed a philosophical path not unlike that of "Alphabet" Browne.[58]

CONCLUSION

Was Browne a self-promoting publicity seeker as his opponents believed, or stoned prophet of our western Jerusalem as Dr. Crosby, the eminent Christian clergyman in New York described him?

Webster defines a prophet as a preacher, as distinguished from a priest, a distinction that applies well in attempting to understand Browne's actions and the vicissitudes that he encountered throughout his career. The priesthood in ancient times was a political office endowed with power and, like that of an American Supreme Court justice, a lifelong tenure. A prophet's platform, on the other hand, depended upon the will of the people and the whim of the sovereign who unquestionably held all power. Browne spoke the truth as he saw plainly, consistently, and frequently to persons of power who could and did punish him for his rash behavior, thereby causing him and his family to suffer. If the definition of a true prophet is someone who acts against his own best interest in order to speak truth for the good of others, then Browne could be considered a modern day prophet.

How does one judge a life lived passionately but not always wisely, read a character complicated by extremes "brilliance flawed by egotism, energy flawed by restlessness and impatience, scholarship flawed by disdain for accepted forms?

Browne was a maverick in a time and place where, although mavericks abounded, an illusion of conformity was usually necessary for success. He was a loner, a non-conformist creative thinker who refused to submit to mainstream opinions or coercion by others. He was not the only charismatic, brilliant, erratic, multi-talented, European,,born maverick rabbi in nineteenth century America who jumped from congregation to congregation and from profession to profession. Many others wrote for and published newspapers as he did, translated early Hebrew literature, developed prayer books, and headed Jewish schools in addition to those affiliated with their congregations. Nor was he the only one to have studied law and medicine, or even to have practiced both at various times, and he was surely not unique in expressing unorthodox views. He may, however, have been the only one in the spotlight of his day who openly defied convention without assurance of support from his congregation and the leaders of Reform Judaism in America.

Observant as he was of national politics, Browne apparently ignored politics on a personal level. Unlike Wise, his teacher and often his role model, who gained success in Cincinnati by skillful and diligent use of personal politics, Browne went forward without such consideration, and therein lay much of his problem.

Browne belonged to two worlds: that of the secularly cultured German-Jewish aristocrats who tended to be conformist and somewhat obsequious in their relationships with Christians, and that of the deeply religious and Jewish-educated Eastern Europeans who usually lacked both the financial means and the American savvy to be effective outside their own circles. He became a spokesman for the latter, much to the displeasure of the former, long accustomed to the role of public voice for the Jewish people. At the outset of Browne's career, few if any of his rabbinic contemporaries could relate to the Christian world as he did. His scholarship in early Christianity as well as in Judaism, expressed by eloquent use of the English language, gave him an early and lasting advantage on the public platform. As this brought him into constant contact with the Christian public, he came to understand mainstream America, interpreting Judaism and the Jewish point of view to Christians without the inhibitions felt by most Jews of the nineteenth and early twentieth centuries. He used his knowledge of American law to test the sincerity of American democracy, often to the dismay of established Jewish leaders who may have been embarrassed by his candor.

While Browne showed signs of rash and unconsidered behavior from the beginning of his rabbinic career, this did not negatively affect his progress until 1878 when he offended Wise. Contrary to previous belief, this research indicates that the irreparable rift between them began not with Browne's tactless publication of a particular story hurtful to Wise, but with the initial publication of the newspaper itself, a vehicle that held the possibility of rivaling Wise influence throughout the South. The rift deepened as Browne increasingly expressed first concern and then contempt for what he considered to be the religiously life, threatening dilutions of Judaism introduced by what is now known as Classical Reform. Significantly, the congregations he served after 1901 ultimately affiliated with either the Conservative movement or with orthodoxy.

Browne was ahead of his time in his ideas and in his perception of what religious Jewish leadership should be. Like many Reform rabbis of the twentieth century, but few in the nineteenth, he addressed the entire community, Christians as well as Jews, forming collegial relationships with Christian ministers and working with them on matters of mutual concern. He viewed particular issues in the context of national and worldwide conditions, and believed that Jews, especially rabbis, had an obligation to speak out publicly and take action against all forms of oppression. Last but not least, he supported Zionism and adhered to a Reform Judaism that retained its distinctiveness in much the same form as that practiced by the majority of Reform congregations today.

Lylah Browne Goldberg, his daughter and my grandmother, dismissed my probing questions about her father by saying, in his later years, "Papa suffered from a bit of paranoia and megalomania." While my research unquestionably bears out her statement, it also gives rise to the suspicion that his paranoia may have been rooted, at least in part, in an actual effort to silence him. Perhaps a future historian will be able to verify this. My purpose here has been to portray a portion of the Jewish experience in America through the life of a fascinating, complicated personality who devoted himself to the betterment of his people and his country during a period of enormous changes and great turmoil for both.

ACKNOWLEDGMENTS

I began my research at home. Browne's book galley contained his own detailed account of experiences in New York and before, as well as encomia to him both from leaders of the Jewish "working men's" committee that presented it and from prominent people such as former Secretary of State Hamilton Fish. My mother lovingly preserved letters and other documents from her grandfather's later years, and I possess many objects that belonged to him or his family--portraits, jewelry and silver serving pieces inscribed with names and dates, his collection of meerschaum pipes, and books of religious content. The inscriptions on jewelry and silver pinpointed significant events. A 267 page handwritten album of poetry that he dedicated to Rabbi Isaac Mayer Wise and Theresa Bloch Wise and gave them for their 25th Wedding Anniversary (later returned to our family) evidenced his vast knowledge of secular subjects, his sense of humor, and views of his student days at the Wise home in Cincinnati. Picture post cards preserved from the family's travels in Europe and the Middle East provided the itinerary and comments on that year-long journey. For this beginning I owe thanks to my forebears, to Great-grandmother Sophie Weil Browne, Grandmother Lylah Browne Goldberg and Mother Carolyn Goldberg Oettinger, preservationists *extaordinaire*.

My first and foremost public resource was the Jacob Rader Marcus Center of the American Jewish Archives (AJA) in Cincinnati where Dr. Marcus began collecting Browne's documents some sixty years ago. I am deeply grateful to Dr. Gary P. Zola, director of the Marcus Center of AJA, first for convincing me that I could and should write a documented biography of Browne, even though I was well into my senior years. Dr. Zola encouraged me throughout, beginning with a grant for research at the Marcus Center. His gracious response to my many requests for advice and for assistance from members of his staff, especially from Kevin Profitt, senior archivist for research and collections, and assistants Ina Remus and Camille Servizzi, were crucial to the development and completion of my work. Archivist Dorothy Smith helped immeasurably by quickly cataloguing the cache of Browne's papers that I contributed to AJA. Fred Krone and Eleanor Lawhorn, both now retired, and Lisa Frankel also gave generously of their time and assistance, as did Dr. Allan D. Satin, senior librarian of the Klau Library of the Hebrew Union College Jewish Institute of Religion in Cincinnati.

As a resident of Washington, D.C., for almost the entire period of my research, I was blessed with easy access to America's National Archives and the Library of Congress, where Peggy Pearlstine and many other gracious librarians led me to records, presidential collections, archival journals and newspapers. I also benefitted from use of the Georgetown University Library, the American University Library, and the generous assistance of Ellen Share, librarian of Washington Hebrew Congregation. No less important were my days spent at the New York Public Library where Faith Jones led me to a treasure trove of information on Browne in the special collection of a nineteenth century New York attorney.

Long before my recent move to Atlanta, Marianna Kaufman, research assistant at the Atlanta Fulton County Public Library gave me invaluable support there. Now retired, she continues to do so as a volunteer research associate in Jewish studies at Emory University's Robert Woodruff Library. I am deeply indebted to her as well as to numerous others for help at the Emory libraries, notably Tarina Rosen, Jana Lonsberger, Joyce Clinkscales, Marian K. Heilbrun, Naomi Nelson of Special Collections at the Woodruff, and Myron McGhee of Pitts Theological Library.

An early resource was via friends at the American Jewish Historical Society--Stanley Remsberg, as well as former directors Michael Feldberg and

Bernard Wax. At the Society's current facility in New York, Lyn Slome and other staffers kindly guided me to the relevant files and gave helpful advice. In Jerusalem, Marcia Lewison led me to professional researchers Naomi Niv and Nancy Shektor-Porat who probed diligently on my behalf, especially in the Central Zionist Archives where Niv also translated her findings from German to English before sending them. I thank Michael Zaft and Rachel Rubenstein at Central Zionist Archives for forwarding copies of the Browne-Herzl correspondence, and my Washington neighbor Leon Leiberg for his gracious contribution of time and effort in initially translating them.

Browne's multiple congregations and diverse activities required numerous inquiries at various locations. The late John Y. Simon, director of the Ulysses S. Grant Foundation, provided valuable insights on the Civil War hero and president. Tweed Roosevelt likewise elucidated on the relationship between his great-grandfather the president, and mine, the rabbi. Barbara Lehmann and Charles Fenyvesi supplied background data on Browne's native Hungary. Rabbi Ronald Sobel, Louise Stern, Frances Hess and Reva Kirschberg assisted me regarding Temple Emanu-El, as did Mariam Touba of the New York Historical Society on other aspects of Jewish life in that city. I am especially grateful to Joel Shapiro for his contribution in researching Browne's life in Chicago, and likewise the help of Rabbi David Sofian and Susan Youdovin in regard to Emanuel Congregation. I thank Z. Hoffman for his information on Browne in Boston; the late Bernice Baron and her daughter, historian Rachel Heimovics Braun on his time in Milwaukee; historian Bobbie Malone and Arden Rice in Madison; Rabbi Frank W. Muller and Allen Cannon in Peoria; Stanley Lasky and Maida Barron in Cleveland; Temple archivist Alice Apelbaum in Toledo as well as Rabbis Samuel Weinstein and Alan Sokobin, Greg Miller of the Toledo Public Library and Barbara Floyd of the University of Toledo; Rabbi Barry

R. Friedman and Marilyn Hufnagel in Evansville as well as Wayne Crowe, Dale Philips, Maxine Brown and Dona Stokes-Lucas of Indiana Freedom Trails throughout Indiana; David B. Farris of Beth Ahabah Archives in Richmond; Shulamith Elster and Jennifer Priest for information regarding Norfolk; Rabbi David Baylinson and Leo Drum for Montgomery; Kay Kole in Savannah; Jean Kiralfy Kent and especially the late Laurette Rothschild Rosenstrauch in Columbus.

The ongoing encouragement, suggestions, and professional assistance of my family and friends was crucial to the completion of my task. My son, Bill Rothschild, provided legal advice as well as many helpful responses to my requests for advice and editorial assistance on portions of the manuscript involving legal procedure. Rabbi W. Gunther Plaut gave generously of his time and expertise to decipher, translate and interpret Browne's correspondence with Theodor Herzl. I am grateful to Ori Z. Soltes for his constant encouragement and thank him especially, along with Rabbi Alvin Sugarman, for their recommendations enabling me to receive the grant from American Jewish Archives. I deeply appreciate the invaluable advice of historians Jonathan Sarna and Eli Evans, as well as the ongoing support of other scholars in the field of American Jewish history; Joyce Antler, Marni Davis, Marcie Cohen Ferris, Bill Ferris, Anton Hieke, Scott Langston, Leonard Rogoff, Cornelia Wilhelm.

As with any manuscript, the most long-suffering and indispensable friends are those who read and critique it. My daughter Marcia Rothschild did this many times over many years, as well as assisting with research and giving of her professional skills as copy editor and frequently summoned computer guru. Her help was paramount throughout. Prize-winning journalist Carole Ashkinaze Kay and publisher Nadine Epstein likewise read the unfinished manuscript and made cogent suggestions which I deeply appreciate. Rabbi

Harold S. White not only read and critiqued the work at various stages of its progress, but facilitated it with valuable suggestions, introductions, and enthusiastic advocacy at every turn. I cannot thank him enough.

Nor can I find words to fully express my appreciation for the crucial assistance of historian and editor Mark K. Bauman. His enormous contribution of time, patience and expertise enabled me to shape an often confusing conglomeration of facts into a meaningful message worthy of publication. Without his mentoring and sharp, sometimes brutal critique, Browne's life would have remained unknown except to his descendants and archivists at the Marcus Center.

This was the ultimate gift, but not Bauman's final one. He is also responsible for suggesting that his neighbor Eric Campos consider my manuscript to fulfill an assignment for the publishing acquisitions course in which he was enroled as an undergraduate at Loyola University Maryland in Baltimore. Campos did so with great success, both for his college record and for me. His enthusiasm for the project adds immeasurably to my delight in achievement and gives me the further pleasure of ongoing friendship and interest in his future. Likewise, I applaud the accomplishments of publisher Kevin Atticks and his team at Apprentice House, especially designer Alyssa Link, and happily anticipate a long and fruitful relationship with them. Their vigor and foresight bode well for the future of budding authors, young or old.

With sincere appreciation,
Janice Rothschild Blumberg
February 2012

THE HEARING OF THE REICH CASE BEFORE GOVERNOR HILL

Precisely at two o'clock p.m., Monday, November 12,1888, the Governor entered his executive office in the Capital. Present, Col. John R. Fellows for the people, Rabbi Edward B. M. Browne for the prisoner, and the Governor's clerks. . . . The Governor shaking hands with the District Attorney and the Rabbi, declared himself ready to hear the case. Col. Fellows [the District Attorney] began his very powerful speech; and having reviewed the trial and sentence of Reich, he argued against the commutation; insisting upon Reich's execution according to the verdict and sentence. Rabbi Browne then rose and thus spoke in behalf of the condemned man:

RABBI BROWNE'S PLEA IN BEHALF OF REICH, BEFORE GOVERNOR HILL

May it please Your Excellency: It is my privilege to be acquainted with the dangerous oratory and convincing arguments of our famous District Attorney, to know the fatal results they carry to any cause he opposes, and under ordinary circumstances, I should not have dared to stand up before his forensic thunder. But fortunately for my client, I am fortified by an impregnable position shielded by a bulwark of facts which Col. Fellows' dynamite eloquence and diamond pointed logic cannot penetrate. Indeed . . . I am not here to combat the views of him who is the people's tried representative, nor to question the legitimacy of his logical conclusions drawn from the premises transmitted to him by his predecessor. . . . My endeavor here is to convince your excellency, and Col. Fellows as well, that the unfortunate man whose cause I plead is a victim of the strangest combination of sad circumstances which led him to make confession of a crime he never committed, and which for him to commit, under the circumstances of the case, was an utter impossibility.

I am here, Mr. Governor, to prove . . . that this poor creature now trembling in the shadow of the gallows, did not commit the crime of which he stands convicted; that an unquestioned and unquestionable alibi had been proven by three reliable witnesses of the people in the course of their cross-examination by the defendant's counsel, but that, that very counsel turned about suddenly, changed his plea to "killing in self-defense" and in the last hour of the trial forced his victim by mental duress, to perjure away his own life in endorsing the false plea made by his mistaken, ignorant, misguided, or willfully corrupt counsel, Chas. F. Kinsley, Jr.

These are strong accusations to bring against an attorney-at-law. It is not easy to believe that he who takes upon himself the heavy responsibility of defending a human life, should all at once turn around and carelessly or willfully jeopardize that imperilled life, particularly after the innocence of the accused had already been conclusively proven. But the unheard-of, the apparently impossible has transpired in this case. . . .

[Browne explains that it is necessary for him to give details that might seem irrelevant but would materialize in the course of his argument.]

On the 11th of April, 1887, about 9 a.m., two Hungarian women called at my house, one was an elderly person, the other a woman of coquettish, bold bearing, over-dressed, and what amongst the ordinary class of Hungarians would be called "good looking." She appeared to me to be about 28 years of age, tall and powerful of build. She told me that she was the wife of a tailor who married her several years ago. They were separated at times, but finally became reunited again about five months ago and have been leading ever since a happy life until a day or two past, when their pleasant domestic relations were interrupted by a man named Brown who had been the cause of her troubles heretofore and which led to an actual fight with her husband.

I ventured the jocose opinion that she did not bear any evidences of rough handling, and she replied with a swagger peculiar to Hungarian peasant women of that kind: "Indeed, I am not afraid to stand up before any man if it comes to fighting" and her clinched fist fully corroborated the assertion.

"No," said the woman, "I am not afraid of my husband's beating me . . . but I have made up my mind not to have any cause for disagreement. I must say it myself that I was not to him always as I should have been and if my neighbors talked about me, they may have had good reasons to do so, but I have made up my mind to be a good and virtuous wife to my old man . . . and I have broken with all my former acquaintances. But your cousin Brown gives me no rest . . . and on his account I had that fight yesterday. Now what I came up for is to ask you to stop your cousin from troubling me."

I told the woman I had no cousin named Brown in this city nor did I know that Brown, in spite of his claims of relationship. . . .

The woman begged me to come down town and have a talk with her husband and make up between them. I declined to do so just then, stating that I had been sick with nose-bleeding these four weeks, and that I should not have been up even now were it not for a very important appointment.

The woman then told me that she herself was addicted to very bad nose-bleeding, and suggested to me to try the remedy which a Hungarian witch had given her. She begged me to come and see her husband as soon as convenient, and told me her name was Mrs. Reich, of 144 Norfolk street. I made so light of the whole affair that I did not even enter the address in my Journal. The woman left and I soon followed.

At the corner of 92nd street and Third avenue I met the two women again. It appeared that they were waiting for me. Mrs. Reich said she would go along with me on the elevated railroad, but her companion was "afraid" and Mrs. Reich gave her a nickel to take the street car. From 89th street until I got out at Houston street the woman kept on a lively talk telling me much of her experience in Hungary and here, boasting—Hungarian peasant characteristic—of the money her husband makes, the jewelry he buys her, etc., etc.

Here again, Your Excellency, I must speak of myself: I am apparently the Attorney-General of the Human Race and the "District Attorney" of the down-town Jews, especially the poorer classes, of all nationalities. My practice is quite extensive and expensive not to my clients, but to myself; and my entire time, excepting the hours I spend in the pulpit, is taken up by these poor people who flock to my house whenever they are in trouble.

[Unlike other rabbis who are asked to arbitrate religious issues, Browne is approached on personal problems, often legal ones]

But it seems I have inherited from my father two cumbersome peculiarities, a string of names and his devotion to the cause of the poor and needy, and I cannot get rid of either. Hence the pilgrimage to my house from downtown, and the Reich woman merely followed the procession.

I attend to urgent cases without delay. Trivial matters like this I have rarely time to take up, hence I never dreamed of the Reich couple any more until the newspaper reported the killing of the woman. The name of Reich recalled my visitor of some time ago, but the description of the woman being so different from the woman I saw—her age was given as near fifty years whilst she seemed to me to be hardly thirty—the name of Reich amongst the Jews being very frequent besides . . . I gave no attention to the murder. Shortly after, I read again about the homicide and when Mr. Brown's name was mentioned it struck me that the murdered woman and my coquettish visitor must have been identical, and I sent one of my down-town friends to Norfolk Street to ascertain particulars, but he brought me no information. . . .

354

I then dropped the matter from my memory altogether.

The 3rd of June, 1887. . . . Coming downstairs about nine o'clock, I found among my other callers a "delegation," as they styled themselves. Mr.Isidor Unger, the spokesman, said that case had been in court for several days, and that my presence was very urgent, there being no one on hand to direct or advise. Rev. Dr. Wise, of the Clinton Street Synagogue, had promised to take charge of the matter, but when the collection of money in the committee's hands proved so small, some $60.00 only, he declined to have anything to do with the case and refused his aid. The accused man, they assured me, was innocent, but the lawyer "acts so . . . funny" that they did not know what he wants—in short, they came to take me into court.

There being, according to the "delegation," no time to lose, I left . . . . direct to the office of one Charles F. Kinsley, unknown to me, a lawyer opposite the Tombs prison. There I met an old gentleman, Mr. Samuel Newman, and a young man, Mr. Herman Roth, both apparently belonging to the most intelligent class of Hungarians. They acquainted me somewhat with the case when Mr. Kinsley came in and they introduced me. Mr. Kinsley was very happy to see me, he thought some one should aid him. There was no money on hand, the court had assigned him to defend Reich, but he expected the Hebrews of New York City would, of course, pay him for his work, etc., etc.

[Before helping Reich, Browne must be convinced of his innocence—not merely that he is Jewish.]

It was near eleven o'clock and we went to the Court of General Sessions, Recorder Smyth being the judge. Your Excellency, that was the first time in my life I ever was in that court, and the first time I ever saw Kinsley, Reich, Newman, Herman Roth, or any of the witnesses in the Reich case.

Samuel Gross, a witness, for the people was testifying, and after listening to his cross-examination, I came to the conclusion that he was the most unmitigated liar the world ever saw, that not one word of his would be believed by the jury. His career in this country was . . . most checkered. Although but two years in the land, he was a peddler, professor of languages, music teacher, cook, waiter, milkman, private tutor, correspondent, tea merchant, picture frame worker and what not. He never remembered one address of his employers, neither the time, month or year, summer or winter. Every one of his employers cheated and swindled him, he got . . . no pay any where, and was always barely making a living. I learned later that Gross was Reich's boarder—the main witness for the people, and that he had caused Reich's arrest. Gross's evidence had in my judgment destroyed all his importance as a witness.

Then came Mrs. Schick, the washerwoman, another witness for the people, whose evidence was very favorable for Reich, and a "widow," Lena Boniface, a boon companion of Mrs. Reich, living in the same house. Whilst trying her worst to injure the prisoner, she was really only proving that she was perjured, as Your Excellency will readily see by perusing her evidence.

I was more interested however, in the evidence of a Mrs. Eckar and her boy, fourteen years of age, both of whom testified to facts which could not have made it possible for Reich to have reached his house before eleven o'clock on the night of the murder. As stated, I came to court to convince myself concerning Reich's guilt or innocence, and when Mrs. Eckar testified to the alibi, I did not yet quite believe in it, for criminal lawyers have ways and means of coaching witnesses, especially an adult of intelligence. But when that child was put on the stand and stood the severe bull dog style examination of District Attorney Purdy, using every fiendish means for confusing that boy, (unprotected by the judge, God bless him) yet failing after hours of torture to bring out the slightest contradiction in little Eckar's statements, then I was convinced that the alibi proven by his parents was really genuine, and I had no fear about the verdict; and Mr. Kinsley triumphantly reminded me of my promises to take interest in the case and help him to save Reich.

The only suspicious feature in the case to be explained away, Kinsley said, were the blood stains which were found on Reich's shirt and undergarments, but the prisoner claimed that these stains were due to nose-bleeding of his wife the night before her death. He could prove that she was subject to very frequent hemorrhages of that kind, and ever so many witnesses could swear having seen the blood stains on his over-shirt the day before his wife was killed and having heard the woman herself talk about it.

I told Kinsley then about the visit of Reich's wife at my house and that she told me of her nose bleeding. . . . Besides, I had an experience similar to Reich in one of my attacks whilst asleep. The entire bed was saturated, so were my garments and my wife's, and when I awoke and hurried to the wash-stand the blood came upon my shirt and undergarments lying on a chair next to my bed. Of course, I did not put on the soiled garments next morning as Reich did, but those who know the habits of his class of people can well understand it. With them the change of garments occurs, as a rule, every Sabbath morning, and come what will, the man has to wear them from Sabbath to Sabbath. Reich being already Americanized, asked for a change of linen, as I was told by him and other witnesses who know of it, but his wife refused on the ground that she had to pay for the washing, and he being anxious to keep up the cordial relations, did not care to rebel against her decision.

When Kinsley heard this, he was overjoyed. "Then you can testify to her nose bleeding, and the incident of your own experience," said he, and I expressed my willingness to do so. Kinsley then began to talk about money—I

should get him at least a thousand dollars next Monday, it was a bad case—
after all, etc., etc. "Why," said I, "Mr. Kinsley, that man is free already. You
have proven a positive alibi, all left to explain away now is the only damaging
feature of the blood stains; which, as you say, are but slight and evident not to
come from a cut throat, all of which you can very easily do. The only thing I
should add now, in your place, would be that evidence, and submit the case
to the jury without argument. I am certain the jury will acquit Reich without
leaving their seats."

These blood stains, however, puzzled me after all, and I thought best to
probe a little deeper.

I took Reich himself into my hands, talking to him in the Hungarian
language, whilst in the cage during recess. I explained the situation fully
and promised to see him through, but said I had my doubts about those
blood stains—it was something that may be true but hard to believe. Reich
reiterated his innocence and insisted that the blood stains came from his
wife's nose bleeding. I then explained that science has means to distinguish
between human blood and blood from other animals. Then I went on
creating my own theory . . . that just as we can distinguish between human
and animal blood, so could we distinguish between human blood that comes
from the throat and from the nose. Hence I urged Reich, who listened
intently, not to let me in the dark—he should tell me as a Rabbi and his
defender, the truth. I would work for him even though he had really killed his
wife, as she was a bad woman etc., etc., etc., but if the blood we claim to have
come from her nose is proven as having come from her throat, then he would
surely hang.

Reich heaved a heavy sigh and said in the pious Jews' jargon style,
"Geloybl is shem Yissborach" (praised be the name of the blessed Lord.)
"Now I am happy, I am not afraid any more; I need no Kinsley and no other

lawyers, nor do I care what Kinsley would have said. Let them take the blood and find out where it came from, and I am a free man."

Reich told me that his lawyer always wanted him to say he killed his wife in self-defense, that he had a man in prison several times to train him how to illustrate the killing, but that he, Reich, would do no such thing, he would not take a false oath and even in self-defense not bear the name of, having killed a human being.

All of the above gave me the conviction that Reich was innocent. . . . I was further convinced that Kinsley was one of the most criminally ignorant lawyers, or that he had sold out the case to the district attorney. Things of that kind I was told had happened before in the history of New York, because the conviction of a murderer is the tallest feather in the cap of an attorney, policemen, detectives, and even the judge.

[Browne notes points of carelessness in Kinsley's conduct of defense; Kinsley refuses to admit Browne as assistant for explaining cultural differences that might prejudicial jury against defendant; Kinsley again asks for money; Hungarians confirm Kinsley's original desire for self-defense plea and having Reich coached to demonstrate it; Browne writes to philanthropists for help, which they accept despite lingering suspicion of guilt; Schiff sends check with note that Temple Emanu-El trustees are hiring Adolph Sanger to represent Reich; Browne makes plea at synagogue service, takes up collection for defense, and swears to Reich's innocence before the open ark.]

After dinner Mr. Unger sent a message that Reich must see me without delay on a matter of his life and death. I hastened to the Tombs prison, which was the first time I ever entered that building. I had difficulty in being admitted, but Warden Walsh happened to be reading just then in the evening paper that I was to speak the same night at the reception given to Mr. William O'Brien on Union Square, asked whether I was that Rabbi Browne, and answering in the affirmative, he ordered the guard to let me in. He received me very politely and introduced me to the Deputy, Mr. Finley, who, took me to Reich, which was, I repeat, the first time I was in his cell. Reich fell down upon his knees, imploring me not to allow Kinsley to change his plea as he had told him he was resolved upon doing. Here I saw another rare opportunity to test Reich's case.

"Mr Reich," said I, "Mr. Kinsley acts according to my instruction."

The poor man was dumbfounded, gasping: "What? you have told him to make me swear to a lie?"

"Mr. Reich," I replied, "it is a terrible thing, but I had to do it and I trust the Lord will forgive me what I have done hastily, but it is your fault. You remember what I told you yesterday, that blood coming through the nose can be distinguished from blood reaching only the throat. You told me that you had no further fear, you were happy and blessed the Lord and asked me to hurry up with the examination of the blood on your shirt. Well, last night the blood was analyzed, and found to be blood coming from the throat, proving that you actually did kill the poor woman. Now then if we persist that you were not at home at the time of the killing and this blood came from your wife's nose, the doctors will show that it came from her throat and you will be hanged beyond question."

Reich was beside himself asking me to summon Mr. Newman and the working men of the shop, a baker and his wife, the installment dealer where Reich was that very morning, and others, all of whom can prove the blood stains to have been on his shirt that morning already; but I insisted these people's evidence will be proven a perjury, and we must take the plea of self-defense.

Reich positively refused to do it: "I will not swear to what is a lie and go the 'gayman' (Hell) forever-let them rather hang me. That is a punishment from the Lord for having made up and lived with her, although I knew of her doings—but she bewitched me. I will die an innocent man but I will not swear to a lie and make of myself a murderer," etc., etc.

I told Reich he had either to swear as Kinsley wanted him or he could make up his mind to hang and I would not come to court any more. Reich wept like a child, but I would not yield and, bidding him good-bye, I went towards the door. The old man jumped at me. "Doctor Browne," said he, "did you analyze that blood?"

I said I did not, but Mr. Kinsley had it done by a physician.

"Well," said Reich, "that doctor is a 'chamer' (an ass). I assure you who is my only defender, dear Rabbi, I swear to God that the blood on my shirt came from my wife's nose bleeding the night before. Have it examined by a good doctor in your presence and you will see I am telling you the truth."

This terrible ordeal which I caused the poor man to pass would convince anybody of Reich's innocence, and I promised to have the blood analyzed under my own supervision, and if it prove as he said, Kinsley will not change the plea of an alibi. The prisoner calmed down again and I left him in a happy frame of mind.

[Sanger consults with Browne, agrees that plea should not be changed, comes to court but departs when Kinsley refuses to admit him as co-counsel; Kinsley repeats request for money and determination to change plea.]

What followed is known to Your Excellency. Kinsley changed his plea, and as he did so, there ensued a scene in the court worthy of a Mosier's brush to paint. Judge Smyth opened his mouth wide and gazed at Kinsley, the jury looked at each other, the spectators were petrified, and Purdy was, or pretended to be, the most surprised man in the world. It took some time before the judge could collect himself, then he wrinkled his brow, and exclaiming "what is that?" he fell back in his chair. Kinsley repeated his confession to the killing, but claimed having done so in self-defense.

Poor Reich never understood a word of what Kinsley spoke, but seeing the consternation all around, he asked what all that meant. I had no heart to tell the sad news, but Mr. Unger did so, and poor Reich was crushed and pale with despair. Order was soon restored again and Mr. Purdy's face was covered with the happiest smiles, shared by the Honorable judge, the policemen and the detectives. I felt first like leaving the court room for good, but the helpless condition of poor Reich seemed to remind me that my duty was by his side, now more than ever before. Kinsley sat down to speak to me and said I must not be so troubled, he was a criminal lawyer and knew how to manage a case, "Reich will be on the sidewalk tomorrow."

[Kinsley calls witnesses, including Browne, who do not help case.]

Finally the climax was reached. Kinsley decided to put Reich on the stand and asked me to interpret his instruction to Reich. He should illustrate the killing of his wife after the manner he had taught him in prison through Mr. Roth. I declined to have a hand in such an outrage, and he prevailed upon Mr. Isidor Unger to serve him. The court then declared a recess of ten or fifteen minutes, which Kinsley utilized for an interview with Reich through Mr. Unger. Reich was told by Kinsley that the blood theory which I gave him was false and that human blood from the nose is just like blood from the throat, that he had already made the self-defense plea and Reich must bear him out or hang, that the Lord would forgive his perjury under the circumstances and he would be a free man "on the sidewalk" next morning.

Poor Reich, thus confused, took the stand and mechanically went through that terrible, scene which I never shall forget if I live a thousand years. Mr. Purdy, of course, made the most of the "confession at this hour." He boasted that Reich at first insisted on an alibi, but after the fatal, links of the circumstances were all found and welded together in a chain that could not be torn asunder, he found himself bound to confess. Kinsley's argument was puerile and feeble, and the judge's strong charge against the prisoner, upon Mr. Purdy's grounds, superadded to all, caused the jury to find the poor man guilty of murder in the first degree, recommending him however, to the mercy of the court.

[Governor Hill asks Browne if he was examined as witness, which Browne confirms, producing the page of the trial record to which he refers, citing each by page, throughout remainder of hearing; Browne tells of Hungarians holding mass meeting with himself as chairman, and cites inability of other members to attend hearing although all had planned to do so.]

I have no doubt my argument thus far, if fortified by legal evidence, will suffice to incline Your Excellency to favor my cause. But there are additional points in this case, the consideration of' which will lead Your Excellency to believe that Reich was not the murderer of his wife, and I beg permission to discuss them. For that purpose it is incumbent upon me to give Your Excellency the history of Reich, which is absolutely necessary for a clear understanding of his case.

Adolph Reich is a man of small stature and slight build. He is about 65 years of age at present, in spite of his claiming to be only 57. To explain this I must inform Your Excellency that these people in reality hardly ever know their exact age, but even if they do, they deny their years upon joining the various Jewish lodges which these foreigners do as soon as their means will permit. The laws of the various orders forbid the admission of men over 45 or 50, hence they all give their ages accordingly. . . . Reich followed simply the rule in that respect and rejuvenated himself to suit the occasion. People in the city who know him from home can prove his age to be about 65.

Adolph Reich was all the days of his life a tailor in a Hungary village. One must be acquainted with the condition of a Jewish country tailor in

Hungary. The working man in Europe even today can no more be compared to the workingmen of America than the lion can be compared with the cat, though both belong to the same genus, and the less could such a comparison be made a generation ago, especially in Hungary. . . . The workingman is looked down upon with contempt in Europe generally, even now, and especially so amongst the Jews, and most so in Hungary. The Jews having been for generations denied the privilege of learning trades, turned to commercial life and probably upon the theory of "sour grapes," began to look with contempt at the workingmen. Later when the trade restrictions were removed the contempt for the trade still survived, and no person of some claim to halfway decency would allow his boy to be a shoemaker. I can recall amongst all the acquaintances of my childhood only two that learned trades, and they were the poorest of the poor.

Reich was working like a beast from early dawn until late at night all the days of his life. He was a Hungarian peasant, uneducated, unrefined; he never saw a newspaper, never knew anything of public affairs, but being Jewish, he knew how to read his prayers in Hebrew and the Jargon-German written in Hebrew characters, and the Jewish newspapers of our downtown brethren gave him access to Jewish story books of ghosts, spirits, etc. Being a Jew, he was raised according to the tenets of the Jewish religion which are taught amongst the common Jews mechanically and are very strictly observed. He would do his oblations every morning, also before and after each meal, recite his prayers four times daily and at meals, mechanically, without giving a thought to the performance. He would not eat forbidden food if you were to kill him, literally speaking. To this day Reich, in all the days of his imprisonment, did not partake of forbidden food. In short his religion was a treadmill of repetition day after day, superstitiously observed. His belief in ghosts, evil spirits and witches is one of the habitual views of the people amongst whom he lived and he swears in his evidence accordingly that he knew of his wife's faithlessness, but with all her faults he loved her still, for she "bewitched" him. The interpreter translated the word "verhext" as "charmed," but it really means bewitched, "hexe" being the same as "witch" in the English language.

Reich was . . . a very quiet, peaceable and sober man, worked day and night and saved his money, and amongst the people with whom he lived from the days of his childhood to the time of his departure for America, he was highly honored and respected as a desirable neighbor, a kind father and husband, and a well-to-do tailor. He raised a family, I believe of four girls and one boy, and gave them a better education than most of his neighbors, his son having even gone to the college, for I find that he knows Latin, Hebrew, and several modern languages. His first wife died some years ago and he married the woman for whose murder he stands convicted. She was at the time a divorced woman. What that means and particularly what it meant amongst the orthodox Jews of Reich's class, Your Excellency can not, of course, conceive. To this day divorces amongst the Jews are very, very rare, and a divorced woman is put down as a bad character. There are hundreds of people in this city who know Reich and that woman for years and years, and there is not one, except those of her American acquaintances interested in her, who does not give her the worst possible character. She was known a public "professional," young and attractive, and having seen that Reich, although an old man, was a very well situated tailor, she set her cap and captured him finally. Nobody in the village could understand how such a nice man could so lower himself as to marry that Cyprian, who several times tried to commit suicide. Poor Reich had only one explanation, to give: "she has bewitched me." The people as a rule believed it, still he lost his former standing, his children were anxious to get rid of the paternal home, and finally Reich felt so out of place in the village of his birth that he left for America, not driven by want, as most of these working people, but by the self-enforced excommunication in consequence of his misalliance.

Arrived in the country, he went to work at once, and during all that time he had only two bosses as a rule. At Mr. Goldwasser, 68 Spring Street, he worked on ready-made clothing during the season peculiar to such work, and after the ready-made clothing season was over, he worked at Mr. Delury's, a very prominent merchant tailor on Sixth Avenue. Reich was always retained for the next season by those two bosses, and Mr. Delury himself and his assistants (all Christians and natives) testified to the quiet, orderly and ever obliging little man Reich. Even his own people, born and raised with him, say he never in his life harmed a living being and never refused a favor, and never was in any dispute or difficulty, whilst just the reverse is said of the woman who was his second wife.

[Browne describes Reich's work routine, his confiding in Newman Goldwasser's (father) who testifies that Reich's only ongoing unhappiness was his wife's insistence on keeping Gross as their the boarder. Rabbi reviews testimony describing Reich's actions with Reich's wife on the day and evening of the murder, his whereabouts when not with his wife, and the fact that Gross had a key to their apartment whereas Reich did not. Browne questioned evidence of the crease in the towel, noting no reason for the blood to have been wiped from knife purported to be the murder weapon.]

Governor Hill: Dr. Browne, you are arguing quite reasonably, but the fact is, the woman has been killed; well, then who did the killing?

Rabbi Browne: May it please Your Excellency, it is not my task here to fasten the crime on anybody, sufficient is it unto me in the success of the showing that Reich was not the man. But since Your Excellency wishes me to do so, I shall gladly name the murderer, for the various strange features noticed just discussed can be understood only if we assume that Gross was the murderer, and every step of his will point to guilt.

First of all, let us look at him. He hates Reich. Reich ordered him out times and again, according to Gross's own confession. Gross lived with the woman during her separation all the time. She makes up with Reich finally again, only upon condition of retaining Gross in the house. The very bitterness Gross displays in giving his evidence, shows the feeling against Reich. See how he tries to cast on Reich the suspicion of trying to borrow his door key. Gross is a wild character; he shot a man in Hungary, and had to leave the country, and the shooting was not accidental either as scores of Hungarians in this city know.

Now let us see: the old man leaves at eight o'clock, Gross says he was at home and knew that Reich went to Eckert's to have his coat made, and wouldn't be back before very late, near twelve o'clock. Gross comes home and spends a pleasant evening. He has no fear of Reich's coming home before midnight, and if he did, Reich cannot surprise him, for he has no key, and Gross can quietly retire in good order to his virtuous couch when Reich knocks for admission.

The coroner's inquest and the towel tell the tale. Something must have transpired of course, between Gross and the woman afterwards. The desperado knew she had money, in short the woman was killed no doubt, in her first sleep. She may have been drugged for all we know, Gross studied chemistry in Hungary. Mrs. Newman heard no noise at all until this dying woman, coming to and regaining consciousness, knocked at the door. Those people go to bed as a rule by ten o'clock. God only knows what led Gross to kill that woman, but after he had stuck the knife into her throat and drew the blade from ear to ear the woman never budged any more and the amount of blood saturating the bed clothes proves that her life must have bled away in bed so suddenly and completely, that he considered her harmless to give any alarm, is a token of his crime. He had time to act and wash without fear of being surprised for Reich was away and had no key and the woman was lifeless.

And now let us return to the "crease" in the towel so tenderly guarded by Mr. Purdy and the officers, showing that the blade of the knife was passed through it for the purpose of wiping off the blood. As stated, I challenge any one to advance a sane theory in explanation of the needless and useless expenditure of most valuable time on the part of the murderer; but I will show Your Excellency that it was quite necessary for the murderer to do so as very essential to his safety, for the knife with which it is alleged the murder was committed did not belong to Reich, as he and Gross both testify. There being no knife in the house capable of doing such bloody work, the knife was introduced later, no doubt by some one of the detectives or policemen who manufacture evidence to suit a given theory.

The knife with which the woman was killed, I insist, was a Hungarian clasp knife, the like of which Hungarian bloods and toughs carry habitually, similar to our Bowie knife, just the thing to cut a throat by plunging the point and drawing it across the neck. Poor Reich never had such a knife—he would be afraid to touch it; but Gross had such a knife. Every one of his kind carries such a weapon and it has been seen in his possession by a number of witnesses. He tried to stab a waiter in Coney Island with that knife. Having killed the woman with his own knife, known to be his, he could not very well leave it there, and being compelled to take it along, be had to wipe off the blood, close the knife in order to put it into his pocket. This explains the crease in the towel which no other theory can illustrate.

At first I was inclined to think the woman committed suicide, she having attempted suicide several times before, and the cuts in her fingers I thought due to her own act, often the case, or to the act of the officers, who, as I was convinced by reliable criminal lawyers, do such things in order to secure convictions; but the crease and the repudiation of the big knife convince me that the woman was killed with a Hungarian Bowie knife—and by Gross. Having killed the woman and wiped off the knife, he goes down stairs to the bar room and awaits the return of Reich, in order to have him arrested. See his own evidence, page 49. "I found Mrs. Reich lying on the floor in the hall-way. Then I thought I will go for some one's arrest, if there is any possible."

"Did you examine her?" asks Mr. Purdy. He answered [that] he did not examine her, but "I went down to look for some policeman some arrest."

Is that the way an innocent man acts on finding his most beloved friend who cured him, saved his mother's life, as Gross testifies? Mark it, Your Excellency, if you please: He finds her lying on the floor in her blood, but does not examine her to ascertain her injuries to see whether she is dead or alive—no, he runs away. What for? To summon a physician? To call an ambulance? No! His first idea is to get somebody arrested, as he tells us twice, and that somebody, he knew, would be poor Reich about coming back with the blood stains of the night before on his garments of which Gross knew, as Reich and others can swear to.

Gross cannot claim having thought the woman dead, for later on, on page 50, he asks the policeman to send for an ambulance. Poor Reich soon comes home. Had he killed that woman and been lucky enough to get out unnoticed, would he have come back with his garments full of blood? Having had time enough to dress, as is supposed so neatly that there was not a wrinkle on his clothes, he could have taken along a set of clean underclothes, changed them somewhere with one of his many friends, and gone home without anybody to betray him as the murderer. But no; poor Reich goes straight home; and his behavior, look at it and contrast it with the demeanor of Gross. I have been told by detectives, and read of what sharp attempts to enforce "confessions," and the most crucial test you can put the criminal to is to make him view the locality where the murder was committed. At the mere sight of the bloody room, or the instrument of death many murderers confessed, but the most hardened criminal will weaken at the sight of his victim, and to make the murderer touch the dead body, is something you can never bring about.

Now let us look at Reich. The witnesses say he was full of sorrow and grief. He goes up, and seeing his wife dead, he bends down, tries to pick her up, and asks Gross to help him carry her in to the room. His first impulse is to take up the dead body of the woman he loved from the doorway, and lay her tenderly on the bed. Gross says (page 67), "I refused to do it." The woman—read his evidence, Your Excellency—whom he said he loved like his mother, he refuses to pick up from the filthy hallway. The murderer dreads to touch his victim even as he dreaded examining her when he first saw her lying dead in her blood. If there were any doubt in my mind still existing as to Gross's innocence, the self-confessed evidence of his terror in the sight of the corpse stamps him as the murderer beyond a doubt.

But Gross the murderer is a tough who had shot his man before, and he had washed his hands, cleansed his knife, possibly changed his garments. The murderer is cool and calculating; he has Reich arrested. The murderer can speak the English language, and is used to policemen and arrests. Poor Reich never was in a court, never knew of a policeman, never had anything to do with lawyers, excepting his intended divorce, and he gladly dropped it as soon as his wife gave him the opportunity. Reich has never in his life been even as much as suspected of the least impropriety, and now all at once he is dragged into what—in his own words—he considered a court. The poor inoffensive man is hustled about by policemen and detectives; strange scenes are enacted before him in strange surroundings by strange men; excited men speak to him in a strange tongue and with strange gestures, and he stood there bewildered, dumbfounded. The only familiar face is that of Gross his mortal enemy, directing the enemies of his life. Gross is used to such scenes; he had been arrested before; he had shot his man in Hungary—read his own admission—he tried to stab a man at Coney Island. Gross, is a "tough" with a dark and bloody history. We must know those characters as they developed occasionally in Hungary, my own home. The rich land owner's son there is just what the "young master" of the southern planter was before the war. You find amongst them here and there an over-bearing fellow who sows his wild oats promiscuously amongst the ignorant peasants as his prototype here did sometimes amongst the ignorant Negroes before the rebellion, and at the least insult or to get out of a scrape, he will whip out his revolver or Bowie knife. It is not often that you find such a rowdy amongst the Hungarians and less frequently yet amongst the Jews, but if you do find him there he is an "outer and outer." Gross is such a character, the son of a rich man in the interior provinces of Hungary, lording over the peasants of his village. He had illicit relations with a peasant girl and when the father came to ask "what will be done in the case?" Gross answered the poor man with a bullet. In the wilds of Hungary a rich man's misdeed can be easily covered up, there being no legal machinery like ours to ferret it out, and the fact that Gross had to flee the country shows his guilt more clearly than the verdict of a jury. He had some fuss with the Reich woman, whose paramour he was, killed her with his clasp-knife, [and] as the evidence shows, wiped the blade on the tell-tale towel with the tell-tale spermatosa, and sneaked downstairs awaiting Reich's return home, to give the alarm after his entrance into the room. But the neighbors discover the murder, they run upstairs. Gross hears it and runs, as he says, not for an ambulance to give aid to the wounded woman still alive, as an innocent man's first impulse would lead him to do especially with a woman, his nurse, who was so dear to him, as he says. No! He runs for a policeman "to make an arrest." He succeeds, for a wonder, in finding a policeman. Reich is arrested. Gross is the manager and inspirer of the examining officers and turn the suspicion from himself against Reich so completely, that he, (Gross) is not examined at all. There is not a wrinkle on Reich's clothes, not the least speck, as would be natural on a man who had just cut a person's throat. "His hands were clean and dry, like mine," (Officer Louis,) and judged by his external appearance, no sane man would have suspected him. But Gross knows that Reich's undergarments were bloody from the dead woman's nose bleeding the night before. (Gross in his evidence admits that it might be, the blood came from that cause) and he directs the attention of the police to make him undress. Poor Reich, handled as is the way of our police, without kid gloves, becomes more confused still, but at once says how his garments became bloody. He has a dozen witnesses to prove it and is anxious to send for them, but hardly has he opened his mouth than Coroner Messemer tells him to keep quiet. He thinks, as he states in the evidence, that he was before a judge who bad the power to hang him on the spot, and he obeyed. Having no witnesses and no defender, with his mortal enemy Gross against him, the jury, of course, upon Gross's evidence, uncontradicted as it was, bound poor Reich over to the Grand jury and the indictment followed as a matter of course.

Right here it may be of interest to say a few words as to the Coroner's inquests, and our detectives, police, district attorneys and judges, and I am speaking upon information from reliable sources. The verdict of "guilty or not guilty" in a murder case is pronounced in reality in the Coroner's court already, and if only one half be true of what has been told me, the most corrupt procedure dominates there. I have been told that it is the easiest thing in the world to get just the kind of a jury you want in the Coroner's office and many a guilty man escapes if he only has the wherewithal to pay for the selection of a jury. It is hard for me to believe, but I have been told so most positively, and I would like Coroner Messemer especially to take notice, that there are certain undertakers in league with certain coroners who will give you just the jury you want if you give them the job, and who will so arrange matters around the corpse that the evidence will be in your favor. I am told that the scene of the murder is not properly watched; that implements of death are introduced meantime which never had a part in the tragedy; that hands are "cut," doors and windows locked or opened by the detectives to show that somebody had killed the "suicide;" that "suicides" for family honor are suppressed, cases nay, often evident cases of murder are often made out to be of mere "accidents."

[Browne continues.]

"If you have money or a good pull," so I was told, the Coroner's jury will be "all right, etc., etc.," and I was pointed also to Ed. Stokes, who killed Fisk, and two other Prominent Tammany bosses, who at the same time were with him in the tombs for killing their men; of course Stokes had his "pile" and the others their "pull," and all of them are this day not only free men, but the rulers of New York City.

Now, since the rich man can free himself, no matter what his crime be, the police and detectives, etc., etc., in order to keep up their reputation, must arrest and convict somebody; hence the poor man, as soon as in their coils, innocent or guilty, is at once doomed. Woe to the poor man in the slums of New York if suspicion be cast upon him, and especially upon the poor Jew. If he escapes the police-man's club—but recently, a Jew on the East side was killed without any reason by a policeman whom he disobeyed—he will not escape his official oath. And the Jew is the worst off in that East Side District. The Irishman, trained at home in resisting the Metropolitan Police, often kills the cop, hence Pat is left alone. The Italian has his stiletto, the Negro his [iron] bar, and the German his bold "French victory prowess" to protect him; but the poor downtrodden Jew, oppressed as a rule in Europe, trembles at the sight of a policeman, and the guardian of the law selects him for the victim as soon as the least occasion offers itself to justify, even remotely, to arrest or "fan" him with a club. And arrests the policeman must make for his own benefit. When a promotion is thought of the policeman who made most arrests is of course selected as the most "zealous and watchful" aid since amongst these arrests only the "convictions" count, the policeman will do anything for a "conviction" and swear to anything that will serve the purpose. The same is the case with our criminal judges and district attorneys, I am told; the claim to re-election or promotion depends upon the "convictions" under their management. Judge Martin's election and Mr. Nichols's nomination were due to the convictions of Sharp, and Mr. Fellows has been scored time and again for the "escape" of the boodle-alderman. Just think of the notorious Jack the ripper in the slums of London. What would the London police not give to get at that cold blooded murderer simply to escape the ridicule and stigma upon their reputation. With our police the Jack-the-ripper problem would have been solved long ago. They would not allow their reputation to suffer. They would catch "Jack" at the commission of his first murder. It might possibly not be "the murderer" at all, but what of that? The detectives would find a theory to involve the first forlorn pauper and fasten the crime on him; the coroner's jury would be selected to suit evidence created at will, and the chain of "circumstantial evidence" be linked so strongly together by Mr. Purdy, with an occasional riveting by of Recorder Smyth, that the jury would find the accused Jack guilty without leaving their seats. Of course it would cost a deal of money and trouble to find "witnesses," etc., but the city pays "incidental expenses" and the people will pay with their votes in advancing the judges, police force, detectives, district attorneys, etc. And what of it if an innocent man is being hung? He was only a poor devil without a "pull;" and prosecutors, police, etc.,must show their efficiency for popularity and promotion. It was useless for Mr. Purdy to come before the jury and pretend disinterestedness in the conviction of Reich. It is Mr. Purdy's and Recorder Smyth's biggest feather and no money nor means are spared to bring about conviction, no matter the blue streaks of sulphurous perjury that follow the policeman's oath; particularly so in this case "the first sheeny to be hung," something clamored for long ago by the Irish criminal classes. Our police are proverbially "the finest;" so they are; and viewing the police parades one must admit them the most superb in physical achievement. Yes, they are as men the finest in body, but their souls—the Lord save them in his endless mercy! Their souls are, with few honorable exceptions, steeped in villainous violence, greed and perjury. When John the Baptist rebuked the Roman soldier he had the prototype of "one of the finest" in his prophetic eye, saying unto him: "Do violence to no man neither accuse any falsely and be content with your wages."

[Invoking recent case of a doctor's wife found murdered for which her husband was wrongfully convicted, Browne points to examples of similar collusion, misrepresentation, and sensationalism by the press as occurred in Reich's case; ultimately, a reporter identified the true murderer who was convicted and the doctor freed.]

If Dr. Hull had been a poor man, an obscure man, a friendless man, a speechless man, a voteless man, an ignorant foreigner and a "sheeney tailor" from the East Side slums, defended by a common "shyster" he would have been hanged long ago. But fortunately for Dr. Hull, he had money, position, character and intelligence, he lived in a fashionable West Side neighborhood, and moved in good society, and above all, he engaged his own counsel, who spared no pains to defend their client, In short, he had all the means to overcome the criminal machinery of the District Attorney's office, hence although the "chain of evidence" against him manufactured by the detectives, was much stronger than the one against Reich. Dr. Hull's innocence was brought to light whilst Reich's innocence was not permitted to come to the surface, being held down by the weight of the "chain" forged by the "detectives" out of whole cloth. The forging, or rather the forgery of the leading links against Reich is just as plain as it proved to be later against Dr. Hull. The "coolness," the key, blood stains on Reich's face, the "freshness" of the blood on Reich's garments, the "big knife" which, even according to Gross never existed in the Reich household, the blood stains on that knife, were all fictitious links, made to order by the detectives, the fellow Gross— the Chastine Cox in the case—the witness Schieck, Lawyer Halberstadt, the "widow" Boniface, all very prominent and honorable characters, as any one can see on reading their printed evidence were each taking the part of the "ex-convict" of the Hull chain. Had poor Reich had money like Dr. Hull, Gross would by this time be moldering in the grave of a murderer. But being, as was stated, a man "without a pull and without a pile" poor Reich had to be utilized at least as the means of official and political capital to establish the efficiency of our detectives, policemen, district attorneys and recorders, as the protectors of our citizens. And in spite of all that, Reich would have been a free man today were not for the ignorance, or rather the connivance and treachery of his so-called defender Kinsley, because on the third day of the trial an unquestionable alibi was proven by three witnesses of the State upon cross examination —a child of thirteen years amongst them, a cross-examination which Kinsley carried on under my supervision on Friday, the first day of mine in the court, when he was still expecting from me a big fee, before he yet knew that I considered him unfit to defend a three-legged yellow dog indicted for high treason and blasphemy; and before he figured out, or was convinced by somebody, that it would pay him better to betray his client than have him surrender the defense to other counsel.

[Browne reiterates his accusations in Reich's case.]

I said before that our police force is an army of perjurers with some honorable exceptions; Schmidt, Louis and Sergeant Allaire are such Ihonorable exceptions. Schmidt is strictly upright and true, whilst Louis does his little bit of lying in a half-hearted way under moral duress as it were, in keeping with the duties imposed by his official position, to contribute some evidence of a damaging nature against the prisoner. Let us look at the report of the officers (P. 130-158) as to the appearance of Reich.

All the officers say that upon examining Reich closely, they found nothing out of the way about his shoes and garments, and his hands were "as clean and dry as mine are now" officer Louis says, adding however "I saw two or three little specks of blood on his forehead," (p.132.)

Officer Schmidt says he saw no blood at all on Reich's face, and as if sorry to see officer Louis testifying to something, he (Schmidt) did not discover, when asked whether Louis called his attention to "the blood" answers with honorable emphasis : "No sir, he did not tell me anything of the kind." (P. 142.)

But officer Young is one of the "regulars," hence whilst he admits that "I and officer Louis looked at his hands, they were perfectly clean," he adds what Lewis did not see "except that on the right hand, between the forefinger and thumb, he had a scrape in there, just the same as if the skin had been scraped off by cutting them" (p. 148), and as to the blood, he says: "I noticed a spot of blood over his right eye, and five or six little specks around his nose, the size of the head of a pin, and one of the spots was not quite dry yet, and I took my finger and wiped it off, and asked him where he got it and he said

'I don't know.'" Officer Young says he kept his eyes closely on Reich, but looking away for a while "I noticed Reich, and he did not have any blood on his face." Did you call his attention to that, asks the District Attorney ? "No, Sir" (P. 145.)

Gross, of course, is better informed still. "I seen his forehead covered with blood, and under his eye, his right eye, (corroborating Young) I saw also blood" and though be says "I looked at him searchingly" he admits on cross examination, (page 68), that he never said a word about the "blood-covered forehead" to either Reich or any of the officers. Gross is apparently well trained and supports Young in saying that soon after, the blood was "everything wiped off." (P. 52.) Logical people will wonder how a "forehead covered with blood" can be "wiped off" suddenly whilst under the "searching" eyes of Gross and Young, and without leaving the least sign or stain at that.

This officer Young finds the "large knife in the cupboard" (the alleged instrument of the murder), he says there was no blood to be seen on it, and Gross when shown the two knives, testifies that he recognizes the small one but the larger one he cannot say he ever saw in Reich;'s household; and Reich swears, after having admitted the killing "that is not my knife; it don't belong to me." (p, 248.) Young and Gross seem to understand each other better than the other officers do.

[Browne reiterates his previous point regarding Reich's demeanor at crime scene, contrasts it with that of Gross, reviews testimony of police officers at coroner's inquest as well as during trial; and notes records of supposed divorce attorney briefly employed by Reich, citing the man's relationship with Mrs. Reich and falsification of status as attorney.]

I have reserved the most infamous witness for the State as a fit climax to the character of the entire cotery, Simon Scheick, to the very last, not simply to show his infamy, but the peculiar ruling of his honor, Recorder Smith. Schieck's wife is an honest, upright woman, and her evidence establishes the facts that she was doing Mrs. Reich's washing, visited the family now and then, and brought the wash to Reich's house on the evening before the woman's death. Reich takes supper with his wife, he brings a pint of beer which they drink jointly; Reich takes a glass of beer, also part of his meat on his plate, and gives it to the poor woman. After supper, Reich takes his coat and goes to Ecker's to have it made. Mrs. Schieck says Reich's behavior and treatment of his wife was "Schoen, still and ruhig," nice, silent and quiet. She knew the Reichs some two years and a half, did the washing for them constantly, she "paid a visit when taking and bringing the wash," and yet she does not remember anything that was not "nice and quiet" in Reich's behavior towards his wife, p. 90 and 91. Mr. Purdy evidently found that woman too honest for "coaching" and when she answers his questions as to Reich's behavior towards his wife as having been "nice . . .and quiet," he drops the witness suddenly, like a hot potato, saying: "I shall not press the other questions, that will do for me." And Mr. Purdy by so doing gave the best evidence as to the principles upon which that trial was conducted. Of the lying evidence by Gross, et. al., he never could get enough, but as soon as he struck a truthful person amongst his own witnesses, a person he could not train, and Mrs. Schieck was the only exception, he had enough, and blurted out in his agony "that will do for me." Kinsley could have brought out from Mrs. Schieck all the evidence necessary to clear Reich, for Mrs. Schieck would have testified that during the two and a half years of her doing the washing for the Reichs, she many a time had washed Reich's shirts, etc., that were made bloody by his wife's profuse nose-bleeding, but Kinsley seemed to understand Mr. Purdy's shriek of agony "that will do for me" and he, Kinsley also, who to my greatest surprise, dropped the noble woman without further questioning. Indeed it is evident to me now that Purdy, intended this peculiar remark "that will do for me" as an order to Kinsley, who, instead of being the defender of Reich, became an assistant to the prosecuting attorney, to do likewise.

But the honesty of Mrs. Schieck which nearly upset Mr. Purdy's plan was to be contradicted by her husband, and the husband was present, but Mr. Purdy could not call Simon Schieck without giving him first the necessary training. Hence in order to gain the opportunity of instructing Simon Schieck, a host of other witnesses are called first. . . . Simon Schieck was left to testify "after recess" during which time Mr. Purdy coached the Simon-pure Schieck what to lie and how to lie, in order to undo the truthful evidence of his wife.

[Browne explains good existing conditions for tinsmiths in New York, hence suspicious reputation of Schieck, a beggar claiming to be an itinerant tinsmith; he also explains Jewish attitude toward men whose wives must do housework for others (Mrs. Schieck was washerwoman for the Reichs); he cites instances of Schieck's lying under oath, and describes a scene which he witnessed personally wherein Schieck was tricked into admitting having been offered money in return for testimony damaging to Reich, Scheick claiming that such false testimony would be absolved by his prayers on Kol Nidre, the eve of Yom Kippur.]

After recess, when Schieck had finished his direct evidence, I gave Kinsley a number of questions to cross examine the witness as found in the report, p. 109-110:

Q. Where do you attend prayer?

A. I go to 22 Rivington street; there is a Hungarian temple where we pray on the day of atonement.

Q. By the Court: What has all this to do with the case; how is this material?

Mr. Kinsley: I want to show that, on the day of atonement, these people resolve that all the oaths they take thereafter during the year shall be null and void.

The Court: I suppose there should be some record of it, if there was anything of the sort; I don't believe that you can show that this man made a promise, on the day of atonement, or any other day, to swear falsely; if you can I will admit it.

Mr Kinsley: Is it not so, that, on the day of atonement, each man solemnly promises three times to God, that all the oaths taken during the year shall be null and void?

The Court: that I will exclude; I will allow you to show that he took such an oath.

Mr. Kinsley: I am asking him if he did it.

The Court: Ask him if he made, on the day of atonement, a solemn oath or promise that all the oaths he took during the year should be null and void.

(Question is put by the interpreter.)

A. It is an old ceremony, and one that says the prayer before every one in the temple; he says that, and every one says "Amen;" it is an old usage since fifteen hundred years.

Mr. Kinsley: It is in evidence, that, this year, he joined in that prayer, and that his oath is not therefore worth anything.

Mr. Purdy: That is an improper remark, I submit.

The Court: Of course it is; the jury will not pay any attention to any improper remarks by either side.

Now may it please Your Excellency this "prayer" called "Kol Nidre" had been recited in the Atonement evening prayer time out of mind amongst our people (the modern Jews have banished it from their liturgy) . . . the

"Kol Nidre" was intended simply to absolve the Jew from frivolous vows and objurgations self-imposed, also from oaths which our oppressed forefathers were often constrained to take, under terrible tortures, in order to disclose the hiding places of their valuables, or to abjure their religion, similar to the oath Harold had to take under duress upon William's box of Norman Saints. The enemies of Israel in olden times such have occasionally revived that malicious perversion of the meaning of "Kol Nidre," and hearing of it, though very rarely, caused some amongst the most ignorant, degraded and unprincipled of our race, to really believe, or make himself to believe for selfish purposes, that by reciting the "Kol Nidre" he could actually commit perjury with impunity. Simon Schieck, the Jewish tramp, is such an individual—first I ever met with—it was my purpose to show that his evidence was not admissible under the law. For a lawful oath depends exclusively upon the subjective effect it has upon the person sworn; and as soon as we ascertain that the witness is impressed with the belief that he cannot be guilty of, nor punished for perjury, his evidence loses all credibility, and especially in this case where the man was ready to testify to anything for money.

Recorder Smyth acknowledges that legal principles, but scoffs the idea and challenges Kinsley to prove that Schieck did recite such a prayer. Kinsley succeeds and Schieck confesses. True, he says, that he did not recite it himself, but he says that the rabbi recited it aloud to all the congregation, and he with the others said "amen" thereto, p. 109; which, (though utterly false, for every one in the congregation repeats every word of the "Kol Nidre" with the reading rabbi) is just as good as if he would have recited it himself. Seeing that Kinsley had proven Scheick's oath not binding upon his conscience, and the evidence inadmissable, Recorder Smyth suddenly veers about, goes back upon his own words of two minutes ago, and rules out the whole part of that evidence as entirely improper. But it must be borne in mind that next to Gross, Schieck was the leading witness of the people and his evidence, especially after Mrs. Schieck's honest statement, was absolutely necessary for Reich's conviction.

And this not only shows the nature of the witness, but particularly the character of the judge, for Smyth violated here most flagrantly, the fundamental principle of justice in admitting the evidence of a witness who testified that the oath he took had no sanctity for him. I told Kinsley to note an exception, and that one "exception" would have been sufficient to secure for poor Reich a new trial, but Kinsley refused to "except." Indeed Recorder Smyth acted so infamously throughout the trial, that he aught to have been impeached for the grossest violation of his duties and ordinary decency. I will cite a few of the many utterances of a judge who is trying a man for his life.

In the case of the alleged blood on Reich's face which, from drops like a pin-head to the covering of the entire face, was testified to by officers Lewis, Young and Gross, (see pages 234-146). . . .

Three times Recorder Smyth called Reich a liar, saying aloud "oh, he lies!" Once when Reich says he did not know his wife's family name (p. 267) it was so incredible to the judge that he called Reich a liar. And yet, if the judge knew the life of Reich in his Hungarian horne, he would have found it very natural for Reich to know the woman only by the name of Lena, without caring for her family name. There was likely only one Lena in that place, and when he married that Lena, the Hebrew Certificate did not mention the name of Lena Weiss, but Leah, "the daughter of so and so." The judge, who, in his justice and mercy was to save or hang a man, did not stop however to enquire but prejudiced the jury by exclaiming with all possible emphasis, "oh, he lies."

Again, when Reich denies having been spoken to in German by Officer Young . . . again the judge said "oh, he lies." And that was after poor Reich had "confessed" to the killing of the woman and the question whether Young did or did not speak to him in German was entirely immaterial. Had the judge been less prejudiced, it might have been established that Young and Reich both testified truthfully on this immaterial point, for the German-jargon of Young compared with the German-jargon of Reich sounds like two different languages and I don't blame Reich for not understanding Young. Yet Young was the interpreter as shown above. And once he calls Reich a liar in his charge to the jury. I hold that a judge who can call a witness a liar in open court is unfit to preside over any case, let alone a case where a human life is in the balance. Of course these "interjections" of His Honor are not reported and the stenographer, most likely familiar with the tastes and wishes of his superior, omits these judicial pleasantries, and "doctors" some uneven utterances. My own evidence has been garbled for I never employed such incorrect, nay ungrammatical language as found in the report of the case (p.226-7).

Had poor Reich had a half-decent defender all these violations of law and humanity in Recorder Smyth would have been censured, but Kinsley was "appointed" by His Honor to defend Reich and of course could not be disrespectful in return for such a rare distinction. I wonder how Recorder Smyth happened to put Reich's case into Kinsley's care? Could His Honor give us some information on that subject? With such a judge, such a defender and such witnesses against him, is it to be wondered at that Reich was found guilty?

[Browne reiterates major points in summation.]

Alas, poor Reich's case was prejudiced as soon as the plea was changed, indeed, all public opinion was against him from that moment on. If a lawyer rests his case three days on an alibi, proves the alibi, and next day surprises the jury with a plea of "killing in self-defense," it is only natural for them to be prejudiced against the prisoner. Add thereto the cruel remarks of the judge during the trial and the "charge" to wind up with, and the result could not be otherwise. Upon hearing the judge's charge everybody knew Reich's doom was sealed. There is in that charge a point which may strike an ordinary judge. Hear him:

> *If it is true, gentlemen, that he lied, to use plain language, at that time, to the officers in respect to who perpetrated the homicide, it must effect his credibility as a witness; the extent to which it should effect it, is for you to say. If this man stated when arrested, "Yes, my wife attacked me with a knife, and I, in self-defense, resorted to the use of the knife, and unfortunately killed her," it would probably go to sustain his defense. But he made no such statement so far as we know, until he made it on this witness stand.*

And the judge tells the jury further that a credibility of a witness is questioned "Where his testimony conflicts with that of other witnesses." Instead of giving Reich the presumption of credibility on account of a "confession against his own interests," the judge shows that because he had "lied" at the Coroner's inquest, in claiming not to have killed his wife, they should not believe him now that he killed her in self-defense. The principle of disbelieving a person who had been proven by other witnesses to have lied before, is altogether different from a person's own changing against his own interest. Where, in the entire evidence, does Reich's evidence "conflict with that of other witnesses"? But we shall not enter upon a legal argument as to that written charge. What I do protest most to is the gestures, the grimaces, the corrogation of his brow, the rolling of his eyes, the fiendish emphasis in his voice, running the gamut down to the scarce audible diminuendo and back to the thundering crescendo, when delivering his charge to the jury. I

385

think a good actor or a sanctimonious priest was sacrificed for the bringing up of an unworthy judge. The charge as it reads in the report, did not effected the jury half as much as the way it was delivered.

In addition to the verbatim report, Smyth's charge to the jury should have been copied by Edison's phonograph and illustrated by instantaneous photographs of His Honor, for it is his mobile features and his vocal modulations that hang the prisoner and not the charge of itself, and I reiterate that no Digger Indian ever scalped victims with more savage delight than does this noble judge pronounce the sentence of death, boastingly informing the public how many scalps of human heads are already hanging on his belt, and in this case he was especially happy to see his trophies increased by one he never attained thus far in spite of all his hopes, i.e., the life of a Jew; or, to employ His Honor's more natural vocabulary, "a Sheeny," and, your Excellency, with all that unhappy combination against poor Reich, the jury had not the heart to find him guilty without a recommendation to mercy. They might as well have recommended a helpless lamb to the mercy of a blood-thirsty hyena.

NOTES

Chapter One

1. Jacob R. Marcus, United States Jewry, Vol. IV, (Detroit, 1993) 718; Jonathan D. Sarna, American Judaism (New Haven 2004) 93.

2. Solomon Grayzel, A History of the Jews (Philadelphia, 1947) 139; Encyclopedia Judaica (Jerusalem 1972) [hereafter cited as EJ.], 13, 1022.

3. Michael Meyer, Response to Modernity: A History of the Reform Movement in Judaism (New York, 1988) 77.

4. Ibid.

5. Ibid.

6. EJ 6, 533.

7. Ibid., 531.

8. Items in possession of author.

9. Phillip Glasberg deposition, Browne v. Burke, Jacob Rader Marcus Center of the American Jewish Archives, Cincinnati [hereafter cited as Browne, AJA]; Eva Glassberg deposition, Browne v. Burke, Browne, AJA.

10. Encyclopedia of Jewish Life Before and During the Holocaust, 1024, Presov; Browne deposition, Box 8, Case Files, Browne, Edward B. M. v. Jones, 1881-1883, Isaiah Thornton Williams Collection, New York Public Library [hereafter cited as Williams, NYPL].

11. Grayzel, History of the Jews, 597.

12. Browne deposition, Williams NYPL; Exhibit H, Browne v. Burke, Browne AJA.

13. Eva Glasberg deposition, Browne, AJA; Ignatz Weingarten deposition, Browne, AJA

14. EJ 6, 532.

15. Browne v. Jones, Williams, NYPL

16. Browne, Sermon The Evolution of Religion, Browne, AJA

17. Ibid.

18. B. L. Jones, War Department, to Browne, September 29, 1919, Browne AJA; Original album in possession of author, copy in Browne, AJA; Browne, letter to the editors, Atlanta Constitution, March 31, 1881, copy in Exhibit H, Browne v Burke, Browne, AJA.

19. Portion of book galley intended for publication as a tribute to Browne by the Hebrew American Republican League in 1889 [hereafter cited as book galley], 52, 167 Browne, AJA.

20. Ibid; American Israelite, June 14, 1872.

21. In possession of author. Copy in Browne, AJA.

22. Bertram W. Korn, American Jewry and the Civil War (Philadelphia 1951) 40; Southern Workman, October, 1904.

23. L.D.C. Lewin to I.M. Wise, Browne, AJA; Browne deposition, Browne v Jones, Williams, NYPL.

24. Ibid; Floral House Weeds, Browne, AJA.

25. American Israelite, July 15, 1887, Vol 34, 3.

Chapter Two

1. Michael Meyer, Response to Modernity, (New York, 1988) 234, 281; Jonathan D. Sarna, American Judaism, (New Haven, 2004) 90-100.
2. Sarna, American Judaism, 90-100.
3. Ibid. 78; Meyer, Response to Modernity, 234.
4. Meyer, Response to Modernity, 255.
5. Attributed to Einhorn, Book galley, Browne, AJA.
6. Meyer, Response to Modernity (New York, 1988) 244-260; Marcus, United States Jewry, v.III, 73. Minhag, literally meaning "custom" or "usage," is generally used by Reform Jews to connote "order of prayer" or "liturgy." For broader use historically see EJ, v.12, 4-25.
7. Meyer, Response to Modernity, 244-260; EJ, Vol 6, 531-532; EJ, Vol 16, 563-565.
8. Israelite, August 16, 1872; Exhibit H, Browne v. Burke, AJA.
9. Ibid.
10. Andee Hochman, Rodeph Shalom: Two Centuries of Seeking Peace (Rodeph Shalom Congregation, Philadelphia, 2000) 12,13; EJ 9, 1298.
11. Browne, book galley, AJA, 171.
12. Alfred G. Moses, "History of the Jews of Montgomery," American Jewish History, v.13, 1905, 86.
13. Moses, Montgomery; Scott Langston, "James K. Gutheim as Southern Reform Rabbi, Community Leader, and Symbol," Southern Jewish History (2002), 78.
14. Sarna, American Judaism, 123; Eli N. Evans, The Provincials (New York, 1973) 93; Marcus, United States Jewry, III, 230.
15. Israelite, August 13, 1869 and subsequent issues.
16. Ibid. August 27, 1869.
17. Ibid, September 17, 1868.
18. Israelite, July 27, 1872; Browne deposition, Williams, NYPL.
19. EJ, v.11, 1588; Louis J. Swichkow and Lloyd P. Gartner, The History of the Jews of Milwaukee (Philadelphia, 1963), 146.
20. Swichkow and Gartner, Jews of Milwaukee, 179; American Israelite, May 5, 1871; EJ, Vol 16, 555.
21. Document in possession of author.
22. Wisconsin State Journal, June 21, 1871.
23. Browne deposition, Williams NYPL; Atlanta Sunday Gazette, September 1, 1880.
24. American Israelite, January 10, 1873.
25. Michael L. Rabkinson, New Edition of the Babylonian Talmud, ed. I. M. Wise (New York, 1903).
26. Sarna, American Judaism, 124.
27. Clipping from unidentified Milwaukee newspaper, September 29, 1912, Browne, AJA; Sarna, American Judaism, 124.
28. Israelite, October 13, 1871.
29. Israelite, March 31, 1871.
30. Marcus, United States Jewry, III, 141.
31. Chumaceiro, JE, v.4, 77.
32. Israelite, September 8, 1871.

33. Highlights of Congregation's History, Congregation B'nai Israel archives, Evansville, Indiana.

34. Deborah Dash Moore, B'nai B'rith and the Challenge of Ethnic Leadership (Albany, New York, 1981) 21; Marcus, United States Jewry, III, 423; Israelite, October 27, 1871.

35. Immigration records, family bible, and photographs in collection of author; stained glass windows in name of Moses and Clara Weil inside present synagogue of B'nai Israel; author conversations with Sophie Weil Browne 1932-1936, and Lylah Browne Goldberg 1940-1960; anonymous History of Congregation, B'nai Israel archives, Evansville.

36. Ibid.

37. Author's conversations with Sophie Weil Browne, 1932-1936.

38. Author's conversation with Wayne Crowe, co-chairman Indiana Freedom Trails, 2004.

39. Ibid; Prayer book in author's collection.

40. Author's conversations with Sophie Weil Browne; Lance Sussman, "The Myth of the Trefa Banquet: American Culinary Culture and the Radicalization of Food Policy in Reform Judaism," Journal of American Jewish Archives, v. 57, 2008.

41. Israelite, October 27, 1871 and November 10, 1871.

42. Undated announcement, Browne, AJA; Israelite, December 29, 1871.

43. Richard Watson, A Biblical and Theological Dictionary, Explanatory of the History, Manners and Customs of the Jews and Neighboring Nation (Nashville,1857).

44. Israelite, January 12, 1872.

45. Unidentified newspaper clippings, Browne, AJA.

46. Objects in collection of author.

47. Ibid.

Chapter Three

1. Israelite, October 13, 1871.

2. Ibid.

3. Israelite, October 13, 1871, February 28, 1873, January 12, 1872 and July 3, 1872; Brochure from Evansville College of Medicine, Browne, AJA.

4. Israelite, October 27, 1871 and December 8, 1871.

5. Israelite, December 22, 1871 (taken from Cincinnati Chronicle and Times by way of Vincennes Sun).

6. Naomi W. Cohen, "The Challenges of Darwinism and Biblical Criticism to American Judaism," Modern Judaism,Vol. 4, No. 2, (May, 1984), 121-125. Also see Benny Kraut, From Reform Judaism to Ethical Culture: The Religious Evolution of Felix Adler (Cininnati, 1979).

7. Ibid.

8. American Israelite, January 10, 1873.

9. Browne, The Book Jashar (New York 1876); Tanach (Philadelphia,1999) 477.

10. American Israelite, January 28, 1876; Jonathan D. Sarna, Jacksonian Jew: The two Worlds of Mordecai Noah, (New York, 1981).

11. Israelite, July 27, 1872,

12. Ibid.
13. Ibid.
14. Ibid.
15. Israelite, August 9, 1872.
16. Myer, Response to Modernity, 282; Marcus, United States Jewry , v.III, 130.
17. Ibid.
18. Israelite, July 12, 1872.
19. Ibid.
20. Ibid.
21. Sefton D.Temkin, Isaac Mayer Wise: Shaping American Judaism (Oxford,1992) 209; Israelite, February 21, 1873.
22. Israelite, February 21, 1873.
23. Israelite, February 28, 1873.
24. Israelite, February 2, 1874.
25. American Israelite, September 1, 1871 and April 11, 1873.
26. Wise to Browne, March 28, 1873, Browne, AJA

Chapter Four

1.www.anshaiemeth.org/history.htm; Stanley E. Powers essay, Anshai Emeth, 1984.
2. Program of Standard Literary Society, March 15, 1874, Browne, AJA.; EJ, Vol. 4, 1145; Israelite, April 25, 1873.
3. Daily Times Herald (Chicago), June 16, 1874.
4. Israelite, November 28, 1873.
5. Ibid.
6.(Illinois) State Journal, January 19, 1874, excerpt reprint in Browne, AJA; Israelite, October 17, 1873.
7. Israelite, February 19, 1874.
8.Http://en.wikipedia.org/wiki/Robert_G._Ingersoll; Meyer, Response to Modernity, 273-274.
9. Peoria Democrat, January, 1874, excerpt reprint in Browne, AJA.
10. J. P. Newman to McBurney, YMCA of New York, February 11, 1881, printed copy in Browne, AJA; Daily Lincoln Nebraska State Journal, undated [July-August, 1891] copy of excerpt in Browne, AJA.
11. UAHC Proceedings, AJA; Israelite, July 11, 1873.
12. Jewish South, June 28, 1878.
13. Israelite, April 17, 1874, Vol 23, 8; Malcolm H. Stern, "Role of the Rabbi in the South", Turn to the South, Nathan M. Kaganoff and Melvin I Urofsky (Charlotteville, 1979) 26-27; George R. Wilke, "Rabbi David Marx and the Unity Club," Southern Jewish History, v 9, 2006, 40; [signature undecipherable] to Browne, January 1, 1874, Browne, AJA; for Chicago Times, see Jewish South June 28, 1878.
14. Browne, book galley, 169, Browne, AJA; Iphigene W. Bettman to Jacob Rader Marcus, May 22, 1988, and "Mayer" to I.M. Wise, Hartford, March 6, 1867, Wise small collections, AJA.
15. Browne, book galley,169; Leo Wise to Browne, November 5, 1874, Browne, AJA.
16. Leo Wise to Browne, December 29, 1867, book galley, 167, Browne, AJA.

17.Israelite, December 11, 1874 and October 1, 1885.

18. Book galley, Browne, AJA; Charles A. Hess to Editor, American Israelite, July 1, 1893, Wise small collections, AJA.

19.Browne deposition, Williams, NYPL ; Israelite, March 19, 1875.

20. Author's conversations with Lylah Browne Goldberg, 1940-1960; (name illegible) to Browne, January 1, 1874; Browne, AJA; Israelite, November 19, 1875.

21. Browne to President Ulysses S. Grant, Grant Calendar, 397, July 30, 1871, Record Group 59, Letters of Application and Recommendation for the Grant Administration, National Archives, College Park, MD., hereafter cited as Grant, NA.

22.The Papers of Ulysses S. Grant, 280.Wise to Grant, August 23, 1875; Ogelsby to Grant, June 23, 1875, Record Group 59, Grant, NA.

23. Ibid.

24. Ibid.

25. Jacob R. Marcus, United States Jewry, v. III, 50.

26. Israelite, July 12, 1872.

27.Bertram Korn, American Jewry and the Civil War (Philadelphia, 1951)146; Marcus, United States Jewry,v.III 50.

28. Marcus, United States Jewry, 1776-1985, v. III, 50; Korn, American Jewry and the Civil War, 121-155. Jewish Independent cited here apparently folded before another of the same name opened in Cleveland in1906. Thus far no copies of the earlier paper have been found, but an excerpt quoted by Bertram Korn in a footnote to his comments on Grant and the Jews in American Jewry and the Civil War confirms its existence and Browne's connection with it.

29. Korn, American Jewry and the Civil War, n.70, 281.

30. Papers of Ulysses S. Grant, 280-281. Browne to Grant, October 30, 1875, Grant, National Archives.

31. Ibid.; Joseph Aub to Browne, November 22, 1875, Browne, AJA; Correspondence Fish to Browne, October 16, 1875; Browne to Fish, October 30, 1875 and July 25, 1876, Grant, NA.

32. See Chapter VI.

33. Israelite, November 19, 1875 and November 26, 1875; Marni Davis, "No Whiskey Amazons in the Tents of Israel," unpublished mss, 2007.

34. See Upton Sinclair, The Jungle, (New York 1906).

35. Undated brochure advertizing lectures, Browne , AJA; Israelite, June 20, 1873.

36. Chicago Tribune, December 1874; Chicago Times, January, 1875, excerpts reprinted in flyer, Browne, AJA; American Israelite, April 13, 1877; New York Dailies, September 22, 1885, excerpt copy in Browne, AJA.

37. Indianapolis Sentinel, January 17, 1876; Excerpt reprinted on flyer, Browne, AJA.

38. Ibid.

39.Ibid.

40. Ibid.

41. American Israelite, April 29, 1876.

42. American Israelite, November 10, 1876.

43. New Orleans Times, March 23, 1877.

44. Columbus Enquirer-Sun, March 30, 1877, excerpt reprinted in flyer, Browne,

AJA.
45. Ibid.; Washington National Republican, January 15, 1895, copy of excerpt in Browne, AJA.
46. Ibid.
47. Hebrew Benevolent Congregation board minutes, 1877; Joseph and Ida Pearl Cohen Archives, William Breman Jewish Heritage Museum, Atlanta; Browne deposition, Williams, NYPL.

Chapter Five

1.. Atlanta Constitution, June 22, 1877, June 23, 1877, and July 12, 1877.
2.. Stephen Hertzberg, Strangers Within the Gate City: Jews of Atlanta, 1845-1915 (Philadelphia, 1978), 231; Atlanta Constitution, September 25, 1870. Reform congregations in America usually referred to their buildings as temples rather than synagogues to emphasize their belief that for them America was the Promised Land and they therefore rejected revival of the Temple cult with an actual rebuilding of the Temple in Jerusalem.
3.. Janice Rothschild-Blumberg, As But A Day to a Hundred and Twenty, 1867-1987 (Atlanta 1987) 30-33. [Hereafter cited as Blumberg, As But A Day].
4.. American Israelite, September 14, 1877; Atlanta Constitution, September 1, 1877.
5.. American Israelite, September 14, 1877; [Atlanta] Daily Constitution, September 1, 1877.
6.. American Israelite, September 14, 1877; Israelite, February 21, 1873 (reflecting patriotism of American Jews, named changed in 1876, anniversary of American Independence).
7.. Ibid.
8.. Atlanta Constitution, September 1, 1877.
9.. Jewish South, October 14, 1877; Blumberg, As But A Day, 4-11; American Israelite, April 30, 1880.
10.. Minutes of the Hebrew Benevolent Congregation, Joseph and Ida Pearl Cuba Archives, Breman Museum, Atlanta [Hereafter cited as Temple minutes, Breman] Jewish South, October 14, 1877.
11.. Blumberg, As But A Day,10-11.
12.. Browne deposition, Williams NYPL; Blumberg, As But a Day, 17; Jewish South, October 14, 1877.
13.. Atlanta Constitution, September 25, 1870.
14.. Meyer, Response to Modernity, 192; Blumberg, As But a Day, 18, 46; see W. Gunther Plaut, The Growth of Reform Judaism (New York, 1965).
15.. Temple records, Breman.
16.16. JE, v. II, 310-311; JE v. V, 628-629.
17.. Temple records, Breman; Proceedings of the Union of American Hebrew Congregations, 1878, 1879, AJA, 404, 564.
18.18. Deborah Dash Moore, B'nai B'rith and the Challenge of Ethnic Leadership (Albany, 1981) 71.
19.. Jewish South, January 24, 1879, 4. This was the forerunner of the Jewish Educational Loan Fund, established in 1876 by B'nai B'rith District 5; NY

Graphic, August 8, 1885.

20.20. Steven Hertzberg, Strangers Within the Gate City (Philadelphia, 1978) 162.

21.. Browne deposition Williams, NYPL.

22.. Jewish South, October 14, 1877 and August 15, 1879; Atlanta Constitution, September 28, 1878 and October 9, 1878; [London] Jewish Chronicle, August 9, 1878; Mark K. Bauman, "Factionalism and Ethnic Politics in Atlanta: The German Jews from the Civil War through the Progressive Era," Georgia Historical Quarterly v.82, 544.

23.. Jewish South, October 14, 1877.Browne later wrote that he had started the Jewish South with his own money, assisted by Herman Jacobs of Charleston, South Carolina, and Charles Wessolowsky.

24.. Ibid.

25.. Ibid.

26.. Jewish South, December 7, 1877, February 22, 1878, April 11, 1879; Henry Heinemann to Browne, January 22, 1880.

27.. See, for example, Jewish South, June 18, 1879 and October 14, 1877.

28.28. American Israelite, February 1, 1878 (see letter from Florence, Alabama, "A Southern Man Pays His Respects to 'The Jewish South.'")

29.. American Israelite February 1, 1878; April 11, 1879 and February 22, 1878.

30.. Jewish South, June 11, 1878.

31.. Ibid.

32.. Jewish South, June 11, 1878.

33.33. See Louis Schmier, Reflections of Southern Jewry (Macon, GA,1982); Jewish South, May 9, 1879; September 27, 1878 and June 11, 1879. Paper later featured a special section on B'nai B'rith.

34.. Jewish South, May 9, 1879; September 27, 1878 and June 11, 1879.

35.35. Jewish South, March 29, 1878.

36.. Jewish South, February15, March 29, April19, September 27, 1878 and April 11, 1879.

37.. Jewish South, March 21, 1879; May 9, 1879; May 18, 1879 and June 8 1879.

38.. Jewish South, January 4, 1878; February 22, 1878; Marni Davis, "No Whiskey Amazons in the Tents of Israel," American Jewish History, v.94, September 2008.

39.. Jewish South, June 28, 1878.

40.. Ibid. and September 20, 1878; Marni Davis, "No Whiskey Amazons in the Tents of Israel," unpublished mss, 2007.

41.. Jewish South, June 7, 1878; Atlanta Constitution, July 23, 1878, reported by Cincinnati correspondent.

42.. Book galley, 164 n.

43.. Jewish South, June 7, 1878; also Atlanta Constitution, July 23, 1878, reported by Cincinnati correspondent, New York World; Browne to Wise, June 9, 1878, Browne Collection, AJA.

44.. Jewish South, January 28, 1878.

45.. Jewish South, February 8, 1878; American Israelite, February 1, 1878.

46.. Hess to Editor, July 1, 1893, I. M. Wise Small Collection, AJA.

47.. Jewish South, October 14, 1877; March 29, 1878; David Philipson, diary, AJA Box 1323 ; Stanley F. Chyet, "Isaac Mayer Wise: Portrait by David Philipson," A

Bicentennial Festschrift for Jacob Rader Marcus (ed. Bertram W. Korn, Waltham, 1976).

48.. Jewish South, March 21, 1879; Suzanne R. White, "Much Good In Small Places", appendix I, (Emory University honors paper, 1982).

49.. Jewish South, October 14, 1877 and March 21, 1879; White,"Much Good In Small Places", appendix I.

50.. Jewish South, September 13, 1878; book galley, n.163-165.

51.. Book galley, n.163-165.

52.. Ibid.

53.. JE, v. XII, 451; Voorsanger File, Wise Collection, AJA. Voorsanger spent the bulk of his career as rabbi of Temple Emanu-El in San Francisco where he was a highly respected spiritual leader, editor, and teacher. Book galley, n. 164.

54.. JE, v.XII, 451; book galley, 165, Browne, AJA.

55.. Southern Workman, September 3,1904

56.. Browne deposition, February 28, 1883, Browne AJA.

57. Ibid.; Southern Workman, September 3, 1904; Temple records, January 2,1881, and January 16, 1881.These and subsequent news releases (n. 61) suggest that two elders of the congregation, Jacob Haas (Aaron's uncle, unrelated to Browne) and Abraham Rosenfeld (at whose wedding in 1867 the congregation was organized) also served on the committee.

58.58. Isaac Frisch testimony, Superior Court, Fulton County, Georgia, May 4, 1889, book galley, 132-135 n., Browne, AJA.

59.. Browne deposition; Frisch testimony; book galley, n. 132-135, Browne, AJA

60.. Frisch testimony, Browne, AJA.

61.61. Ibid., Jewish South, November 22, 1878.

62.. Browne deposition, Browne, AJA; Wise's confrontation with Louis Spanier, the president of his congregation, occurred when Wise attempted to officiate at Rosh Hashana services after being fired by Spanier two days before. The controversy was over Wise's theology of reform. Sarna, American Judaism, 96-97.

63.. Washington Star, February 3,1881; National Republican, February 3, 1881.

64.. Exhibit B, Browne deposition, Browne, AJA.

65.65. Blumberg, As But a Day, 23-41.

66.. Exhibit D, Browne deposition, Browne, AJA.

67.. Book galley, n.134; Browne deposition, AJA; Browne to Williams, March 23, 1881, Browne, American Jewish Historical Society, New York; Browne to Williams, February 1881, Browne, AJA; Browne, Williams, NYPL.

68.68. Browne to Williams, March 23, 1881, Williams, NYPL.

69.. Temple Minutes, March 24, 1881, Breman; Browne to Temple Board, April 6, 1881, published in American Israelite April 22, 1881.

70.. Browne deposition, Browne, AJA.

71.. American Israelite, April 22, 1881.

72.. Sunday Gazette, January 23, 1881, copy in Browne deposition, Browne, AJA; American Israelite, January 28, 1881; Charles A. Hess to the editor, American Israelite,

73.. Atlanta Sunday Gazette, January 23, 1881; Blumberg As But a Day, 18-19 ; Browne deposition, Browne, AJA, Temple minutes, January 16,1881, Breman.

Contrary to other reports, these state that the minority report was signed by Jacob Haas and Aaron Haas, the majority by Elsas, Franklin, Fleischel and Teitlebaum.

74.. Browne deposition, Browne, AJA.
75.. Ibid.
76.. Ibid.
77.. Jewish South, March 29, 1878, May 10, 1878; Browne deposition, Browne, AJA.
78.. Browne deposition, Browne, AJA.
79.. Ibid.
80.. Ibid.
81.81. See Joshua Stampher, Rabbi of the West: The Life and Times of Julius Eckman, (Portland, OR, 1988).
82.82. Atlanta Constitution, January 7, 1895; Blumberg, As But a Day, 45.

Chapter Six

1.. Gerald Sorin, A Time for Building: The Third Migration (Baltimore 1992) 136; Diane Ravitch, The Great School Wars: A History of New York City Public Schools (Baltimore 1874/2000)109; See Stephen Birmingham, Our Crowd, (New York, 1967); W. Gunther Plaut, The Growth of Reform Judaism (New York, 1965) 342; EJ v. XII, 1078.
2.2. Sarna, American Judaism, 160; The Jewish Encyclopedia, v. IX (New York, 1901, hereafter cited as JE) 271.
3.. New York Jewish Herald, March 9, 1883.
4.4. Hebrew American Republican League Committee, book galley, Browne, AJA
5.. New York Sunday Herald, February 4, 1883; Temple Gates of Hope Dedication (New York,1883); The [New York] Daily Graphic, August 8, 1885.
6.. Browne again displayed ecumenism when in 1883 he invited Bishop John P. Newman, to deliver a Friday night sermon on his recent trip to the Holy Land. Browne stated—perhaps erroneously—that this was the first instance of a Christian minister speaking at Jewish services in a New York synagogue, a practice which he favored as a means of "loosening the tight lines of sectarianism." New York Jewish Herald, March 9, 1883, book galley, AJA,133.
7.. Ibid.
8.. Sorin, A Time for Building (Baltimore, 1992) 47-49.
9.. Marcus, United States Jewry, v. III,103, 442. HEAS should not be confused with the Hebrew Immigrant Aid Society (HIAS) which was established in the early 1900s.
10.. David L. Harris, Sod Jerusalems: Jewish Agricultural Communities in Frontier Kansas, Chapter II, thesis, University of Oklahoma, 1984; EJ v.VI, 679.
11.. Zosa Szajkowski, "The Alliance Israelite Universelle in the United States, 1860-1949," Publications of the American Jewish Historical Society, XXXXIX, (June, 1950), 402-403.
12.. Book galley, Browne, AJA, 101.
13.. Hebrew Leader; quoted in Book galley, Browne, AJA, 179.
14. Book galley, Browne, AJA, 101-102, 179. Ann Novotny, Strangers at the Door (Riverside, CN, 1971) 52; Edward Corsi, In the Shadow of Liberty: The Story of Ellis Island. (New York, 1937) 61, 283.

15.. Book galley, 179-180, Browne, AJA.

16.. New York Tribune, October 15, 1882.

17.. New York Tribune, October 15, 1882.

18.18. Jewish Herald, January 23, 1883; Book galley, Browne, AJA, 101-102.

19.. Sun, February 9, 1883; February 12, 1883; February 18, 1883; February 26, 1883; Jewish Herald, March 2, March 9, 1883.

20.. American Israelite, August 8, 1881; Jewish Herald, March 2, 1883.

21.. Jewish Herald, July 27 and August 17, 1883; March 28, February 8, and February 29, 1884.

22.22. Lance Sussman, "The Myth of the Trefa Banquet: American Culinary Culture and the Radicalization of Food Policy in American Reform Judaism," American Jewish Archives Journal, 2005.

23.. Batya Miller, "Enforcement of the Sunday Closing Laws on the Lower East Side, 1882-1903", American Jewish History, v. 91, #2, 2003, 269-285; Hasia R. Diner, A Time for Gathering: The Second Migration, 1820-1880 (Baltimore 1992)131-133; Azriel,Yaakov, "The Evangelist at Our Door: The American Jewish Response to Christian Missionaries, 1880-1920", American Jewish Archives Journal, v. XLVIII, Fall-Winter 1996, No. 2, 139; W. G. Plaut, The Rise of Reform Judaism (New York 1963) 192-3; Meyer, Response to Modernity, 236.

24.. New York Tribune, March 23, 1886; book galley, 20- 21, Browne, AJA.

25.. Michael Feldberg, Chapters in American Jewish History, American Jewish Historical Society, Part V.

26.. Kerry M. Olitzky, "The Sunday Sabbath Movement in American Reform Judaism: Strategy or Evolution?" American Jewish Archives,v. XXXIV, April 1982, #1, 75; Jewish Herald, March 2, 1883; Meyer, Response to Modernity, 290; book galley, 290; Howard Crosby to Alexander S. Rosenthal, January 9, 1889, book galley, Browne, AJA, n.137.

27.. Jewish Messenger, April 29, 1887; Marcus, United States Jewry, v. III, 117.

28.. Olitzky, "The Sunday Sabbath Movement,"75.

29.. Fish to Isaac Frisch, Esq., January 16, 1889,quoted in book galley, Browne, AJA, n.139; Fred Grant to Browne, October 10, 1889; February 17, 1893; January 26, 1895; September 18, 1908; Julia Cantacuzene to Browne, December 4, 1927, Browne, AJA.

30.. [New York] Daily Graphic, August 9, 1885.

31.. Daily Graphic, August 8, 1885; conversations with Lylah Browne Goldberg, 1940-1960.

32.. Reprint of telegram B to Fred Grant, August 6, 1885; Browne, AJA.

33.. [New York] Daily Graphic, August 8, 1885.

34.. Daily Graphic, August 9, 1885.

35.. Daily Graphic, August 8, 1885; American Israelite, February 9, 1883.

36.. New York Sun, November 27, 1885, from Associated Press dispatch, reprint with illustration in book galley, 14, Browne, AJA.

37.. Daily Telegraph, January 7, 1896, reprint in book galley, Browne, AJA, 24-25; Col. Elliot F. Sheppard to Isaac Frisch, January 15, 1889, quoted in book galley, n.140, Browne, AJA.

38.. Browne to Benjamin Harrison, September 25, 1889, Benjamin Harrison

Correspondence, Presidential Collection, Library of Congress; book galley, Browne, AJA, 119.

39.. Associated Press to New York Herald, October 22, 1886; copy of text in book galley, 15, 173, Browne, AJA; New York Tribune, September 27, 1884.

40.. New York Tribune, September 27, 1884.

41.. Associated Press, New York Herald, October 22, 1886, text with illustration in book galley,15; Lazare Isidor to Browne, September 3, 1884, Browne, AJA.

42.. New York Tribune, January 2, 1887.

43.. Cleveland Gazette, April 1, 1893; Col. Elliot F. Shepherd to Isaac Frisch, January 15, 1889, text in book galley, n.140, Browne, AJA; Southern Workman, September 3, 1904.

44.44. New York Herald, March 2, 1887; Jewish Messenger, February 22, 1887.

45.45. Jewish Messenger, February 22, 1887.

46.. New York Herald, March 2, 1887, text in book galley, 16, Browne, AJA; Jewish Messenger, February 25, 1887 and March 25, 1887.

47.47. Congressional Record, May 27, 1884.

48.. New York Tribune, October 2, 1882; New York Daily Graphic, August 8, 1885, reprint in portion of book, Browne, AJA; Jewish Messenger, March 11, 1887; Congressional Record, May 27, 1884; New York Daily Graphic August 8, 1885; Washington Times, August 13, 1918; Washington Post, May 27, 1884.

49.. New York Tribune, summer 1884 [source undated, copy in Browne, AJA]

50.. Book galley, 23, Browne, AJA; New York Tribune, October 30, 1884.

51.. E.B.M.Browne, secretary, and H.H.Boody, chair, Union League Club Political Committee to Congress, December 13, 1884; James G. Blaine to Browne, December 29, 1884, text in book galley, 123-4, document Browne to Congress; Browne, AJA.

52.. Marcus, United States Jewry v. III, 134, 214.

53.. Book galley, 13, Browne, AJA; New York Daily Tribune, May 17, 1886.

54.. Book galley, 13, Browne, AJA.

55.. Copy of correspondence, Browne to Elihu Root, Sept. 23, 1886, Browne, AJA

56. Irving Howe, World of Our Fathers (New York,1976) 366-7; Sorin, Gerald, A Time For Building (Baltimore, 1992) 193.

57.. Rosenberg, Stuart E.,"Notes on the Political Attitudes of The Jewish Tidings," Jewish Social Studies, October, 1955, 323; Jewish Tidings, June 11, 1887 and January 20, 1888.

58.. New York Jewish Daily News, June 30, 1887; Southern Workman, July 3, 1904.

59.. Browne to Benjamin Harrison, November 16, 1888, Special Collections, Benjamin Harrison Presidential Papers, Library of Congress, hereafter cited as Harrison, LoC.

60.. This and following, Browne to Benjamin Harrison, October 5, 1888, Harrison, LoC.

61.. Browne to Wise, August 15, 1888, Browne, AJA; Hebrew Leader; quoted in book galley,179, Browne, AJA; Browne to Harrison, November 16, 1888, Harrison, LoC.

62.. Book galley, n.120, Browne, AJA; Browne to Harrison, October 5, 1888, Harrison, LoC.; unspecified press release, Harrison, LoC.

63.. Book galley, n.121, Browne, AJA.

64.. Browne to Harrison, October 23, 1888, Harrison, LoC.

65.. Book galley, 122-124

66.. Harrison to Browne, October 9, 1888; Browne to Harrison, November 16, 1888, January 7, April 22, September 9, 1889, Harrison, LoC.

67.. New York Tribune, October 23, 1888.

68.68. Carl Schuirz was a German-born reformer and journalist who served in the Hayes cabinet, 1877-1881.

69.. Browne to Harrison, November 16, 1888, Harrison, LoC.

70.. Senator William Sherman to Browne, April 2, 1887, Browne, AJA.

Chapter Seven

1. New York Times, April 21, 1887; April 22, 1887; April 26, 1887; book galley, 51-54.

2. New York Times, June 7, 1887.

3. New York Times, June 20, 1887.

4. New York Times, April 10, 1903.

5. New York Times, July 13, 1887.

6.New York Times, June 10, 1887.

7. New York Times, June 20, 1887.

8. Book galley, Browne, AJA, 78-110, 121-127.

9. New York Times, October 11, 1888.

10. New York Sun, November 27, 1888.

11.11. Ibid.

12. Ibid.; book galley 44-49.

13. Book galley, Browne, AJA 102, 121-122; New York Daily Tribune, April 3, 1889.

14. Book galley, Browne, AJA, 102, 121, 122.

15. New York Times, June 10, 1887; book galley 130, 131.

16. Myers, Response to Modernity, 288.

17. American Israelite, July 29, 1887; New York Times, July 1, 1887.

18. New York Times, July 1, 1887.

19. Atlanta Constitution, July 16, 1887.

20. Ibid.

21. Book galley, 25, 147-150, Browne, AJA; Voucher, Mt. Sinai Congregation to Moses Weil, Browne, AJA.

22. Book galley, 147-150, Browne, AJA.

23. Book galley, 150, 173, and notes 119, 122 , 132, Browne, AJA.

24. Book galley, 25, Browne, AJA.

25. Book galley, 26-27, Browne, AJA.

26. Book galley, 28-29; Jacob Schiff to Browne, October 10, 1904, Browne, AJA.

27. Alexander Rosenthal comments, book galley, Browne, AJA, 29.

28. Book galley, Browne. AJA, 32-39.

29. Book galley, Browne, AJA, 30. Cane head with inscription in author's possession.

30. Book galley, 30, Browne, AJA.

31. Book galley, 9-26, Browne, AJA.

32. Book galley, 181, Browne, AJA.

33. Adolph L. Sanger to Committee, January 14, 1889, copy in book galley, n.142, Browne, AJA.
34. Elliot F. Sheppard to Committee, copy in book galley, n.140-1,Browne, AJA; Cleveland Gazette, April 1, 1893.
35. Howard Crosby to Committee, book galley, n. 137-8, Browne, AJA.
36. Browne to Harrison, January 7, 1889, Harrison, LoC

Chapter Eight

1. Benjamin Peixotto to Harrison, March 25, 1889; Browne to Halford, March 31, 1889, B. Harrison, LoC.
2. Browne to Halford, September 9, 1889, B. Harrison, LoC.
3. Ibid.
4. Browne to Halford and Harrison, September 25, 1889, B. Harrison, LoC.
5. Browne to Harrison, March 5, 1890, B. Harrison, LoC.
6. Other presidents had appointed Jewish chaplains for special units during wartime but not as a permanent assignment to serve all of the armed forces.
7. Ibid.
8. Browne to Halford, March 5, 1890, B. Harrison, LoC.
9. Browne to Halford, March 26, 1890, B. Harrison, LoC.
10. Browne to Harrison, November 24, 1891, B. Harrison, LoC.
11. Ibid; M. M. Parkhurst to Browne, January 8, 1892, Browne, AJA.
12. Browne to Harrison, November 28, 1892, B. Harrison, LC.
13. Elaine S. Anderson, PhD dissertation, 262-266, Box 1635, Toledo Collection, AJA; unnumbered pages attributed to Anderson, Congregation Shomer Emunim archives, Toledo.
14. Ibid.; Jesse Browne to Sophie Weil Browne, January 1890, in author's possession; American Israelite, October 17, 1889, June 19, August 28, and September 11, 1890; Toledo Blade, September 15, 1890.
15. Conversations with Lylah Browne Goldberg, 1940-1960; Frederick Grant to Browne, October 10, 1889, Browne, AJA.
16. Toledo Blade, October 4, 1890; Browne to Lylah Browne, July 8, 1891; Zadoc Kahn to Browne, June 29, 1891, Browne, AJA; Zosa Szajkowski, "The Alliance Israelite Universelle in the United States, 1840-1949," Publications of the American Jewish Historical Society, XXXXIX, June 1950, 402.
17. Toledo Blade, September 14, 1891.
18. Toledo Bee, June 27, 1892.
19. JE v. IV, 25;.H. L.Meites, History of the Jews of Chicago (Chicago, 1924) 516-517.
20. Ibid.; Chicago Herald, March 10, 1892.
21. San Francisco Chronicle, July 19, 1891.
22. John P. Newman to Browne, October 31, 1891, book galley, Browne, AJA.
23. Minneapolis Tribune, July 6, 1891; reprint from Chicago Tribune, undated; John P. Newman, copy of quote, Browne, AJA.
24. State Journal, Lincoln, Nebraska, undated, copy in Browne, AJA.
25. Ibid.
26. Ibid.

27. John M. Thurston to Browne, August 29, 1891, Browne, AJA.

28. Ibid.

29. Thurston to Browne, December 21, 1892, Browne, AJA.

30. Chicago Times, February 15, 1892; Chicago Inter-Ocean, April 6, 1892.

31. Chicago Blue Book, 1893 (Chicago, 1892); calling card undated, Browne, AJA.

32. Ida Honore Grant to Bertha Honore Palmer, undated, enclosed in Grant to Browne, December 15, 1891, Browne, AJA; June Shochen, "Volunteer Activists,"American Jewish History, September, 1980, 24; undated newspaper clipping, Browne, AJA.

33. Morris A. Gutstein, A Priceless Heritage (New York, 1953) 87-88; Clipping from unidentified and undated New York newspaper, Browne, AJA; National Council of Jewish Women to Sophie Weil Browne, in author's possession; June Schochen, "Volunteer Activists", American Jewish History, September, 1980, 24.

34. Zadok Kahn to Browne, June 20, 1893, Browne, AJA; Browne business card, Browne, AJA; Certificate of admittance to Cook County Bar Association in family collection (recertification, John Gibbons to whom it may concern, May 27, 1910, Browne, AJA.)

35. Jean Kiralfy Kent, Temple Israel of Columbus, Georgia, 1854-2000 (Columbus, 2000).

Chapter Nine

1. Conversations with Laurette Rothschild Rosenstrauch, 2003. See Clason Kyle, Images: A Pictorial History of Columbus, Georgia (Norfolk,1986).

2. Jean Kiralfy Kent, Temple Israel of Columbus, Georgia, 1854-2000 (Columbus, 2000) 4,5.

3. Ibid., 15, 16.

4. Columbus Enquirer, January 6, 1894; Congregation B'nai Israel minutes, November 21, 1893.

5. Author's recollections; author's conversations with Sophie Weil Browne, 1930-1936.

6. Ibid.

7. Confirmation program, Browne, AJA; Records of Congregation B'nai Israel, Columbus, 1895.

8. Records of Congregation B'nai Israel, Columbus.

9. Kent, Temple Israel, 24, 26, 27.

10. Thurston to Browne, January 5, 1895; Grant to Browne, January 26, 1895, Browne, AJA.

11. See Edmund Morris, The Rise of Theodore Roosevelt (New York, 1979) 403-405.

12. Alexander S. Rosenthal to Browne, April 29, 1895. The apointment was apparently based on merit since President Cleveland was known to be averse to patronage.

13. Chicago Times-Herald, May 8, 1895.

14. Daily Press, Albany, NY, undated, probably 1903 (referring to New York Herald, June 11, 1896), Browne, AJA

15. New York Herald, August 20, 1896.

16. HIGH WATER MARK, dispatch to Commercial Cable Company, New York Herald, August 20, 1896, reprint in Browne, AJA.

17. Peter Balakian, The Burning Tigris (New York 2003) 35-62; Deborah Lipstadt, Princeton Alumni Weekly, April 17, 1996.

18. Proof copy, flyer for lectures, August 15, 1897, Browne, AJA; New York Herald, Paris edition, July 11, 1896, July 26, 1896, August 5, 1896; Milwaukee Journal, September 29, 1912; Daily Press (Albany, New York) undated, probably 1903 (referring to New York Herald, June 11, 1896) Browne, AJA; Toledo Blade, February 21, 1905.

19. Thurston to William McKinley, copied to Browne, March 14, 1897, Browne, AJA

20. Ibid.

21. Jewish Chronicle (London) May 30, 1898.

22. Jewish Chronicle (London) June 17, 1898.

23. Ibid.

24. American Israelite, April 28, 1898. See Jeanne Abrams, "Remembering the Maine: The Jewish Attitude Toward the Spanish American War as Reflected in The American Israelite," American Jewish History, June 1987, 439-455; Korn, "Jewish Welfare Activities for the Military During the Spanish-American War," Eventful Years and Experiences (Cincinnati, 1954)

23. Augusta R. Crawford to Sophie Weil Browne, August 1, 1898 and August 3, 1898, possession of author; Jewish Chronicle (London) May 20, 1898 and June 17, 1898.

24. Korn, "Jewish Welfare Activities for the Military During the Spanish-American War," American Jewish Historical Society, 1951-1952, Vol.41 #1, n.2, 358. The National Jewish Welfare Board was organized in April, 1917, with roots that began in 1913; yearbok of the Central Conference of American Rabbis, 1898-1899, vol. VIII.

25. Richard Weightman to Browne, January 21, 1899; George Dewey to Browne, November 17, 1899, Browne, AJA.

26. Atlanta Journal, June 5, 1899.

27. Ibid.

28. Columbus Daily Enquirer, August 14, 1900.

29. William Sulzer to Browne, October 30, 1900, Browne, AJA; Browne to McKinley, October 15, 1900, McKinley, LoC.

30. Columbus Ledger Enquirer, November 16, 1897.

31. Columbus Ledger Enquirer, November 17, 1897. Ib

32. Ibid; author's conversations with Lylah Browne Goldberg, 1939-1959.

33. George R. Wilkes, "Rabbi David Marx and the Unity Club: Organized Jewish-Christian Dialogue, Liberalism, and Religious Diversity in Early Twentieth Century Atlanta," Southern Jewish History, vol. 9, 2006, 35.

34. Atlanta Constitution, December 28, 1899; Atlanta Journal, December 28, 1899.

35. Universalist Souvenir, December 26, 1899.

36. Ibid.

37. Atlanta Journal, December 26, 1899.

38. Ibid.

39. Ibid.

40. Ibid.
41. Possession of author.
42. Ibid.

Chapter Ten

1. Marcus, United States Jewry, v. I, 64-67.
2. American Israelite, May 6, 1897.
3. Ibid.
4. Ibid.
5. Browne to Max Nordau, August 18, 1897, Herzl collection, Central Zionist Archives, Jerusalem [hereafter cited as Herzl, CZA] ; EJ12, 1211; JE VIII, 51-53; Bobbie Malone, Rabbi Max Heller (Tuscaloosa, 1997) 109.
6. Undated Browne memoir, Browne, AJA.
7. Southern Workman, September 3, 1904.
8. Ibid.
9. Undated memoir, Browne, AJA.
10. Ibid.
11. Ibid.
12. Ibid.
13. Michael Singer to Herzl, August 6, 1897, Herzl, CZA.
14. Michael Singer to Browne, August 13, 1897, Herzl, CZA.
15. Browne to Herzl, August 9, 1897, Herzl, CZA
16. Browne to Herzl, August 9, 1897- March 24, 1898, Herzl, CZA.
17. Ariel Yaakov, "Roots of Christian Zionism", Modern Judaism, v 26 # 1, February 2006, 75.
18. Browne to Herzl, portion undated, mid-August, 1897, Browne, AJA.
19. Ibid.
20. B'nai Israel minutes, August 11, 1897.
21. Browne to Herzl, August 16, 1897, Herzl, CZA.
22. Browne to Zionist Congress, August 18, 1897, Herzl, CZA.
23. Ibid.
24. Central Conference of American Rabbis record, Montreal, 1897.
25. Browne to Zionist Congress, August 18, 1897, Herzl, CZA
26. Ibid.
27. Ibid.
28. Ariel Yaakov, "Roots of Christian Zionism", Modern Judaism, February 2006, 75.
29. Ibid.
30. Ibid.
31. Browne to Zionist Congress, August 18, 1897, CZA; Psalms 137:5.
32. Browne to Max Nordau, August 18, 1897, Herzl, CZA; New York Herald, August 20, 1896; JE IX, 330- 332
33. Browne to Max Nordau, August 18, 1897, Herzl, CZA; EJ12, 1211; JE VIII, 51-53.
34. Browne to Herzl, August 29, 1897, Herzl, CZA.
35. Browne to Herzl, August 30, 1897, Herzl, CZA.

36. Shochet—ritual kosher slaughterer. Browne to Herzl, September 5, 1897, Herzl, CZA.

37. Ibid.

38. Browne to Herzl, September 12, 1897.

39. Marcus, United States Jewry, v. III, 682; American Israelite, September 16, 1897 and November 4, 1897.

40. Browne to Herzl, October 11, 1897, Herzl, CZA; Josef Fraenkel, Moritz Gudemann and Theodor Herzl, Leo Baeck Institute Yearbook 1966 11 (1) 67; JE, VI, 105.

41. Ibid.

42. Browne to Herzl, October 17, 1897 and October 19, 1897, Herzl, CZA.

43. For this and following see Browne to Herzl, November 8, 1897, Herzl, CZA. (Blaine quote from book galley, n. 123-132, Browne, AJA.)

44. Richard Gottheil, unknown at the time, became a distinguished Zionist and scholar.

45. Herzl to Browne, November 22, 1897, Herzl, CZA

46. Ibid.

47. For this and following see Browne to Herzl, December 8, 1897, Herzl, CZA.

48. For following see Browne to Herzl, December 9, 1897, Herzl, CZA.

49. M. Singer to Herzl, December 10 and December 14, 1897, Herzl, CZA

50. American Israelite, November 4, 1897.

51. Portion of correspondence Browne to Herzl, undated, Herzl, CZA

52. Carl Hermann Voss, Stephen S. Wise, Servant of the People, JPS, Philadelphia, 1969, 7.

53. Browne to Herzl, January 26, 1898, Herzl, CZA.

54. Ibid.

55. Stephen S. Wise to Herzl, June 26, 1898, Carl Hermann Voss, Stephen S. Wise, Servant of the People, JPS, Philadelphia, 1969, 7.

56. Browne to Herzl, February 11, 1898.

57. Browne to Herzl, March 16, 1898, Herzl, CZA.

58. Browne to Herzl, March 24, 1898.

59. Alex Bein, "Herzl," Jewish Publication Society, 1940, 435 ; Browne, AP dispatch from Cairo, April 3, 1903, Browne, AJA; Southern Workman, July 9, 1904.

60. Browne to Nordau, June 3, 1904, Browne Files, Herzl, CZA; Stephen S. Wise to Richard Gottheil, April 21, 1904, Stephen S. Wise to Herzl, May 6, 1904, Stephen S. Wise: Servant of the People, JPS Philadelphia, 1969; Browne's presence in Cairo corroborated by correspondence to family and newspaper articles, Series A & C, Browne, AJA.

61. Simon B. Hilf to Herzl, January 3, 1898; July 11, 1898; May 10, 1900; Herzl, CZA.

62. Browne to Nordau, August 29, 1905, Herzl, CZA.

63. Knickerbocker Press, August 4, 1913, Browne, AJA.

Chapter Eleven

1. See previous chapter, n. 56 and n. 57.

2. Mark K. Bauman, "Southern Jewish Women and Their Social Service

Organizations," Journal of American Ethnic History, 22, Spring, 2003, 42-45; Century Club programs, 1900-1927, in author's possession; Janice Rothschild Blumberg, "Sophie Weil Browne: From Rabbi's Wife to Clubwoman," Southern Jewish History, v 9, 2006, 1-33.

3. Temple Israel minutes, April 25, 1900 and May 30, 1902, Book I, 213..215; .Atlanta Journal, February 19,1901.

4. Columbus Ledger, November 11, 1902; J. P. Spanier to Browne, August 26, 1902, Captain Ambrozy to Browne, October 16, 1902, Browne, AJA.

5. Browne to family, July 8, 1896; Lylah Browne to Browne, August 1, and August 4, 1896, Browne, AJA; New York Herald, August 26, 1896.

6. W. Neale to Browne, August 25, 1902; Sophie to family, October 30, 1902, Browne, AJA.

7. Browne to Beckwith, January 30, 1897, Browne, AJA; Petersburg (Pennsylvania) Town and Country, May 17, 1905.

8. R. K. Pelton to D. S. Goldberg, January 1, 1903, Browne, AJA.

9. Le Nicois, undated clipping June 1896, Browne, AJA; Echo, undated enclosure, Taft Presidential Papers, Manuscripts, Library of Congress [hereafter cited as Taft, LC.]

10. Sophie Browne to family, March 23 and 28,1903, Browne, AJA; Bowne to Max Nordau, June 3, 1904; Alex Bein, Theodor Herzl, 435; (Philadelphia, 1940) Richard Gottheil, Zionism (Philadelphia,1914) 122.

11. Browne to Associated Press, April 3, 1903, copy in Browne, AJA; Toledo Daily Blade, February 21, 1905.

12. Sophie Browne to family, October 10, 1902, Browne, AJA

13. Sophie Browne to family, April 10, 12, 13 and undated, 1903; statement from Kaminitz Hotel, Jerusalem, April 22, 1903, Browne, AJA

14. Toledo Daily Blade, February 21, 1905.

15. EJ, v. 10, 1063-1065.

16. Youngstown Daily Vindicator, Saturday, April 9, 1911; Sophie to family, April 22, 1903, Browne AJA Echos, Moniteur Oriental, undated, Taft, LC; Milwaukee Journal, September 22, 1912.

17. Boston Journal, May 11, 1912.

18. Sophie Browne to family, May 29, 1903; Christian Vogely to Browne, June 9 and June 12, 1903; Alvin Adec to Browne, March 5, 1904, Browne, AJA.

19. Browne to family, August 29, 1903 and September 1, 1903, Browne, AJA

20. Sophie Browne to Lylah Browne Goldberg, October 30, 1903; items in possession of author.

21. Saloon Passenger List, S.S. Cambroman, October 13, 1903, Sophie Browne to Lylah Browne Goldberg, October 30, 1903, Browne, AJA.

22. Items in possession of author. See Blumberg, "Sophie Weil Browne: From Rabbi's Wife to Clubwoman," Southern Jewish History, v.9, 1-33.

Chapter Twelve

1. Jack Fischel and Sanford Pinsker, Jewish-American History and Culture: an Encyclopedia (New York 1992) 544.

2. Unidentified to Browne at addresses in Cleveland, June 21 and 26, 1901, August

5, 1901 and September 27, 1901; J. C, Drayhan to Browne, April 15, 1901, Drayhan to E. Kahn, April 26, 1901, Browne, AJA; Browne to William Howard Taft, October 9, 1908, Taft, LoC; Fischel and Pinsker, ed., Jewish-American History and Culture, 35. See Naomi W. Cohen, "Antisemitism in the Gilded Age: The Jewish View," Jewish Social Studies, v. 41 #3/4 1979, 182-210.

3. N. J. Younger to Browne, June 4, 1900, Theodore Roosevelt, Manuscripts, Presidential Papers, Library of Congress (hereafter cited as T Roosevelt, LoC). Roosevelt letter copied in flyer for benefit lecture in Toledo, June 4, 1905, attachment to EBM Browne correspondence, T.Roosevelt presidential correspondence, manuscript division, Library of Congress.

4. Roosevelt to Editor-in-Chief, National Encyclopedia Company, May 15, 1901, Browne, AJA.

5. Eric Goldstein, "The Unstable Other: Locating the Jew in Progressive Era American Racial Discourse", American Jewish History, Vol.89 Number 4, 383-409.

6. Dov Peretz Elkins, God's Warriors (Middle Village, New York, 1974) introduction, 10-14 Bertram W. Korn, "Jewish Welfare Activities for the Military During the Spanish-American War," American Jewish Historical Society, 1951-1952, v. 41 #1, n.2, 358 (The National Jewish Welfare Board was organized in April, 1917, with roots that began in 1913); John Higham, Send These to Me, Immigrants in Urban America, revised edition (Baltimore, 1984) 101.

7. T.C. Platt to Browne, September 27, 1901; Browne to Elihu Root, June 8, 1904, Browne, AJA Higham, Send These to Me.

8. Browne to Taft, September 2, 1904, Taft, LC

9. Southern Workman, July 9, 1904.

10. Ibid.

11. Ibid.

12. Ibid.

13. Browne to Taft, September 2, 1904, Taft, LC; see Esther L. Panitz, Simon Wolf (Cranbury, NJ, 1987).

14. Ibid.

15. Inscribed photograph Roosevelt to Browne, October 25, 1904, in author's possession.

16. Flyer for lecture benefitting City's Relief Committee, Columbus, Georgia, October 11, 1904, copy on microfilm, Taft, LoC; The Southern Workman, July 2, 1904 ("Miss Alice" was eldest Roosevelt daughter.)

17. Southern Workman, July 2, 1904; see Edmund Morris, Theodore Rex (New York, 2001.)

18. Southern Workman, July 2, 1904.

19. Browne to Taft, September 2, 1904 (enclosure) Taft, LoC.

20. See William Blood, Apostle of Reason: A Biography of Joseph Krauskopf, (Philadelphia, 1973)

21. Toledo Blade, February 21, 1905, and September 8, 1905; Foraker to Herrick, April 17, 1905; Herrick to Browne, October 21, 1905, Browne, AJA.

22. Blade, Toledo, September 8, 1905.

23. Browne to Taft enclosure (lecture announcement) June 4, 1905, Taft, LoC; Blade,

Toledo, September 8, 1905.

24. Blade, Toledo, September 8, 1905.
25. Ibid.
26. Browne to Taft enclosure (note on lecture announcement) June 4, 1905, Taft, LoC.
27. See Bobbie Malone, Rabbi Max Heller (Tuscaloosa, 1997; Browne to Sophie (letterhead) March 10, 1925, Browne, AJA; Reform Advocate, May 3, 1919; Miami News, March 10, 1925.
28. Exodus: 18:13-26; The Legal Aid Society Company History, www. fundinguniverse.com/company-histories.
29. World, July 8, 1906; Naomi Cohen, "Antisemitism in the Gilded Age: The Jewish View," Jewish Social Studies, v. 41 #3/4 1979, 182-210(McGlynn, minister of St. Stephen's Church in New York, was an outspoken supporter of Henry George and political economist who expounded the single tax theory.)
30. World, July 8, 1906; for anti-Semitism during this era see Eric L. Goldstein, "The Unstable Other", American Jewish History, v.89 n. 4, 383- 409, Higham, Send These To Me, 127-136.
31. World, July 8, 1906.
32. See Paul M. Rego, American Ideal: Theodore Roosevelt's search for American Individualism, (New York, 2008)1-23; Wayne Andrews, ed., Concise Dictionary of American History (New York, 1962); Richard B. Morris, ed., Encyclopedia of American History (New York, 1953); Sarna, American Judaism,158; Irving Howe, World of Our Fathers (New York, 1976) 101-115.
33. New York Times, September 9, 1906 (Activist Rose Pastor Stokes embraced a form of socialism based on the teachings of social economist Henry George, identified especially with George's single tax theory [see Chapter VI, n.56.] This was also advocated by Democrat William Randolph Hearst while seated in Congress, 1903-1907).
34. Ibid.
35. World, April 2, 1907.
36. Foraker to Browne, October 12, 1907, Browne, AJA
37. Ibid.
38. Foraker to Browne, December 16, 1907, Browne, AJA.
39. Woodford to Browne, February 21,1908.
40. Ibid. (Reference to pogroms in Russia fomented by government backed organization, the Black Hundreds, exacerbated by 1905 publication of notoriously anti-Semitic Protocols of the Elders of Zion.)
41. Woodford to Browne, April 30, 1908, Browne, AJA.
42. Lauterbach to Browne, July 2, 1908, Browne, AJA.
43. Woodford to Browne, July 7, 1908, Browne, AJA.
44. Browne to Taft, August 10, 1908, Taft, LoC
45. Ibid.
46. Ibid
47. Ibid.
48. Browne to Taft, September 17, 1908, Taft, LoC
49. Ibid.

50. Ibid.

51. Meyer Koteen to Taft, September 19, 1908.

52. Browne to Taft, October 9, 1908, Taft, LoC.

53. Browne to Taft, October 9, 1908, Taft, LoC; Malcolm H. Stern, "Some Notes on the History of the Organized Jewish Community of Norfolk, Virginia", Journal of the Southern Jewish Historical Society, v. 1, # 3, November 1963 (Beth El Congregation, organized 1870, membership largely increased by Eastern European immigrants during Browne's tenure.)

54. Browne to Taft, October 31, 1908, Taft, LoC

55. Browne to Taft, November 18, 1908, Taft, LoC.

56. Browne to Joseph Distillator, August 21, 1908; partial outline of contents, Browne, AJA.

57. Browne to Taft enclosure, fragment, unidentified, undated Brooklyn newspaper, Taft, LoC; Fred Grant to Browne, September 18, 1908, Browne, AJA.

58. Announcement, The Immigrants' National Encyclopedia of Biography, 1907, Browne, AJA.

59. William Bennet to Brown, November 10, 1909; fragment, unidentified newspaper, Boston, December 11, 1910, Browne, AJA; Boston Journal, May 11, 1912.

60. Boston Journal, May 11, 1912.(Browne's attitude toward Storrow may have been reaction to Storrow's position on labor unions.)

61. Boston Journal, May 11, 1912; see Timothy George, ed., Mr. Moody and the Evangelical Tradition, (New York, 2004); William Gerald McLoughlin, Modern Revivalism: Charles Grandison to Billy Graham (New York, 1959) 166. U. S. Senator (signature illegible) to New York State Senator John Raines, March 1, 1909, Browne, AJA.

62. Summary from congregational records, Mishkan Tefila, Boston; Sunday Herald, Boston, August, 1909, Browne, AJA

63. Archives of Beth Ahabah Congregation, Richmond, Virginia; records in possession of author.

64. W.H. O'Connell to Browne, March 12, 1910, Browne, AJA Summary of congregational records, Mishkan Tefila, Boston; Boston Journal, May 11, 1912.

65. EJ, 2, 822.

Chapter Thirteen

1. Century Club programs, 1900-1927, items in possession of author.

2. St. Louis Daily Globe-Democrat, undated; unidentified fragment, Boston newspaper, December 11, 1910, Browne, AJA.

3. Jonathan D. Sarna, "Anti-Semitism in American History", Commentary 71 (March 1981) 47; Henry L. Feingold, A Time for Searching: Entering the Mainstream (Baltimore 1992)1-34; Jacob Rader Marcus, United States Jewry 1776-1985 , III (Detroit 1993) 359-371; Leonard Dinnerstein, Anti-Semitism in America (New York, 1994) 58-77.

4. Jack Fischel and Sanford Pinsker, Jewish-American History and Culture: an Encyclopedia (New York 1992) 544.

5. Joseph Green Butler, History of Youngstown and the Mahoney Valley in Ohio, I

(Cleveland, 1912), 323.

6. Youngstown Daily Vindicator, undated fragment, Browne, AJA.

7. Youngstown Daily Vindicator, April 9, 1911; see Edna Nahshon, ed., From The Ghetto to The Melting Pot: Israel Zangwill's Jewish Plays: Three Playscripts (Detroit, 2006), introduction and commentary; Julius Novick, Beyond the Golden Door (New York, 2008); Chloe Veltman, Zangwill Coined America's Most Enduring Metaphor (Jewish Theatre News, http://www.jewish-theatre.com/visitor/article).

8. For this and following, Youngstown Daily Vindicator, April 9, 1911.

9. Edmund Morris, The Rise of Theodore Roosevelt (New York, 2001); Paul M. Rego, American Ideal: Theodore Roosevelt's Search for American Individualism (New York, 2008)

10. Inscription on candlesticks, possession of author.

11. Boston Journal, May 11, 1912.

12. Ibid.

13. Blumberg, "Sophie Weil Browne: From Rabbi's Wife to Clubwoman," Southern Jewish History, v 9 (2006) 1-33; candlesticks in possession of author.

14. Blumberg, "Sophie Weil Browne;" Century Club programs, 1906-1928; Columbus Enquirer-Sun, January 4, 1925.

15. Milwaukee Journal, September 15, 1912 and September 29, 1912.

16. Hugh L. Nichols to Browne, April 4, 1911; W. C. Adamson to Browne, June 1, 1911; Julius Harburger to Browne, August 18, 1911, Browne, AJA.

17. William Sulzer to Browne, February 19, 1912; February 21, 1912, March 23, 1912; May 1, 1912, May 17, 1912, July 5, 1912, Browne, AJA.

18. For this and following, Browne to Otto T. Bannard, April 21, 1912, Taft, LoC.

19. For this and following, Record of 65th Congress, 2nd Session, April 21, 1912, Congressional Records, LoC.

20. See Chapter VI for Corrigan, Newman, and Gottheil.

21. Marcus, United States Jewry, III, 104-107; Ann Healy, "Tsarist Anti-Semitism and Russian American Relations," Slavic Review, v 42 n 3 (Autumn, 1983, 408-425.

22. Lewis Barish, ed, Rabbis in Uniform (New York, 1952); Seymour Brody, Rabbis as Chaplains in America's Military: A Tradition of Service, Dedication and Bravery, www library: fau.edu/depts/spc/brody; Champ Clark to Browne, April 27, 1914, July 10, 1918, May 12, 1919, December 12, 1919, Browne, AJA

23. Browne to Woodrow Wilson, September 18, 1910, Wilson Presidential Papers, Manuscripts, Library of Congress [hereafter cited as Wilson, LoC.]

24. Ibid.; Warold S. Wechsler, "Rabbi Bernard C. Ehrenreich: A Northern Progressive Goes South," Samuel Proctor, Louis Schmier, Malcolm Stern, ed., Jews of the South (Macon, Georgia, 1984) 46; Wikipedia, http://en.wikipedia.org/wiki/woodrow_wilson.

25. Browne to Woodrow Wilson, September 18, 1910, Wilson, LoC.

26. Browne to Woodrow Wilson, July 14, 1911, Wilson, LoC.

27. Browne to Woodrow Wilson, December 22, 1912, Wilson, LoC.

28. The American Jewish Congress, a major voice for Jewish issues whose leaders more closely fit Browne's definition of "genuine" Jews, was established in 1918.

29. Browne to Woodrow Wilson, January 9, 1913, Wilson, LoC.
30. Ibid.
31. Browne to Joseph P. Tumulty, February 6, 1913, February 26, 1913, Wilson, LoC.
32. EJ 4,1297; Melvin I. Urofsky, Louis D. Brandeis: A Life (New York, 2009); Mordechai M. Kaplan, Judaism as a Civilization: Toward a Reconstruction of American-Jewish Life (Philadelphia, 1981)
33. Albert Gleaves to Browne, May 4, 1914, Browne, AJA
34. Alexander S. Rosenthal to City and State of New York, Kings County, re. Browne application for admittance to the Bar, March 20, 1913; Edward Lauterbach to Browne, October 20, 1913; unidentified and undated Poughkeepsie newspaper, 1913; Knickerbocker Press, March (date unclear) 1913; New York Times, August 11, 1913; Announcement of service, Sunday, November 1, 1914, Browne, AJA.
35. World, letter to ed., November 20, 1915; New York Times, February 13, 1916. Frank Moss to Browne, January 19, 1916; Hamilton Holt to Browne, January 18, 1916; Browne, AJA.
36. Frank Moss to Browne, January 19, 1916, Browne, AJA.
37. Governor Martin Glynn to Browne, October 18, 1914; publication announcement for The Talmud, December 18, 1914; Arthur V. Briesen to Browne, December 29, 1914; Frank Moss to Browne, January 10, 1915 and August 27, 1915; Temple Zion, announcement of reception and resolutions, September 5, 1915; Frank Moss to Browne, November 5, 1915, George B. Gamsby to Browne, September 7, 1915, Browne, AJA.
38. Edward B. M. Browne deposition, Washington, D.C., January 6, 1919, Browne, AJA; Washington Star, January 12, 1919.
39. Edward B. M. Browne deposition, Washington, D.C., January 6, 1919, Browne, AJA.
40. Newton D. Baker to Browne, July 22, 1920; Jacob Schiff undated note, copy on letterhead of The American Jewish Seventy Elders, March 10, 1925, Browne, AJA.
41. Governor E. J. Henning to Browne, May 26, 1921, Browne, AJA.
42. Thomas A. Edison to Browne, January 14, 1913, Browne, AJA.
43. W. E. Gillmore to Browne, September 29, 1919, Browne, AJA..
44. George Foster Peabody to Browne, March 6, 1915; Newton D. Baker to Browne, July 22, 1920, William G. McAdoo to Browne, June 18, 1920; Robert E. Goode to Browne, January 24, 1922; James J. Davis to Browne, January 11, 1921; Louis Marshall to Browne, March 3, 1921; Laura Harlau to Browne, June 9, 1921; Edward Lauterbach to Jacques Poliachek, November 15, 1921; Sophie Irene Loeb to Browne, October 5, 1922 and May 27, 1924; Clark Howell to Browne, December 22, 1922; William Jennings Bryan to Browne, February 2,1923; William Dawe to Browne, March 13, 1923; Henry S. New to Browne, August 20, 1923 and February 20, 1925; George R. Van Namee, to Browne, March 6, 1924; Oscar W. Underwood to Browne, June 5, 1924; Robert M LaFollette Jr. to Browne, August 4, 1924; Albert Ottinger to Browne, September 20, 1924; Oscar of the Waldorf to Browne, February 23, 1926;, Harry S. New to Louis Berman, February 19, 1925; Browne, AJA.
45. Congressional Record, House of Representatives, December 13, 1917.

46. Ibid.
47. Congressional Record, Senate, August 30, 1918; Washington Times, August 30, 1918, copy of text, Browne, AJA.
48. Program of Grant Memorial, 1919, Browne, AJA.
49. Program of Grant Memorial, August 15, 1920, Browne, AJA.
50. Ibid; Browne to Sophie Browne, photograph on 70 Elders letterhead, December 7, 1922; Browne, AJA.
51. Conversations with Lylah Browne Goldberg, 1940 - 1960.
52. Author's experience, 1928.
53. Pincess Julia Cantacuzene to Browne, December 4, 1927, Browne, AJA.
54. Record in family Bible, possession of author.
55. Ibid.
56. Bernard Drachman to Lylah Browne Goldberg and Carolyn Goldberg Oettinger, October 29, 1929, Browne, AJA.
57. [New York] Jewish Guardian, November 28, 1929.
58. JE v.6, 191; Jeffrey S. Gurock, "From Exception to Role Model: Bernard Drachman and the Evolutiom of Jewish Religious Life in America, 1880 - 1920," American Jewish History, June 1987, 464-484; Yitzhok Levine, Rabbi Dr. Bernard Drachman (1861-1945) http://personl.stevens.edu/Levine/ Drachman; Bernard Drachman to Browne, March 2, 1921; William F. Crafts to Browne, January 20, 1921, Browne, AJA.

ABOUT THE AUTHOR

Janice Rothschild Blumberg is a native Atlantan who returned here after many years in Washington, D.C. She graduated in the arts from the University of Georgia, and subsequently studied American Jewish history while experiencing it, often at close range as the wife - now widow - of two outspoken Jewish leaders, civil rights activist Rabbi Jacob M. Rothschild of

 Atlanta and David M. Blumberg of Knoxville, Tennessee, international president of B"nai B'rith, 1971-1978.

Ms. Blumberg is the author of two books dealing with Atlanta Jewish history, *One Voice: Rabbi Jacob M. Rothschild and the Troubled South*, and *As But a Day*, the story of Atlanta's Hebrew Benevolent Congregation; and co-author of *Deadly Truth*, a fact-based novel about a Jewish family coping with apartheid in South Africa. She has written various articles for newspapers, magazines and scholarly journals as well as the entries about Atlanta and Georgia for the *Encyclopedia Judaica*.

In addition to her writing, Ms. Blumberg held leadership positions in numerous organizations in both Atlanta and Washington. Currently a Martin Luther King Jr. Collegium Scholar at Morehouse College, she served for many years on the board of the American Jewish Historical Society, is a past president of the Southern Jewish Historical Society, and chaired the board of the B'nai B'rith Klutznick National Jewish Museum from 1991 to 1998. Her most recent commitment is as a volunteer docent at the William Breman

Jewish Heritage Museum in Atlanta.

Her newest work, *Prophet in a Time of Priests*, recounts the extraordinary life of "Alphabet" Browne, whose colorful and eccentric life is a study in the history of American Judaism.

The future of publishing...today!

Apprentice House is the country's only campus-based, student-staffed book publishing company. Directed by professors and industry professionals, it is a nonprofit activity of the Communication Department at Loyola University Maryland.

Using state-of-the-art technology and an experiential learning model of education, Apprentice House publishes books in untraditional ways. This dual responsibility as publishers and educators creates an unprecedented collaborative environment among faculty and students, while teaching tomorrow's editors, designers, and marketers.

Outside of class, progress on book projects is carried forth by the AH Book Publishing Club, a co-curricular campus organization supported by Loyola University Maryland's Office of Student Activities.

Eclectic and provocative, Apprentice House titles intend to entertain as well as spark dialogue on a variety of topics. Financial contributions to sustain the press's work are welcomed. Contributions are tax deductible to the fullest extent allowed by the IRS.

To learn more about Apprentice House books or to obtain submission guidelines, please visit www.ApprenticeHouse.com.

Apprentice House
Communication Department
Loyola University Maryland
4501 N. Charles Street
Baltimore, MD 21210
Ph: 410-617-5265 • Fax: 410-617-2198
info@apprenticehouse.com

CPSIA information can be obtained
at www.ICGtesting.com
Printed in the USA
EDOW020920120413
1177ED

9 781934 074732